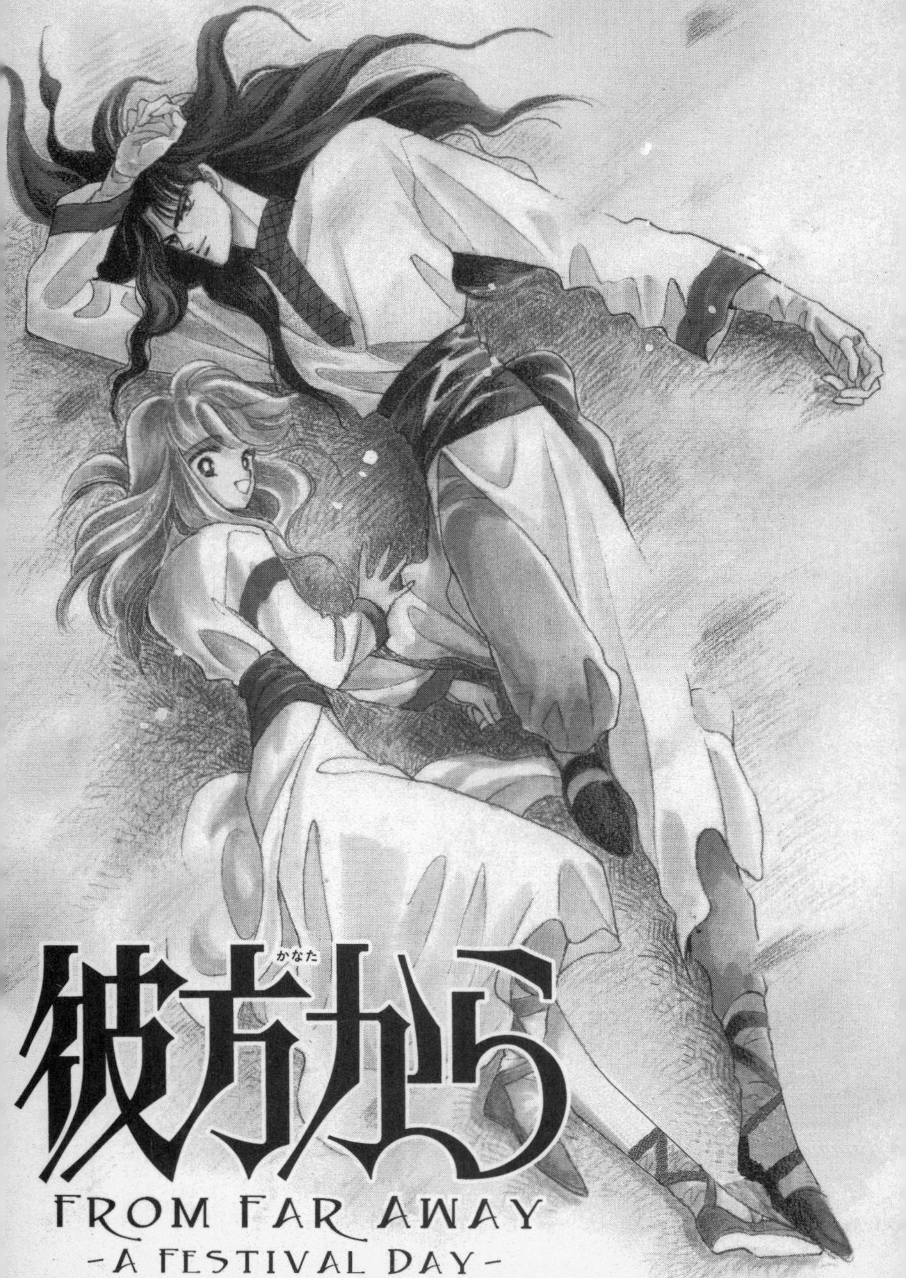
彼方から
かなた
FROM FAR AWAY
-A FESTIVAL DAY-

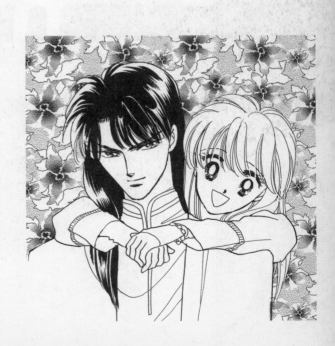

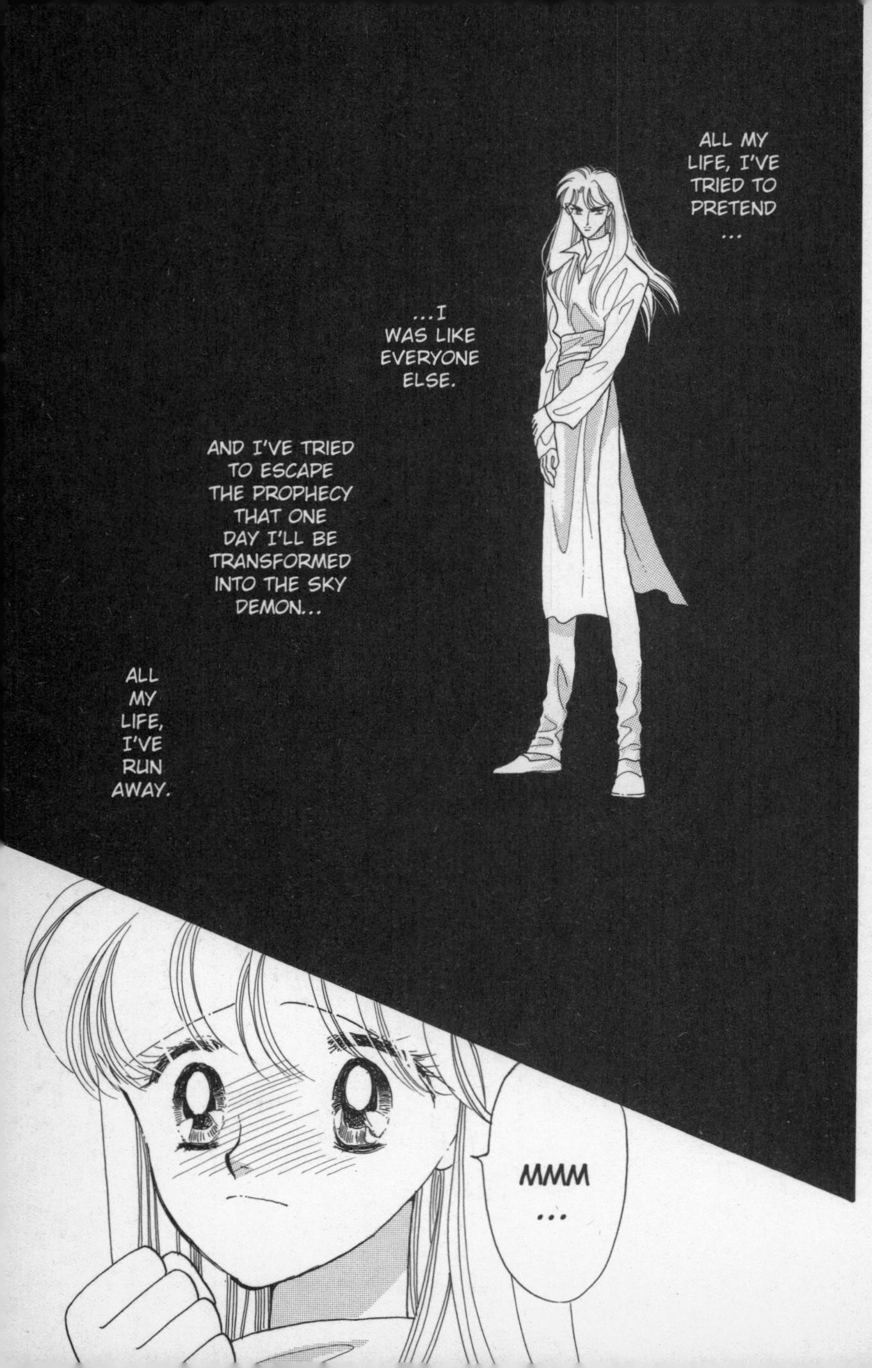
ALL MY LIFE, I'VE TRIED TO PRETEND ...
...I WAS LIKE EVERYONE ELSE.
AND I'VE TRIED TO ESCAPE THE PROPHECY THAT ONE DAY I'LL BE TRANSFORMED INTO THE SKY DEMON...
ALL MY LIFE, I'VE RUN AWAY.
MMM ...

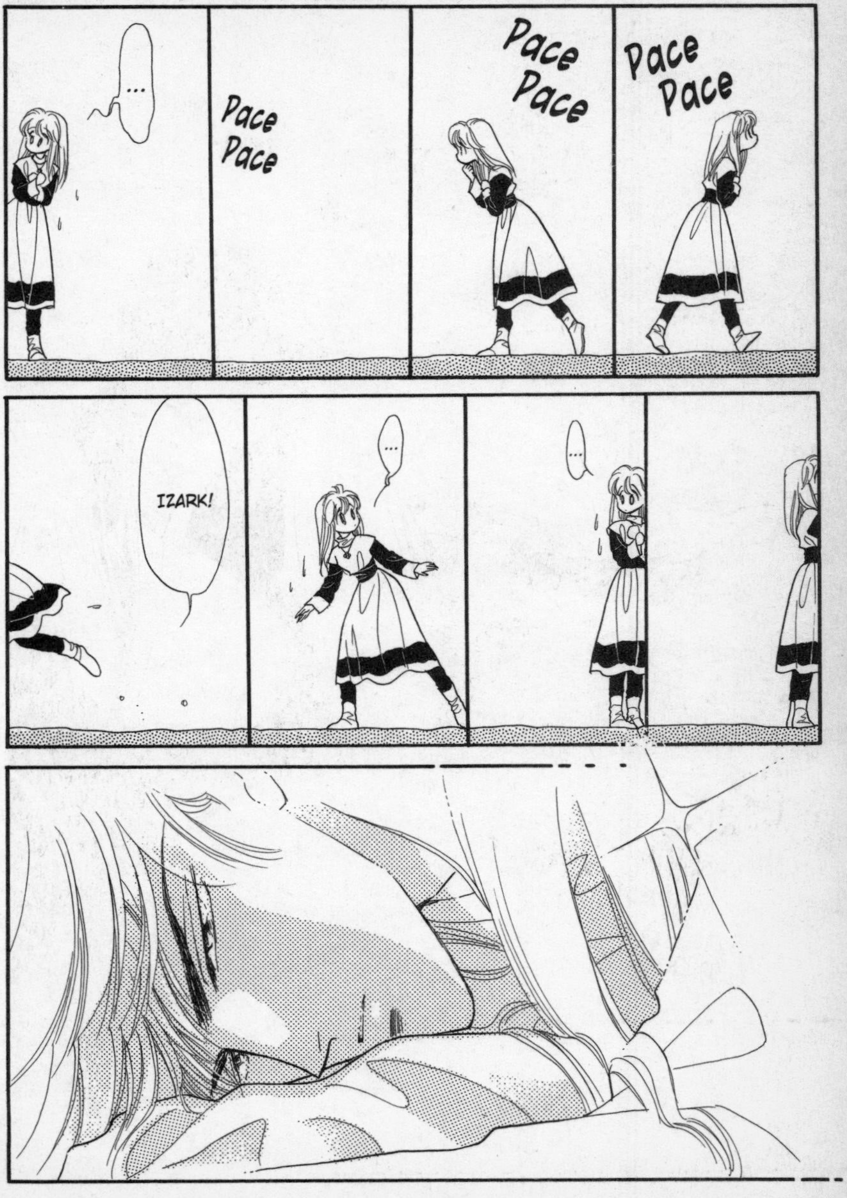
Pace Pace
Pace Pace
Pace Pace
...
...
...
IZARK!

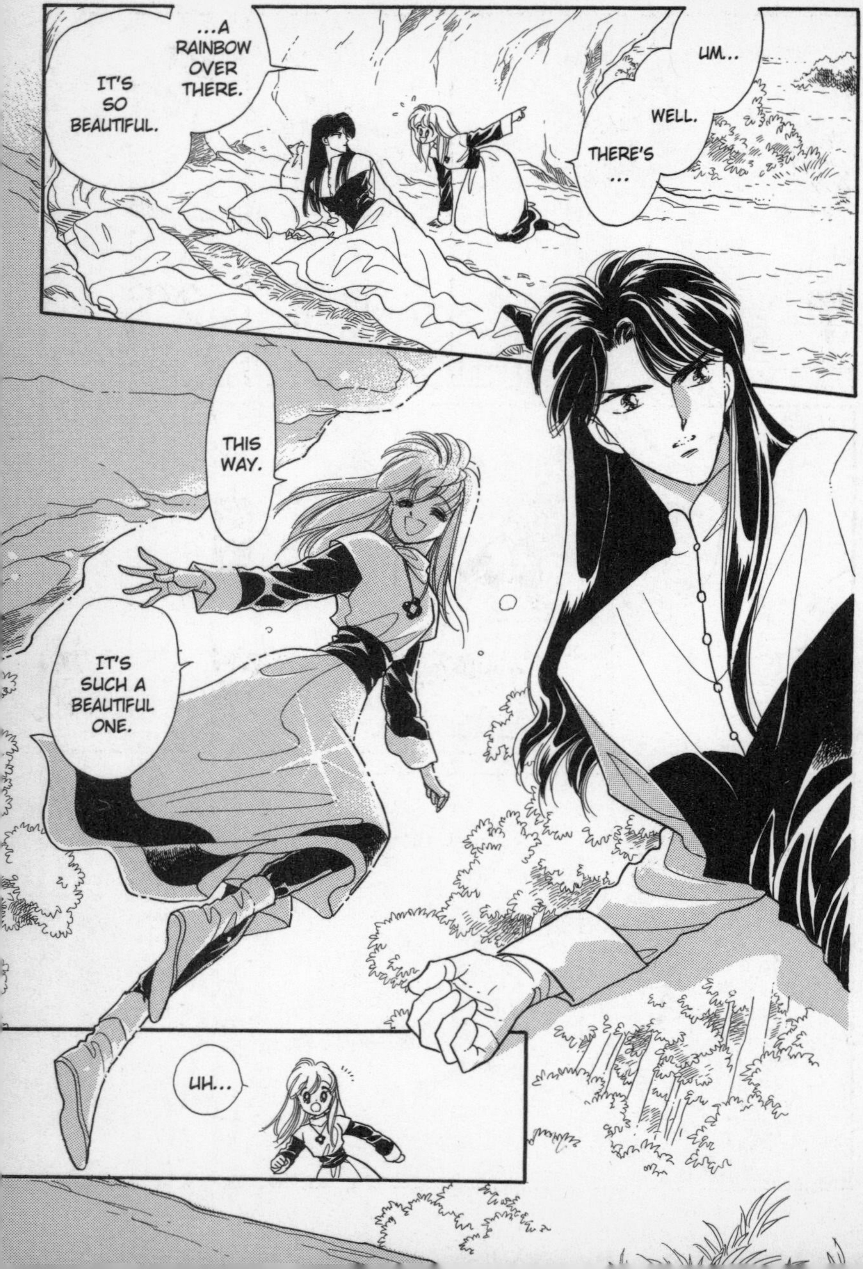
UM.. WELL. THERE'S ...
...A RAINBOW OVER THERE.
IT'S SO BEAUTIFUL.
THIS WAY.
IT'S SUCH A BEAUTIFUL ONE.
UH...

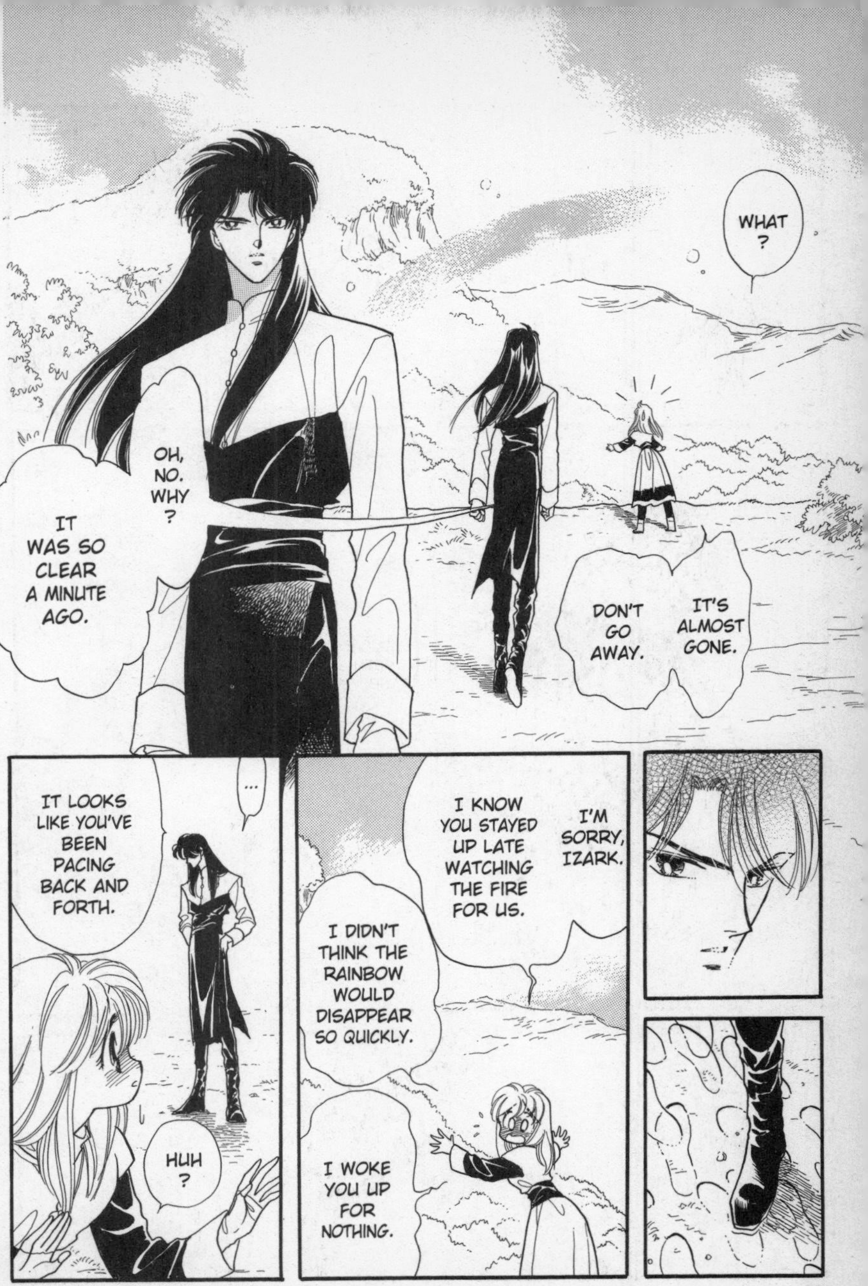

WHAT?
IT'S ALMOST GONE.
DON'T GO AWAY.
OH, NO. WHY?
IT WAS SO CLEAR A MINUTE AGO.
I'M SORRY, IZARK.
I KNOW YOU STAYED UP LATE WATCHING THE FIRE FOR US.
I DIDN'T THINK THE RAINBOW WOULD DISAPPEAR SO QUICKLY.
I WOKE YOU UP FOR NOTHING.
...
IT LOOKS LIKE YOU'VE BEEN PACING BACK AND FORTH.
HUH?

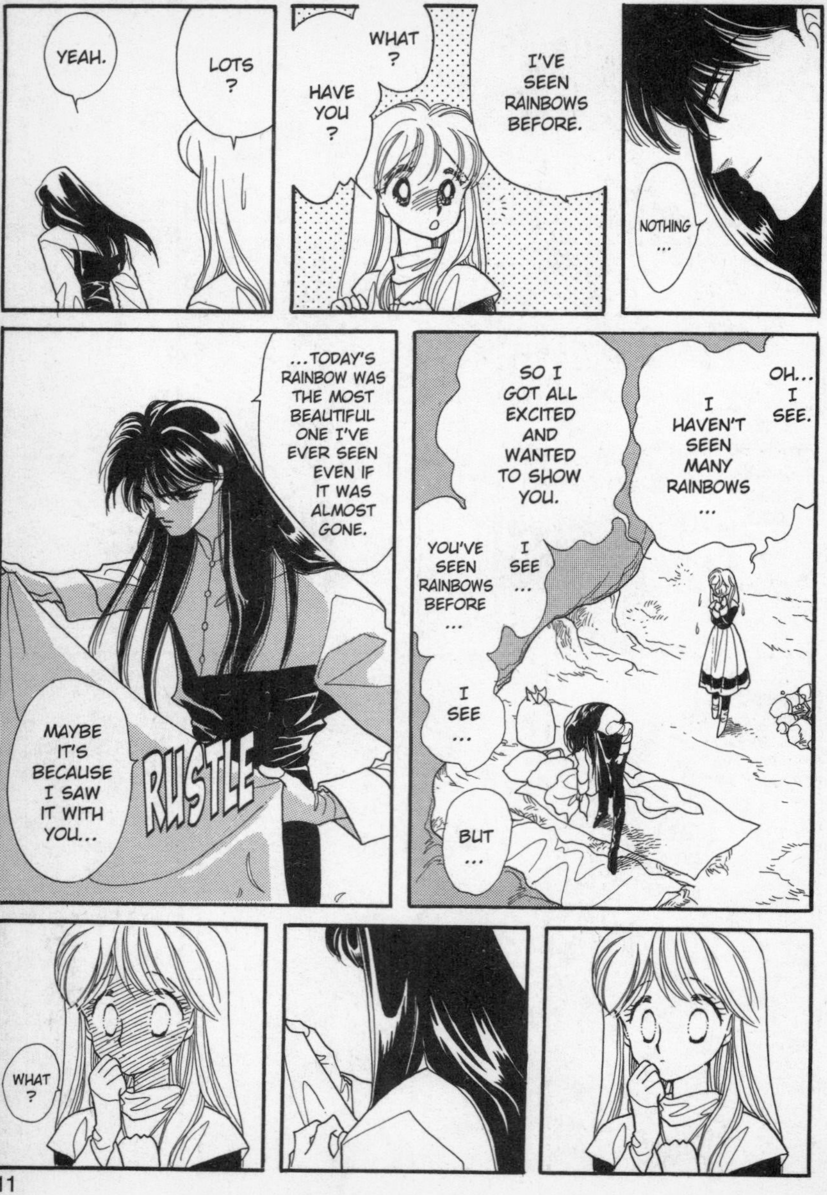
NOTHING ...
I'VE SEEN RAINBOWS BEFORE.
WHAT ?
HAVE YOU ?
LOTS ?
YEAH.
OH... I SEE.
I HAVEN'T SEEN MANY RAINBOWS ...
SO I GOT ALL EXCITED AND WANTED TO SHOW YOU.
I SEE ...
YOU'VE SEEN RAINBOWS BEFORE ...
I SEE ...
BUT ...
...TODAY'S RAINBOW WAS THE MOST BEAUTIFUL ONE I'VE EVER SEEN EVEN IF IT WAS ALMOST GONE.
RUSTLE
MAYBE IT'S BECAUSE I SAW IT WITH YOU...
WHAT ?

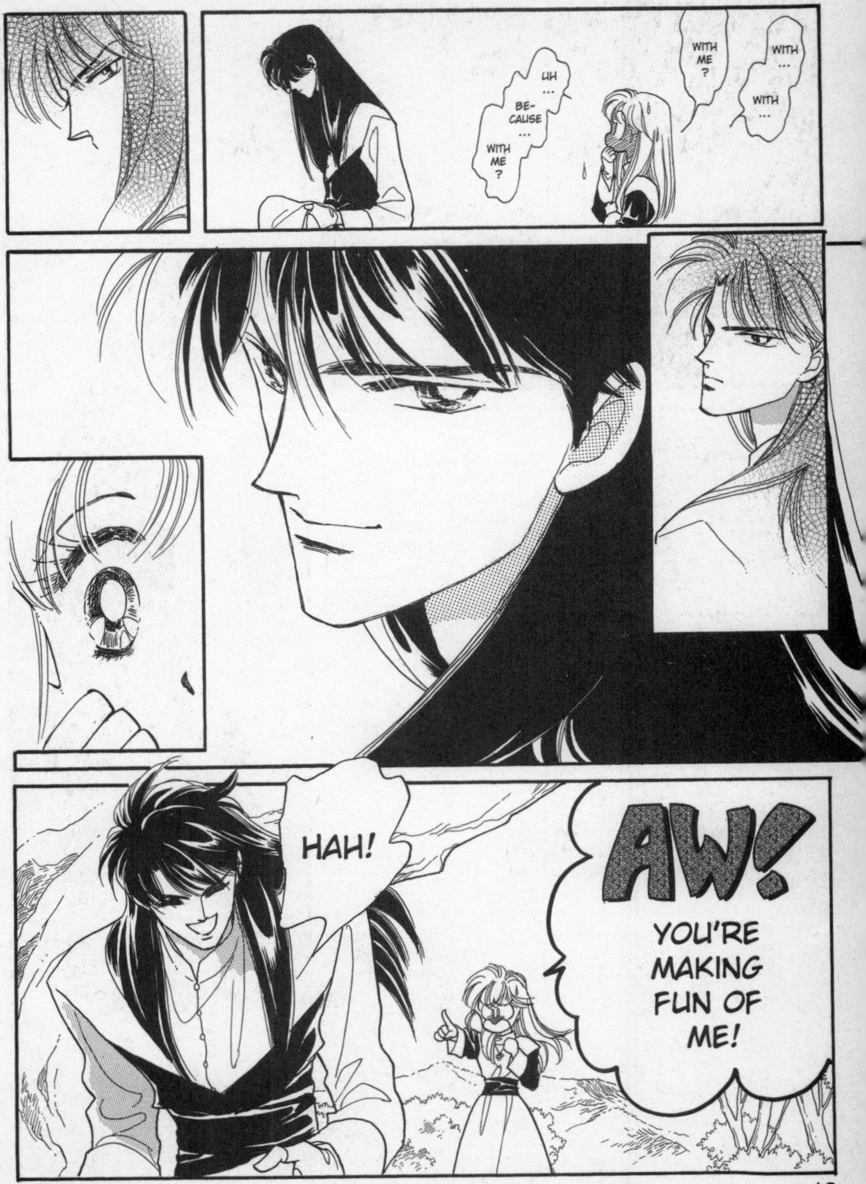
WITH ... WITH ...
WITH ME ?
UH ... BE-CAUSE ... WITH ME ?
AW! YOU'RE MAKING FUN OF ME!
HAH!

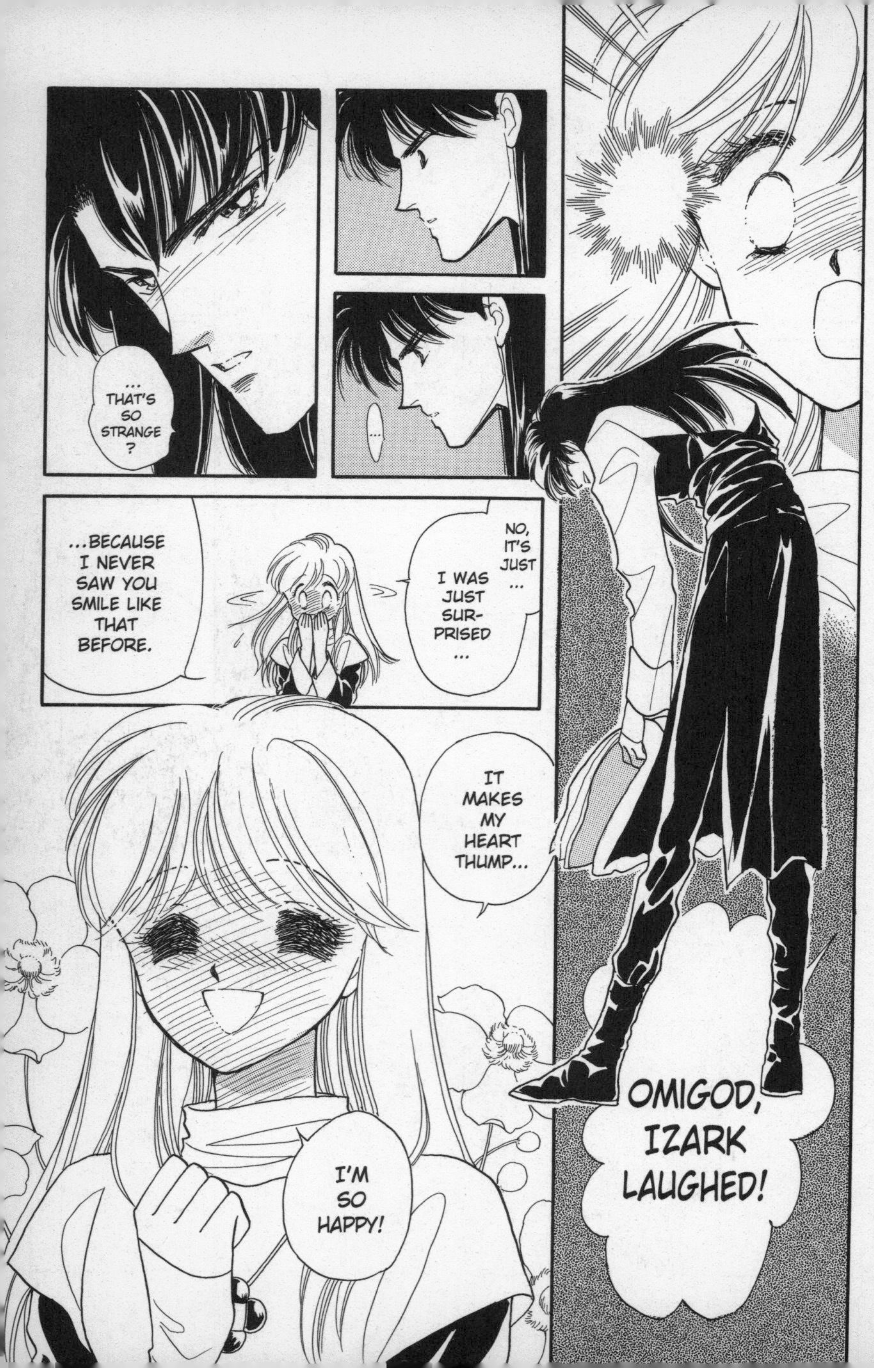
OMIGOD, IZARK LAUGHED!
...
... THAT'S SO STRANGE ?
NO, IT'S JUST ... I WAS JUST SURPRISED ...
...BECAUSE I NEVER SAW YOU SMILE LIKE THAT BEFORE.
IT MAKES MY HEART THUMP...
I'M SO HAPPY!

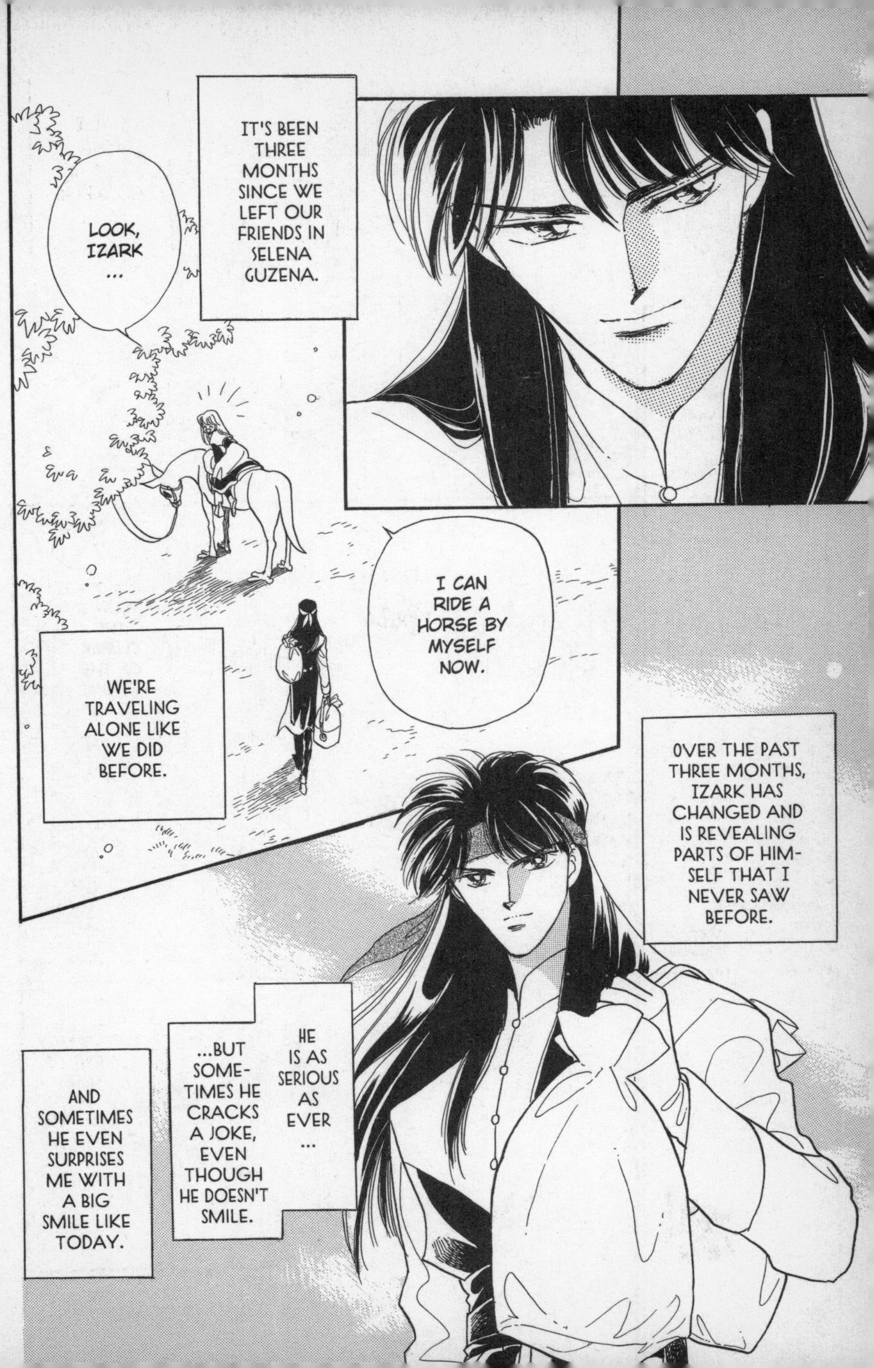
IT'S BEEN THREE MONTHS SINCE WE LEFT OUR FRIENDS IN SELENA GUZENA.
LOOK, IZARK ...
I CAN RIDE A HORSE BY MYSELF NOW.
WE'RE TRAVELING ALONE LIKE WE DID BEFORE.
OVER THE PAST THREE MONTHS, IZARK HAS CHANGED AND IS REVEALING PARTS OF HIM-SELF THAT I NEVER SAW BEFORE.
HE IS AS SERIOUS AS EVER ...
...BUT SOME-TIMES HE CRACKS A JOKE, EVEN THOUGH HE DOESN'T SMILE.
AND SOMETIMES HE EVEN SURPRISES ME WITH A BIG SMILE LIKE TODAY.

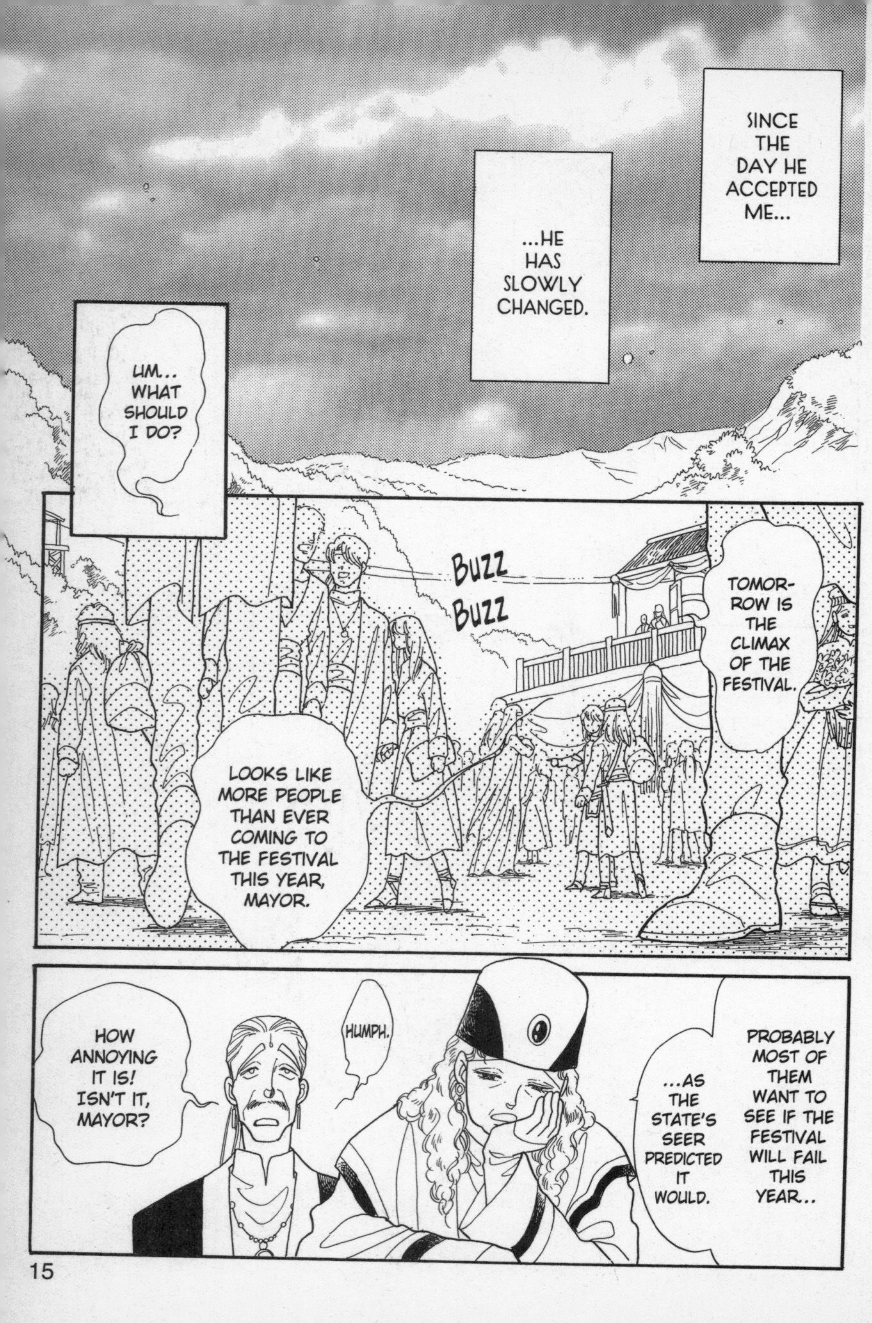
SINCE THE DAY HE ACCEPTED ME...
...HE HAS SLOWLY CHANGED.
UM... WHAT SHOULD I DO?
TOMOR-ROW IS THE CLIMAX OF THE FESTIVAL.
BUZZ BUZZ
LOOKS LIKE MORE PEOPLE THAN EVER COMING TO THE FESTIVAL THIS YEAR, MAYOR.
PROBABLY MOST OF THEM WANT TO SEE IF THE FESTIVAL WILL FAIL THIS YEAR...
...AS THE STATE'S SEER PREDICTED IT WOULD.
HUMPH.
HOW ANNOYING IT IS! ISN'T IT, MAYOR?

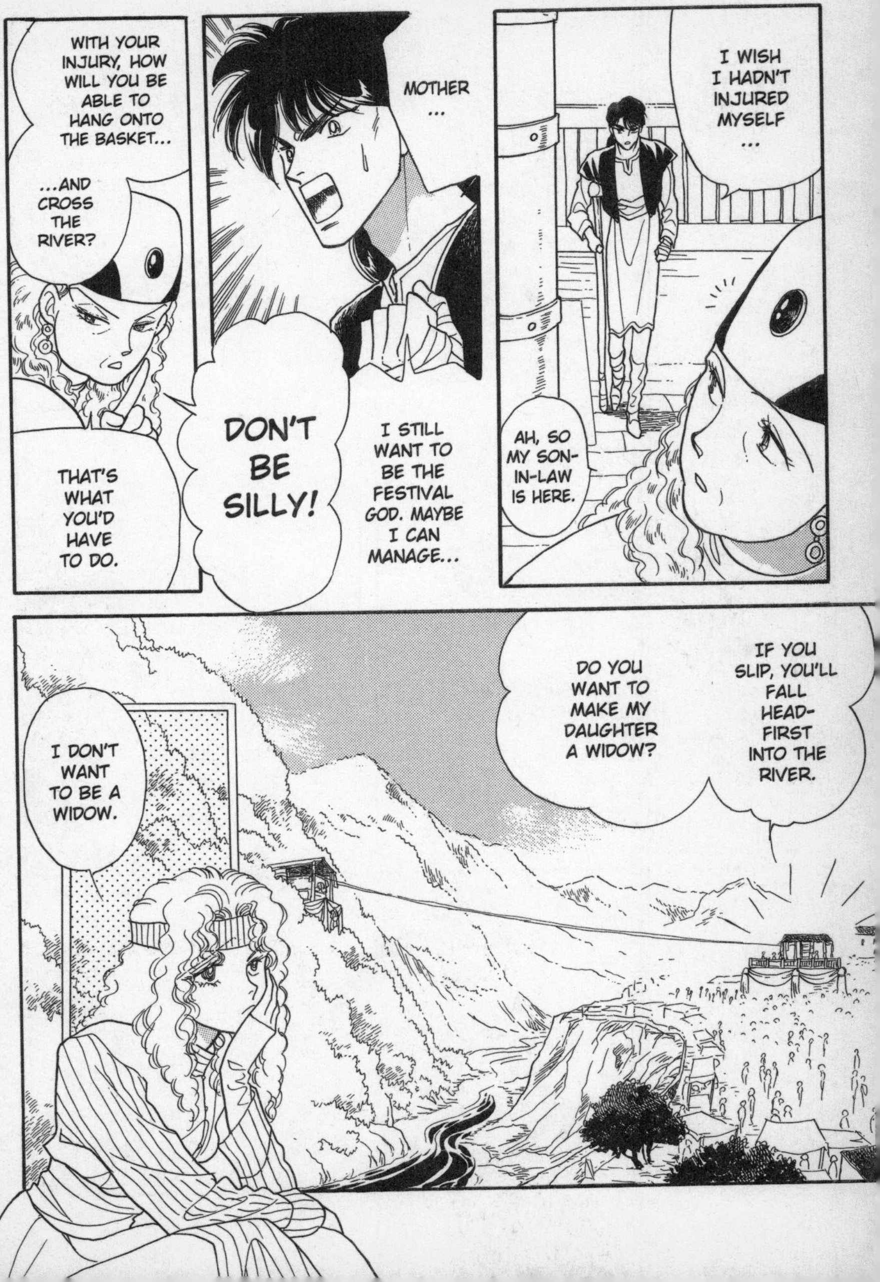
I WISH I HADN'T INJURED MYSELF ...
AH, SO MY SON-IN-LAW IS HERE.
MOTHER ...
I STILL WANT TO BE THE FESTIVAL GOD. MAYBE I CAN MANAGE...
DON'T BE SILLY!
WITH YOUR INJURY, HOW WILL YOU BE ABLE TO HANG ONTO THE BASKET...
...AND CROSS THE RIVER?
THAT'S WHAT YOU'D HAVE TO DO.
IF YOU SLIP, YOU'LL FALL HEAD-FIRST INTO THE RIVER.
DO YOU WANT TO MAKE MY DAUGHTER A WIDOW?
I DON'T WANT TO BE A WIDOW.

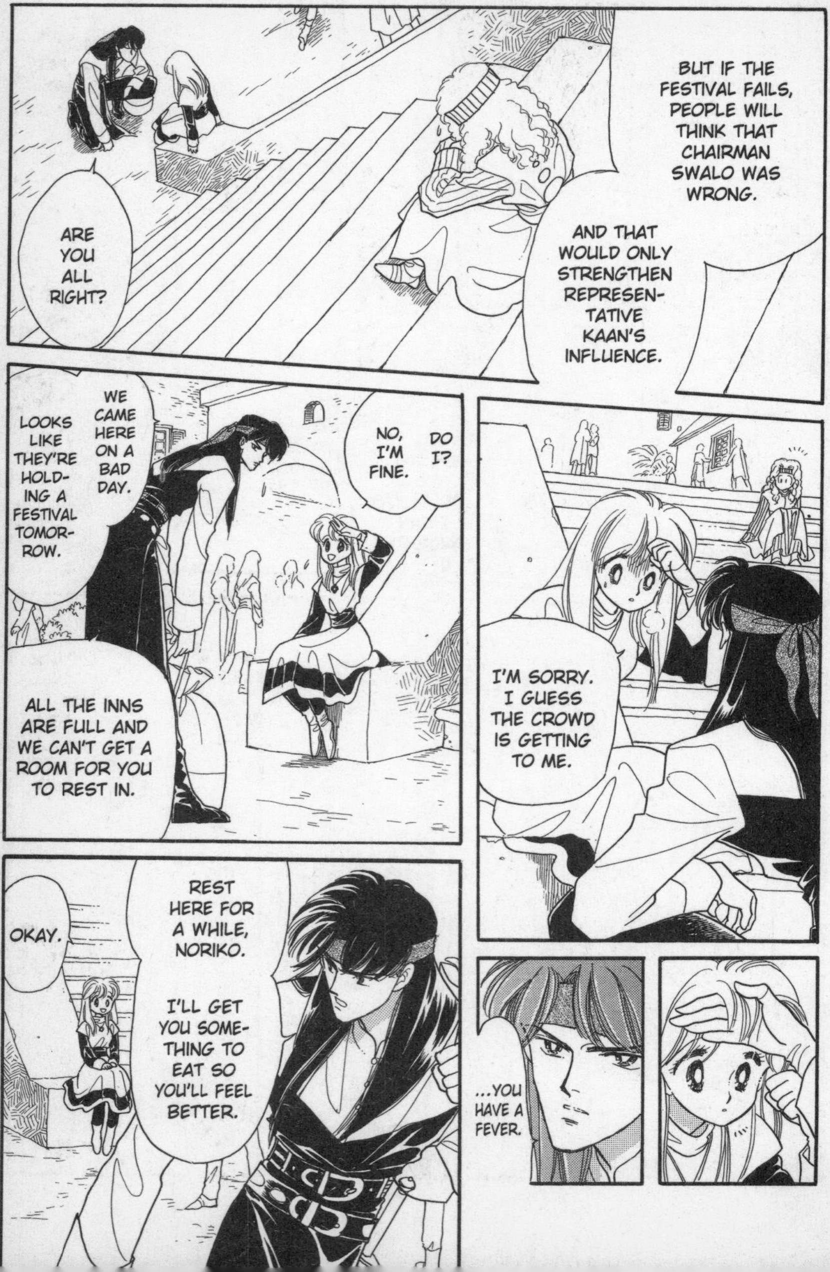
BUT IF THE FESTIVAL FAILS, PEOPLE WILL THINK THAT CHAIRMAN SWALO WAS WRONG.
AND THAT WOULD ONLY STRENGTHEN REPRESEN-TATIVE KAAN'S INFLUENCE.
ARE YOU ALL RIGHT?
I'M SORRY. I GUESS THE CROWD IS GETTING TO ME.
...YOU HAVE A FEVER.
DO I?
NO, I'M FINE.
WE CAME HERE ON A BAD DAY.
LOOKS LIKE THEY'RE HOLD-ING A FESTIVAL TOMOR-ROW.
ALL THE INNS ARE FULL AND WE CAN'T GET A ROOM FOR YOU TO REST IN.
REST HERE FOR A WHILE, NORIKO.
I'LL GET YOU SOME-THING TO EAT SO YOU'LL FEEL BETTER.
OKAY.

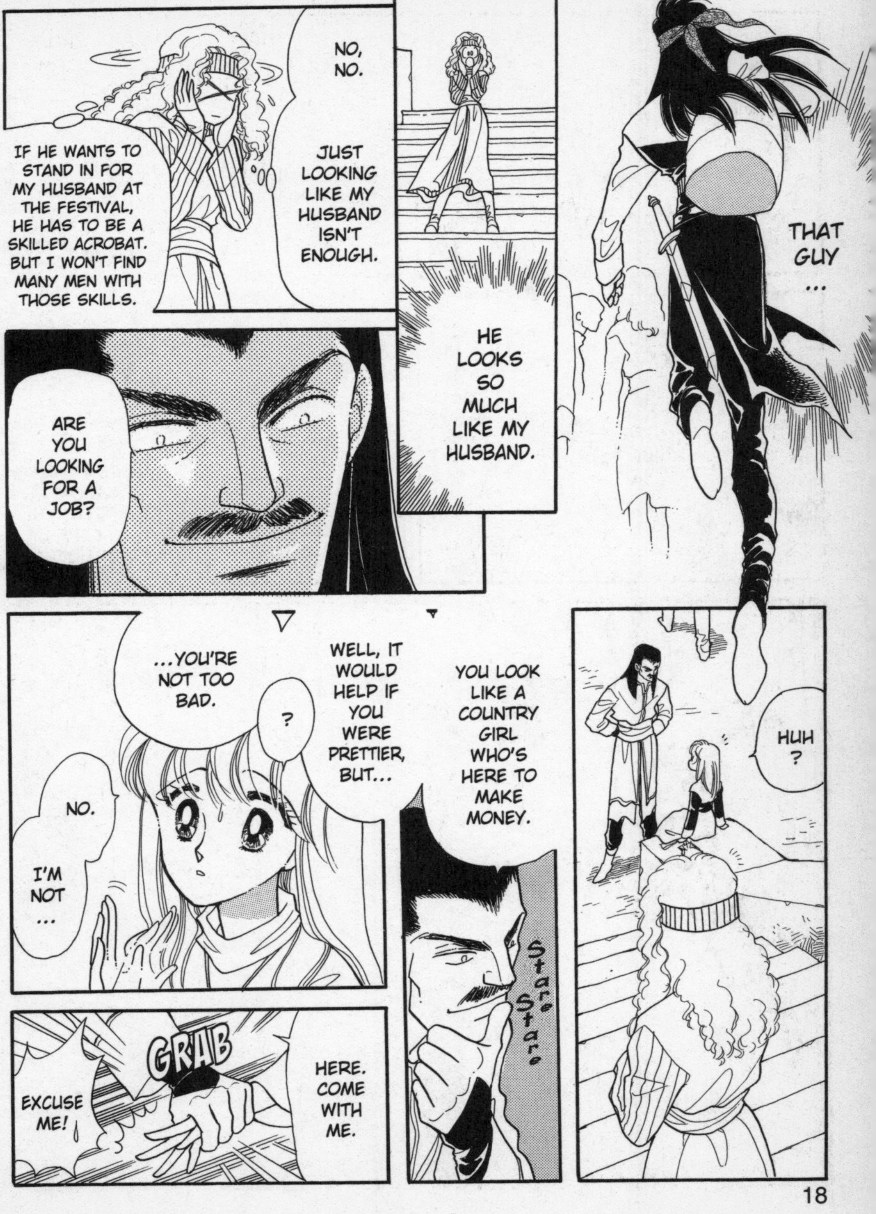

THAT GUY ...
HE LOOKS SO MUCH LIKE MY HUSBAND.
NO, NO.
JUST LOOKING LIKE MY HUSBAND ISN'T ENOUGH.
IF HE WANTS TO STAND IN FOR MY HUSBAND AT THE FESTIVAL, HE HAS TO BE A SKILLED ACROBAT. BUT I WON'T FIND MANY MEN WITH THOSE SKILLS.
ARE YOU LOOKING FOR A JOB?
HUH?
YOU LOOK LIKE A COUNTRY GIRL WHO'S HERE TO MAKE MONEY.
Stare Stare
WELL, IT WOULD HELP IF YOU WERE PRETTIER, BUT...
...YOU'RE NOT TOO BAD.
?
NO.
I'M NOT ...
HERE. COME WITH ME.
GRAB
EXCUSE ME!

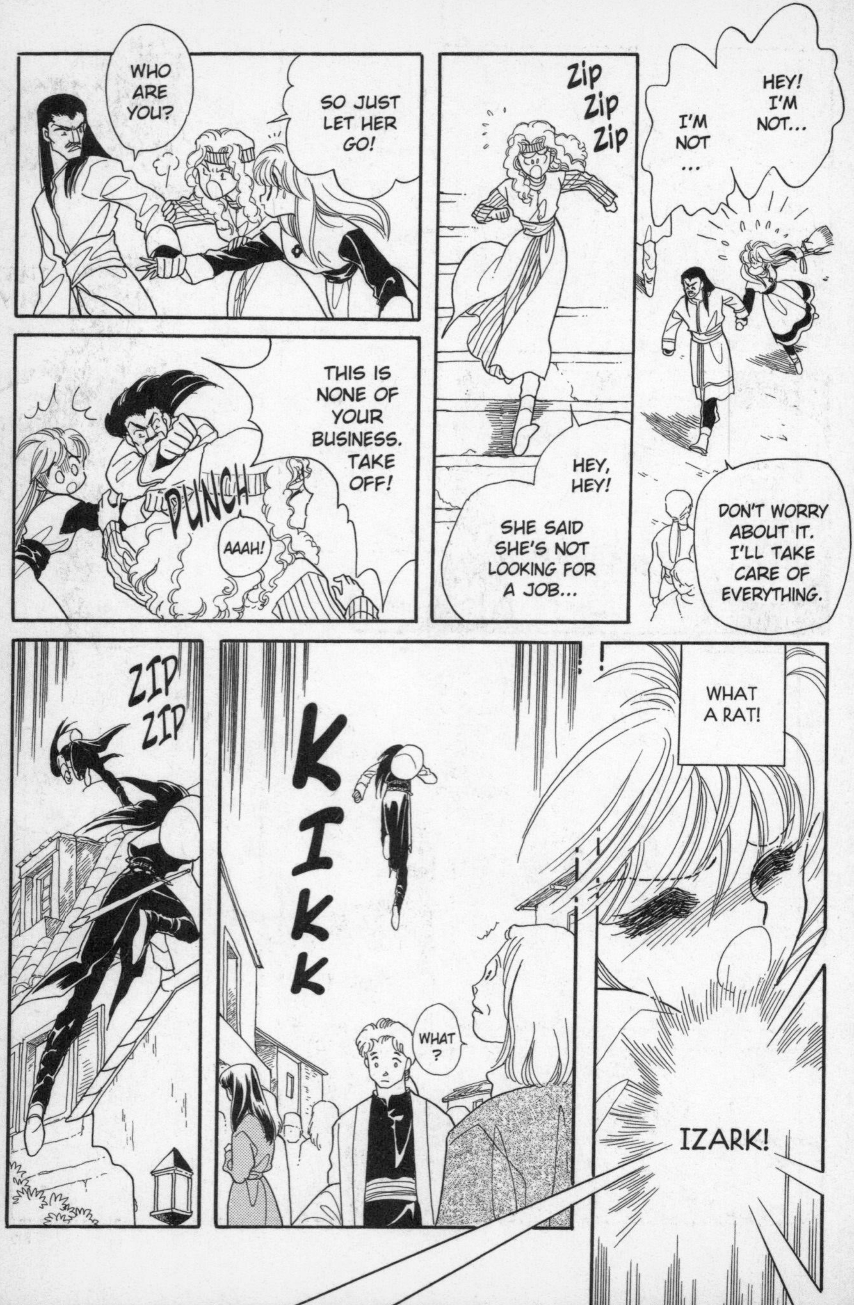
HEY! I'M NOT...
I'M NOT ...
DON'T WORRY ABOUT IT. I'LL TAKE CARE OF EVERYTHING.
Zip Zip Zip
HEY, HEY!
SHE SAID SHE'S NOT LOOKING FOR A JOB...
SO JUST LET HER GO!
WHO ARE YOU?
THIS IS NONE OF YOUR BUSINESS. TAKE OFF!
PUNCH
AAAH!
WHAT A RAT!
IZARK!
KIKK
WHAT ?
ZIP ZIP

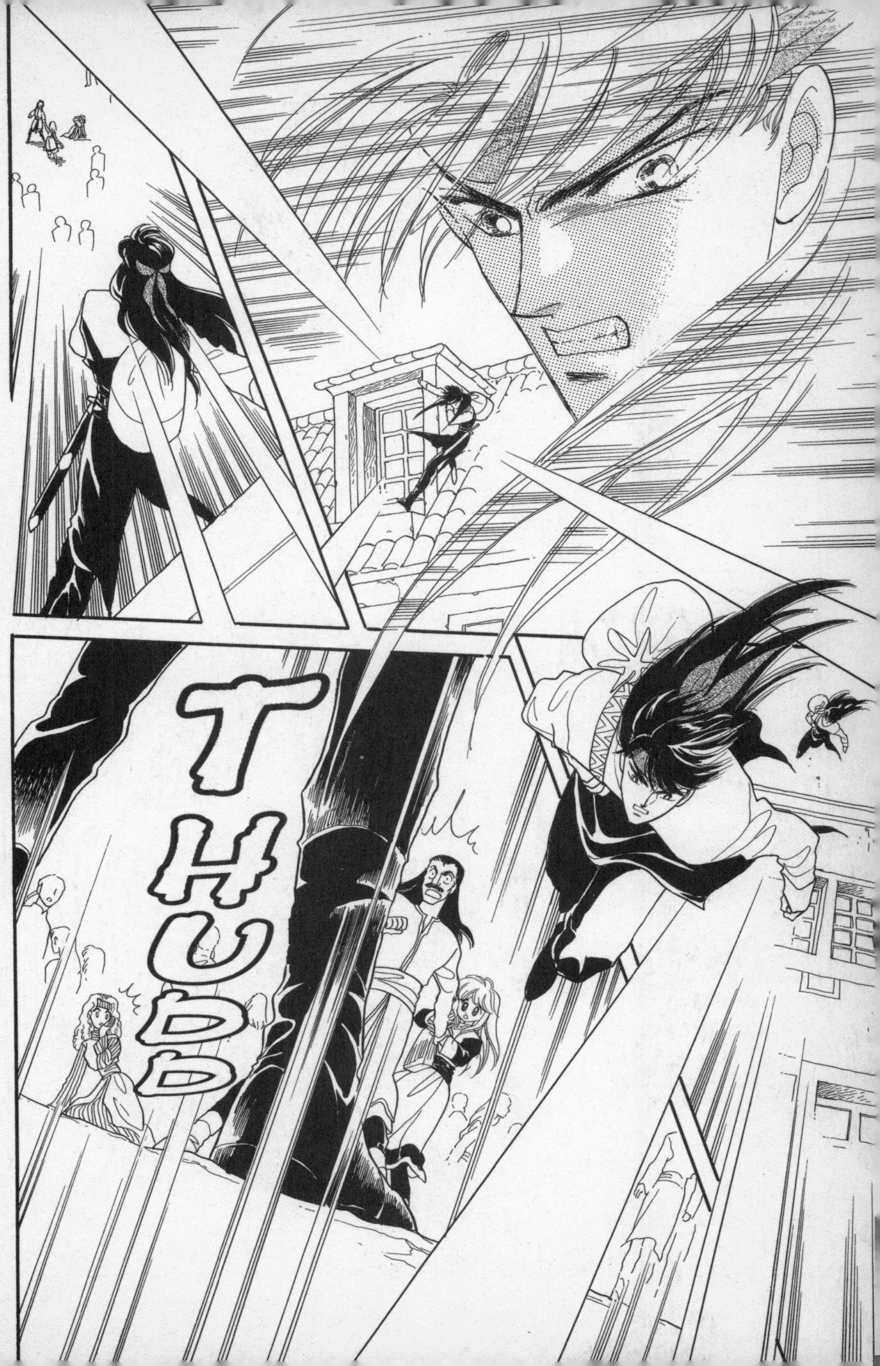
THUD

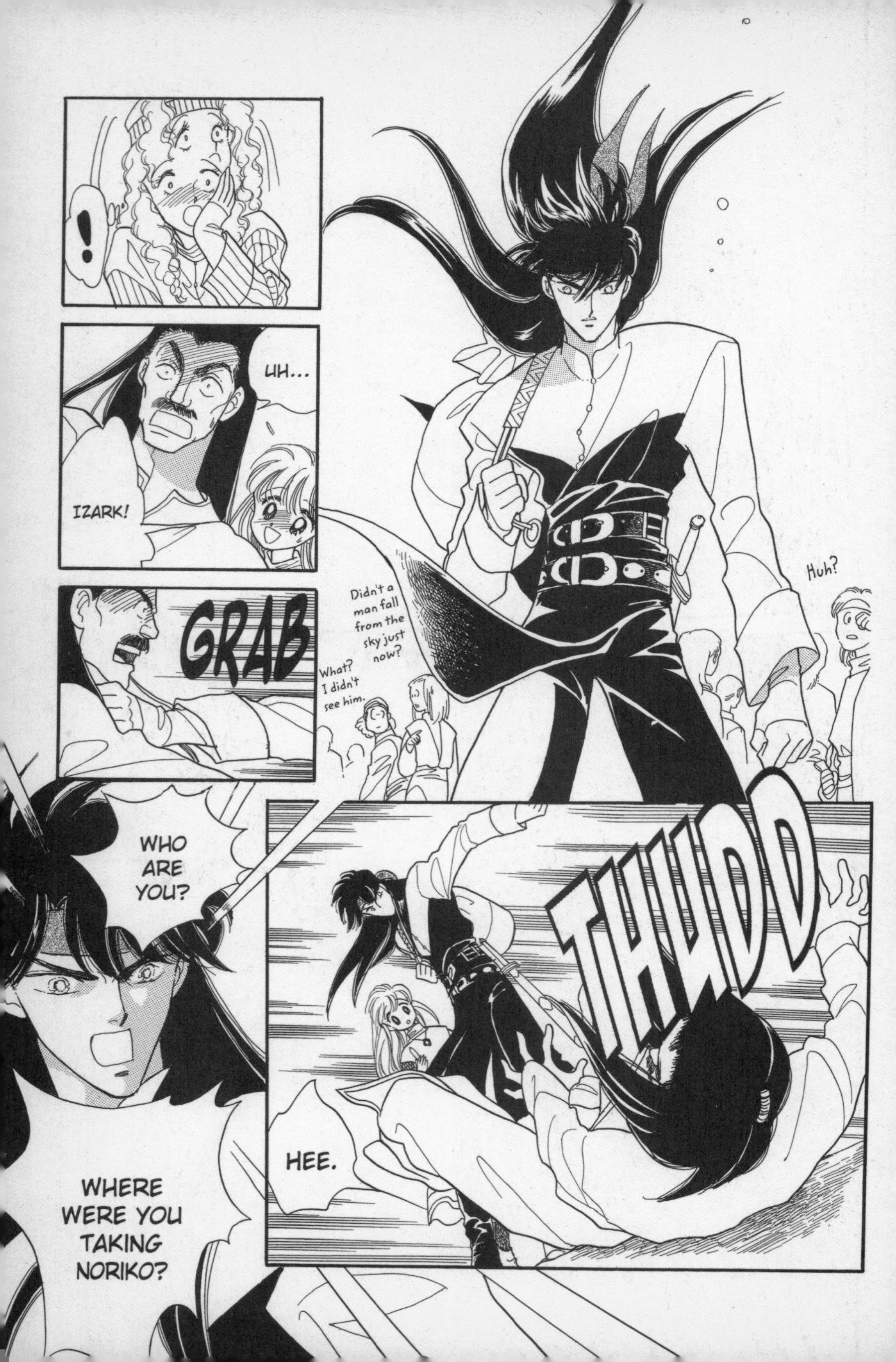
Huh?
Didn't a man fall from the sky just now?
What? I didn't see him.
!
UH...
IZARK!
GRAB
THUDD
HEE.
WHO ARE YOU?
WHERE WERE YOU TAKING NORIKO?

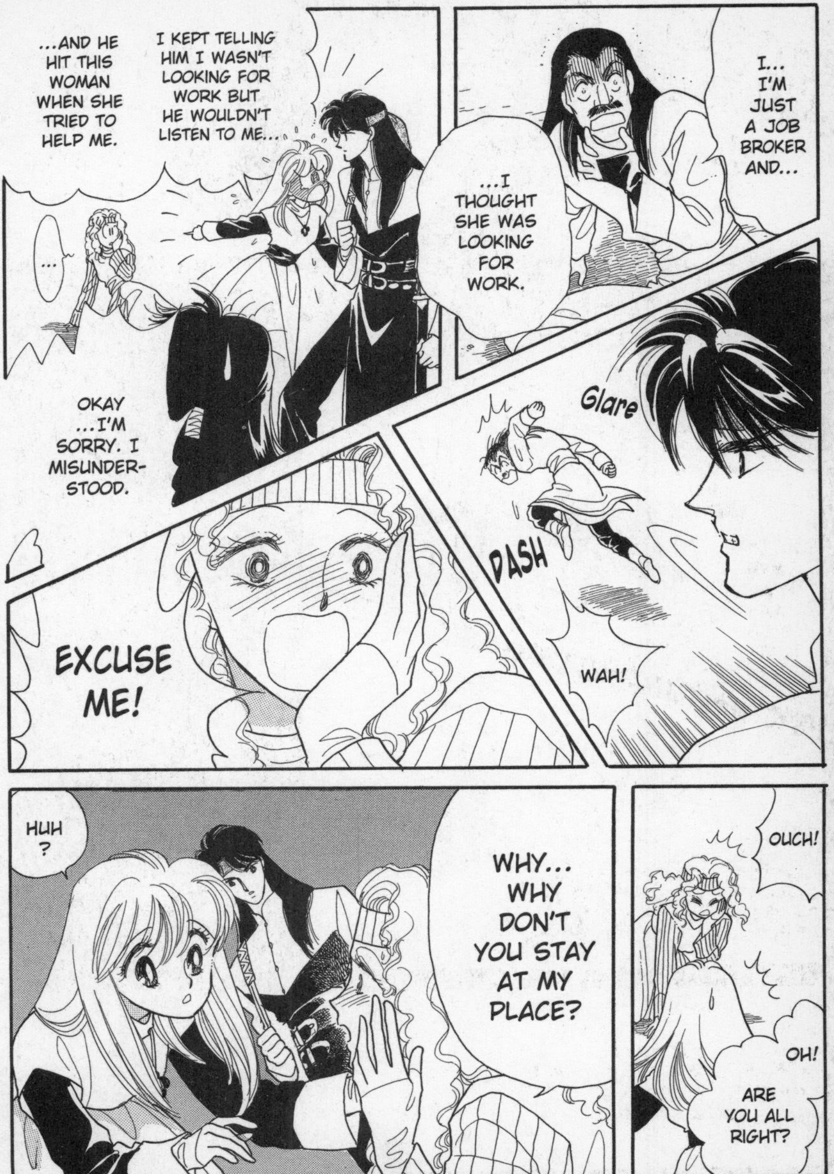
I... I'M JUST A JOB BROKER AND...
...I THOUGHT SHE WAS LOOKING FOR WORK.
I KEPT TELLING HIM I WASN'T LOOKING FOR WORK BUT HE WOULDN'T LISTEN TO ME...
...AND HE HIT THIS WOMAN WHEN SHE TRIED TO HELP ME.
...
OKAY ...I'M SORRY. I MISUNDERSTOOD.
Glare
DASH
WAH!
EXCUSE ME!
OUCH!
OH!
ARE YOU ALL RIGHT?
WHY... WHY DON'T YOU STAY AT MY PLACE?
HUH ?

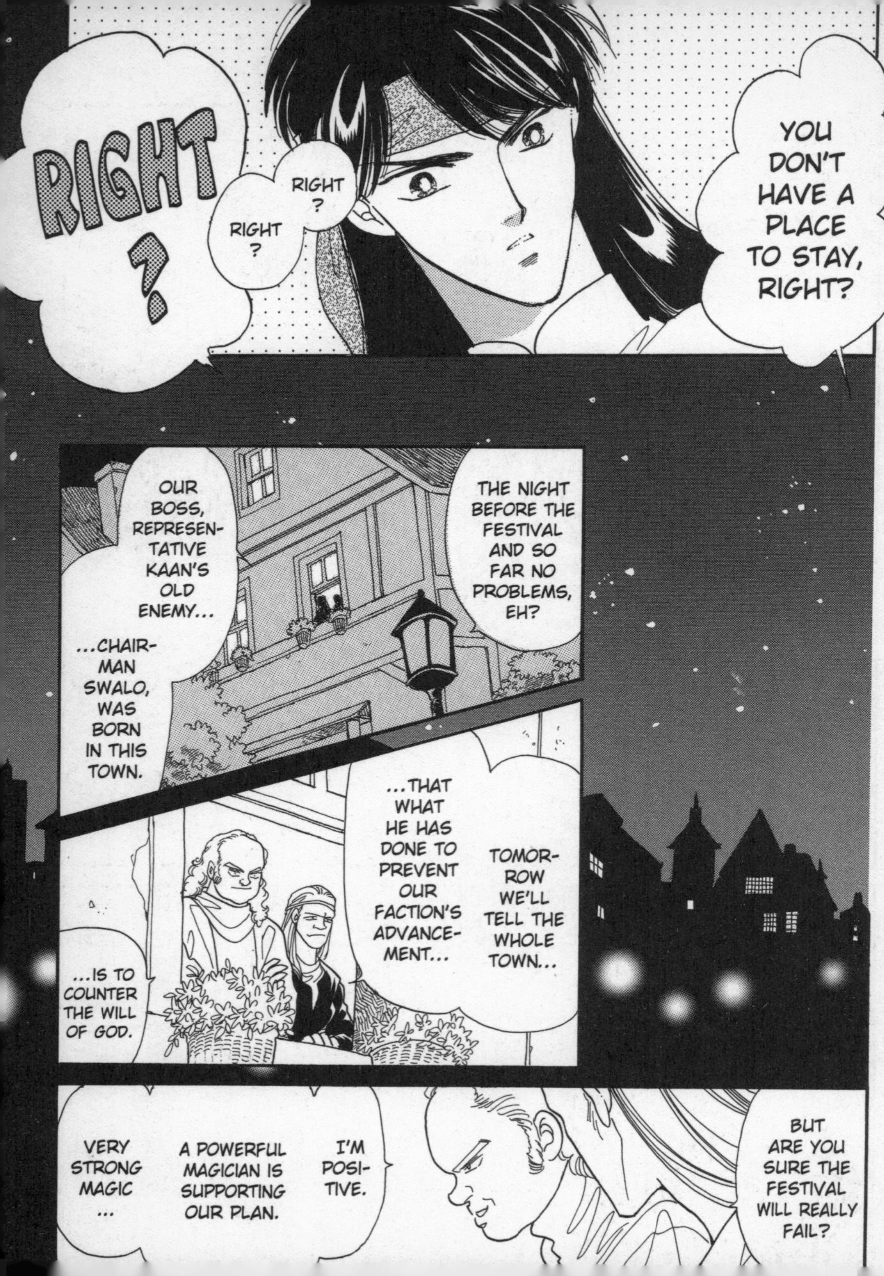
YOU DON'T HAVE A PLACE TO STAY, RIGHT?
RIGHT ?
RIGHT ?
RIGHT ?
THE NIGHT BEFORE THE FESTIVAL AND SO FAR NO PROBLEMS, EH?
OUR BOSS, REPRESENTATIVE KAAN'S OLD ENEMY...
...CHAIRMAN SWALO, WAS BORN IN THIS TOWN.
TOMORROW WE'LL TELL THE WHOLE TOWN...
...THAT WHAT HE HAS DONE TO PREVENT OUR FACTION'S ADVANCEMENT...
...IS TO COUNTER THE WILL OF GOD.
BUT ARE YOU SURE THE FESTIVAL WILL REALLY FAIL?
I'M POSITIVE.
A POWERFUL MAGICIAN IS SUPPORTING OUR PLAN.
VERY STRONG MAGIC ...

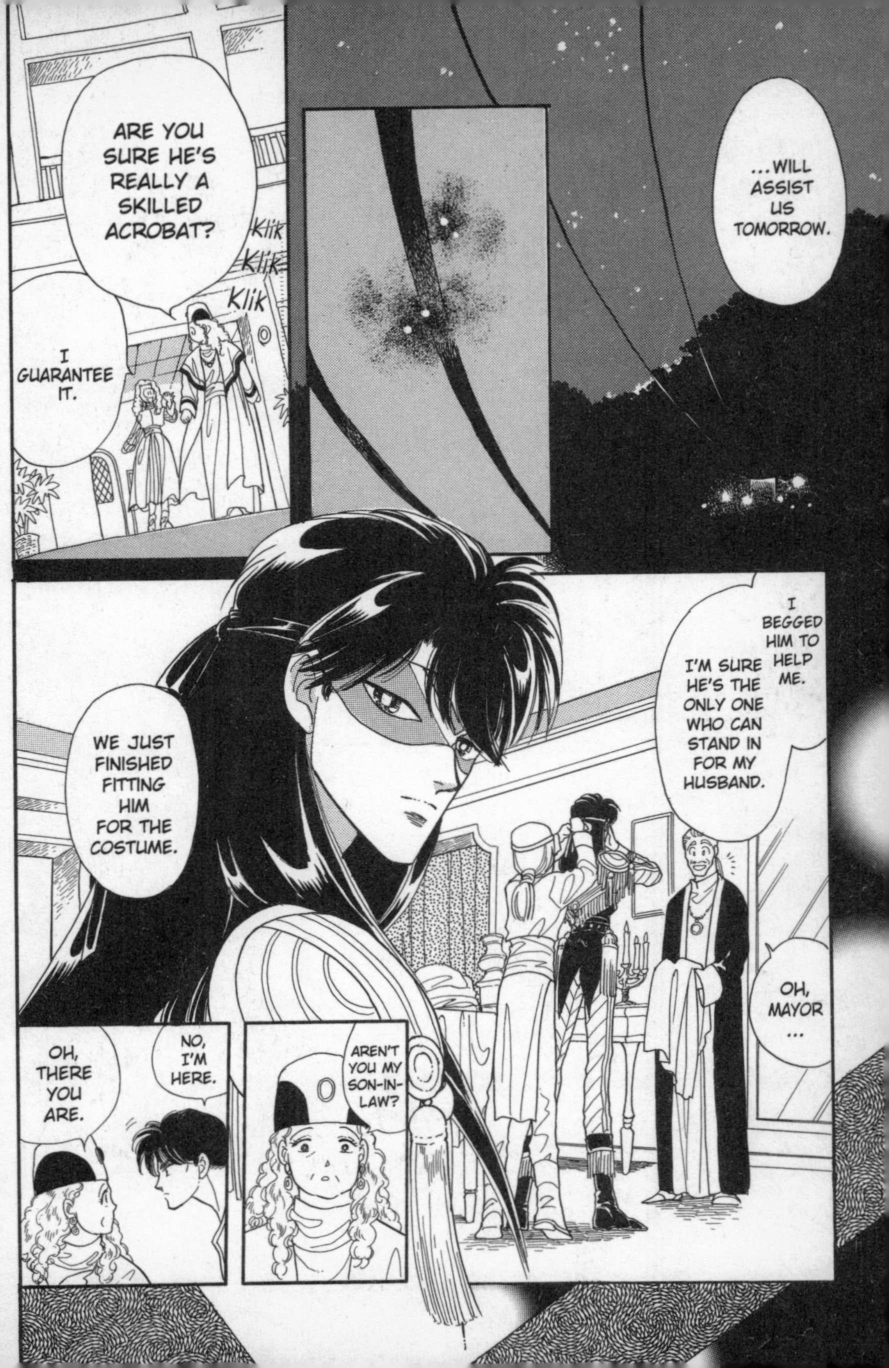
...WILL ASSIST US TOMORROW.
ARE YOU SURE HE'S REALLY A SKILLED ACROBAT?
Klik Klik Klik
I GUARANTEE IT.
I BEGGED HIM TO HELP ME.
I'M SURE HE'S THE ONLY ONE WHO CAN STAND IN FOR MY HUSBAND.
WE JUST FINISHED FITTING HIM FOR THE COSTUME.
OH, MAYOR ...
AREN'T YOU MY SON-IN-LAW?
NO, I'M HERE.
OH, THERE YOU ARE.

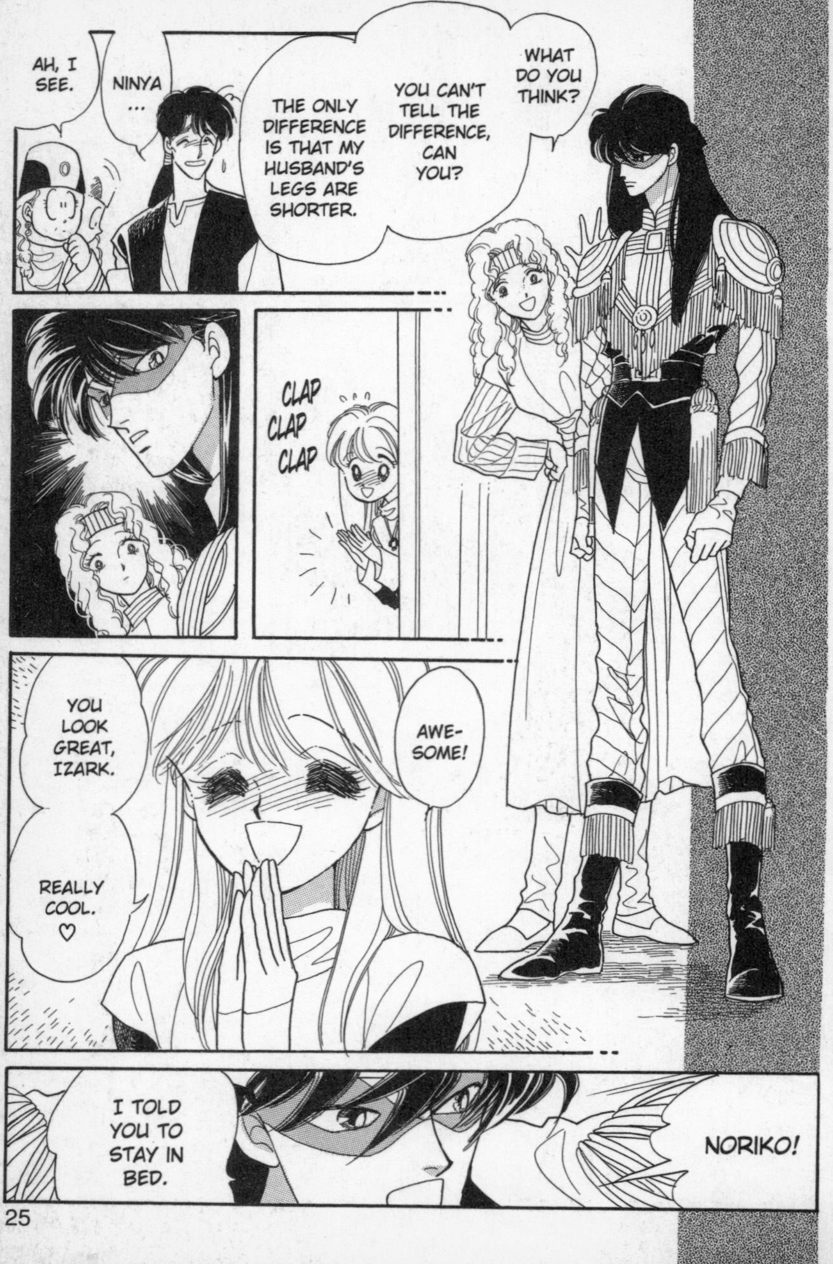
WHAT DO YOU THINK?
YOU CAN'T TELL THE DIFFERENCE, CAN YOU?
THE ONLY DIFFERENCE IS THAT MY HUSBAND'S LEGS ARE SHORTER.
NINYA...
AH, I SEE.
CLAP CLAP CLAP
AWE-SOME!
YOU LOOK GREAT, IZARK.
REALLY COOL. ♡
NORIKO!
I TOLD YOU TO STAY IN BED.

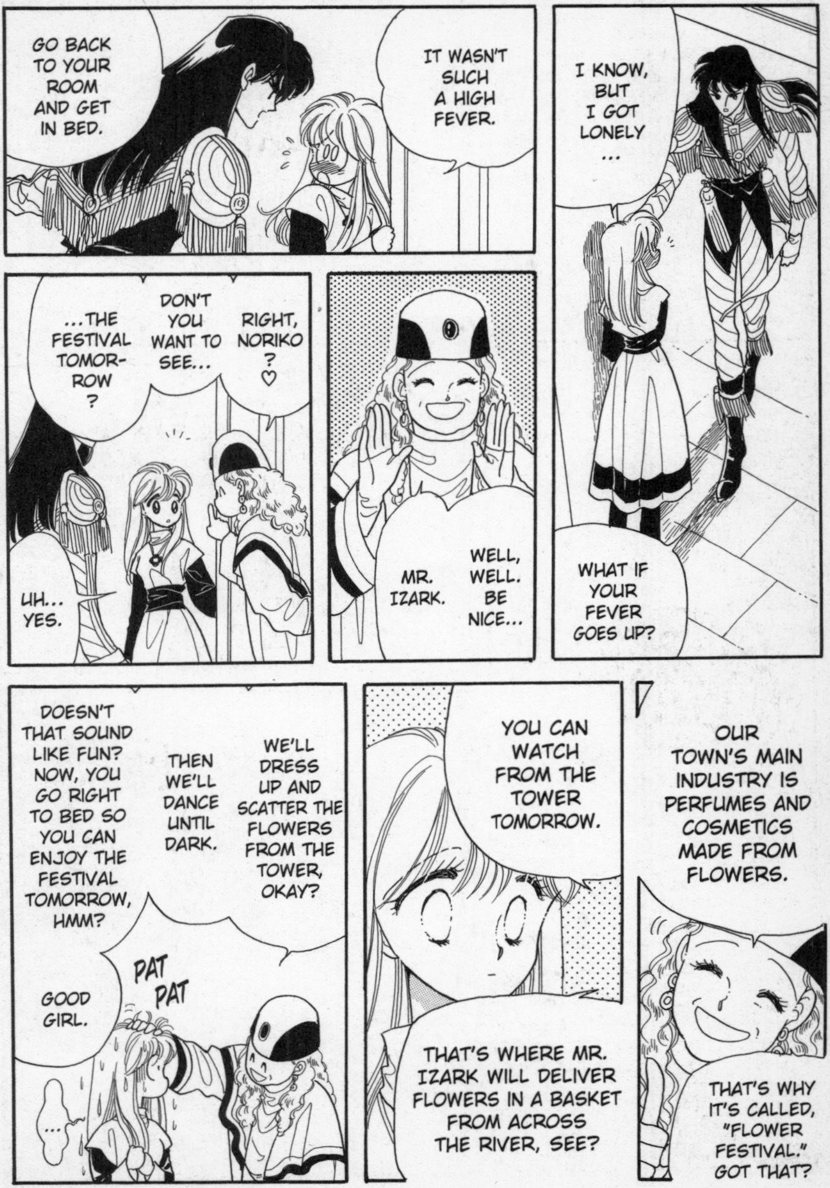
I KNOW, BUT I GOT LONELY ...
WHAT IF YOUR FEVER GOES UP?
IT WASN'T SUCH A HIGH FEVER.
GO BACK TO YOUR ROOM AND GET IN BED.
WELL, WELL. BE NICE...
MR. IZARK.
RIGHT, NORIKO ? ♡
DON'T YOU WANT TO SEE...
...THE FESTIVAL TOMORROW ?
UH... YES.
OUR TOWN'S MAIN INDUSTRY IS PERFUMES AND COSMETICS MADE FROM FLOWERS.
THAT'S WHY IT'S CALLED, "FLOWER FESTIVAL." GOT THAT?
YOU CAN WATCH FROM THE TOWER TOMORROW.
THAT'S WHERE MR. IZARK WILL DELIVER FLOWERS IN A BASKET FROM ACROSS THE RIVER, SEE?
WE'LL DRESS UP AND SCATTER THE FLOWERS FROM THE TOWER, OKAY?
THEN WE'LL DANCE UNTIL DARK.
DOESN'T THAT SOUND LIKE FUN? NOW, YOU GO RIGHT TO BED SO YOU CAN ENJOY THE FESTIVAL TOMORROW, HMM?
PAT PAT
GOOD GIRL.
...

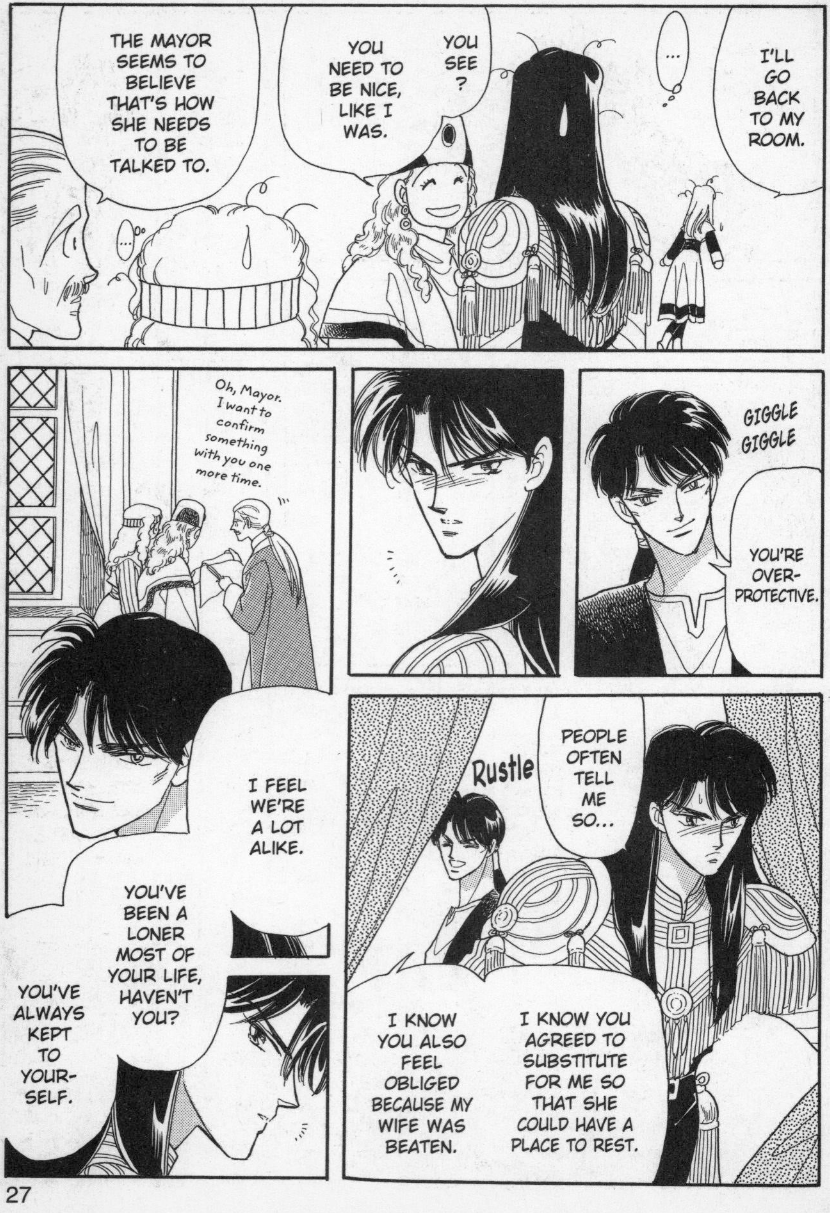
I'LL GO BACK TO MY ROOM.
...
YOU SEE?
YOU NEED TO BE NICE, LIKE I WAS.
THE MAYOR SEEMS TO BELIEVE THAT'S HOW SHE NEEDS TO BE TALKED TO.
...
GIGGLE GIGGLE
YOU'RE OVER-PROTECTIVE.
PEOPLE OFTEN TELL ME SO...
Rustle
I KNOW YOU AGREED TO SUBSTITUTE FOR ME SO THAT SHE COULD HAVE A PLACE TO REST.
I KNOW YOU ALSO FEEL OBLIGED BECAUSE MY WIFE WAS BEATEN.
Oh, Mayor. I want to confirm something with you one more time.
I FEEL WE'RE A LOT ALIKE.
YOU'VE BEEN A LONER MOST OF YOUR LIFE, HAVEN'T YOU?
YOU'VE ALWAYS KEPT TO YOUR-SELF.

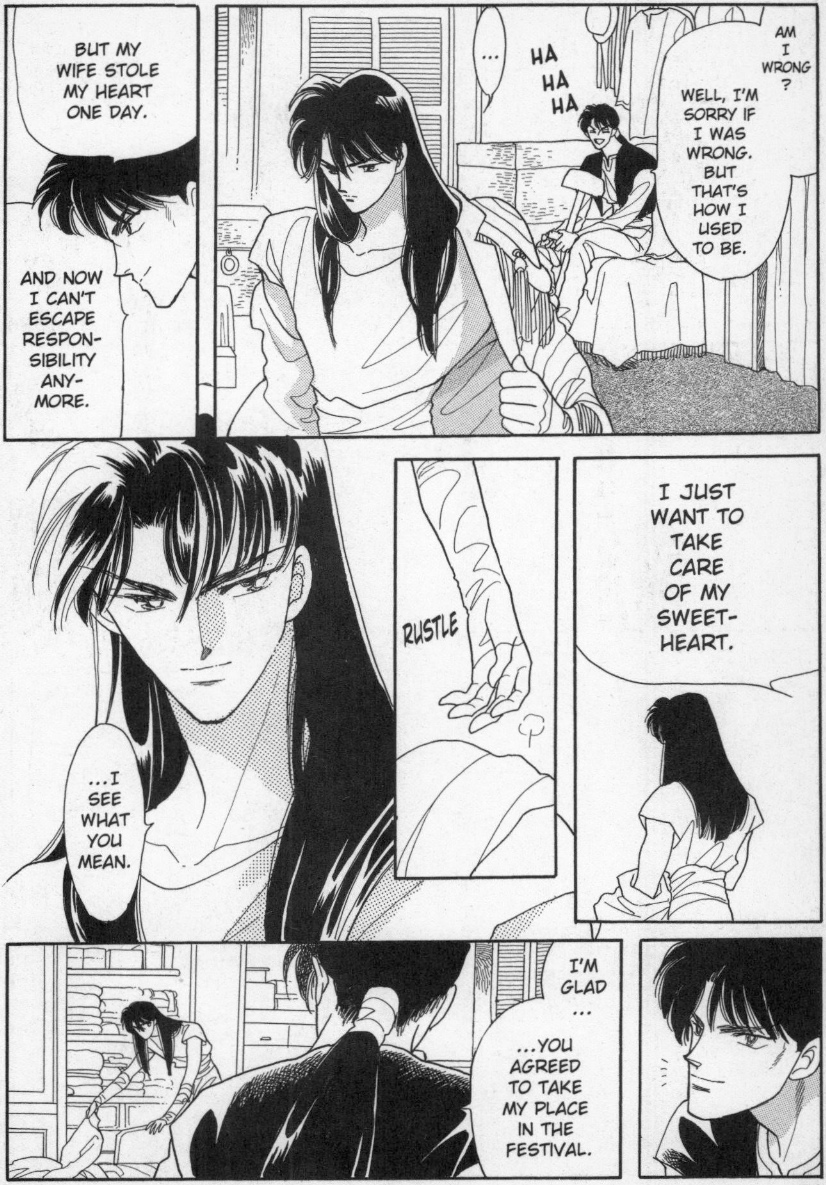
AM I WRONG?
WELL, I'M SORRY IF I WAS WRONG. BUT THAT'S HOW I USED TO BE.
HA HA HA
...
BUT MY WIFE STOLE MY HEART ONE DAY.
AND NOW I CAN'T ESCAPE RESPONSIBILITY ANYMORE.
I JUST WANT TO TAKE CARE OF MY SWEETHEART.
RUSTLE
...I SEE WHAT YOU MEAN.
I'M GLAD...
...YOU AGREED TO TAKE MY PLACE IN THE FESTIVAL.

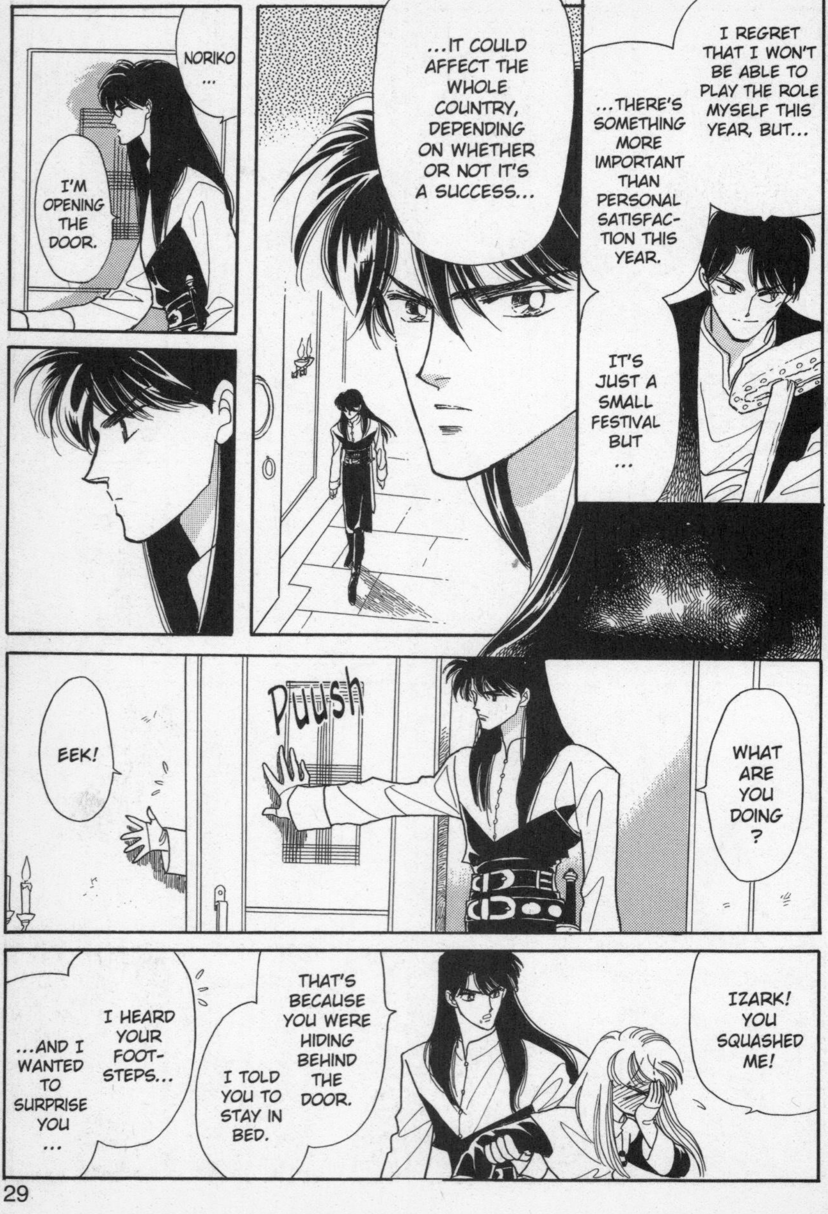
I REGRET THAT I WON'T BE ABLE TO PLAY THE ROLE MYSELF THIS YEAR, BUT...
...THERE'S SOMETHING MORE IMPORTANT THAN PERSONAL SATISFACTION THIS YEAR.
IT'S JUST A SMALL FESTIVAL BUT ...
...IT COULD AFFECT THE WHOLE COUNTRY, DEPENDING ON WHETHER OR NOT IT'S A SUCCESS...
NORIKO ...
I'M OPENING THE DOOR.
WHAT ARE YOU DOING ?
Puush
EEK!
IZARK! YOU SQUASHED ME!
THAT'S BECAUSE YOU WERE HIDING BEHIND THE DOOR.
I TOLD YOU TO STAY IN BED.
I HEARD YOUR FOOT-STEPS...
...AND I WANTED TO SURPRISE YOU ...

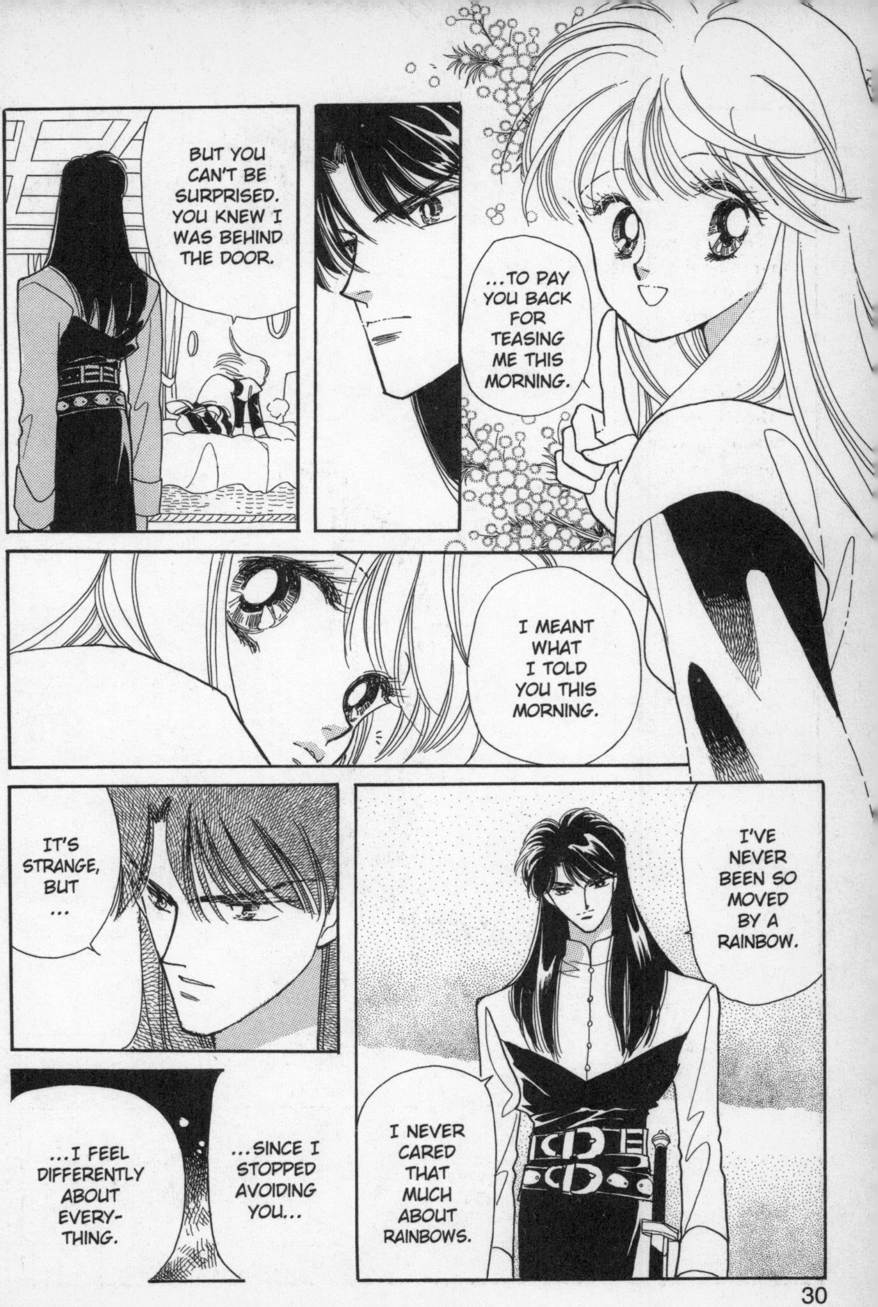
...TO PAY YOU BACK FOR TEASING ME THIS MORNING.
BUT YOU CAN'T BE SURPRISED. YOU KNEW I WAS BEHIND THE DOOR.
I MEANT WHAT I TOLD YOU THIS MORNING.
I'VE NEVER BEEN SO MOVED BY A RAINBOW.
I NEVER CARED THAT MUCH ABOUT RAINBOWS.
IT'S STRANGE, BUT ...
...SINCE I STOPPED AVOIDING YOU...
...I FEEL DIFFERENTLY ABOUT EVERY-THING.

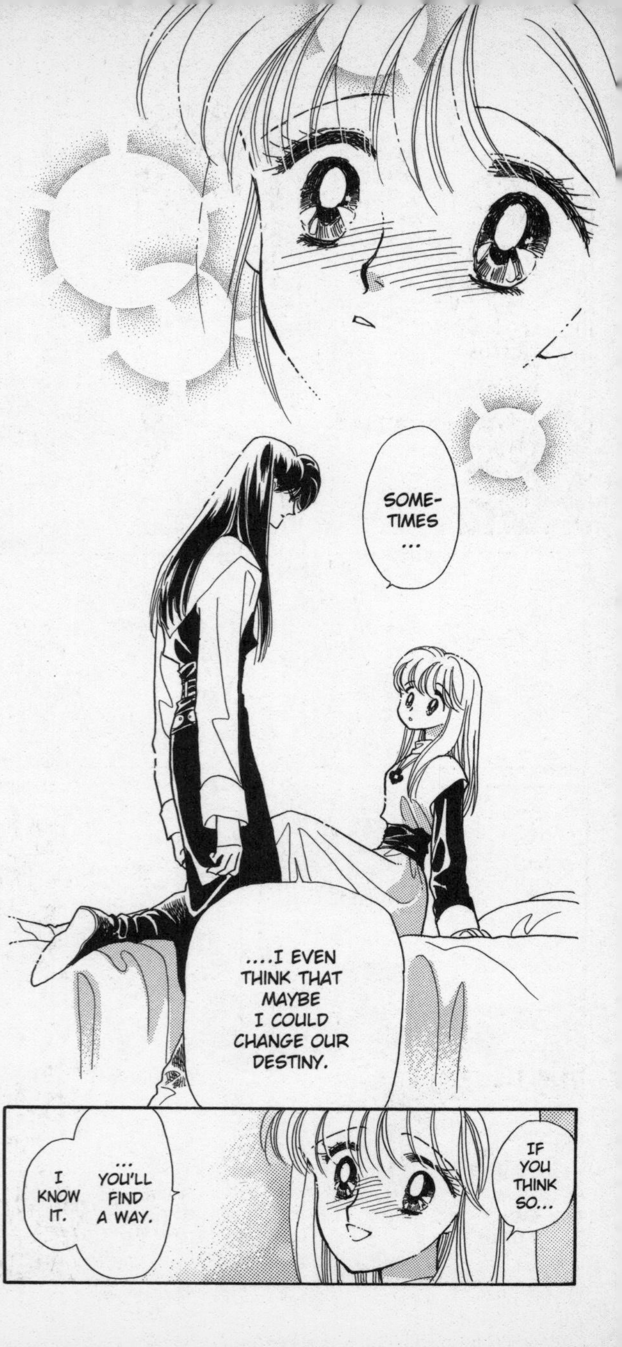
SOME-TIMES ...
....I EVEN THINK THAT MAYBE I COULD CHANGE OUR DESTINY.
IF YOU THINK SO...
... YOU'LL FIND A WAY.
I KNOW IT.

Cat Story (1)

Cats are my favorite animal. I never miss TV shows about cats.

But I don't like them enough to want to keep one at home.

That's about how much I "like" them.

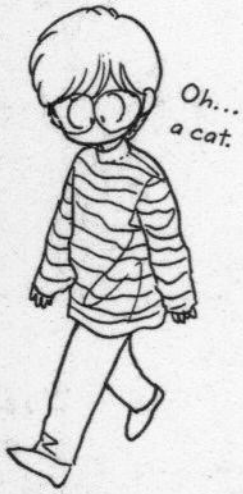
Oh... a cat.

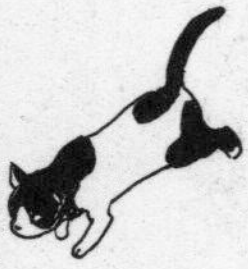

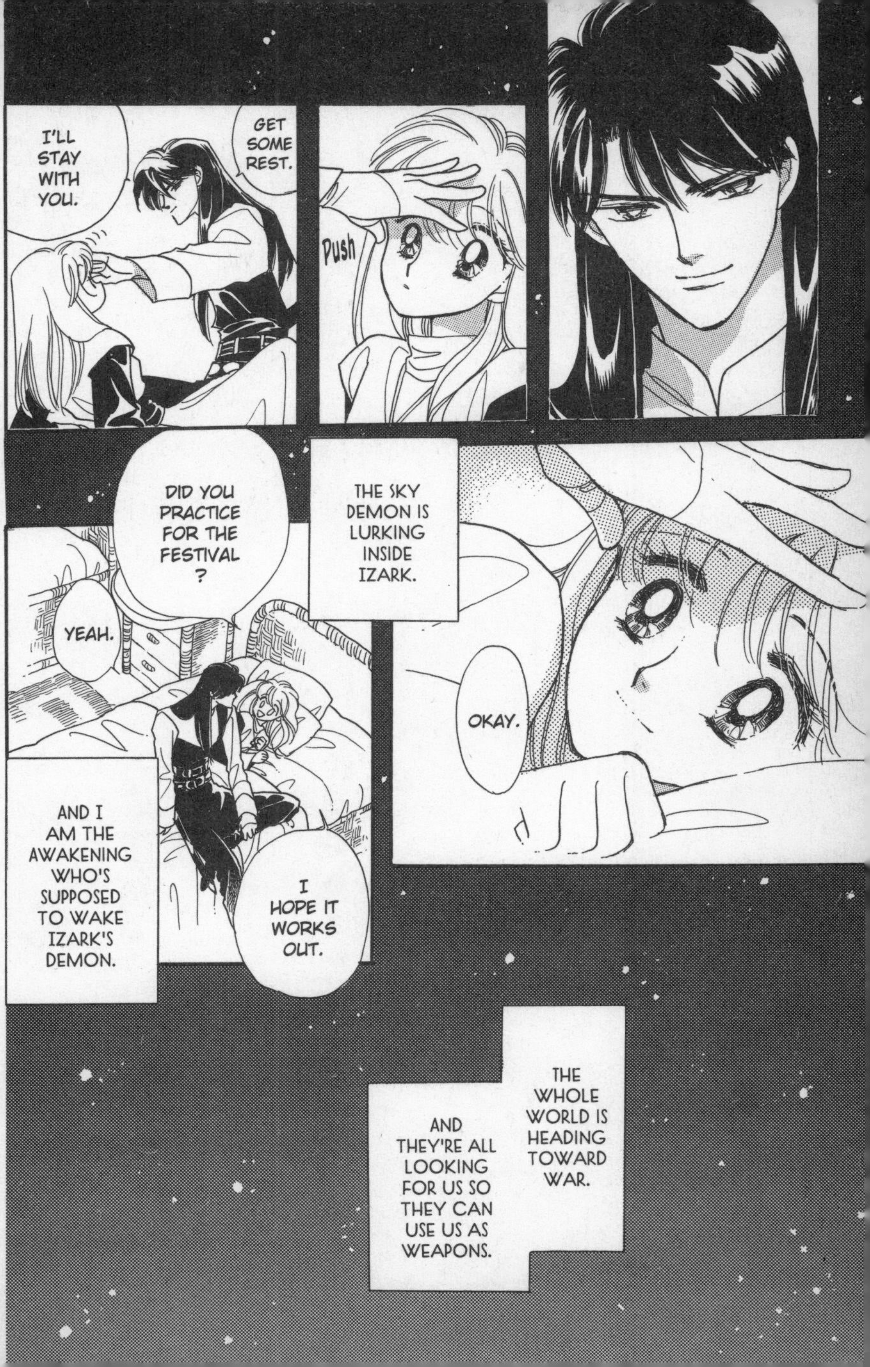
Push
GET SOME REST.
I'LL STAY WITH YOU.
THE SKY DEMON IS LURKING INSIDE IZARK.
OKAY.
DID YOU PRACTICE FOR THE FESTIVAL ?
YEAH.
I HOPE IT WORKS OUT.
AND I AM THE AWAKENING WHO'S SUPPOSED TO WAKE IZARK'S DEMON.
THE WHOLE WORLD IS HEADING TOWARD WAR.
AND THEY'RE ALL LOOKING FOR US SO THEY CAN USE US AS WEAPONS.

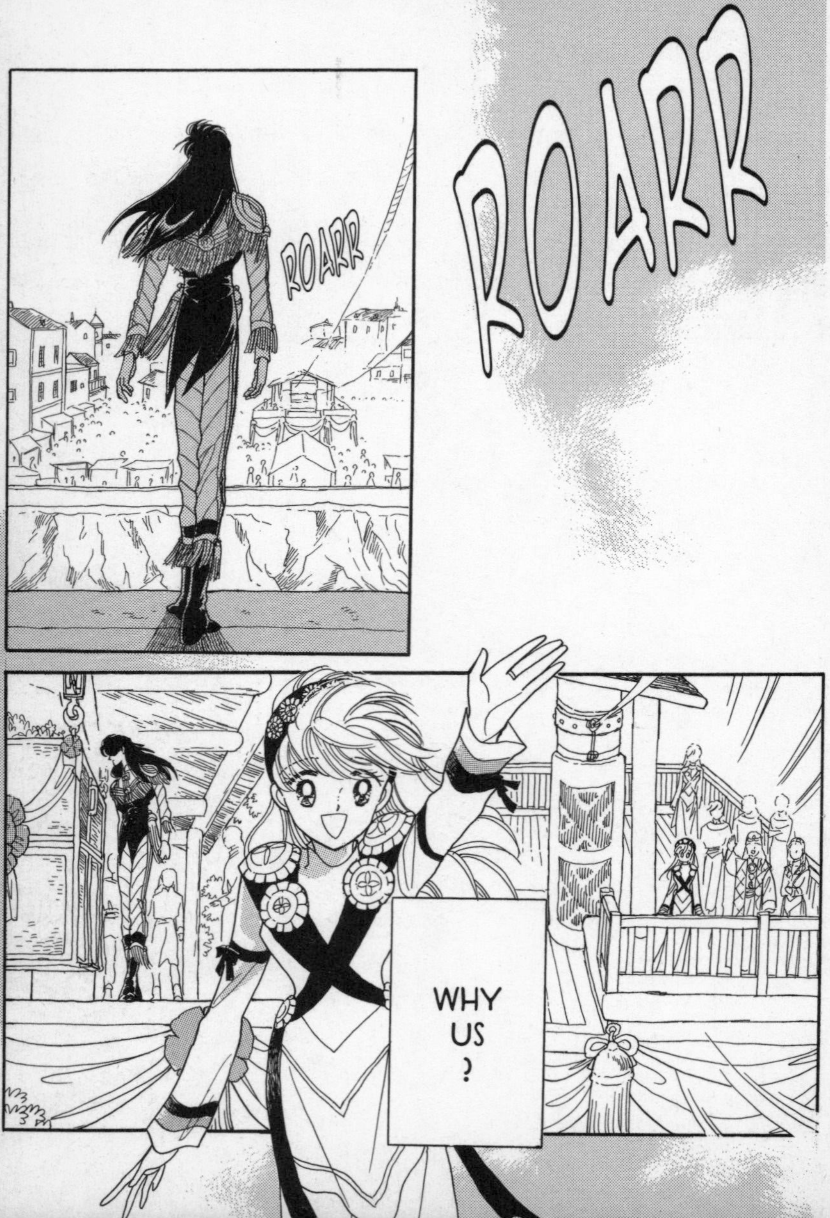
ROARR
ROARR
WHY US ?

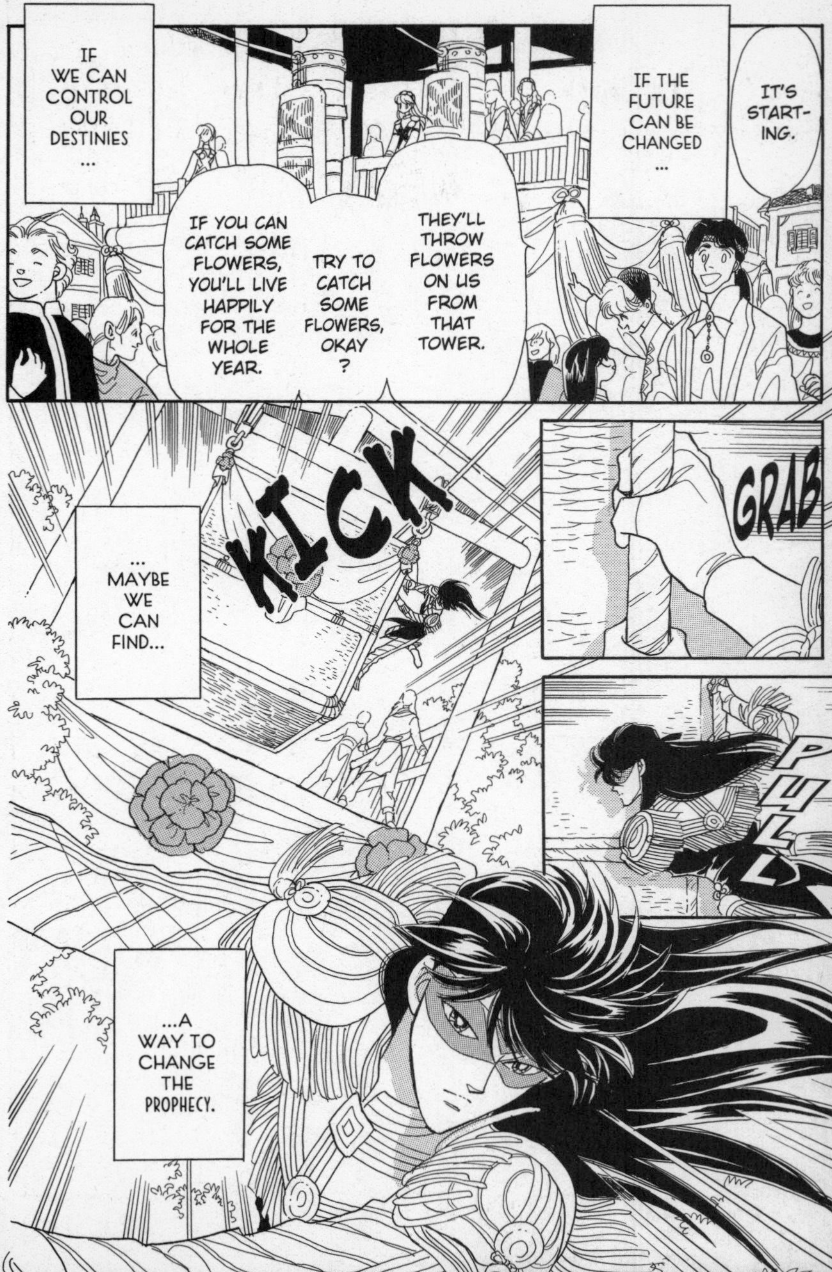
IT'S STARTING.
IF THE FUTURE CAN BE CHANGED ...
IF WE CAN CONTROL OUR DESTINIES ...
THEY'LL THROW FLOWERS ON US FROM THAT TOWER.
TRY TO CATCH SOME FLOWERS, OKAY ?
IF YOU CAN CATCH SOME FLOWERS, YOU'LL LIVE HAPPILY FOR THE WHOLE YEAR.
GRAB
PULL
KICK
... MAYBE WE CAN FIND...
...A WAY TO CHANGE THE PROPHECY.

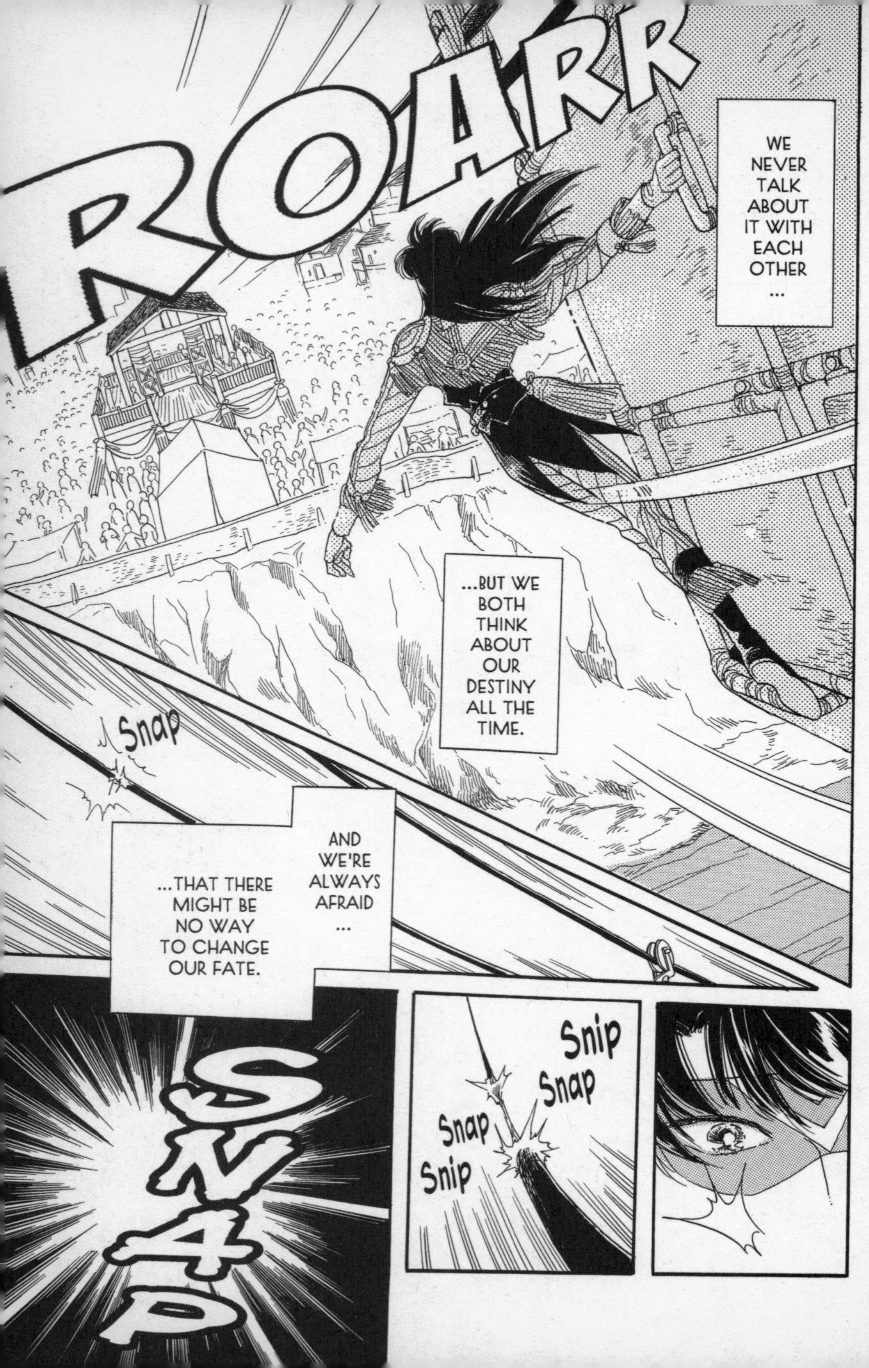
ROARR
WE NEVER TALK ABOUT IT WITH EACH OTHER ...
...BUT WE BOTH THINK ABOUT OUR DESTINY ALL THE TIME.
Snap
AND WE'RE ALWAYS AFRAID ...
...THAT THERE MIGHT BE NO WAY TO CHANGE OUR FATE.
Snip
Snap
Snap
Snip
SNAP

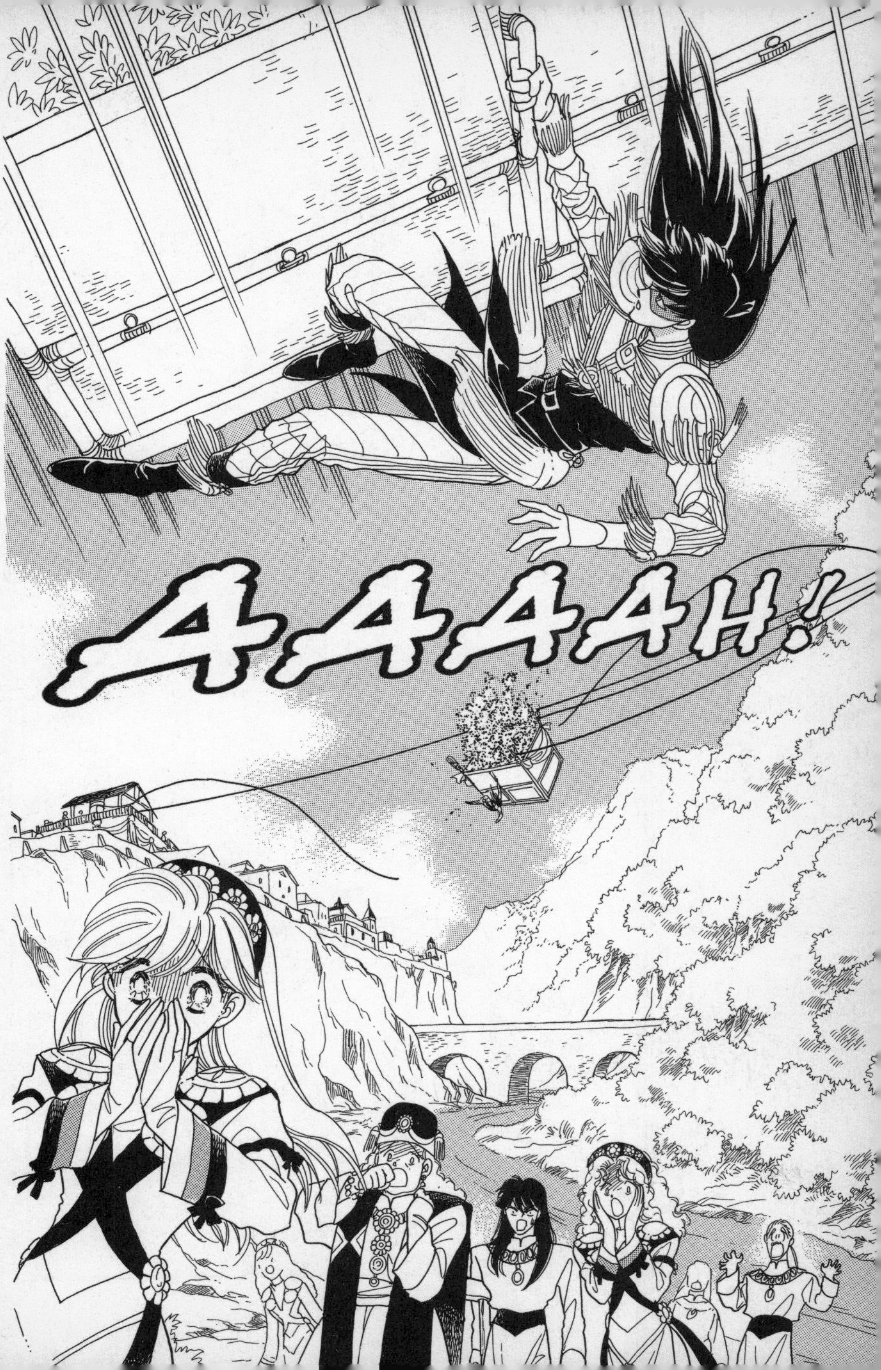
AAAAH!

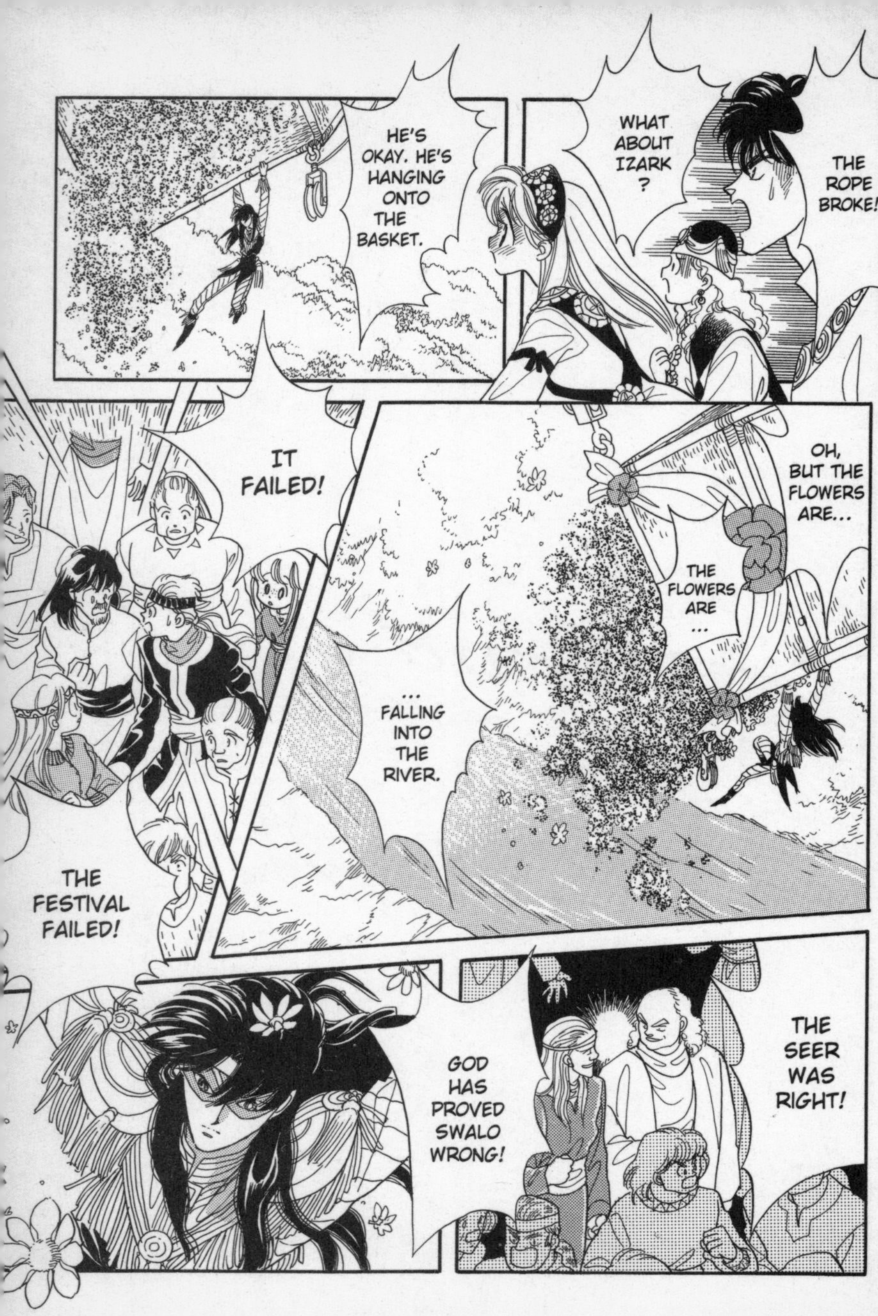
THE ROPE BROKE!
WHAT ABOUT IZARK ?
HE'S OKAY. HE'S HANGING ONTO THE BASKET.
OH, BUT THE FLOWERS ARE...
THE FLOWERS ARE ...
... FALLING INTO THE RIVER.
IT FAILED!
THE FESTIVAL FAILED!
THE SEER WAS RIGHT!
GOD HAS PROVED SWALO WRONG!

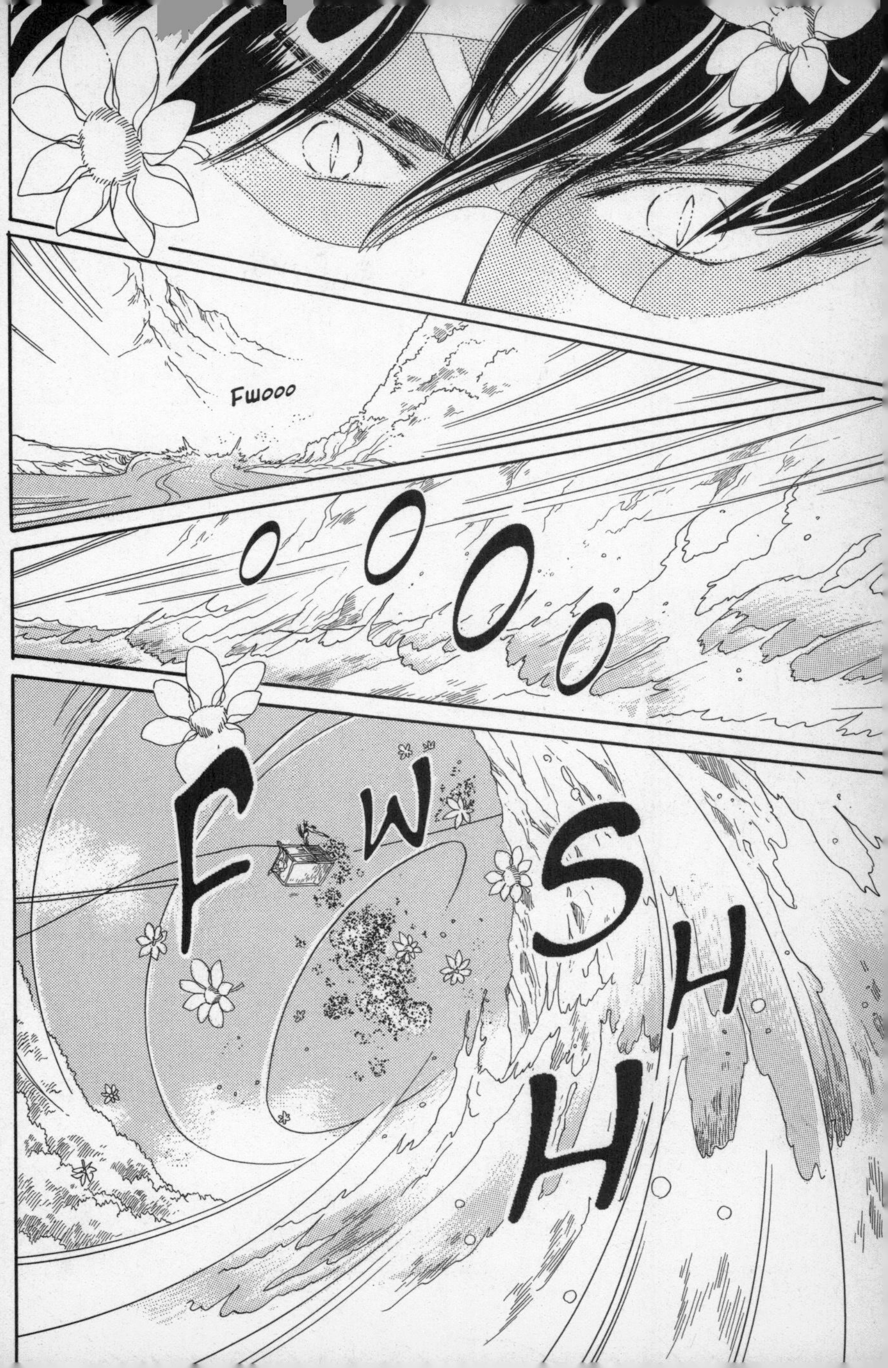
Fwooo
ooooo
FWSHH

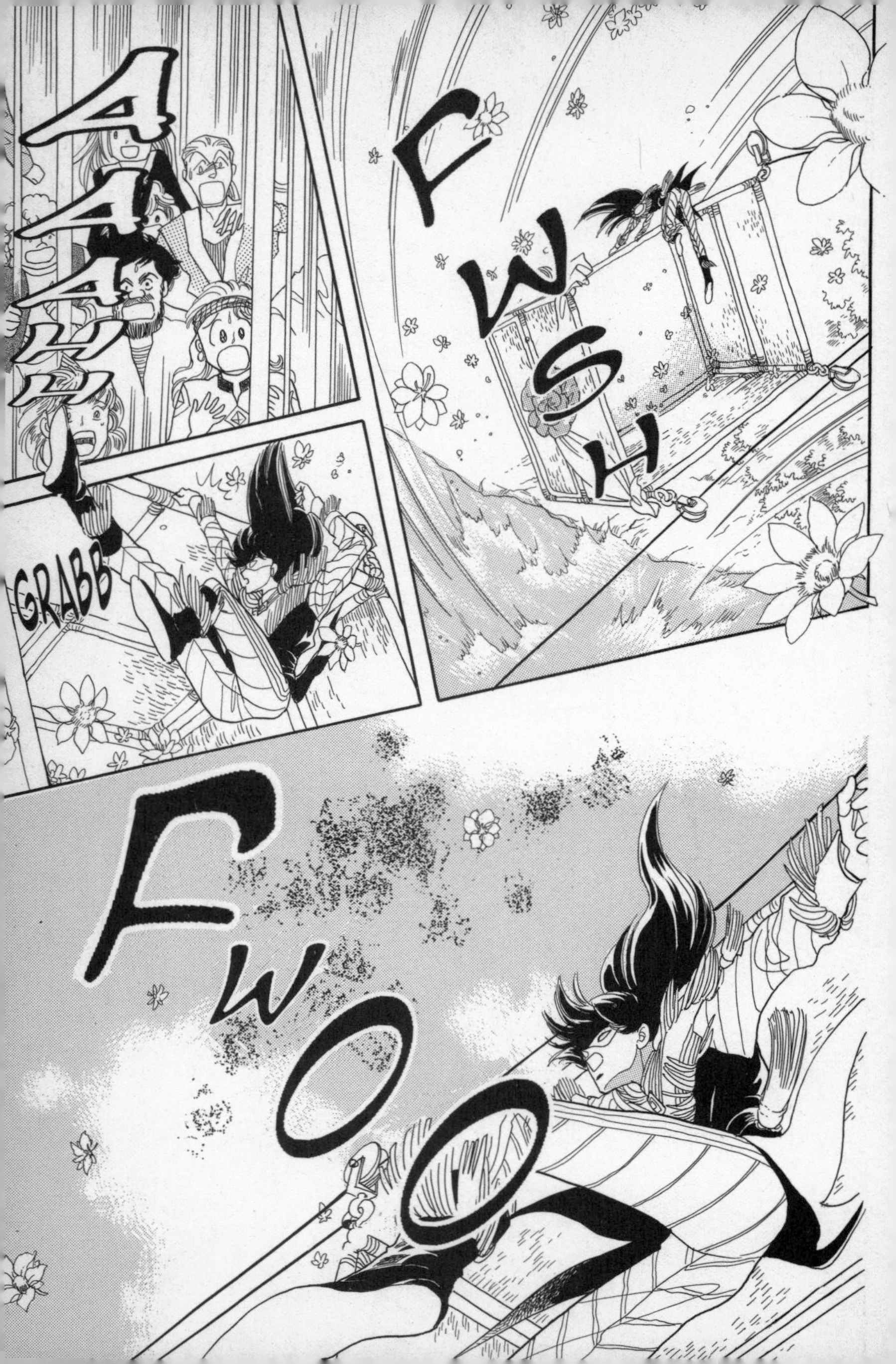
FWSH
AAAHH
GRABB
FWOO

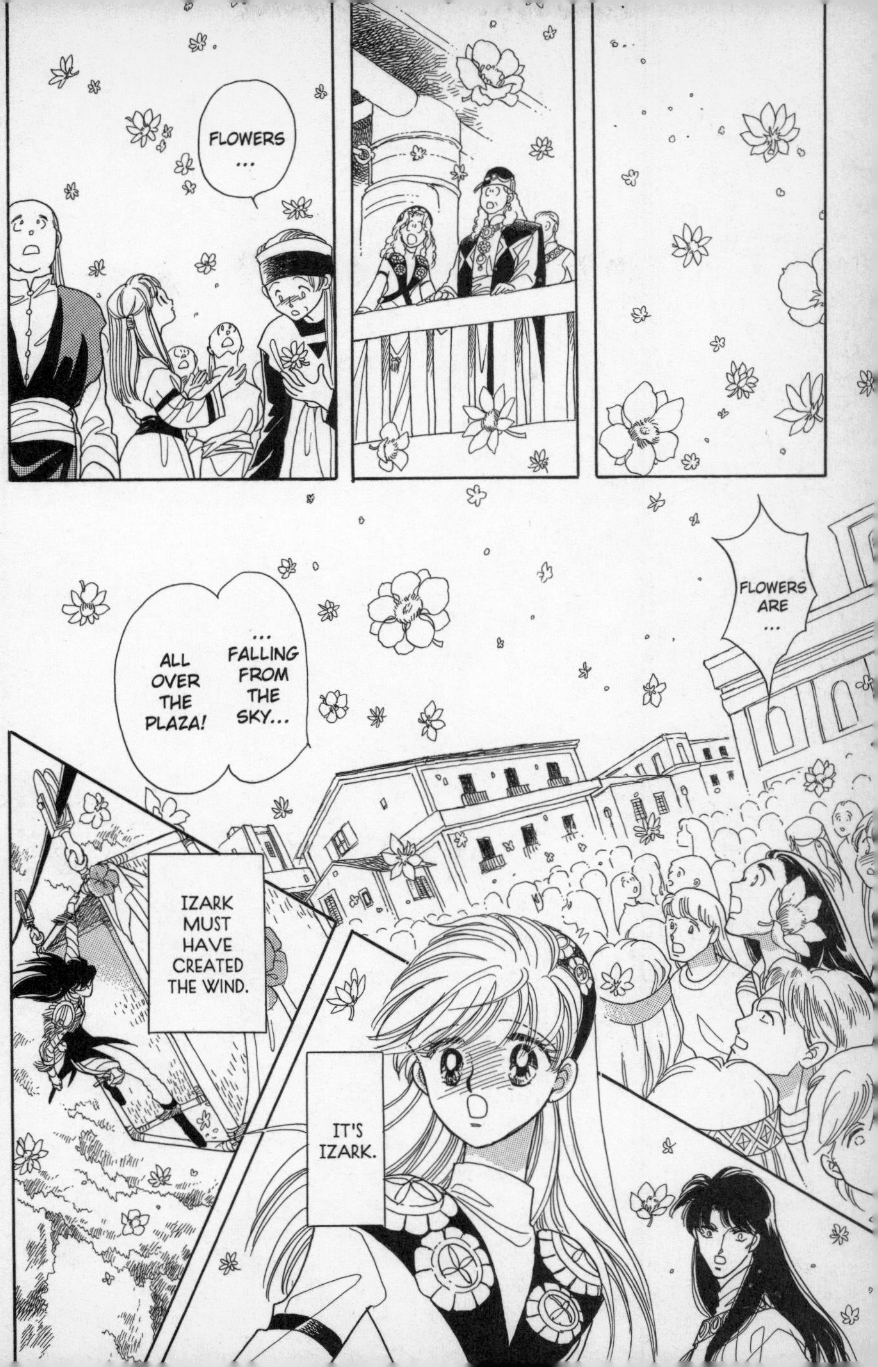
FLOWERS ...
FLOWERS ARE ...
... FALLING FROM THE SKY...
ALL OVER THE PLAZA!
IT'S IZARK.
IZARK MUST HAVE CREATED THE WIND.

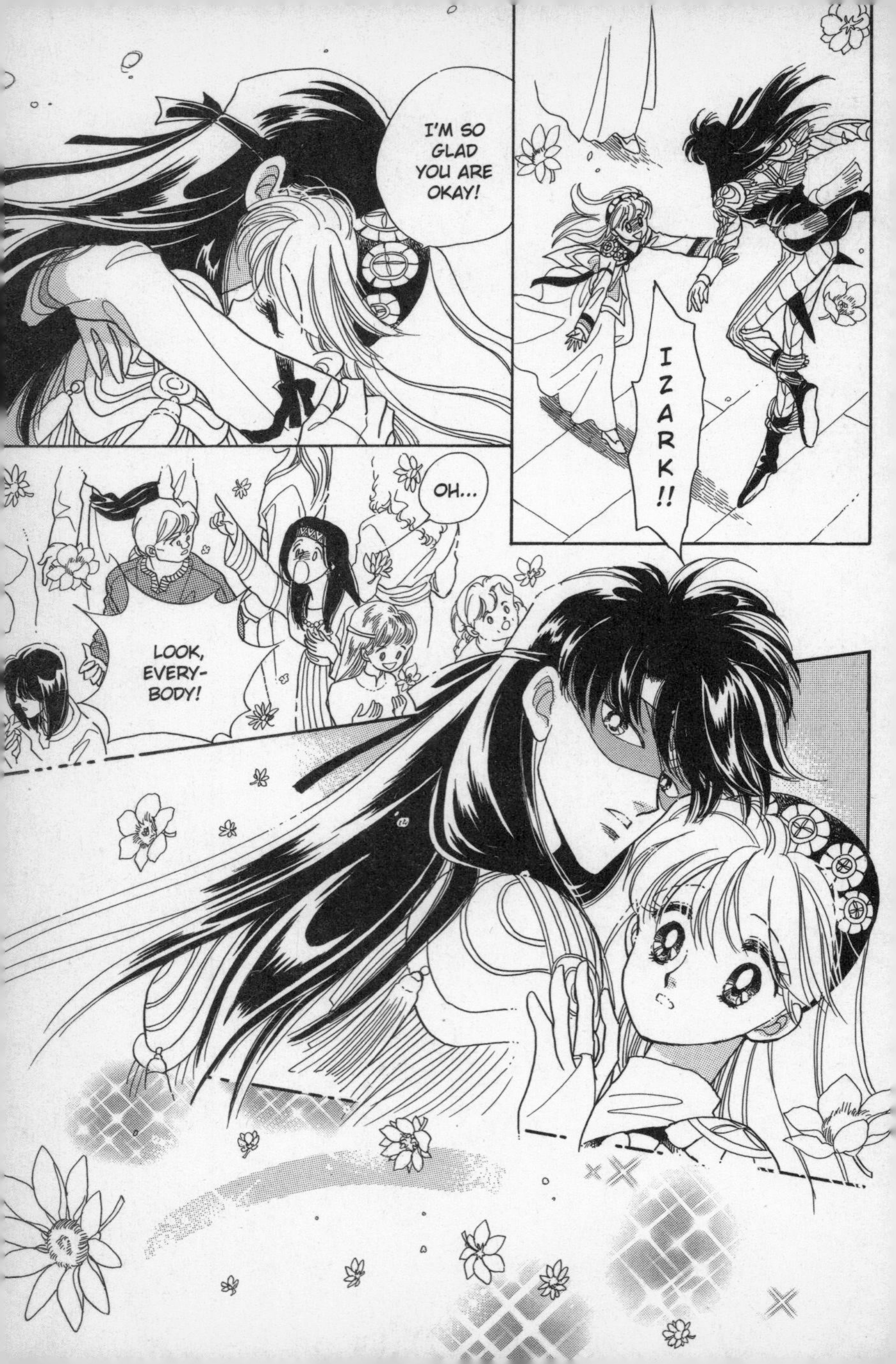
IZARK!!
I'M SO GLAD YOU ARE OKAY!
OH...
LOOK, EVERY-BODY!

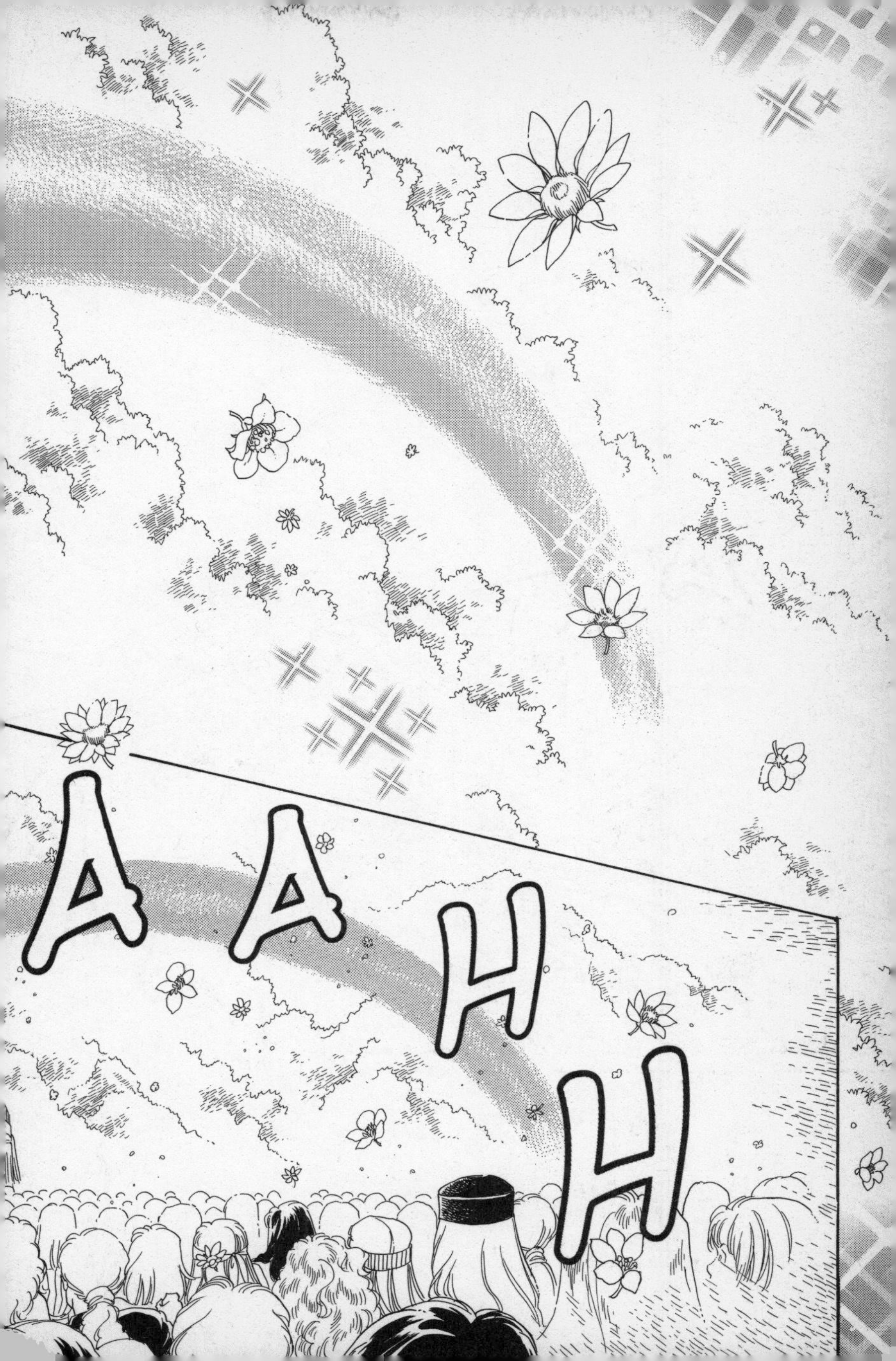
AAHH

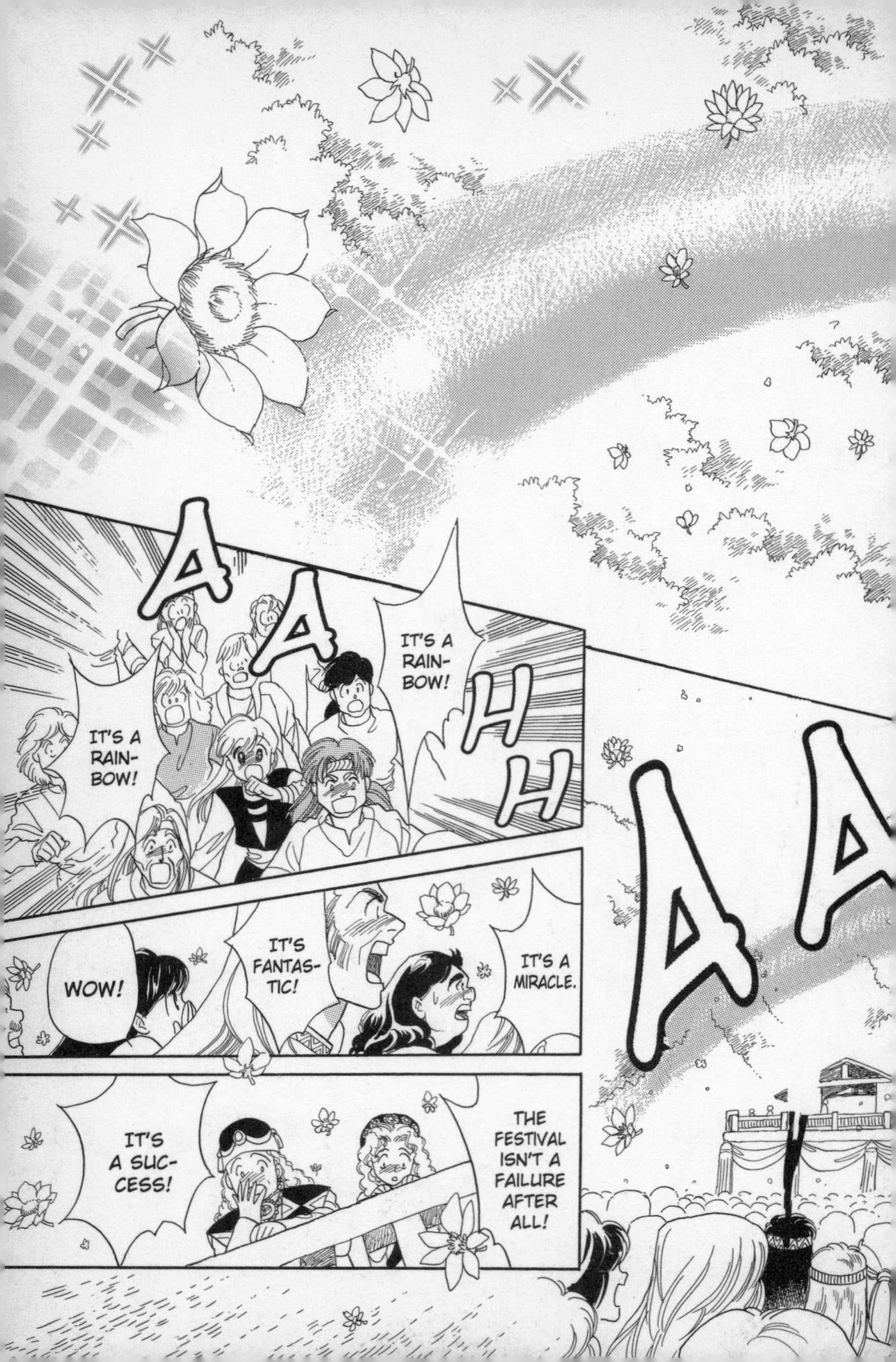

AA
AAHH
IT'S A RAINBOW!
IT'S A RAINBOW!
IT'S A MIRACLE.
IT'S FANTASTIC!
WOW!
THE FESTIVAL ISN'T A FAILURE AFTER ALL!
IT'S A SUCCESS!

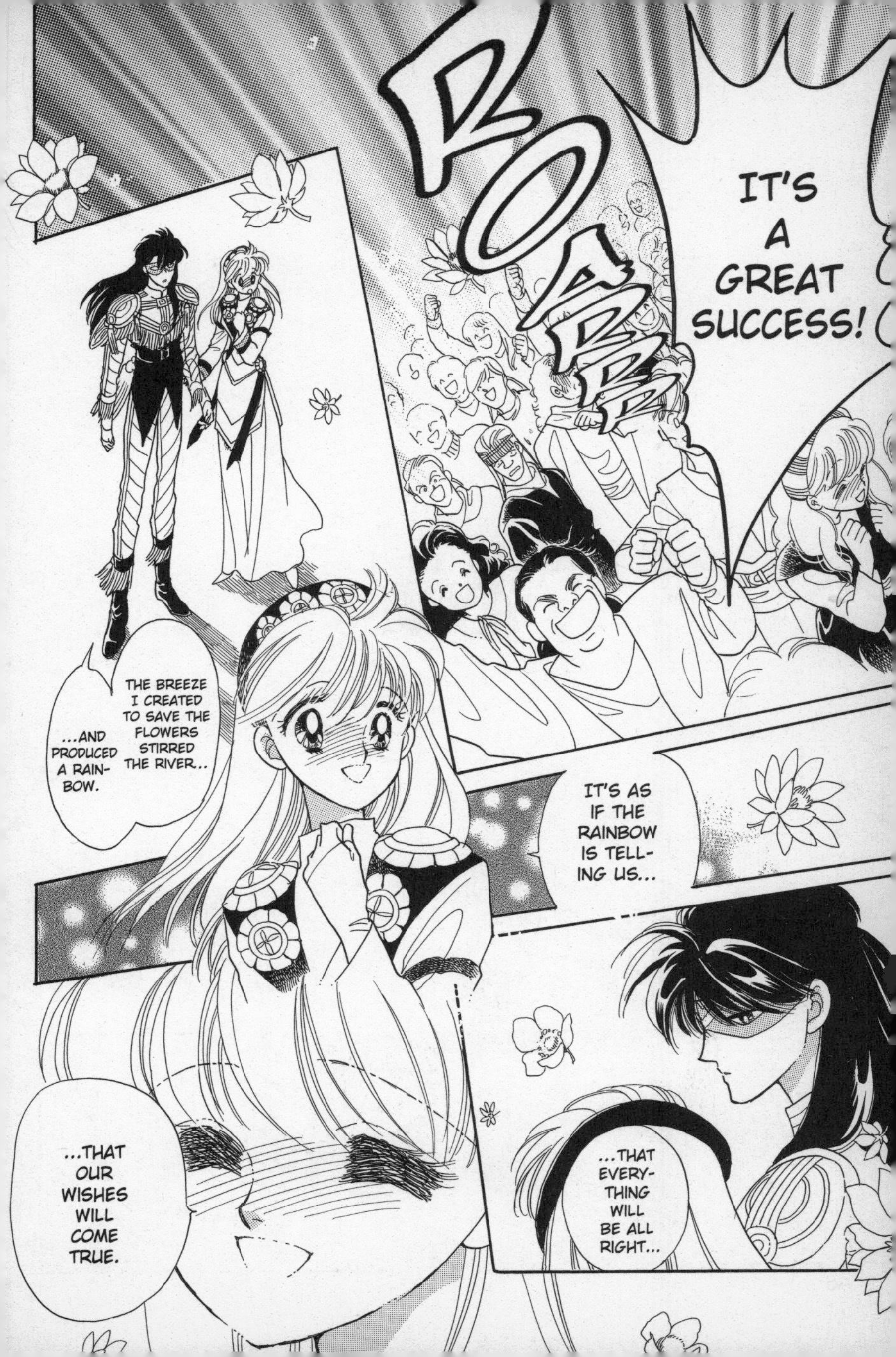
IT'S A GREAT SUCCESS!
THE BREEZE I CREATED TO SAVE THE FLOWERS STIRRED THE RIVER...
...AND PRODUCED A RAIN-BOW.
IT'S AS IF THE RAINBOW IS TELL-ING US...
...THAT EVERY-THING WILL BE ALL RIGHT...
...THAT OUR WISHES WILL COME TRUE.

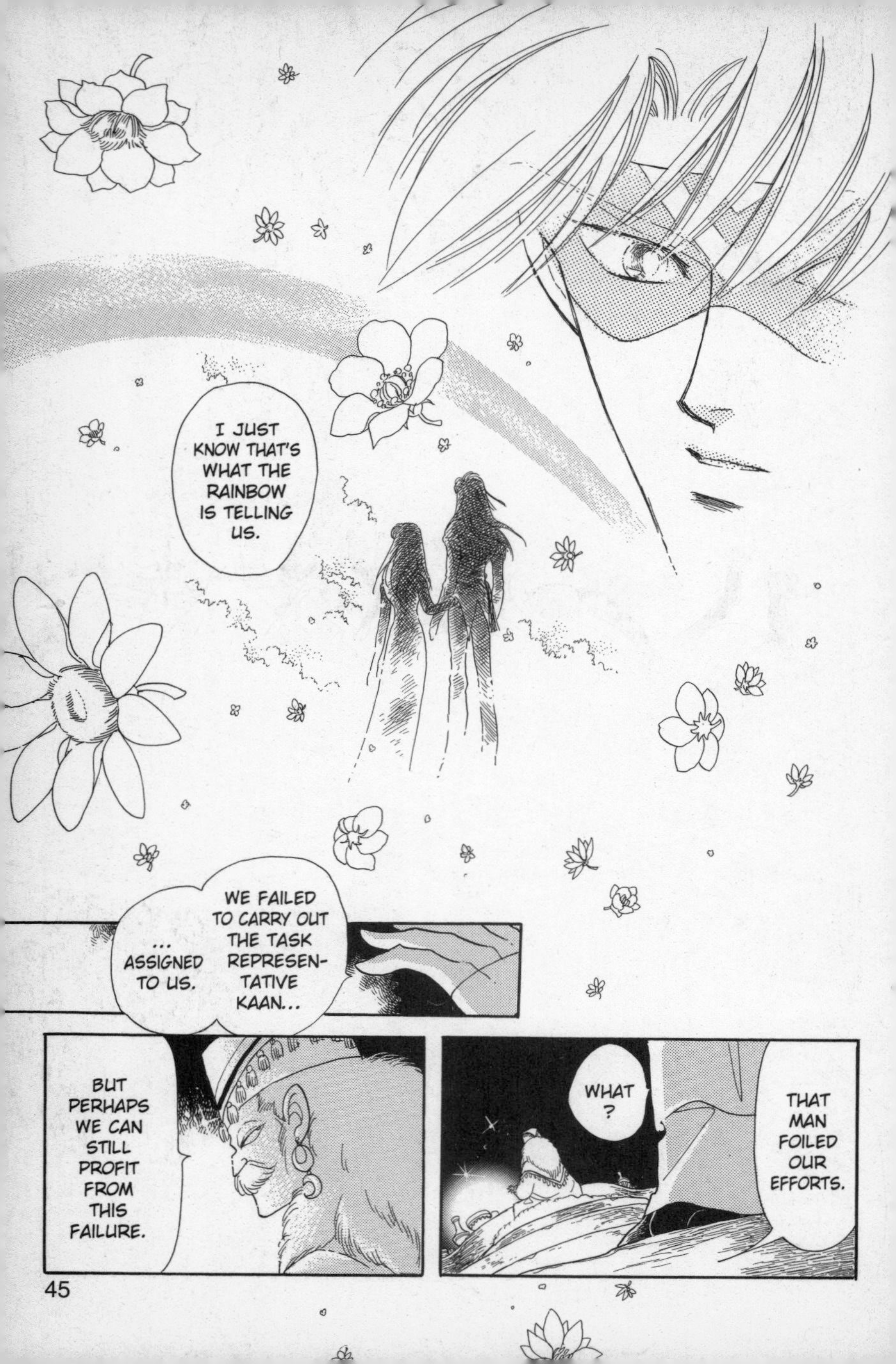
I JUST KNOW THAT'S WHAT THE RAINBOW IS TELLING US.
WE FAILED TO CARRY OUT THE TASK REPRESENTATIVE KAAN...
... ASSIGNED TO US.
THAT MAN FOILED OUR EFFORTS.
WHAT ?
BUT PERHAPS WE CAN STILL PROFIT FROM THIS FAILURE.

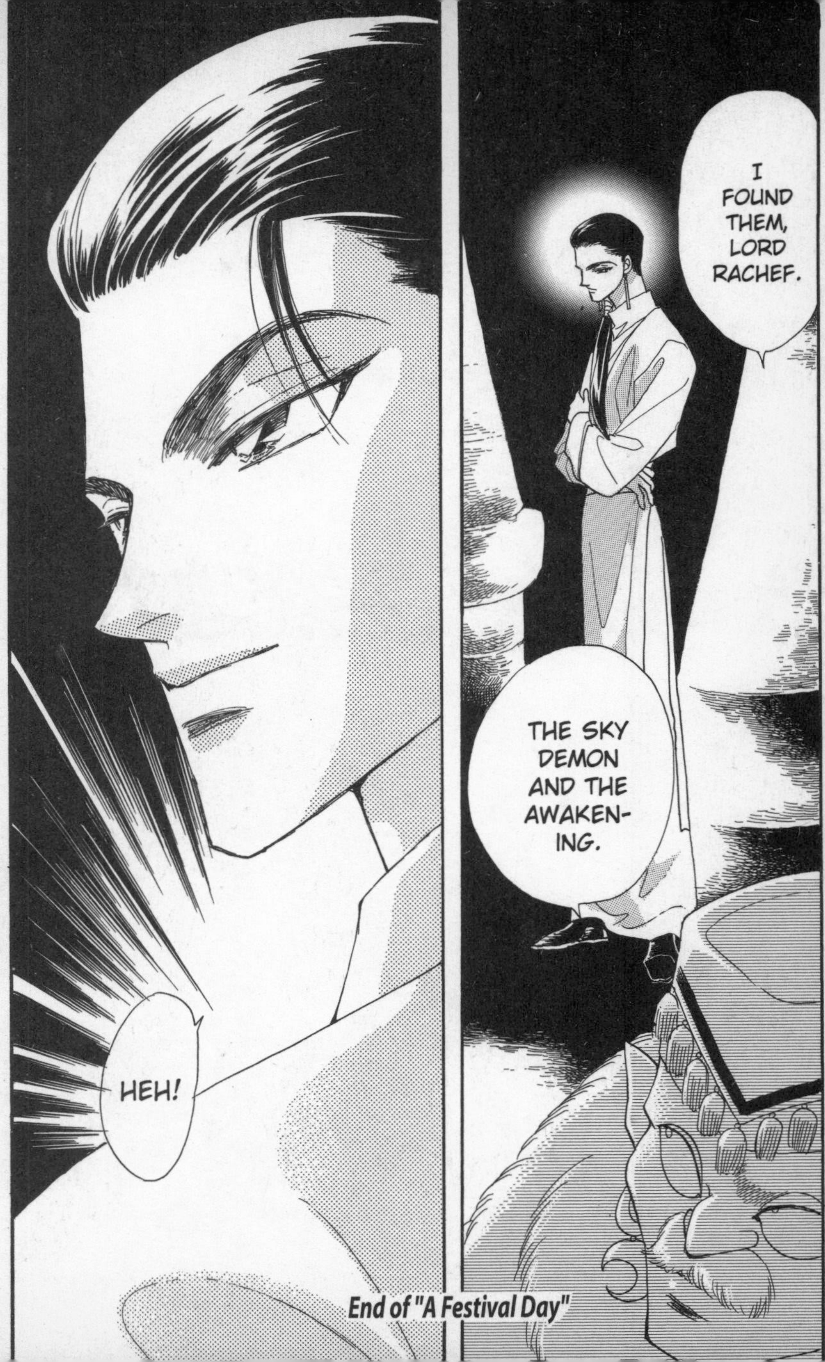
I FOUND THEM, LORD RACHEF.
THE SKY DEMON AND THE AWAKEN-ING.
HEH!

End of "A Festival Day"

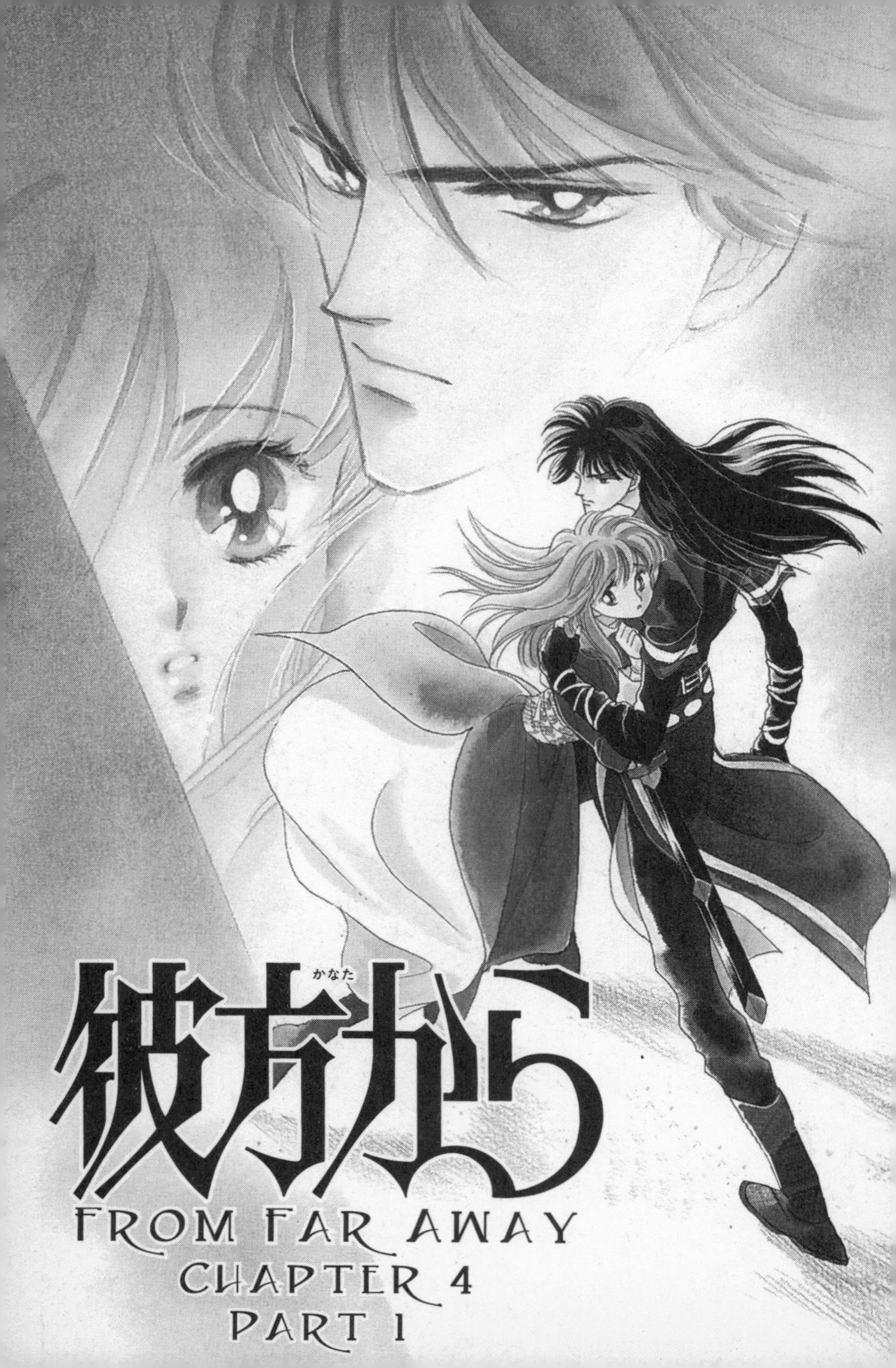
彼方(かなた)から
FROM FAR AWAY
CHAPTER 4
PART 1

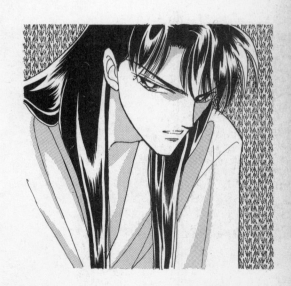

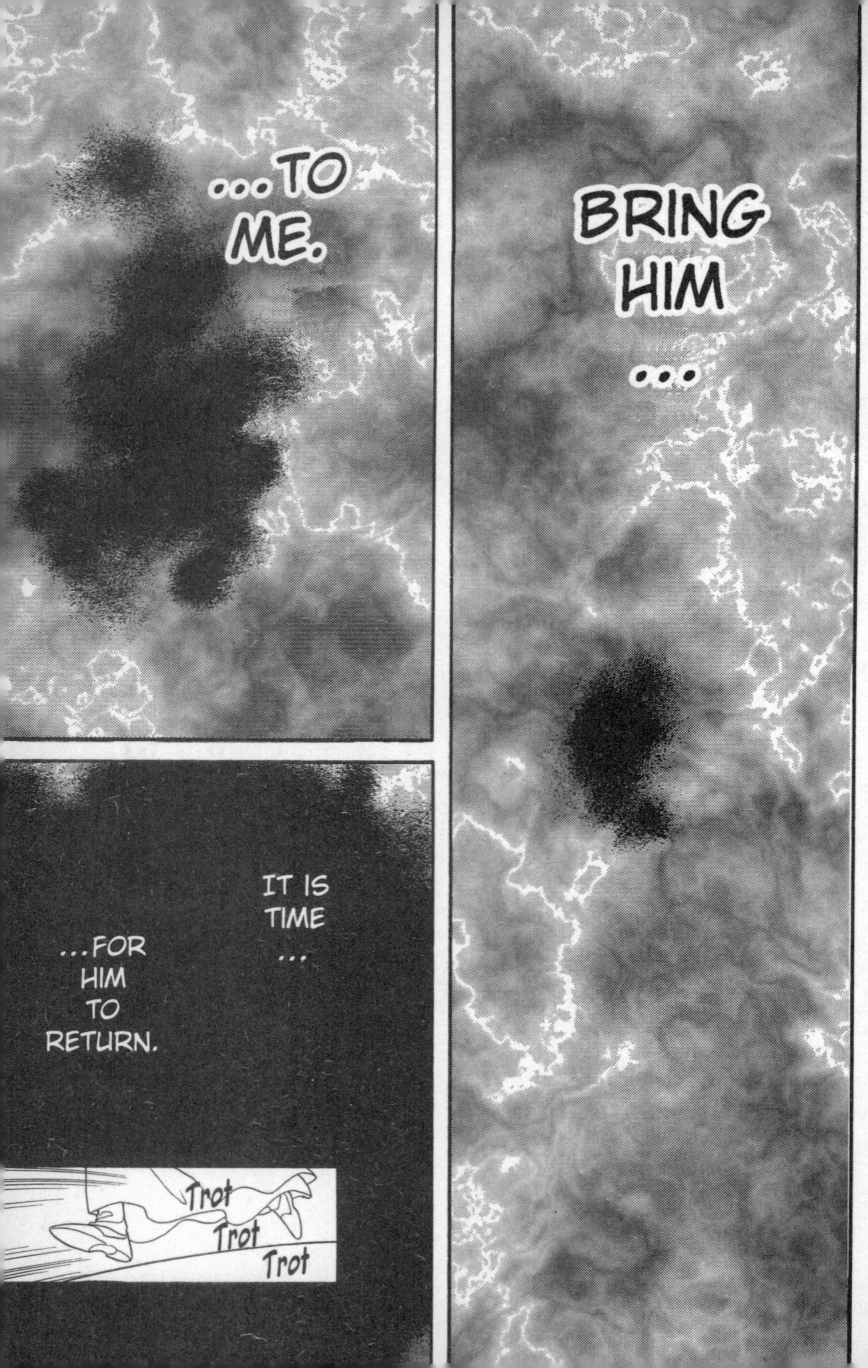
BRING HIM ...
...TO ME.
IT IS TIME ...
...FOR HIM TO RETURN.
Trot
Trot
Trot

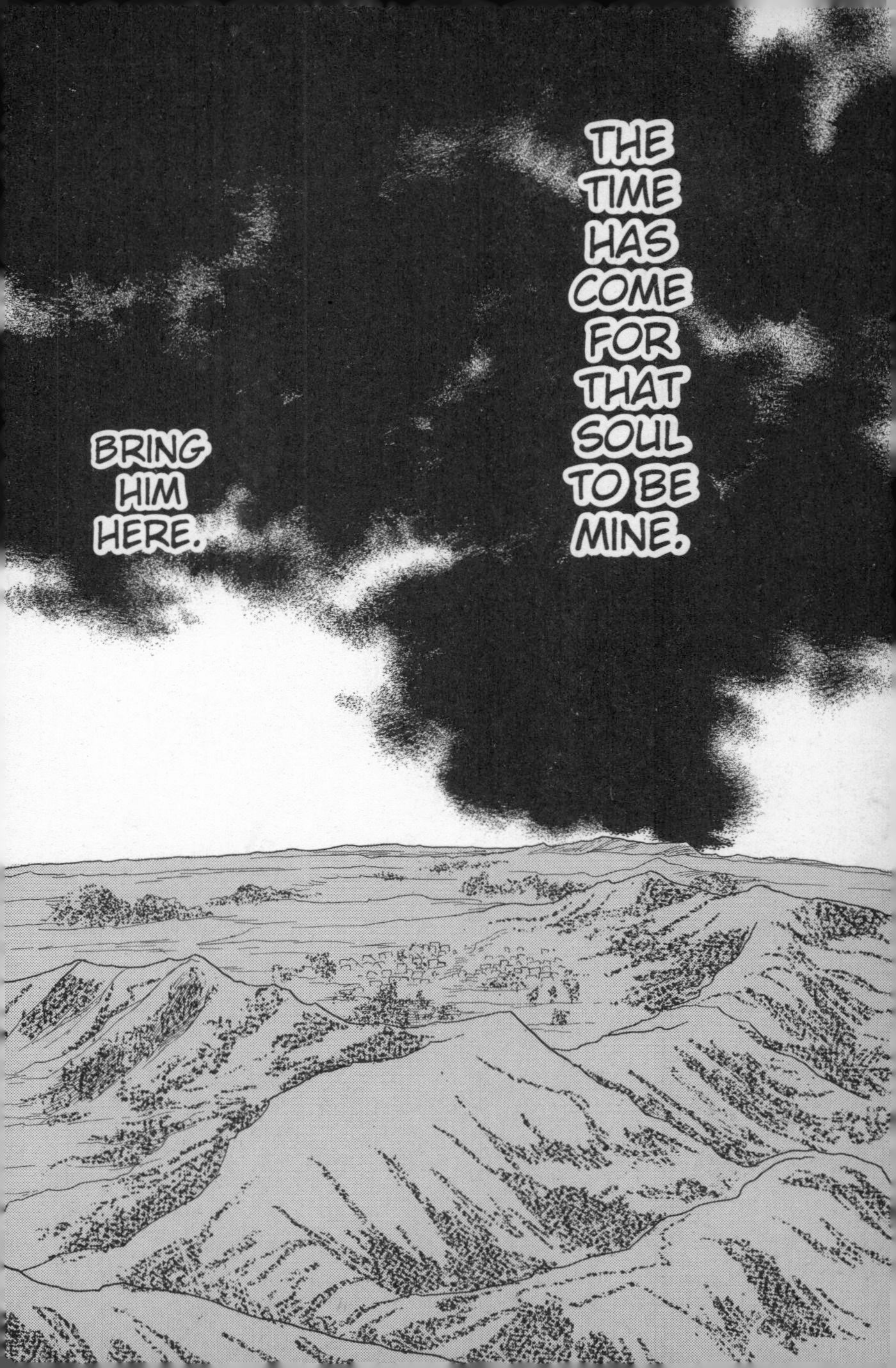
THE TIME HAS COME FOR THAT SOUL TO BE MINE.
BRING HIM HERE.

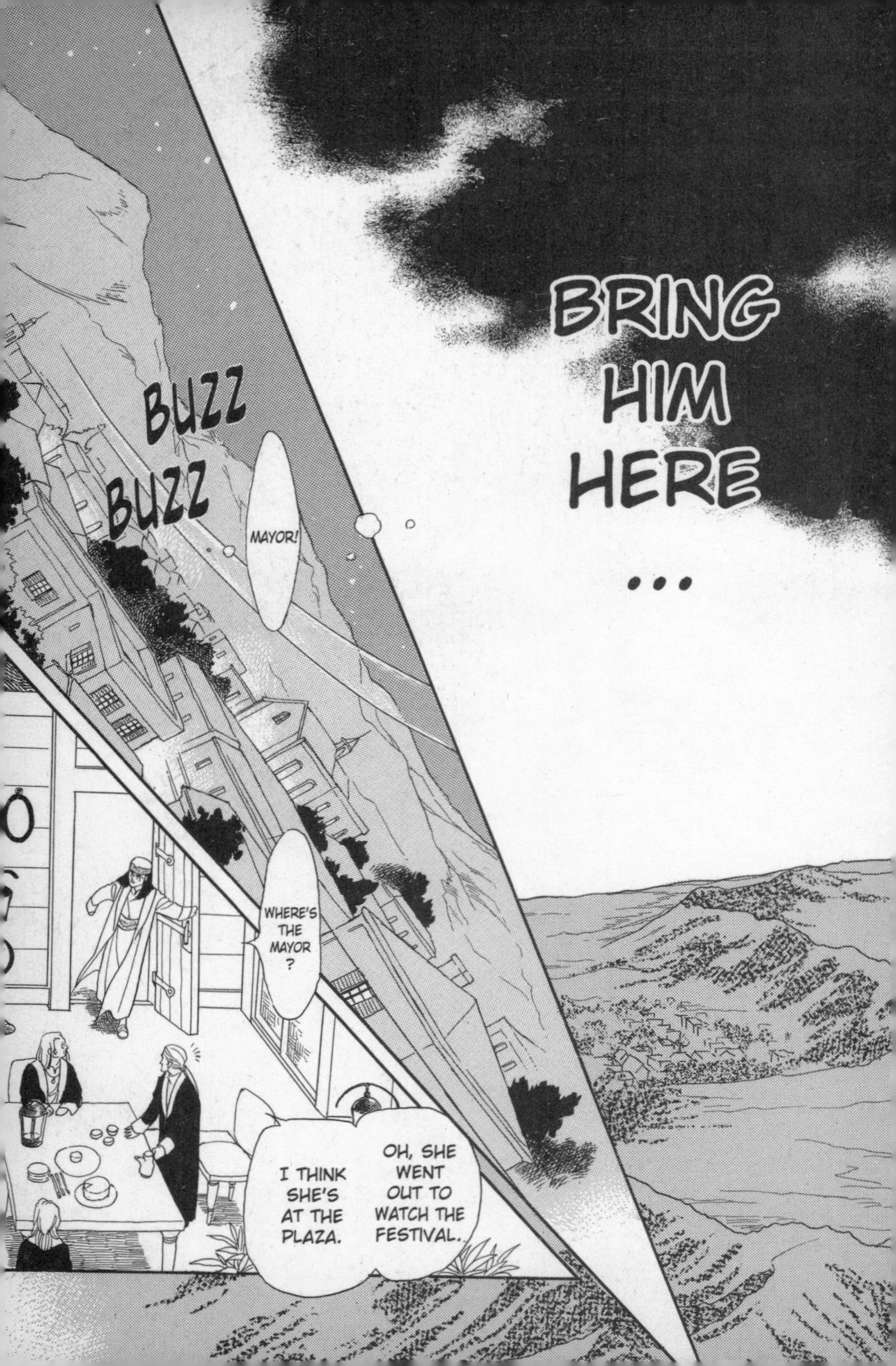
BRING HIM HERE ...
BUZZ BUZZ
MAYOR!
WHERE'S THE MAYOR?
OH, SHE WENT OUT TO WATCH THE FESTIVAL.
I THINK SHE'S AT THE PLAZA.

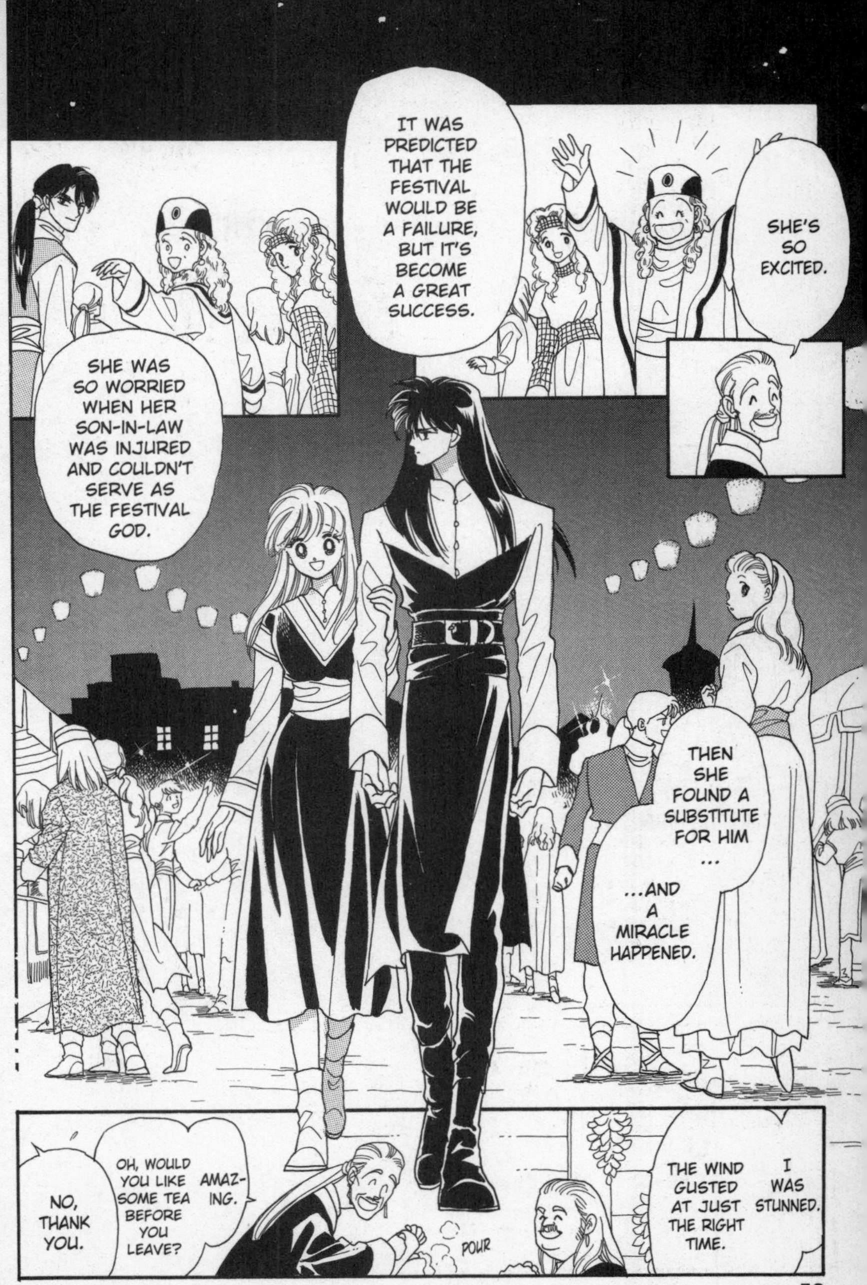
IT WAS PREDICTED THAT THE FESTIVAL WOULD BE A FAILURE, BUT IT'S BECOME A GREAT SUCCESS.
SHE'S SO EXCITED.
SHE WAS SO WORRIED WHEN HER SON-IN-LAW WAS INJURED AND COULDN'T SERVE AS THE FESTIVAL GOD.
THEN SHE FOUND A SUBSTITUTE FOR HIM ...
...AND A MIRACLE HAPPENED.
I WAS STUNNED.
THE WIND GUSTED AT JUST THE RIGHT TIME.
POUR
AMAZ-ING.
OH, WOULD YOU LIKE SOME TEA BEFORE YOU LEAVE?
NO, THANK YOU.

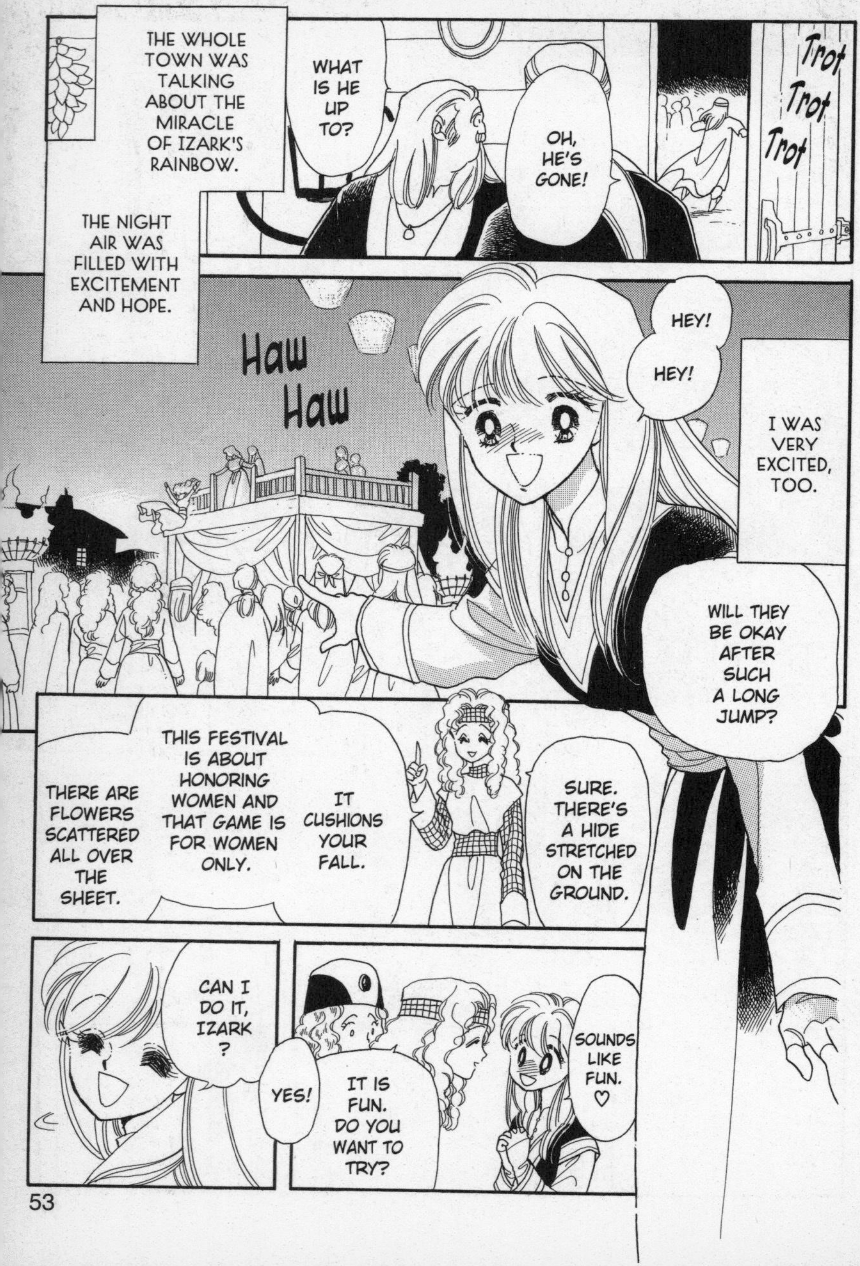
Trot Trot Trot
OH, HE'S GONE!
WHAT IS HE UP TO?
THE WHOLE TOWN WAS TALKING ABOUT THE MIRACLE OF IZARK'S RAINBOW.
THE NIGHT AIR WAS FILLED WITH EXCITEMENT AND HOPE.
I WAS VERY EXCITED, TOO.
HEY!
HEY!
Haw Haw
WILL THEY BE OKAY AFTER SUCH A LONG JUMP?
SURE. THERE'S A HIDE STRETCHED ON THE GROUND.
IT CUSHIONS YOUR FALL.
THIS FESTIVAL IS ABOUT HONORING WOMEN AND THAT GAME IS FOR WOMEN ONLY.
THERE ARE FLOWERS SCATTERED ALL OVER THE SHEET.
SOUNDS LIKE FUN. ♡
IT IS FUN. DO YOU WANT TO TRY?
YES!
CAN I DO IT, IZARK ?

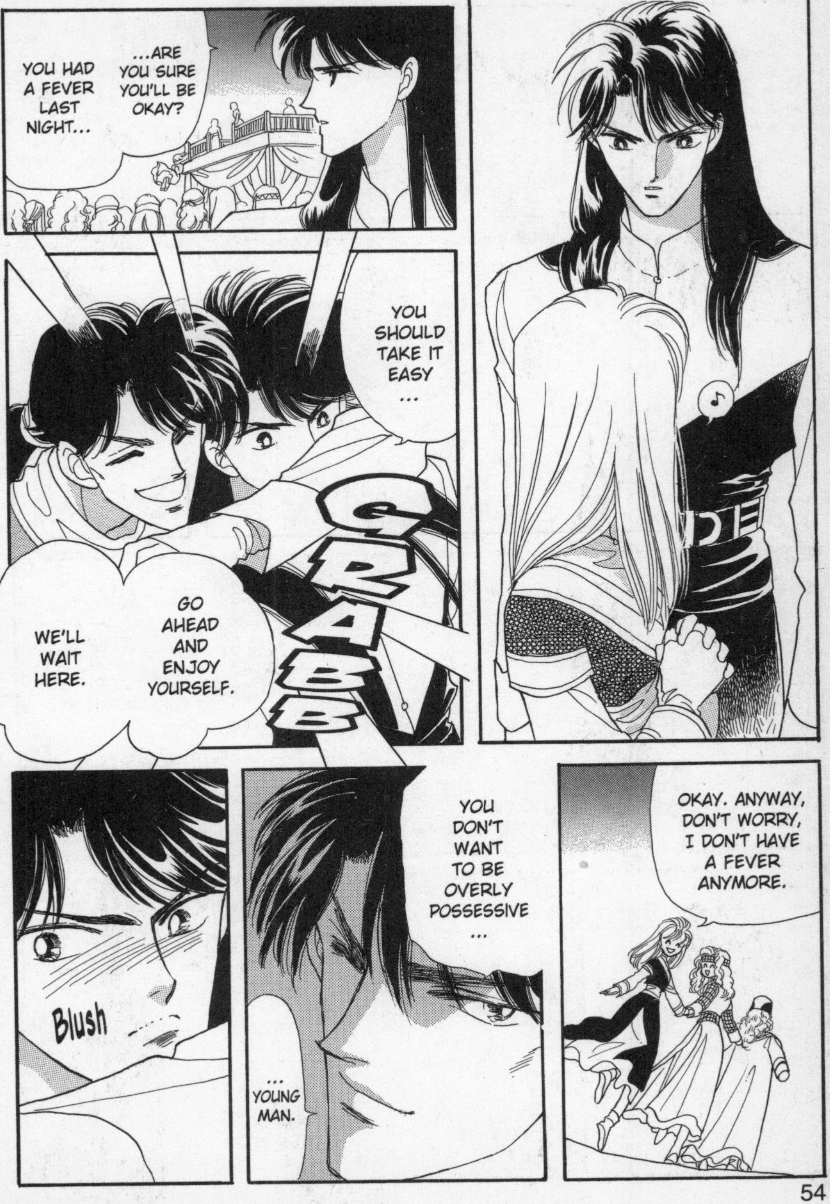
♪
YOU HAD A FEVER LAST NIGHT... ...ARE YOU SURE YOU'LL BE OKAY?
YOU SHOULD TAKE IT EASY ...
GRABB
WE'LL WAIT HERE. GO AHEAD AND ENJOY YOURSELF.
OKAY. ANYWAY, DON'T WORRY, I DON'T HAVE A FEVER ANYMORE.
YOU DON'T WANT TO BE OVERLY POSSESSIVE ...
... YOUNG MAN.
Blush

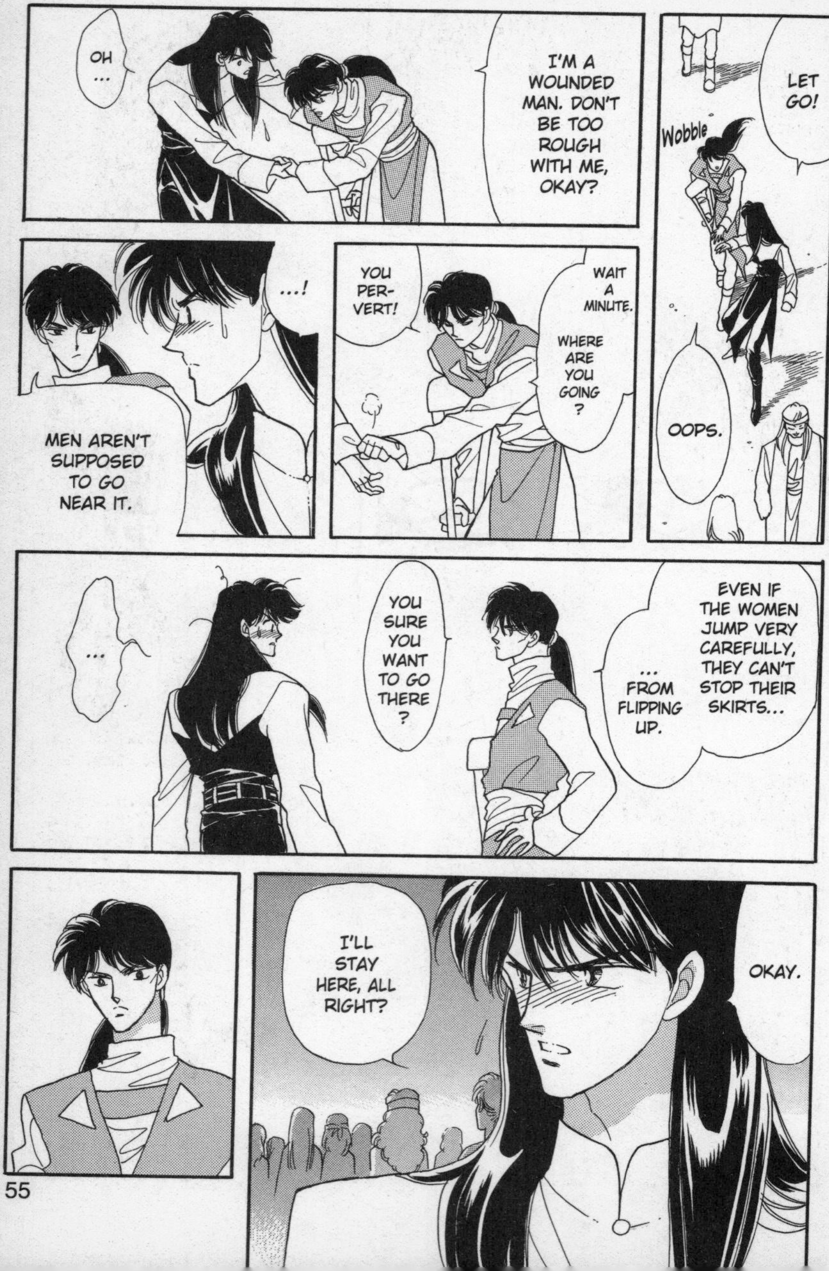
LET GO!
Wobble
OOPS.
I'M A WOUNDED MAN. DON'T BE TOO ROUGH WITH ME, OKAY?
OH ...
WAIT A MINUTE.
WHERE ARE YOU GOING ?
YOU PER-VERT!
...!
MEN AREN'T SUPPOSED TO GO NEAR IT.
EVEN IF THE WOMEN JUMP VERY CAREFULLY, THEY CAN'T STOP THEIR SKIRTS...
... FROM FLIPPING UP.
YOU SURE YOU WANT TO GO THERE ?
...
OKAY.
I'LL STAY HERE, ALL RIGHT?

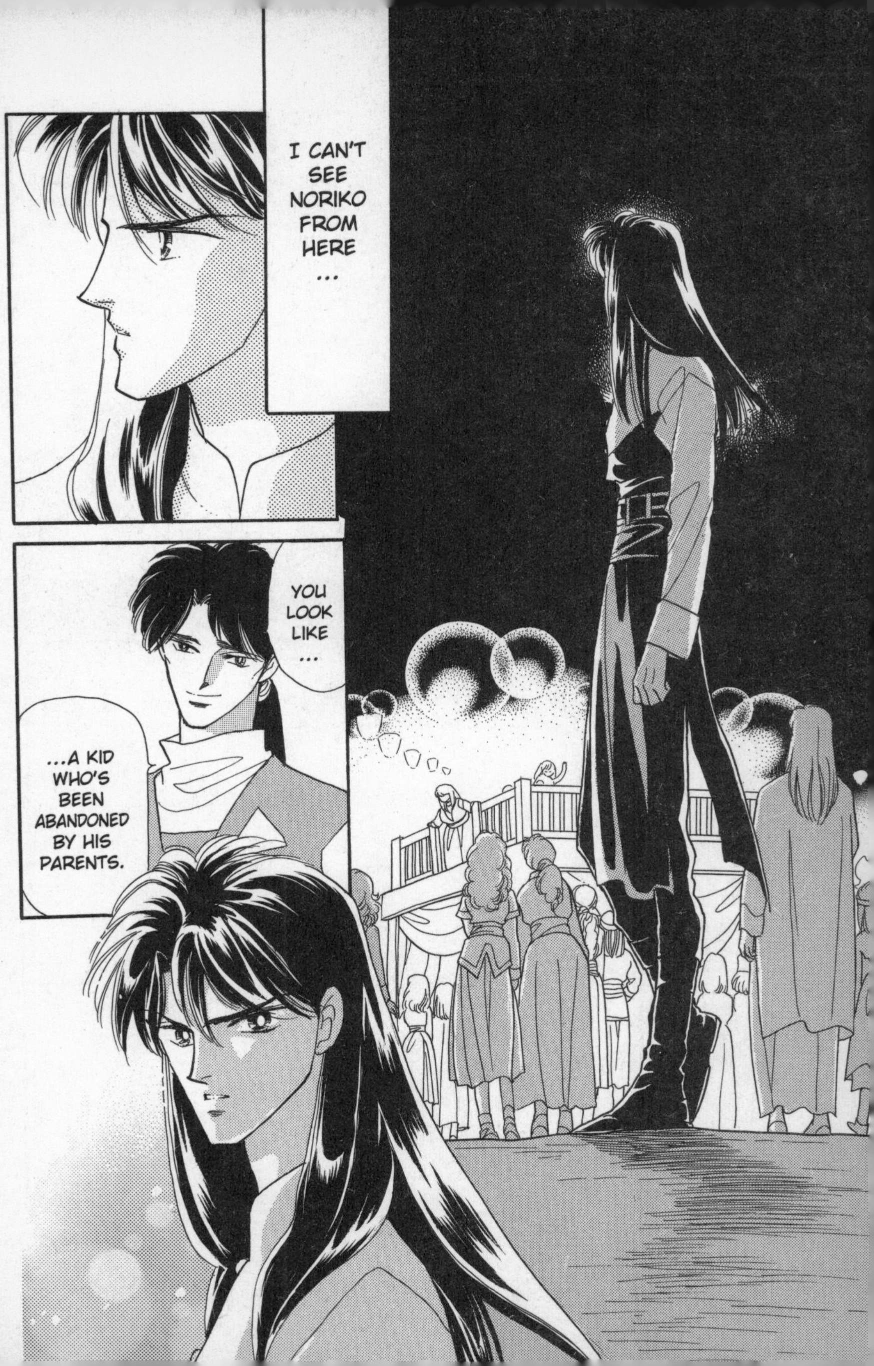
I CAN'T SEE NORIKO FROM HERE ...
YOU LOOK LIKE ...
...A KID WHO'S BEEN ABANDONED BY HIS PARENTS.

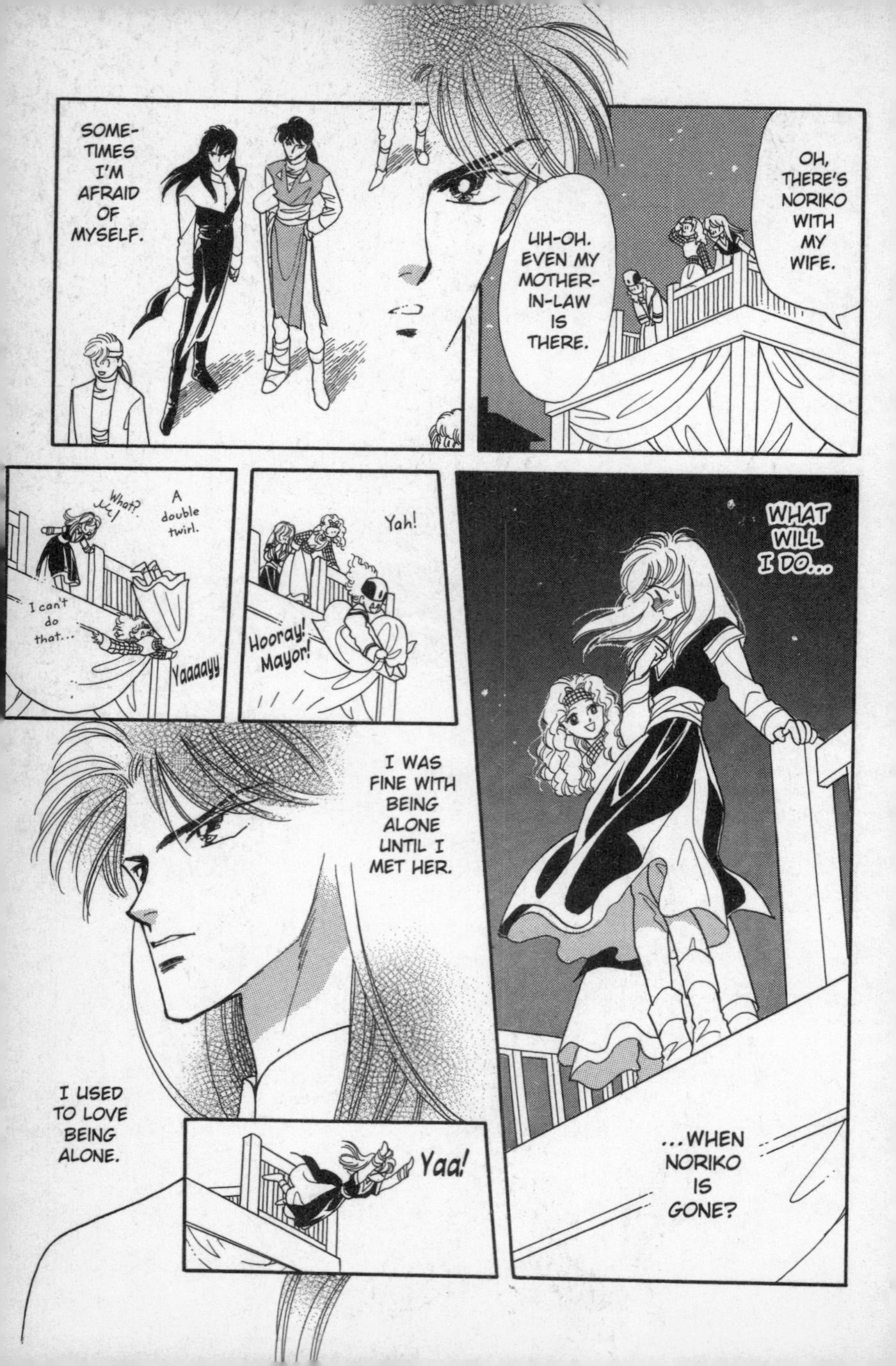
OH, THERE'S NORIKO WITH MY WIFE.
UH-OH. EVEN MY MOTHER-IN-LAW IS THERE.
SOME-TIMES I'M AFRAID OF MYSELF.
WHAT WILL I DO...
...WHEN NORIKO IS GONE?
Yah!
Hooray! Mayor!
What?
A double twirl.
I can't do that...
Yaaaayy
I WAS FINE WITH BEING ALONE UNTIL I MET HER.
I USED TO LOVE BEING ALONE.
Yaa!

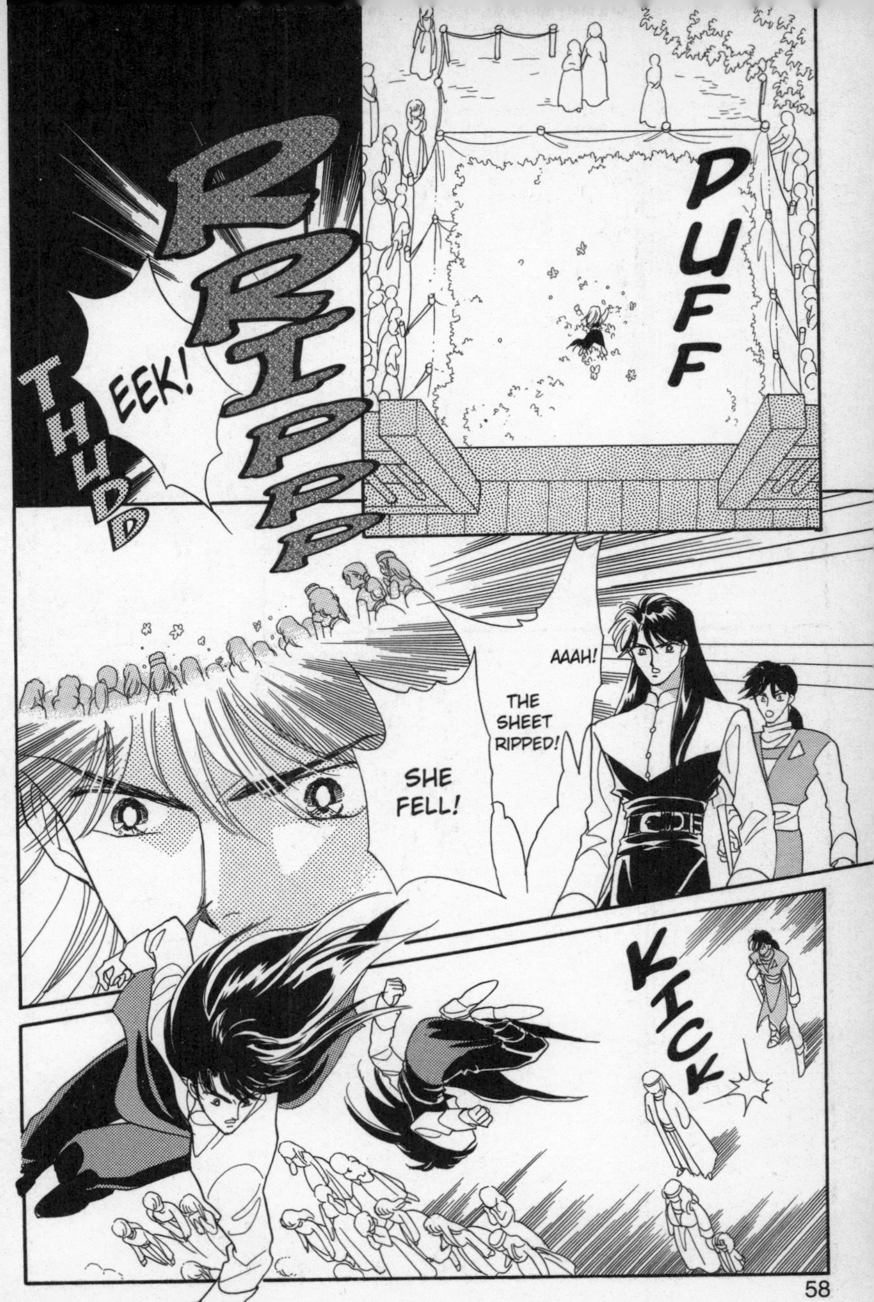
DUFF
RRIPPP
EEK!
THUDD
AAAH!
THE SHEET RIPPED!
SHE FELL!
KICK

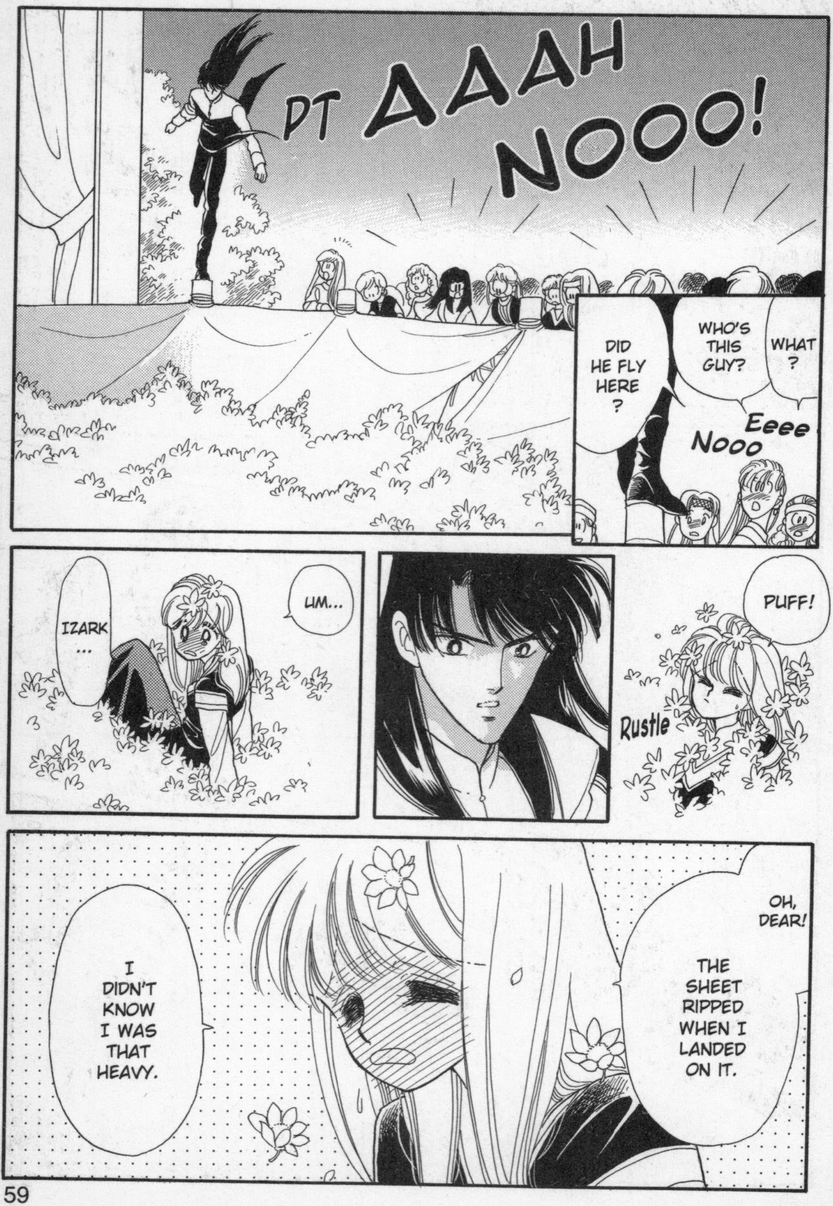
AAAH NOOO!
PT
WHAT ?
WHO'S THIS GUY?
DID HE FLY HERE ?
Eeee
Nooo
PUFF!
Rustle
UM...
IZARK ...
OH, DEAR!
THE SHEET RIPPED WHEN I LANDED ON IT.
I DIDN'T KNOW I WAS THAT HEAVY.

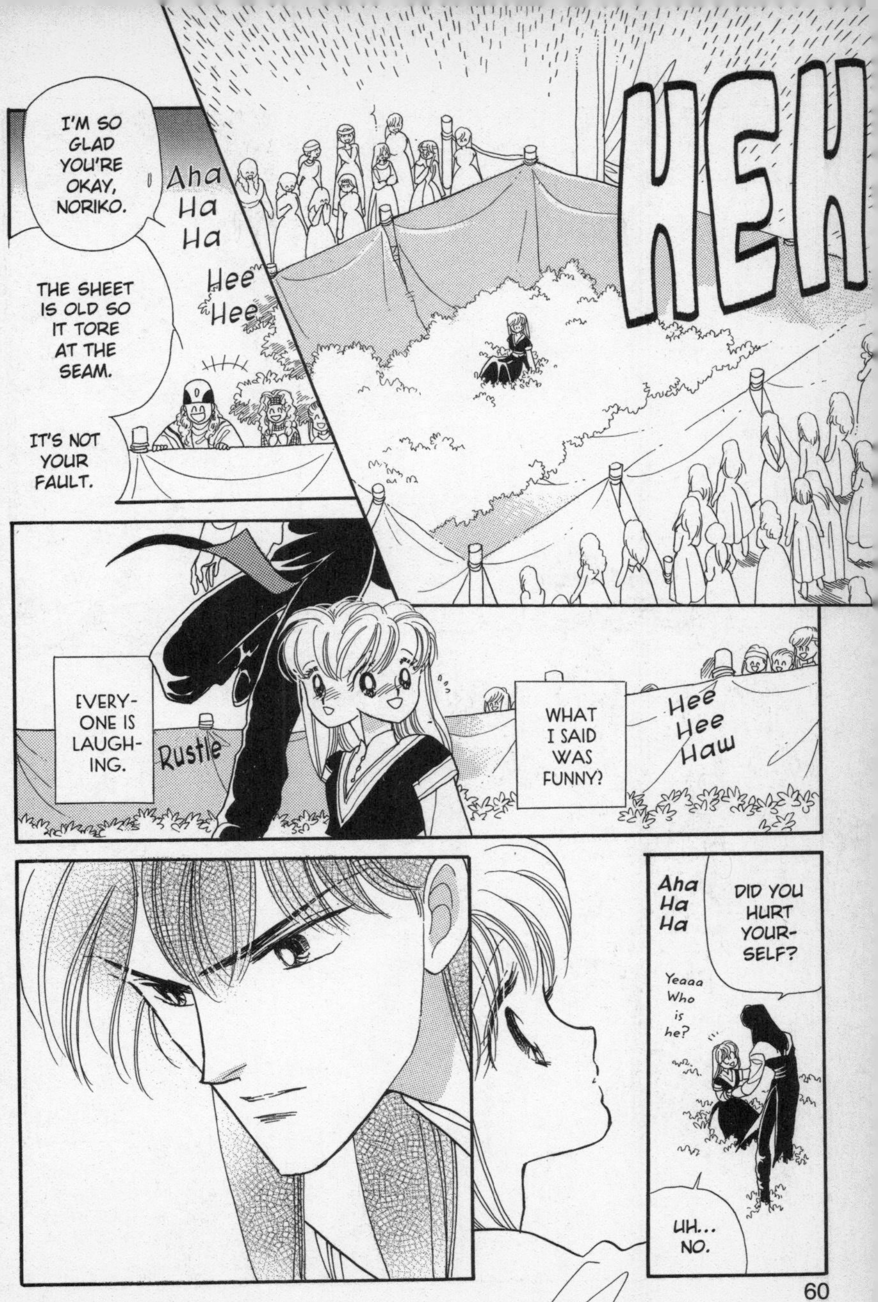
HEH
I'M SO GLAD YOU'RE OKAY, NORIKO.
Aha Ha Ha
THE SHEET IS OLD SO IT TORE AT THE SEAM.
Hee Hee
IT'S NOT YOUR FAULT.
Hee Hee Haw
WHAT I SAID WAS FUNNY?
EVERY-ONE IS LAUGH-ING.
Rustle
DID YOU HURT YOUR-SELF?
Aha Ha Ha
Yeaaa Who is he?
UH... NO.

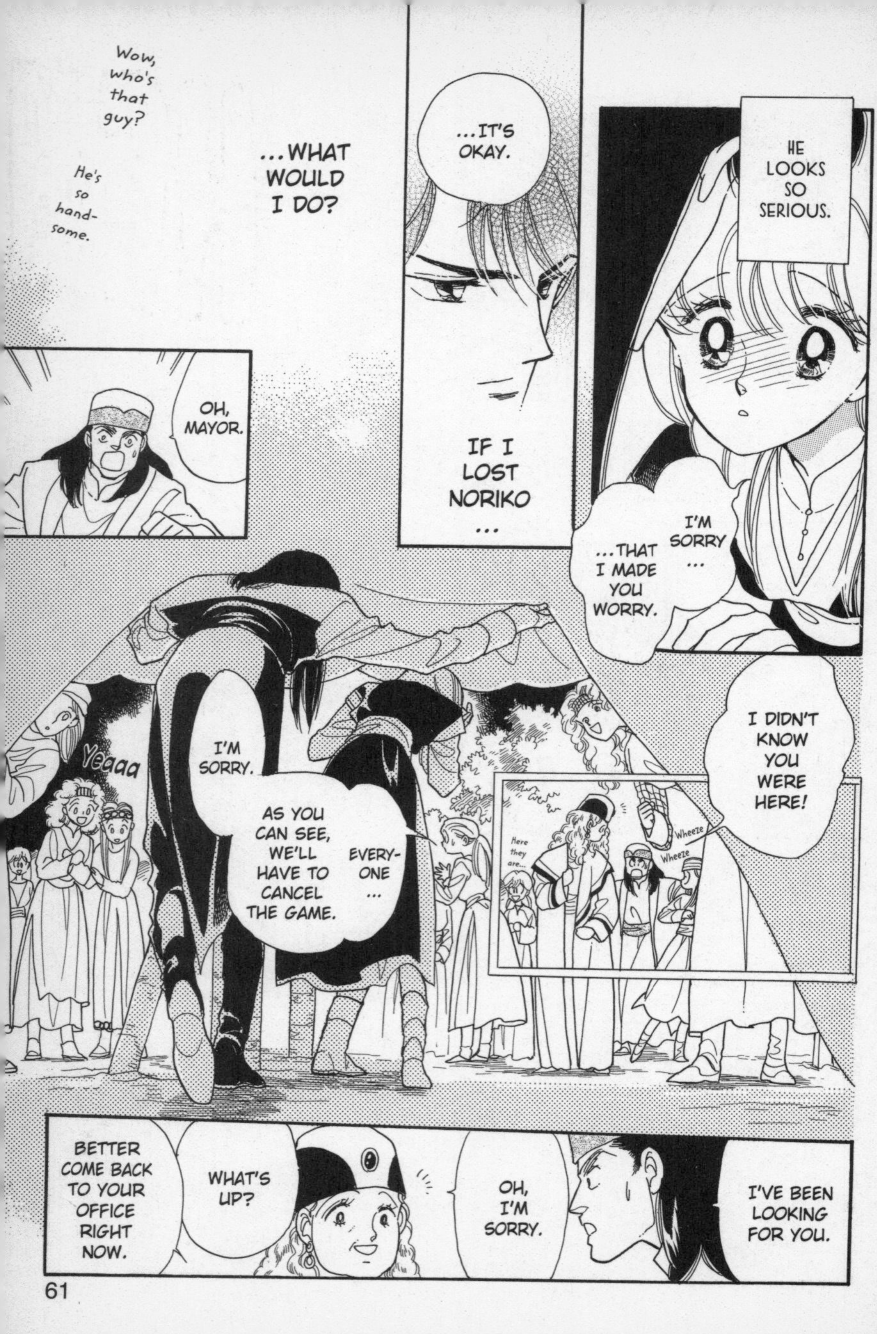
HE LOOKS SO SERIOUS.
I'M SORRY ...
...THAT I MADE YOU WORRY.
...IT'S OKAY.
IF I LOST NORIKO ...
...WHAT WOULD I DO?
Wow, who's that guy?
He's so hand-some.
OH, MAYOR.
I DIDN'T KNOW YOU WERE HERE!
Wheeze
Wheeze
Here they are...
EVERY-ONE ...
AS YOU CAN SEE, WE'LL HAVE TO CANCEL THE GAME.
I'M SORRY.
Yeaaa
I'VE BEEN LOOKING FOR YOU.
OH, I'M SORRY.
WHAT'S UP?
BETTER COME BACK TO YOUR OFFICE RIGHT NOW.

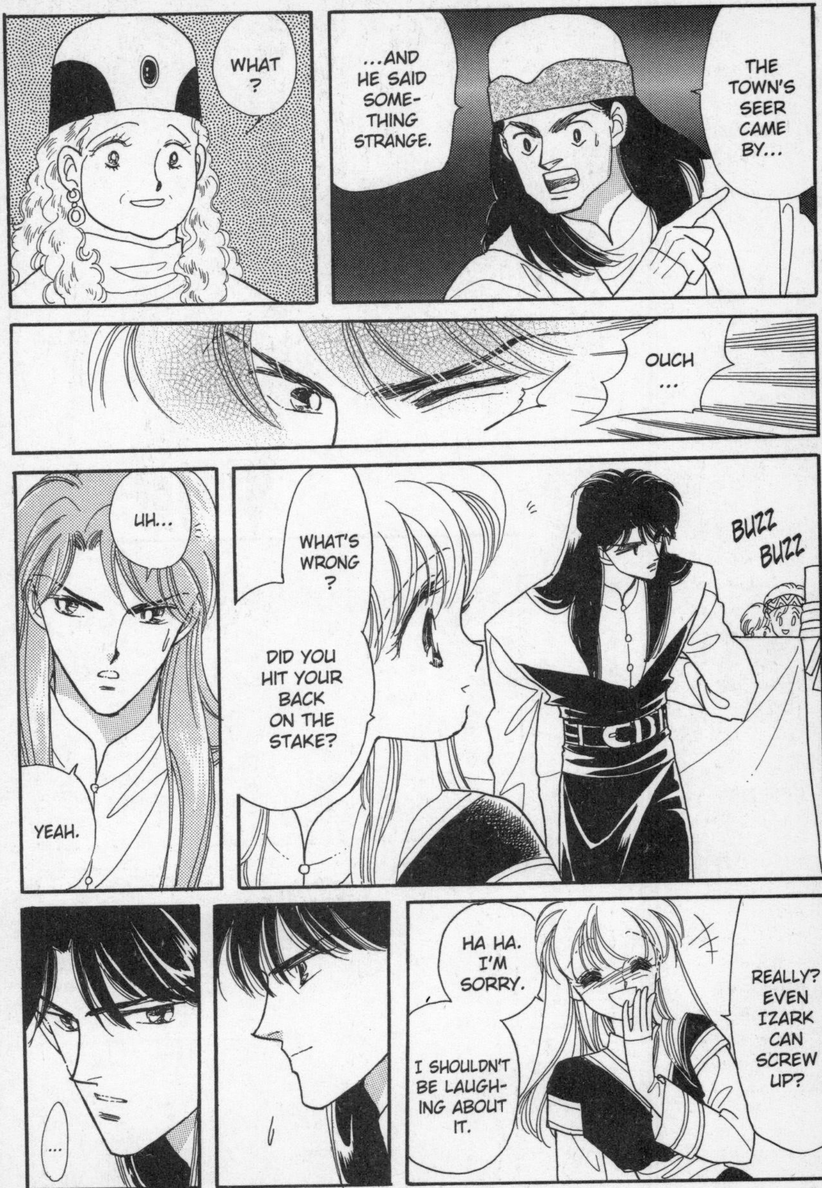
THE TOWN'S SEER CAME BY...
...AND HE SAID SOME-THING STRANGE.
WHAT ?
OUCH ...
BUZZ BUZZ
WHAT'S WRONG ?
DID YOU HIT YOUR BACK ON THE STAKE?
UH...
YEAH.
REALLY? EVEN IZARK CAN SCREW UP?
HA HA. I'M SORRY.
I SHOULDN'T BE LAUGH-ING ABOUT IT.
...

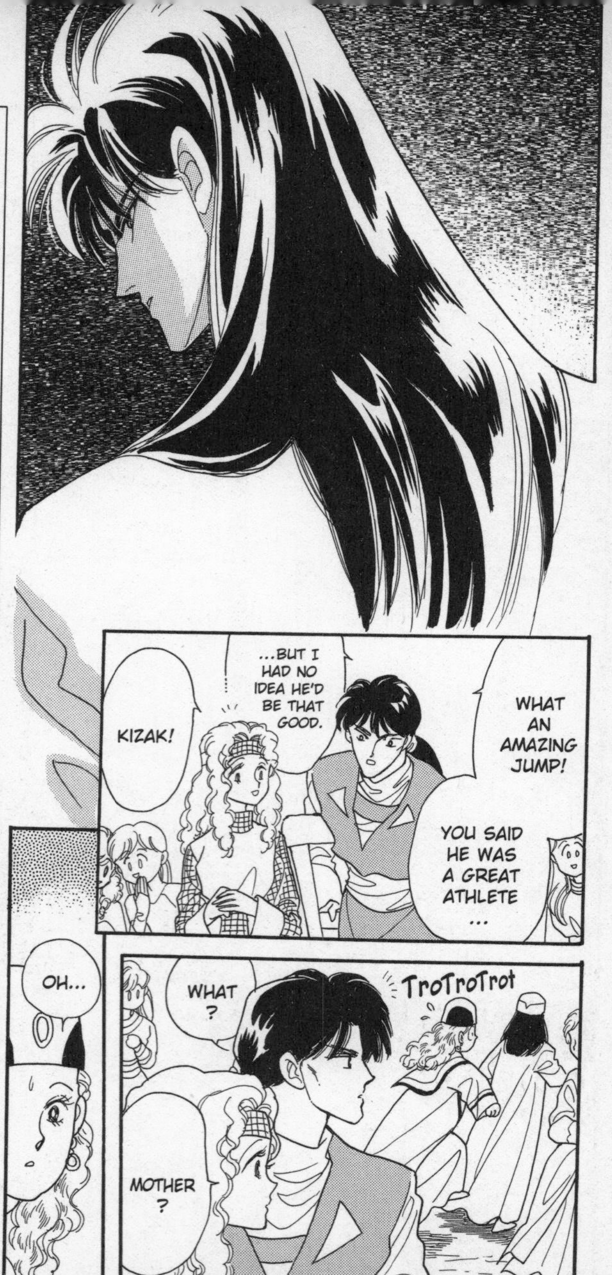
WHAT AN AMAZING JUMP!
YOU SAID HE WAS A GREAT ATHLETE ...
...BUT I HAD NO IDEA HE'D BE THAT GOOD.
KIZAK!
TroTroTrot
WHAT ?
MOTHER ?
OH...

Cat Story (2)

This cat often visits my garden.

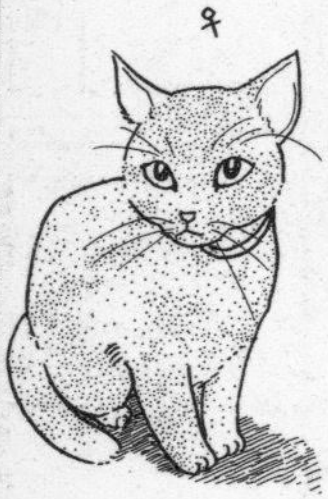

She must belong to someone because she wears a collar. Her coat is brown with black patches so I call her "Tortoise."

(What a straightforward name!)

She's not friendly at all. When she sees me, she either runs away or ignores me. I've never heard her meow.

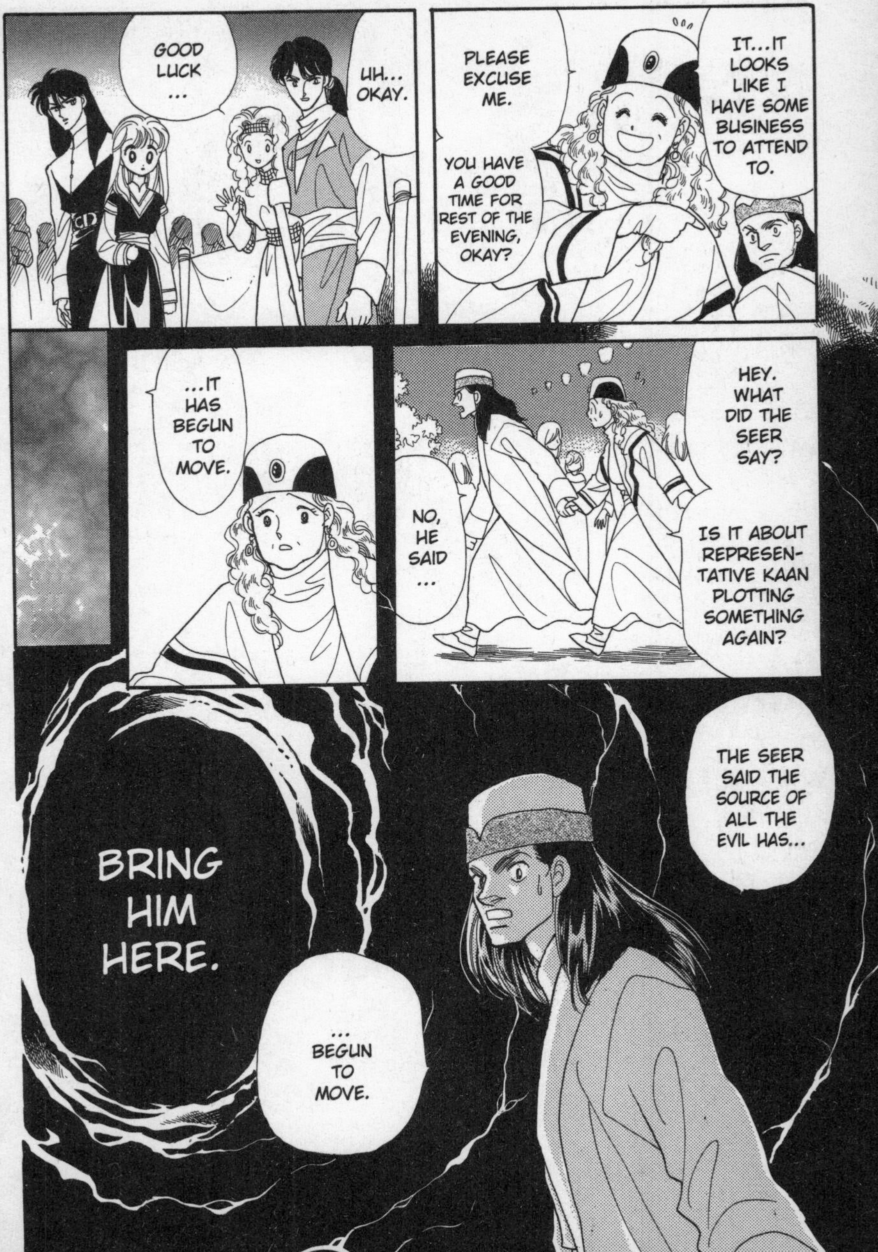
IT...IT LOOKS LIKE I HAVE SOME BUSINESS TO ATTEND TO.
PLEASE EXCUSE ME.
YOU HAVE A GOOD TIME FOR REST OF THE EVENING, OKAY?
UH... OKAY.
GOOD LUCK ...
HEY. WHAT DID THE SEER SAY?
IS IT ABOUT REPRESENTATIVE KAAN PLOTTING SOMETHING AGAIN?
NO, HE SAID ...
...IT HAS BEGUN TO MOVE.
THE SEER SAID THE SOURCE OF ALL THE EVIL HAS...
BRING HIM HERE.
... BEGUN TO MOVE.

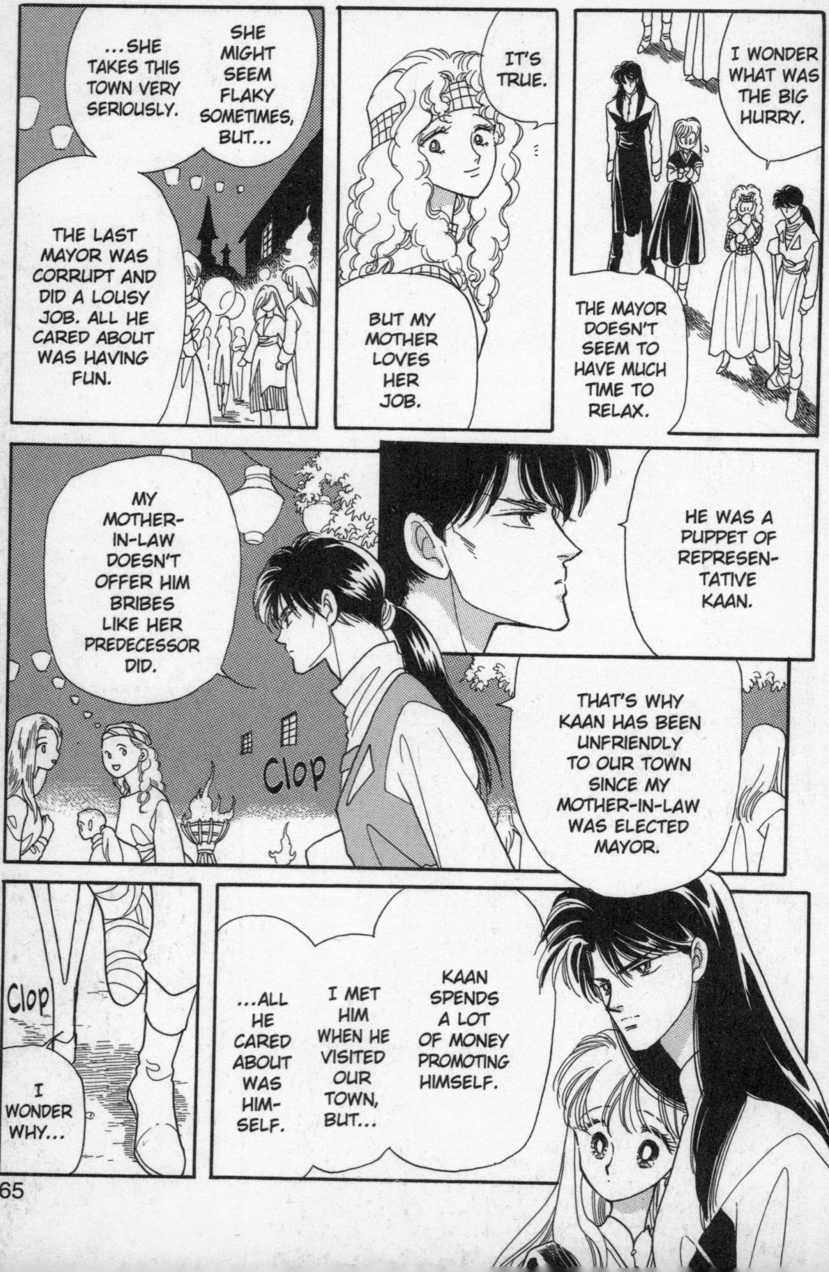
I WONDER WHAT WAS THE BIG HURRY.
THE MAYOR DOESN'T SEEM TO HAVE MUCH TIME TO RELAX.
IT'S TRUE.
BUT MY MOTHER LOVES HER JOB.
SHE MIGHT SEEM FLAKY SOMETIMES, BUT...
...SHE TAKES THIS TOWN VERY SERIOUSLY.
THE LAST MAYOR WAS CORRUPT AND DID A LOUSY JOB. ALL HE CARED ABOUT WAS HAVING FUN.
HE WAS A PUPPET OF REPRESENTATIVE KAAN.
THAT'S WHY KAAN HAS BEEN UNFRIENDLY TO OUR TOWN SINCE MY MOTHER-IN-LAW WAS ELECTED MAYOR.
MY MOTHER-IN-LAW DOESN'T OFFER HIM BRIBES LIKE HER PREDECESSOR DID.
Clop
KAAN SPENDS A LOT OF MONEY PROMOTING HIMSELF.
I MET HIM WHEN HE VISITED OUR TOWN, BUT...
...ALL HE CARED ABOUT WAS HIMSELF.
Clop
I WONDER WHY...

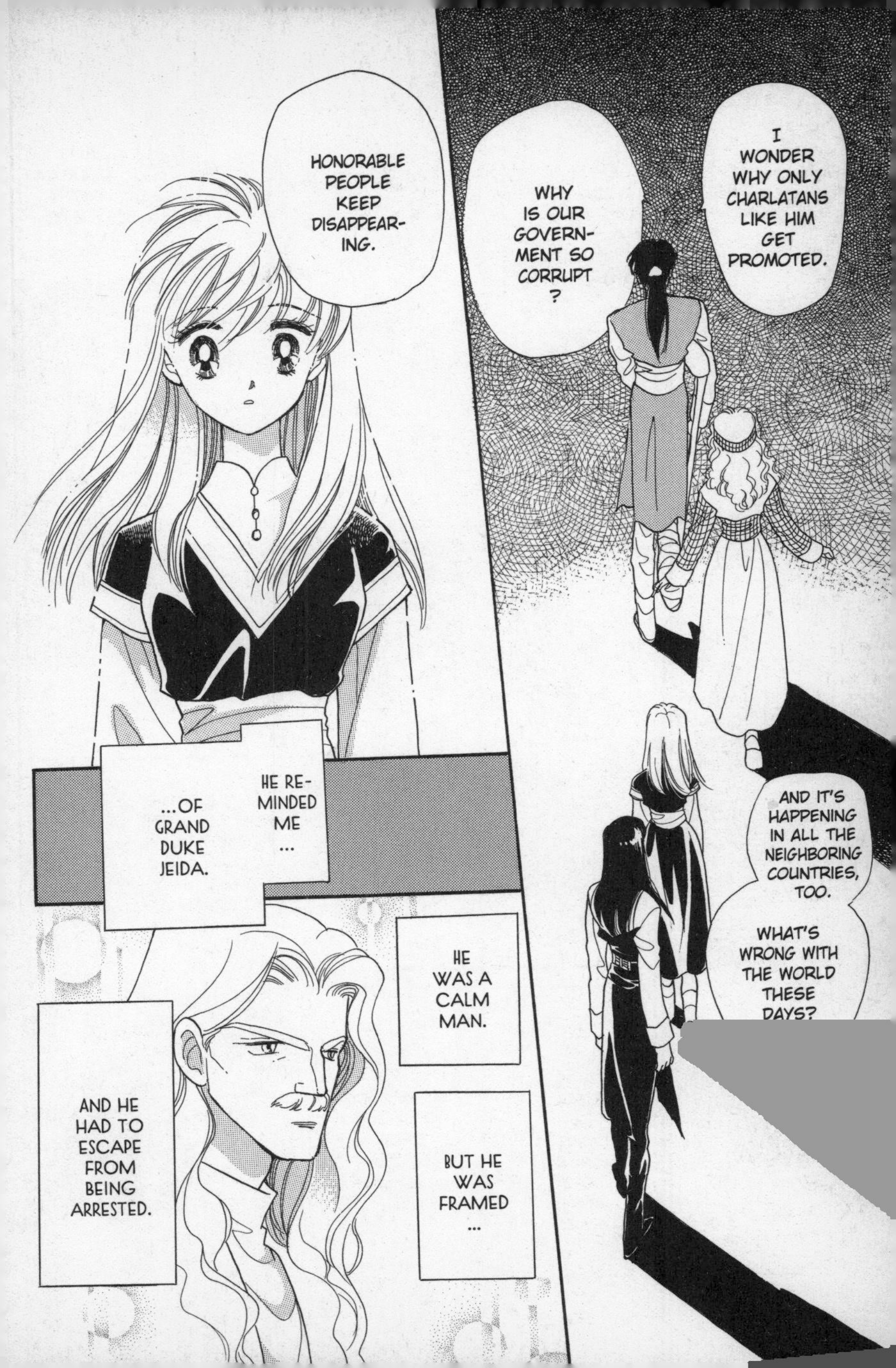
I WONDER WHY ONLY CHARLATANS LIKE HIM GET PROMOTED.
WHY IS OUR GOVERNMENT SO CORRUPT?
AND IT'S HAPPENING IN ALL THE NEIGHBORING COUNTRIES, TOO.
WHAT'S WRONG WITH THE WORLD THESE DAYS?
HONORABLE PEOPLE KEEP DISAPPEARING.
HE REMINDED ME...
...OF GRAND DUKE JEIDA.
HE WAS A CALM MAN.
BUT HE WAS FRAMED...
AND HE HAD TO ESCAPE FROM BEING ARRESTED.

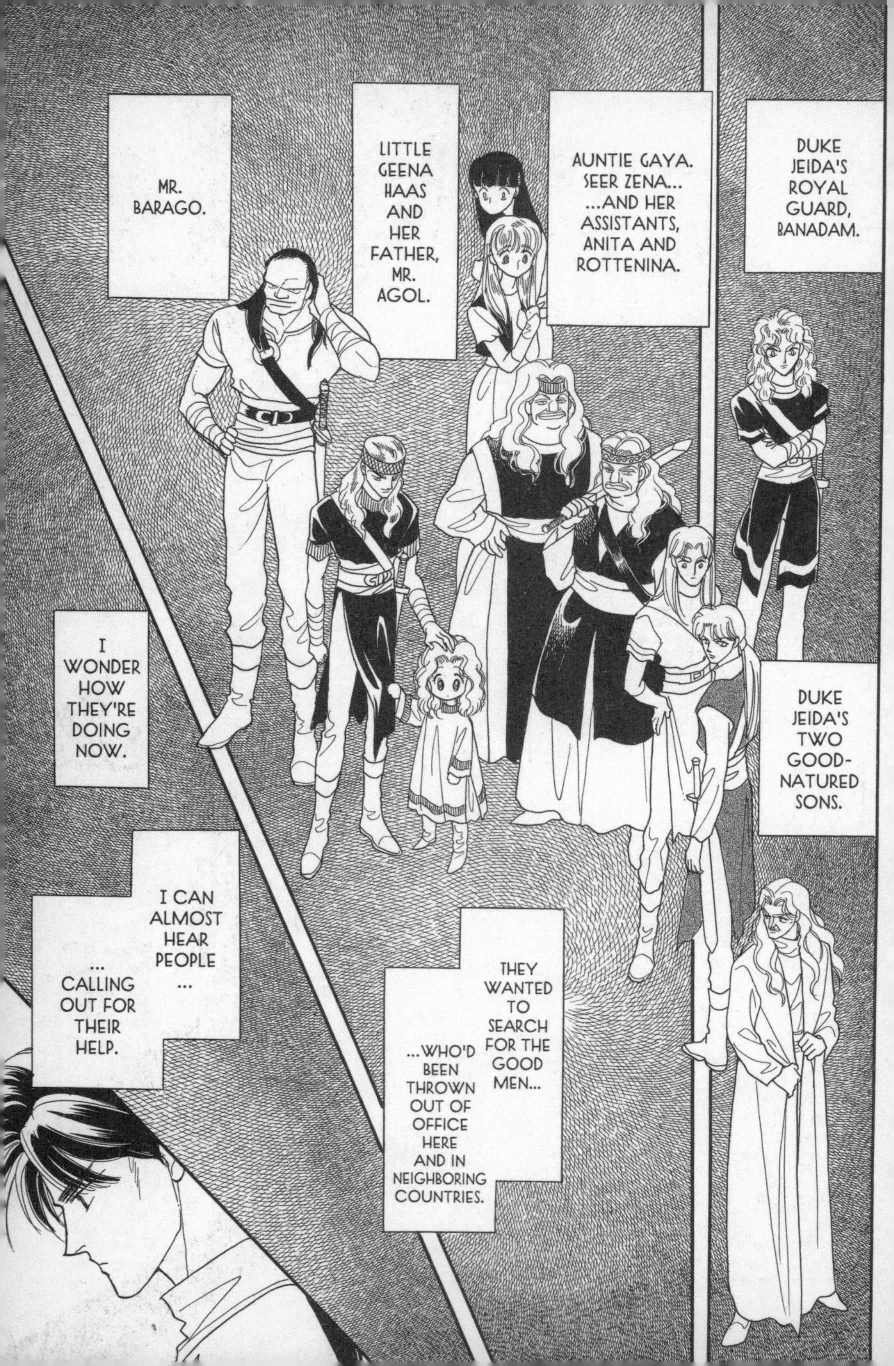
DUKE JEIDA'S ROYAL GUARD, BANADAM.
AUNTIE GAYA. SEER ZENA... ...AND HER ASSISTANTS, ANITA AND ROTTENINA.
LITTLE GEENA HAAS AND HER FATHER, MR. AGOL.
MR. BARAGO.
DUKE JEIDA'S TWO GOOD-NATURED SONS.
THEY WANTED TO SEARCH FOR THE GOOD MEN...
...WHO'D BEEN THROWN OUT OF OFFICE HERE AND IN NEIGHBORING COUNTRIES.
I WONDER HOW THEY'RE DOING NOW.
I CAN ALMOST HEAR PEOPLE...
...CALLING OUT FOR THEIR HELP.

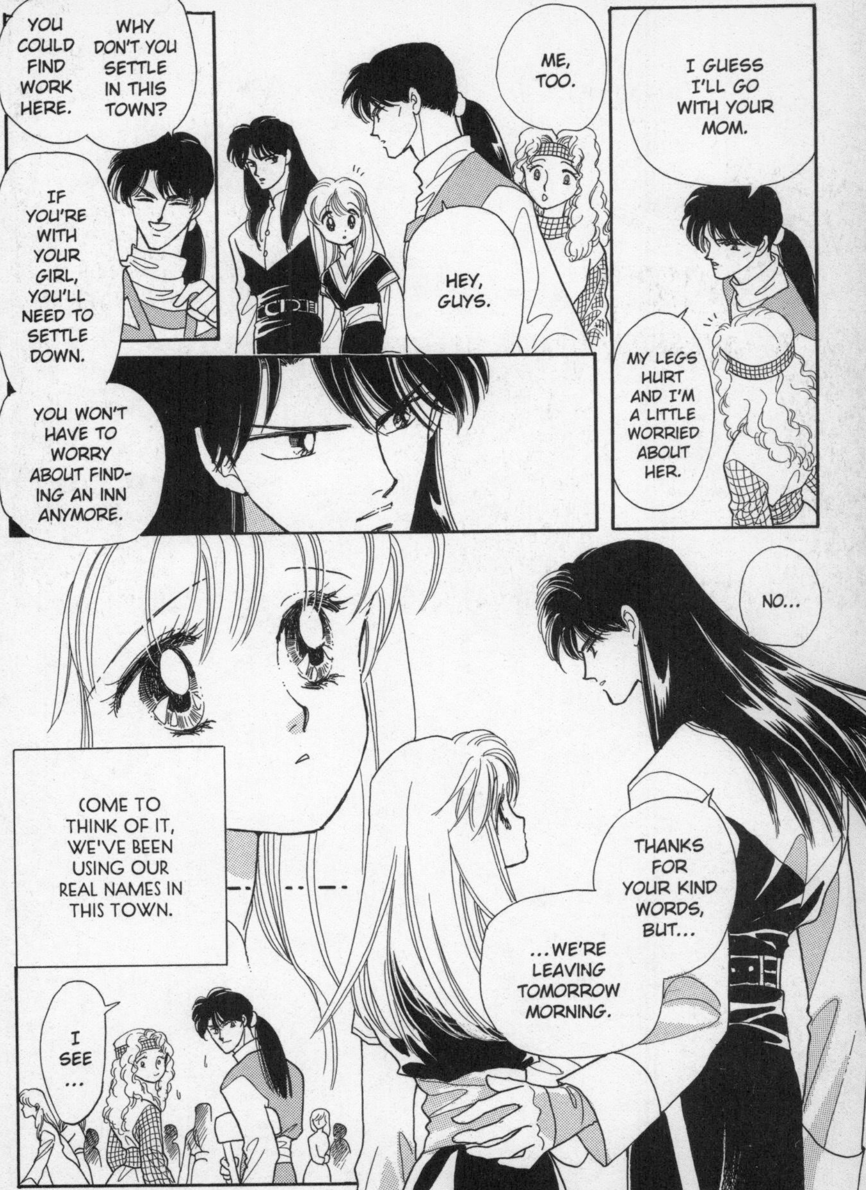
I GUESS I'LL GO WITH YOUR MOM.
MY LEGS HURT AND I'M A LITTLE WORRIED ABOUT HER.
ME, TOO.
HEY, GUYS.
YOU COULD FIND WORK HERE. WHY DON'T YOU SETTLE IN THIS TOWN?
IF YOU'RE WITH YOUR GIRL, YOU'LL NEED TO SETTLE DOWN.
YOU WON'T HAVE TO WORRY ABOUT FINDING AN INN ANYMORE.
NO...
THANKS FOR YOUR KIND WORDS, BUT...
...WE'RE LEAVING TOMORROW MORNING.
COME TO THINK OF IT, WE'VE BEEN USING OUR REAL NAMES IN THIS TOWN.
I SEE...

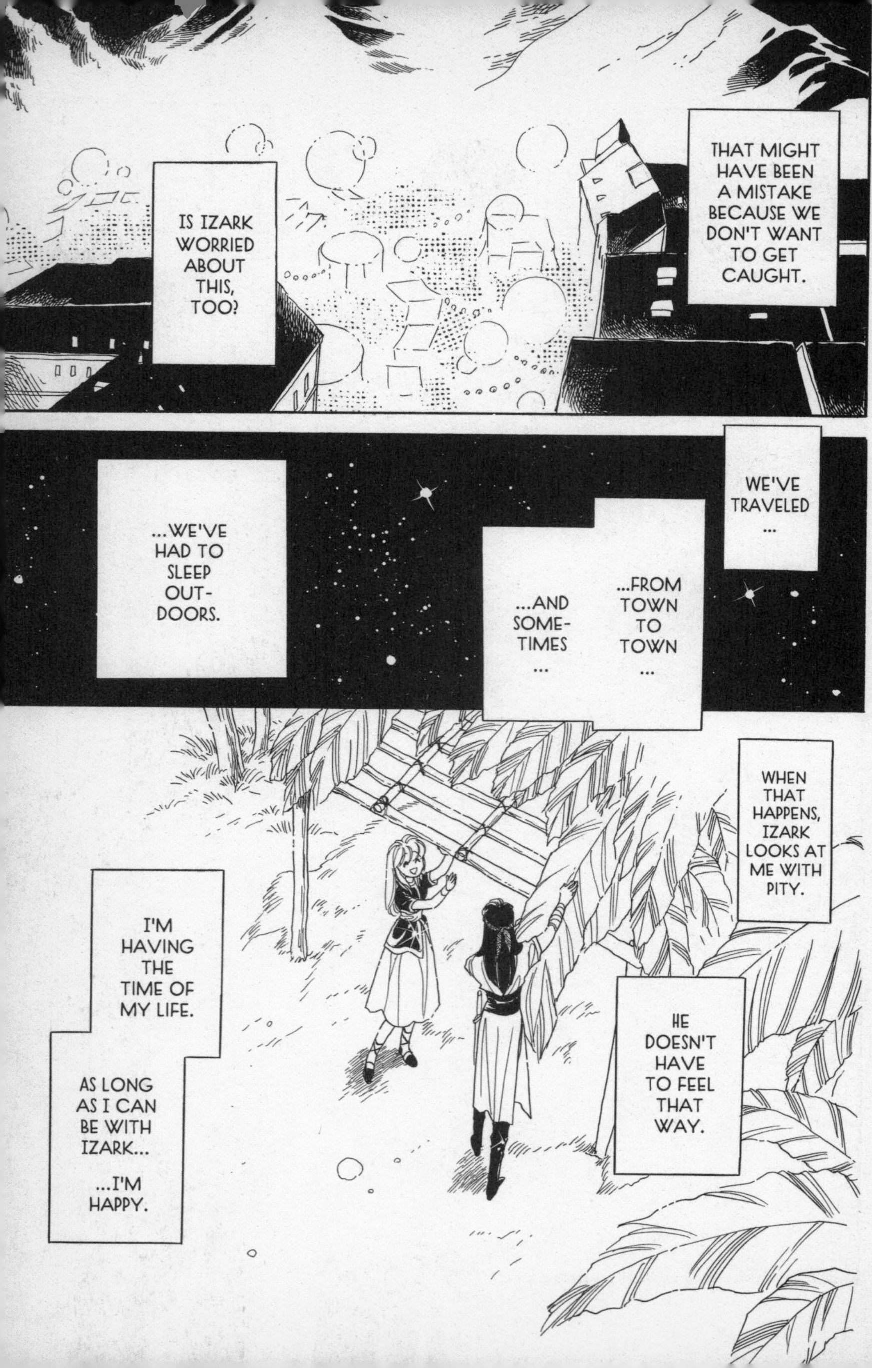
THAT MIGHT HAVE BEEN A MISTAKE BECAUSE WE DON'T WANT TO GET CAUGHT.
IS IZARK WORRIED ABOUT THIS, TOO?
WE'VE TRAVELED ...
...FROM TOWN TO TOWN ...
...AND SOME- TIMES ...
...WE'VE HAD TO SLEEP OUT- DOORS.
WHEN THAT HAPPENS, IZARK LOOKS AT ME WITH PITY.
HE DOESN'T HAVE TO FEEL THAT WAY.
I'M HAVING THE TIME OF MY LIFE.
AS LONG AS I CAN BE WITH IZARK...
...I'M HAPPY.

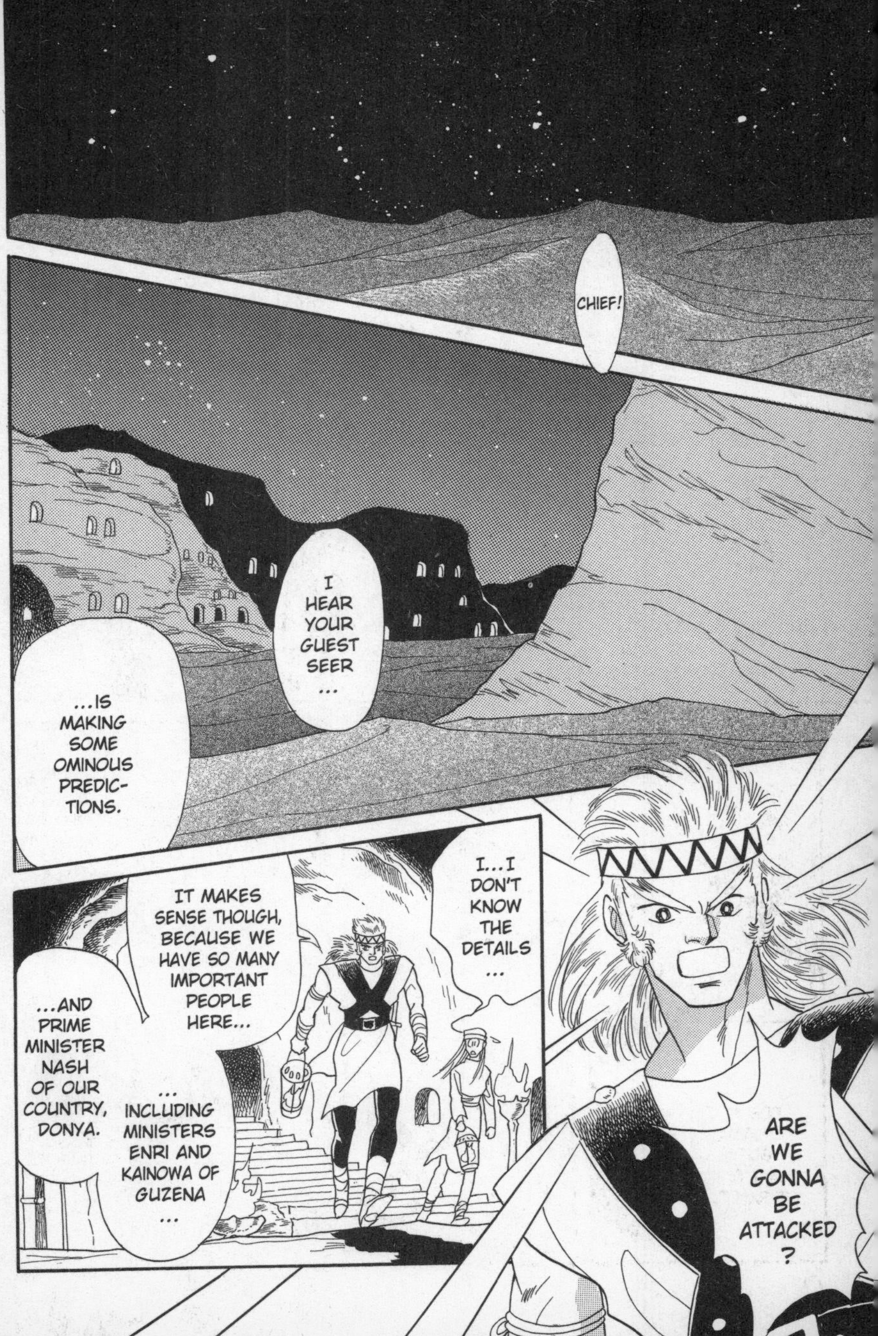
CHIEF!
I HEAR YOUR GUEST SEER ...
...IS MAKING SOME OMINOUS PREDICTIONS.
ARE WE GONNA BE ATTACKED?
I...I DON'T KNOW THE DETAILS...
IT MAKES SENSE THOUGH, BECAUSE WE HAVE SO MANY IMPORTANT PEOPLE HERE...
...INCLUDING MINISTERS ENRI AND KAINOWA OF GUZENA...
...AND PRIME MINISTER NASH OF OUR COUNTRY, DONYA.

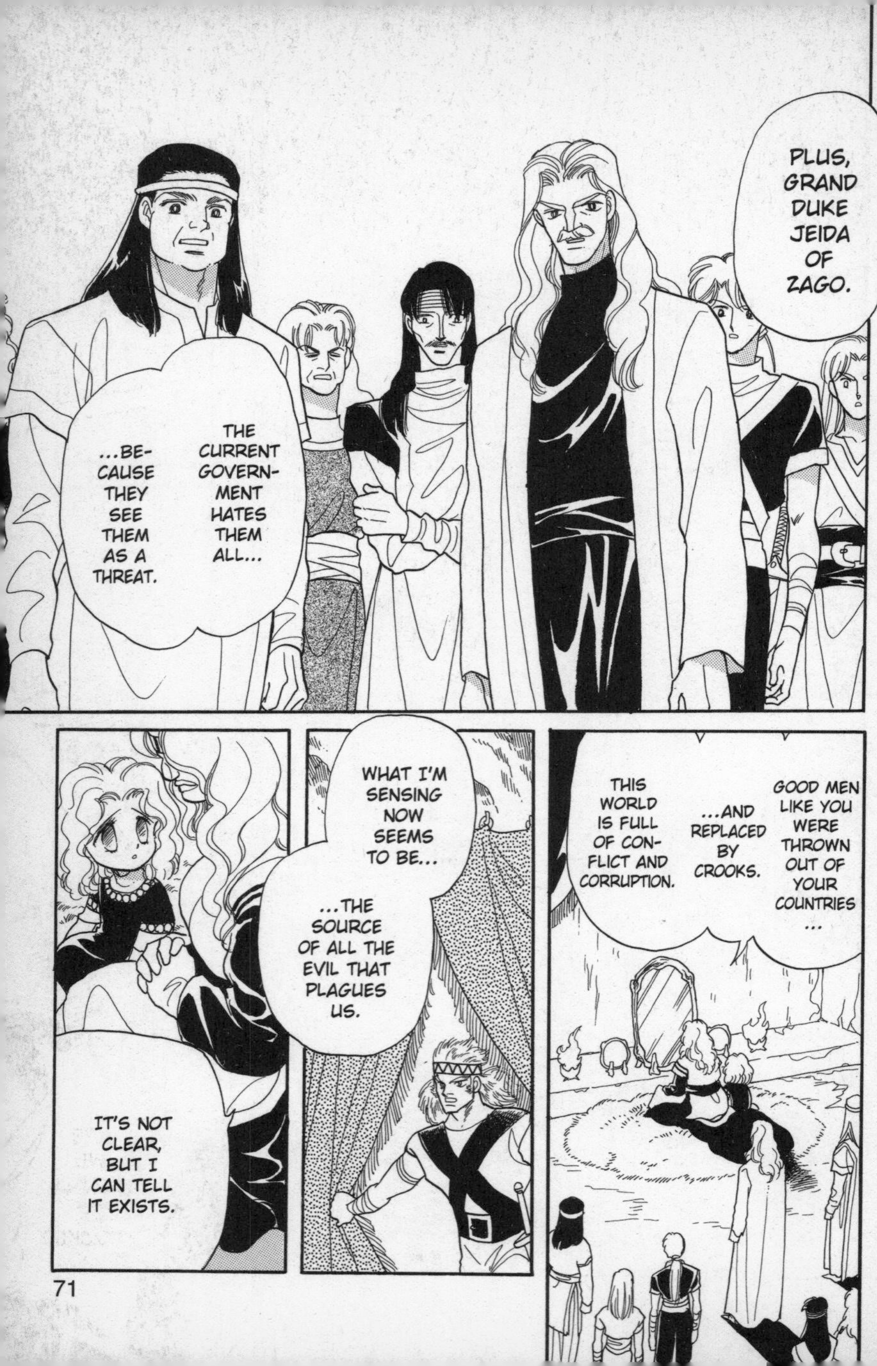
PLUS, GRAND DUKE JEIDA OF ZAGO.
THE CURRENT GOVERN-MENT HATES THEM ALL...
...BE-CAUSE THEY SEE THEM AS A THREAT.
GOOD MEN LIKE YOU WERE THROWN OUT OF YOUR COUNTRIES ...
...AND REPLACED BY CROOKS.
THIS WORLD IS FULL OF CON-FLICT AND CORRUPTION.
WHAT I'M SENSING NOW SEEMS TO BE...
...THE SOURCE OF ALL THE EVIL THAT PLAGUES US.
IT'S NOT CLEAR, BUT I CAN TELL IT EXISTS.

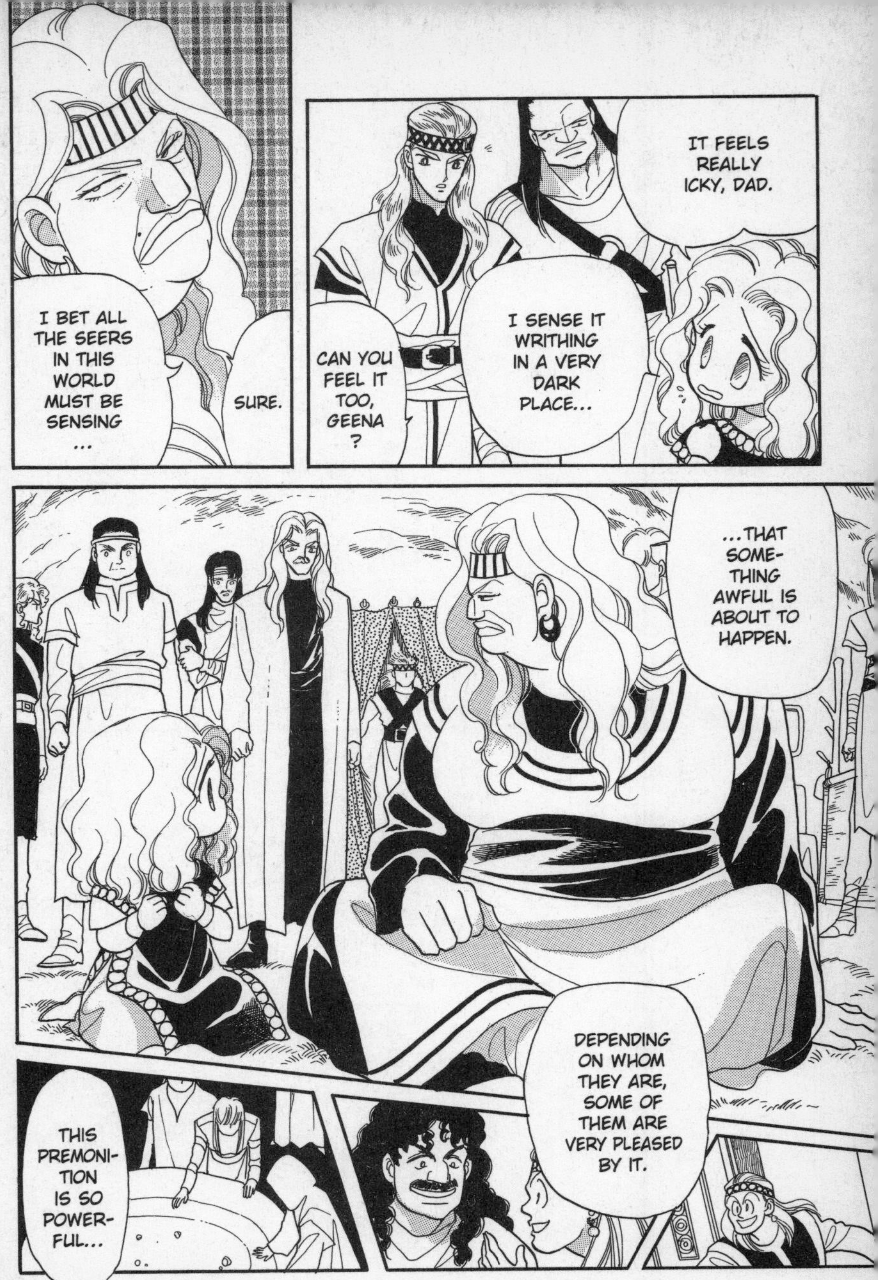
IT FEELS REALLY ICKY, DAD.
I SENSE IT WRITHING IN A VERY DARK PLACE...
CAN YOU FEEL IT TOO, GEENA?
SURE.
I BET ALL THE SEERS IN THIS WORLD MUST BE SENSING ...
...THAT SOMETHING AWFUL IS ABOUT TO HAPPEN.
DEPENDING ON WHOM THEY ARE, SOME OF THEM ARE VERY PLEASED BY IT.
THIS PREMONITION IS SO POWERFUL...

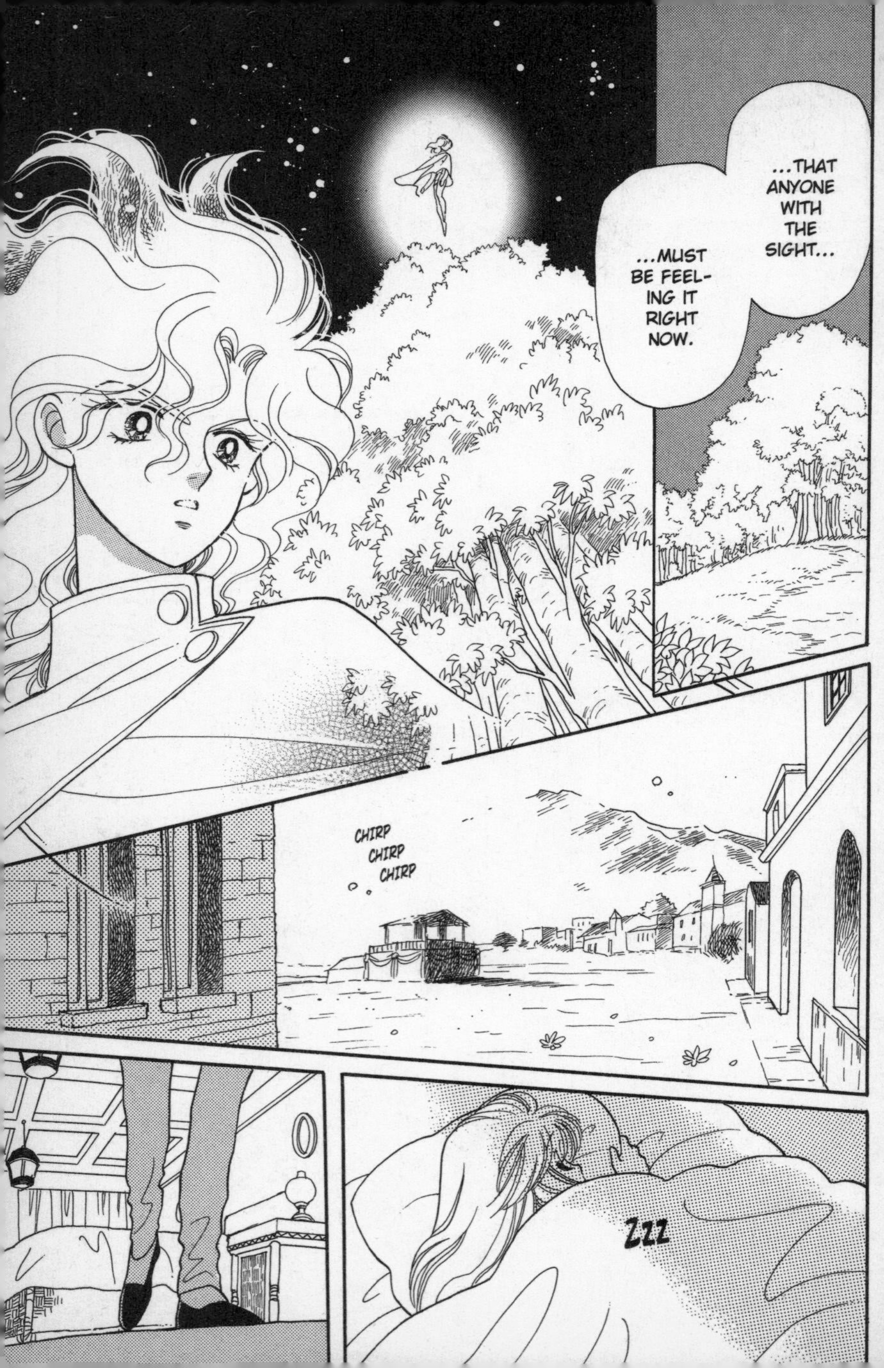
...THAT ANYONE WITH THE SIGHT...
...MUST BE FEELING IT RIGHT NOW.
CHIRP CHIRP CHIRP
ZZZ

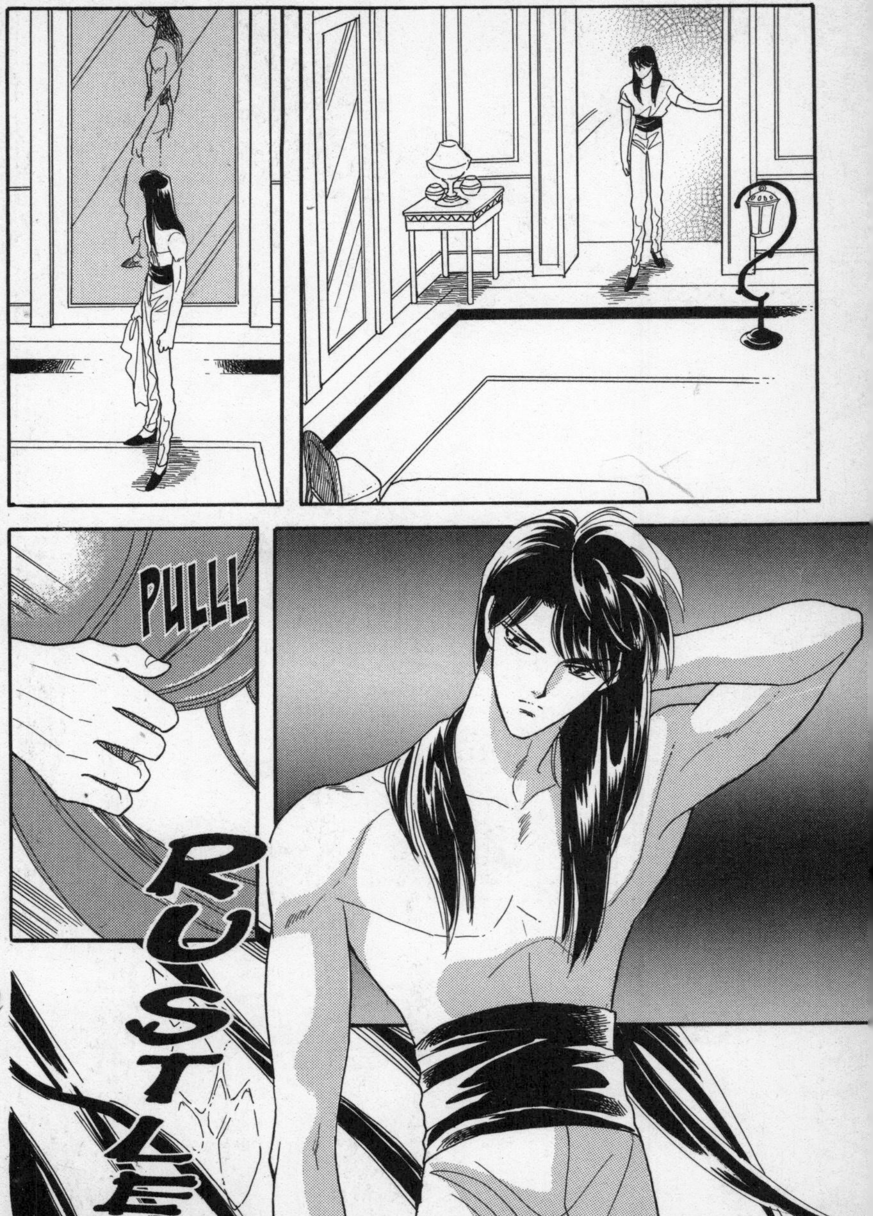
PULLL
RUSTLE

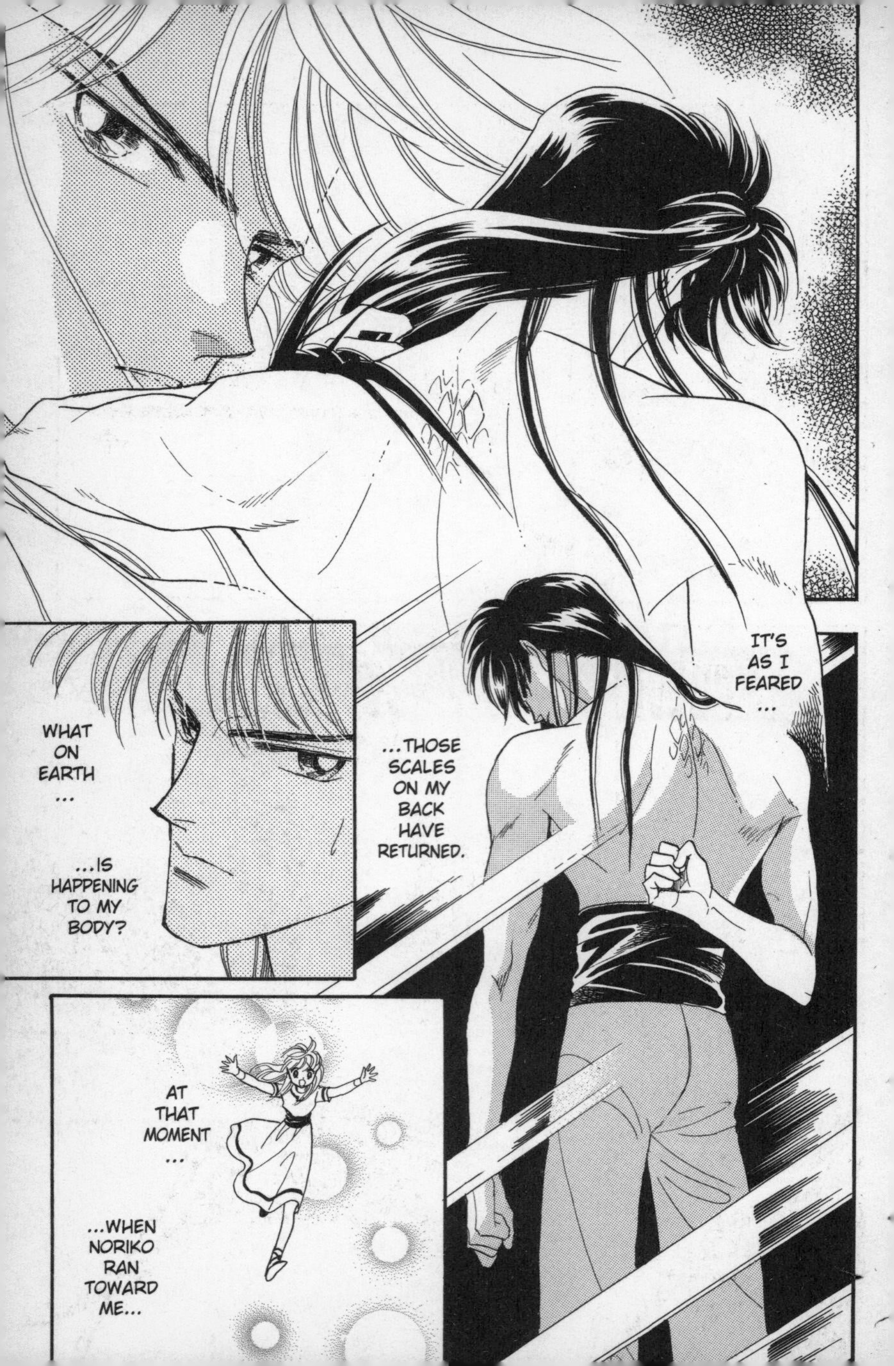
IT'S AS I FEARED...
...THOSE SCALES ON MY BACK HAVE RETURNED.
WHAT ON EARTH...
...IS HAPPENING TO MY BODY?
AT THAT MOMENT...
...WHEN NORIKO RAN TOWARD ME...

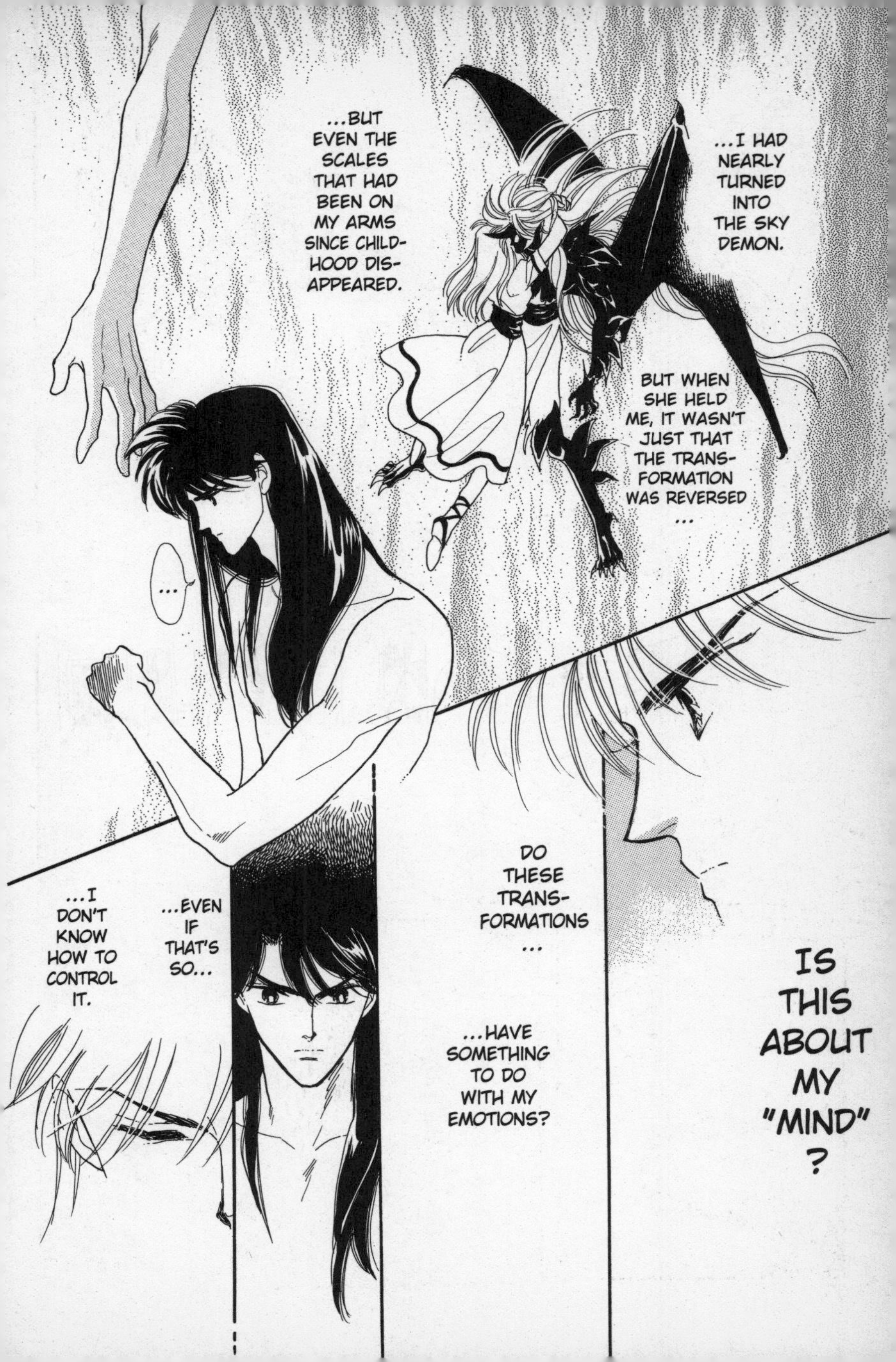
...I HAD NEARLY TURNED INTO THE SKY DEMON.
BUT WHEN SHE HELD ME, IT WASN'T JUST THAT THE TRANSFORMATION WAS REVERSED ...
...BUT EVEN THE SCALES THAT HAD BEEN ON MY ARMS SINCE CHILDHOOD DISAPPEARED.
...
IS THIS ABOUT MY "MIND" ?
DO THESE TRANSFORMATIONS ...
...HAVE SOMETHING TO DO WITH MY EMOTIONS?
...EVEN IF THAT'S SO...
...I DON'T KNOW HOW TO CONTROL IT.

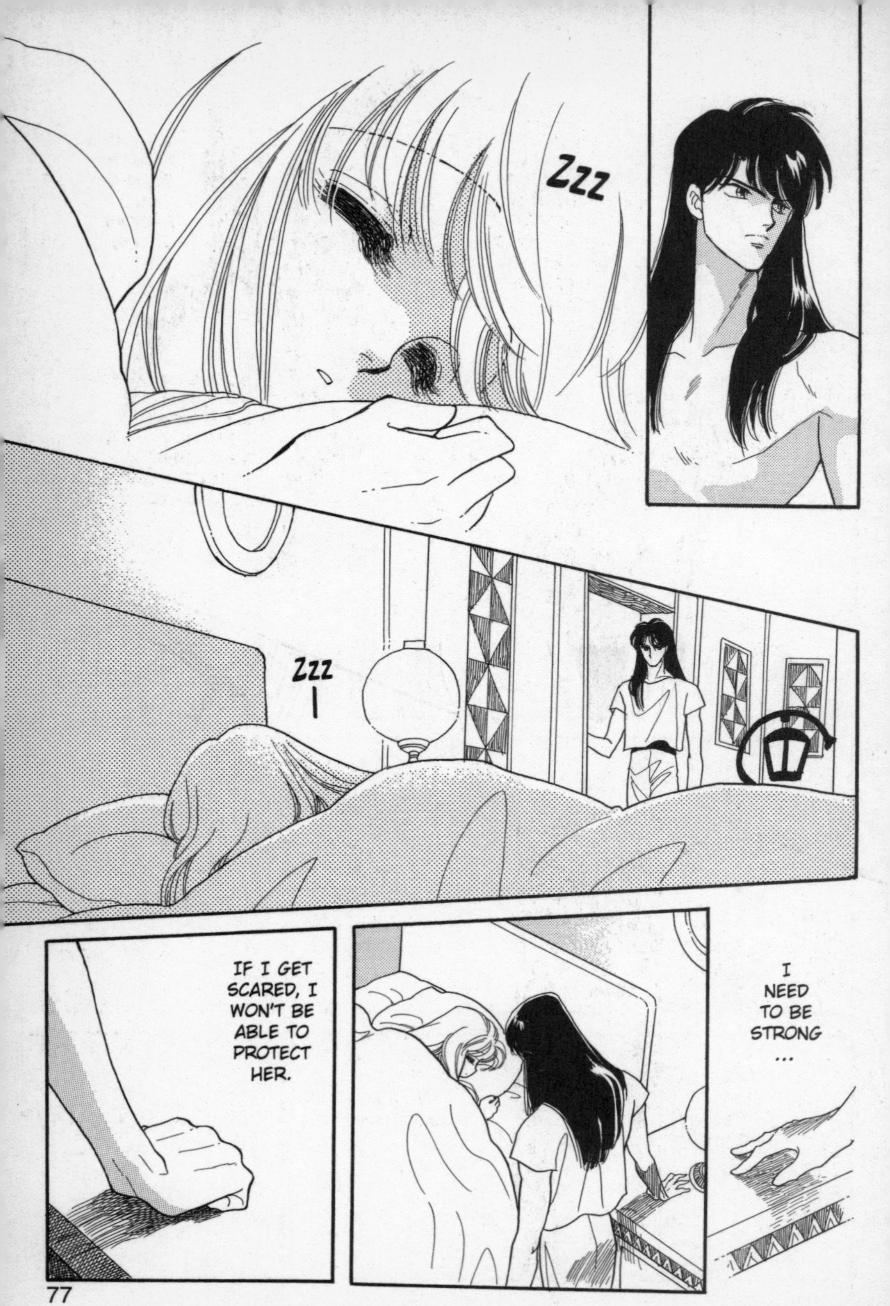
Zzz
Zzz
I NEED TO BE STRONG ...
IF I GET SCARED, I WON'T BE ABLE TO PROTECT HER.

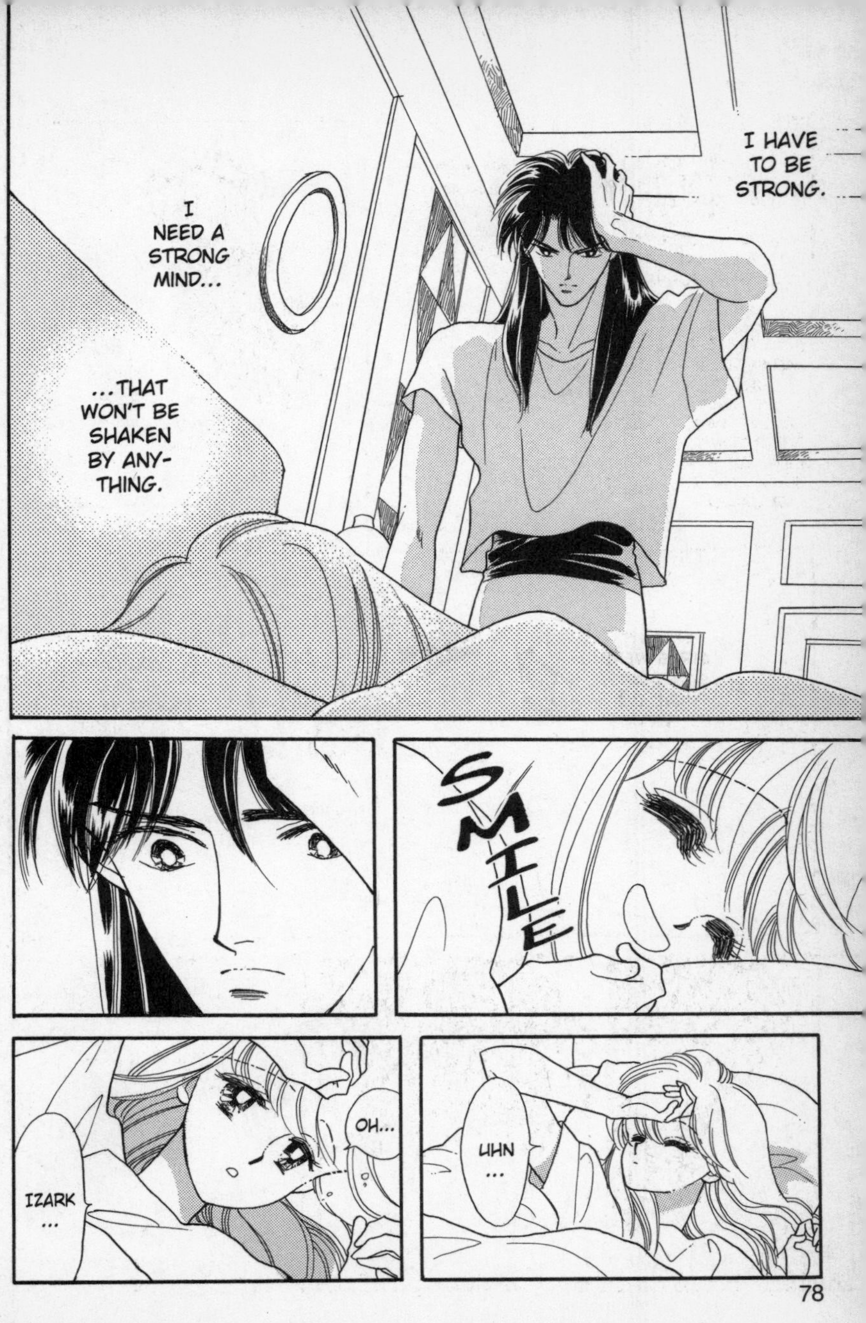
I HAVE TO BE STRONG.
I NEED A STRONG MIND...
...THAT WON'T BE SHAKEN BY ANY-THING.
SMILE
UHN ...
OH...
IZARK ...

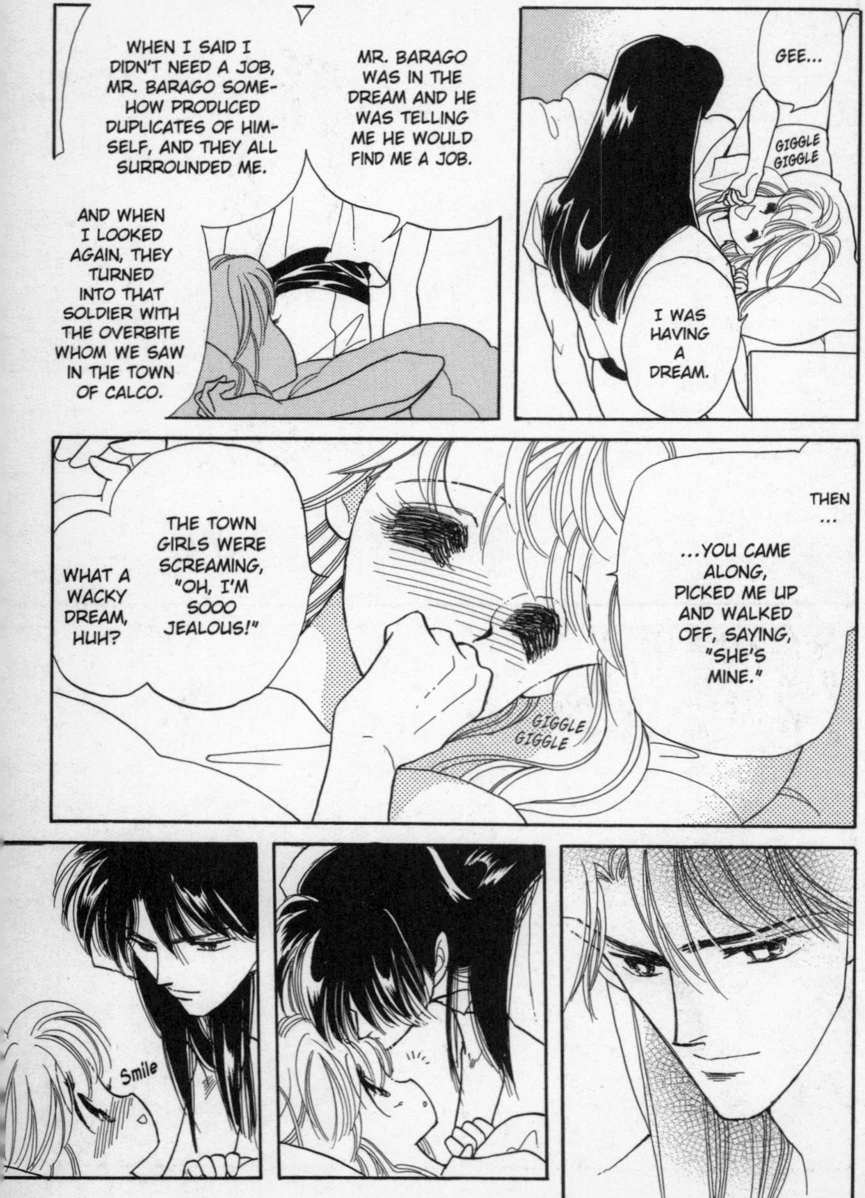
GEE...
GIGGLE GIGGLE
I WAS HAVING A DREAM.
MR. BARAGO WAS IN THE DREAM AND HE WAS TELLING ME HE WOULD FIND ME A JOB.
WHEN I SAID I DIDN'T NEED A JOB, MR. BARAGO SOME-HOW PRODUCED DUPLICATES OF HIM-SELF, AND THEY ALL SURROUNDED ME.
AND WHEN I LOOKED AGAIN, THEY TURNED INTO THAT SOLDIER WITH THE OVERBITE WHOM WE SAW IN THE TOWN OF CALCO.
THEN ...
...YOU CAME ALONG, PICKED ME UP AND WALKED OFF, SAYING, "SHE'S MINE."
GIGGLE GIGGLE
THE TOWN GIRLS WERE SCREAMING, "OH, I'M SOOO JEALOUS!"
WHAT A WACKY DREAM, HUH?
Smile

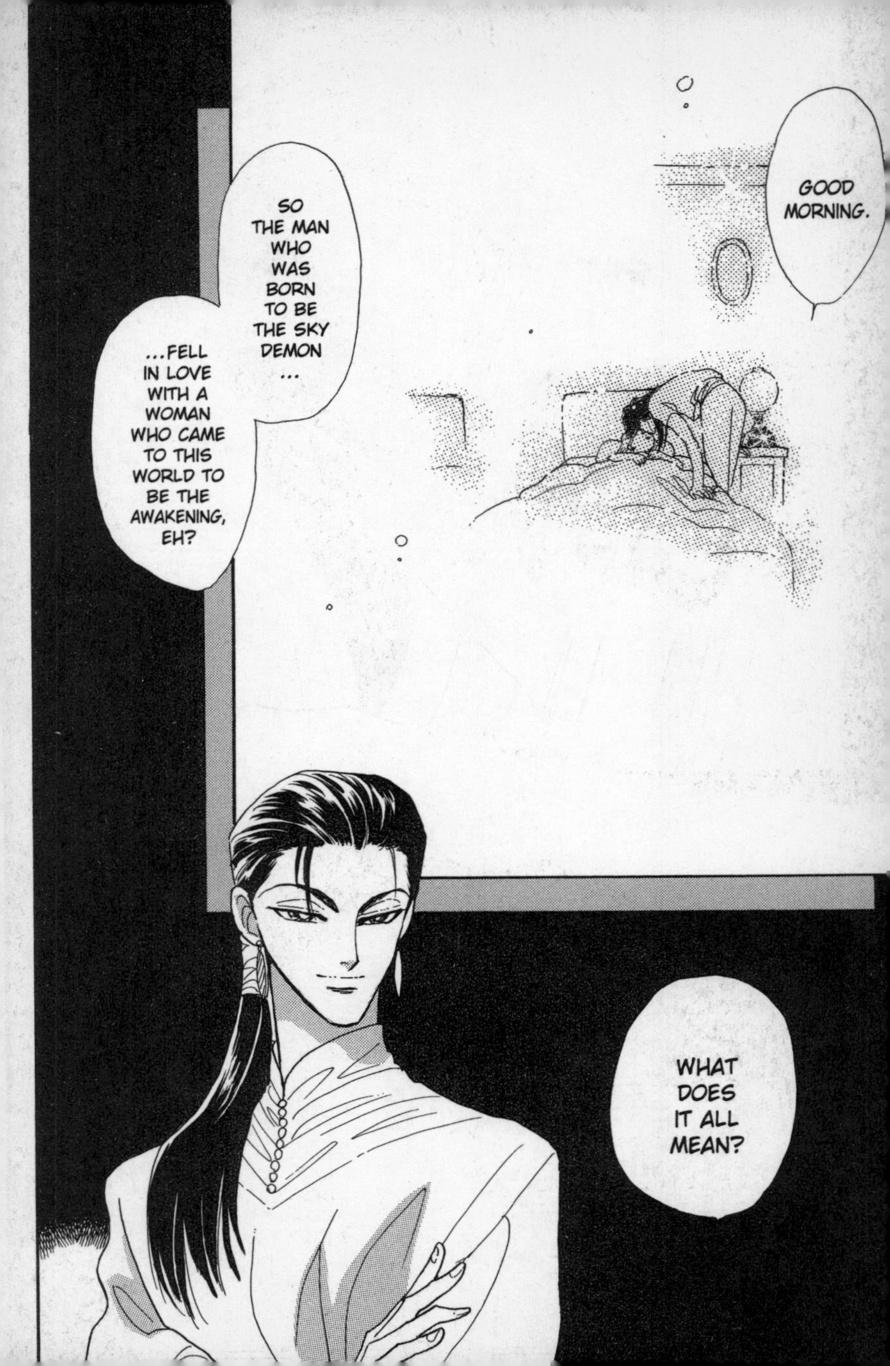
GOOD MORNING.
SO THE MAN WHO WAS BORN TO BE THE SKY DEMON ...
...FELL IN LOVE WITH A WOMAN WHO CAME TO THIS WORLD TO BE THE AWAKENING, EH?
WHAT DOES IT ALL MEAN?

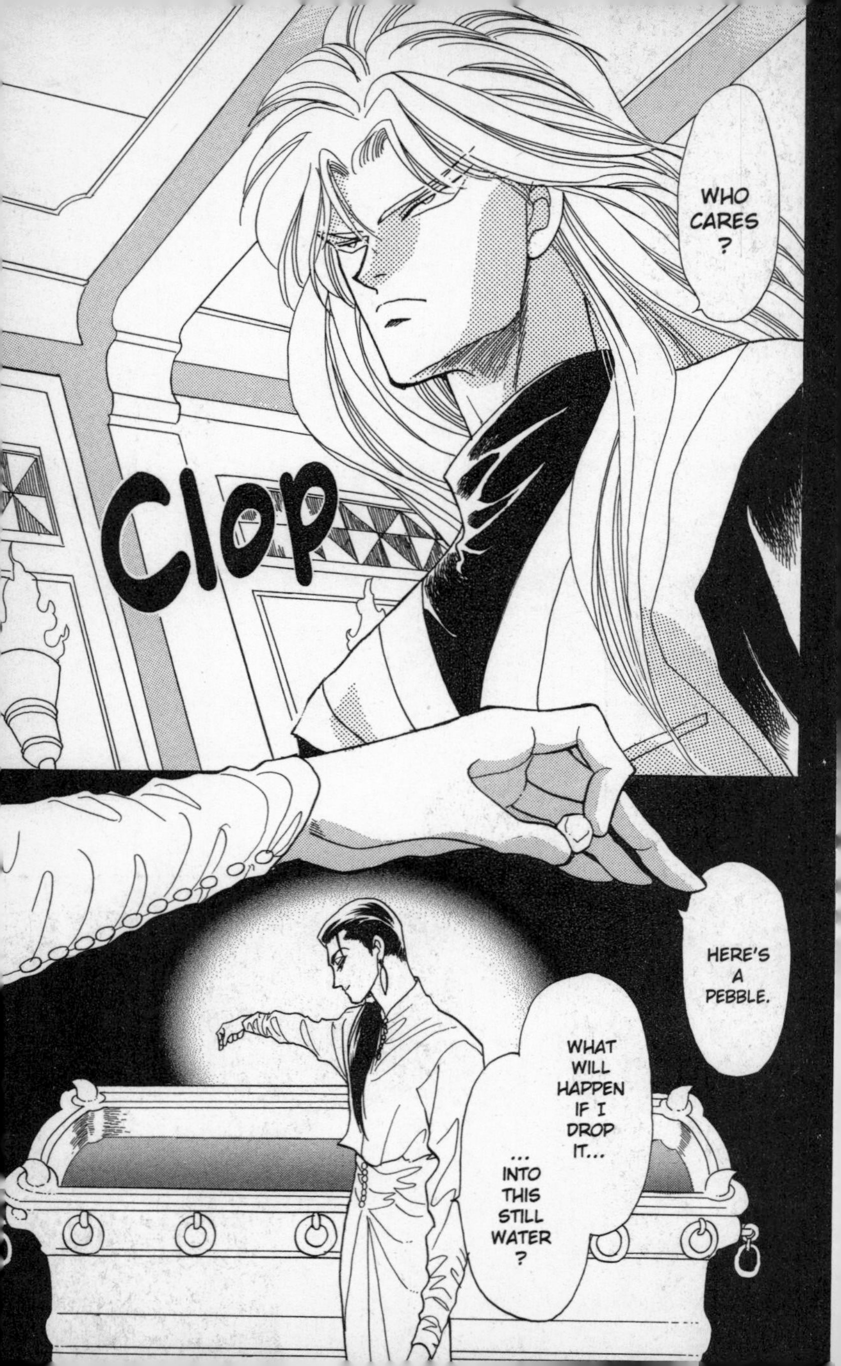
WHO CARES ?
CLOP
HERE'S A PEBBLE.
WHAT WILL HAPPEN IF I DROP IT...
... INTO THIS STILL WATER ?

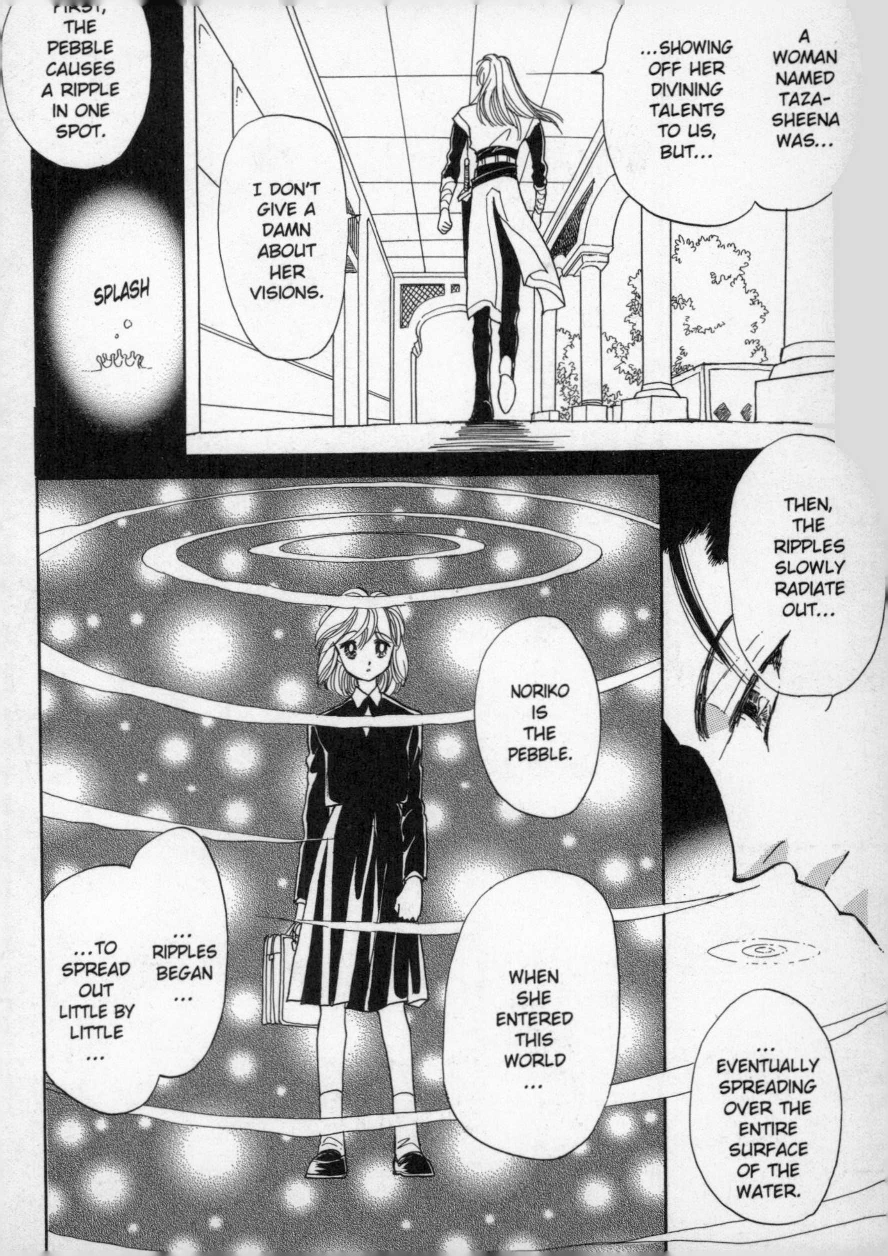
A WOMAN NAMED TAZA-SHEENA WAS...
...SHOWING OFF HER DIVINING TALENTS TO US, BUT...
I DON'T GIVE A DAMN ABOUT HER VISIONS.
THE PEBBLE CAUSES A RIPPLE IN ONE SPOT.
SPLASH
THEN, THE RIPPLES SLOWLY RADIATE OUT...
...EVENTUALLY SPREADING OVER THE ENTIRE SURFACE OF THE WATER.
NORIKO IS THE PEBBLE.
WHEN SHE ENTERED THIS WORLD...
...RIPPLES BEGAN...
...TO SPREAD OUT LITTLE BY LITTLE...

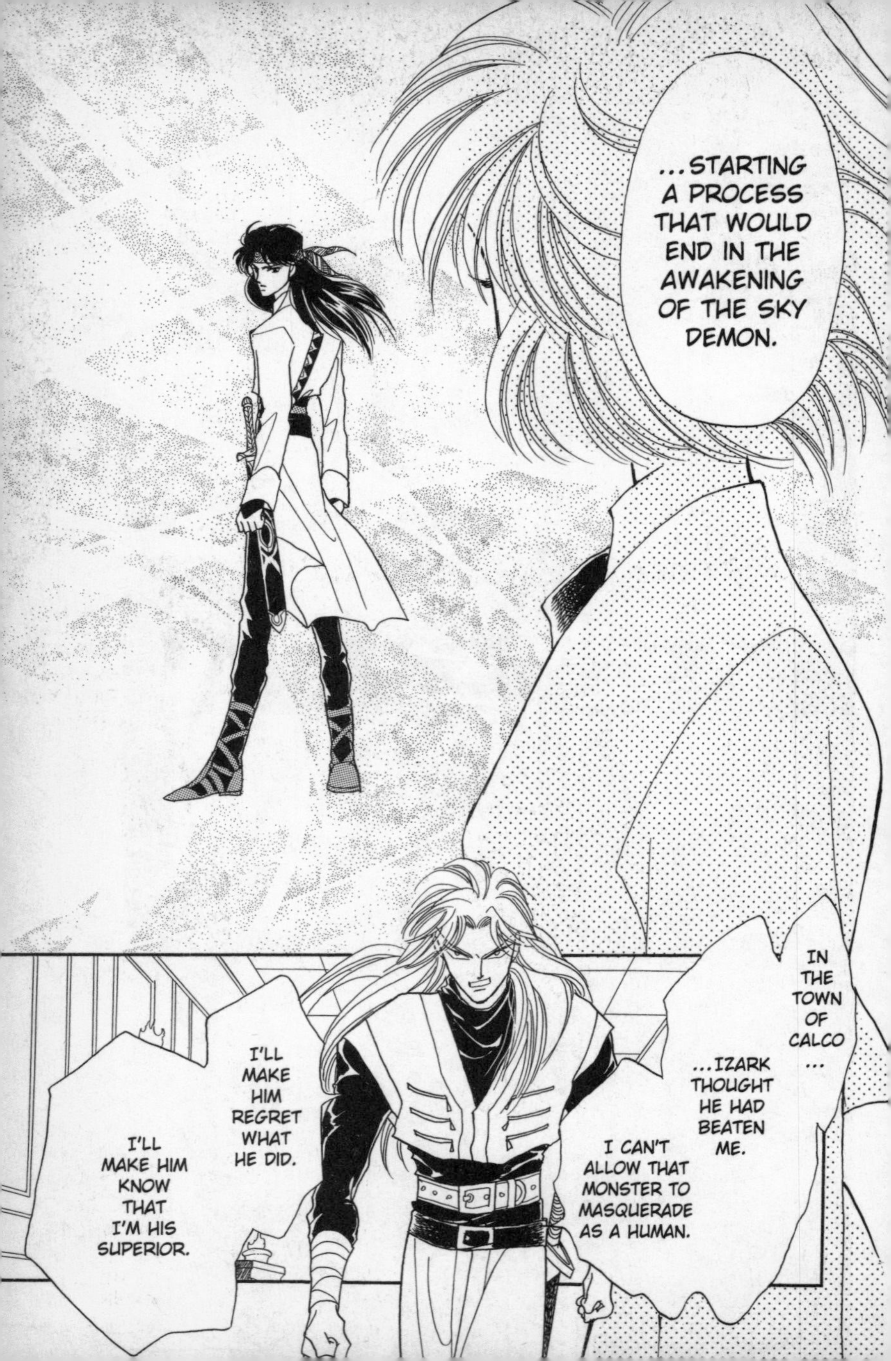
...STARTING A PROCESS THAT WOULD END IN THE AWAKENING OF THE SKY DEMON.
IN THE TOWN OF CALCO...
...IZARK THOUGHT HE HAD BEATEN ME.
I CAN'T ALLOW THAT MONSTER TO MASQUERADE AS A HUMAN.
I'LL MAKE HIM REGRET WHAT HE DID.
I'LL MAKE HIM KNOW THAT I'M HIS SUPERIOR.

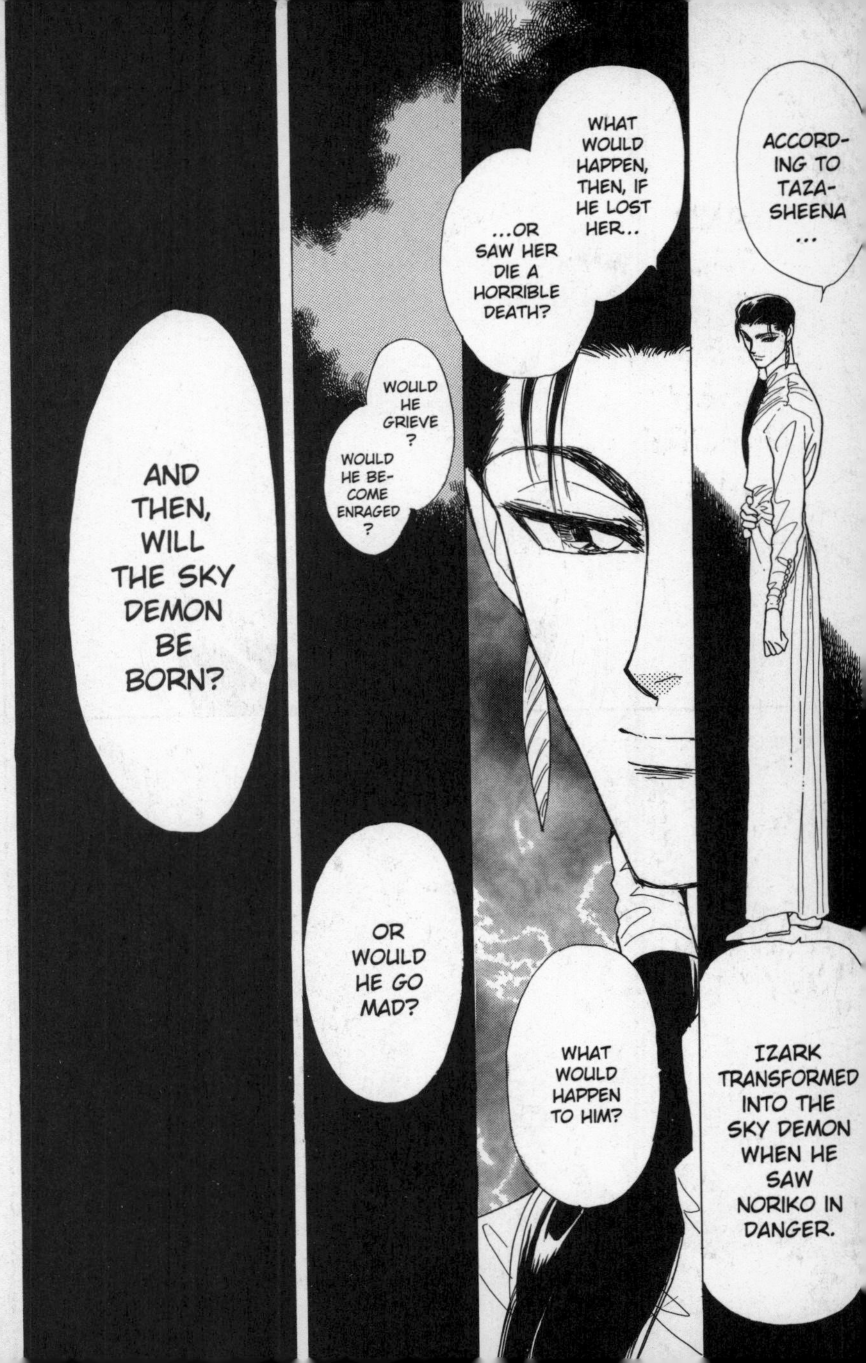
ACCORDING TO TAZA-SHEENA ...
IZARK TRANSFORMED INTO THE SKY DEMON WHEN HE SAW NORIKO IN DANGER.
WHAT WOULD HAPPEN, THEN, IF HE LOST HER...
...OR SAW HER DIE A HORRIBLE DEATH?
WHAT WOULD HAPPEN TO HIM?
WOULD HE GRIEVE ?
WOULD HE BE-COME ENRAGED ?
OR WOULD HE GO MAD?
AND THEN, WILL THE SKY DEMON BE BORN?

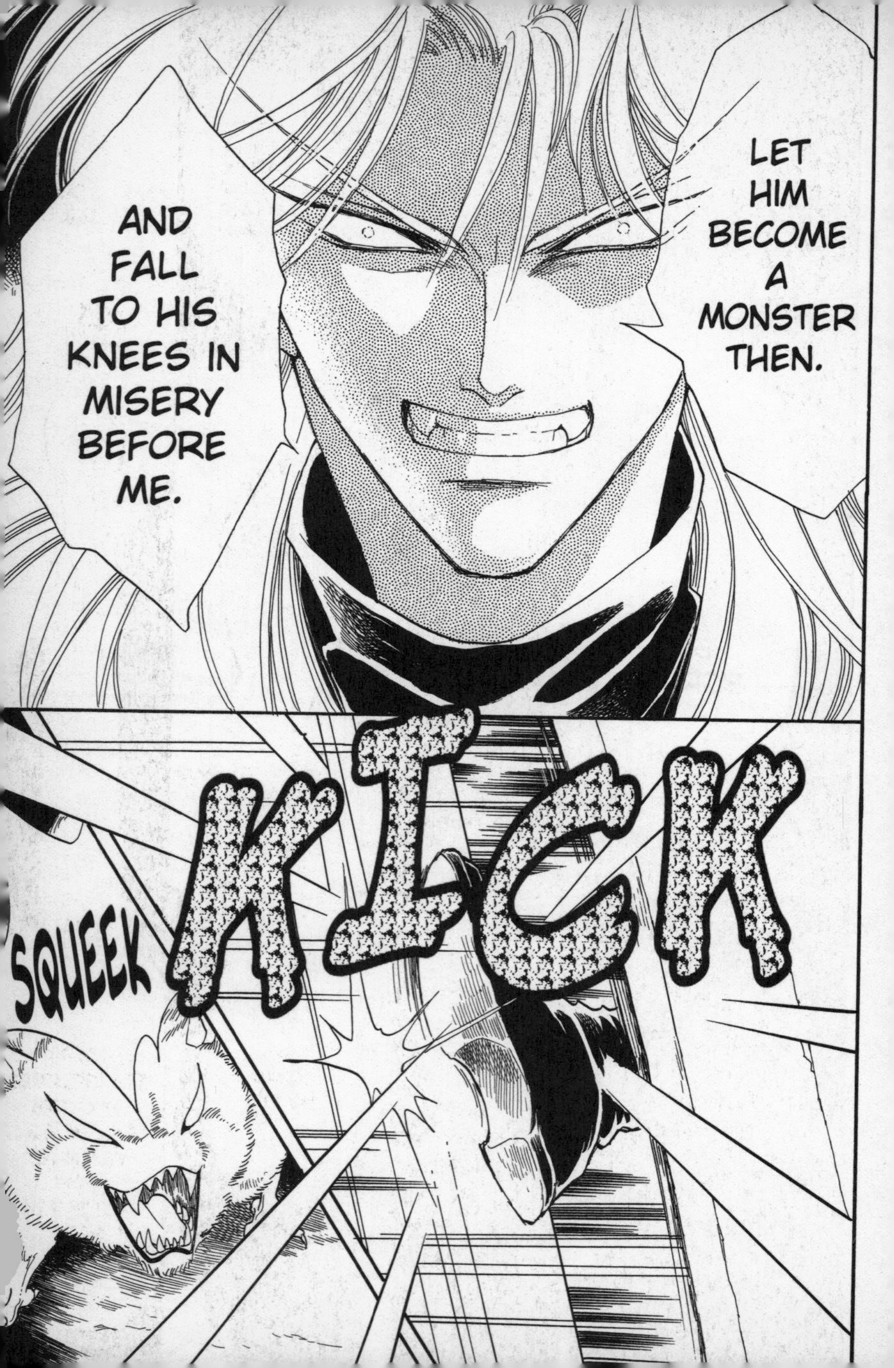
LET HIM BECOME A MONSTER THEN.
AND FALL TO HIS KNEES IN MISERY BEFORE ME.
KICK
SQUEEK

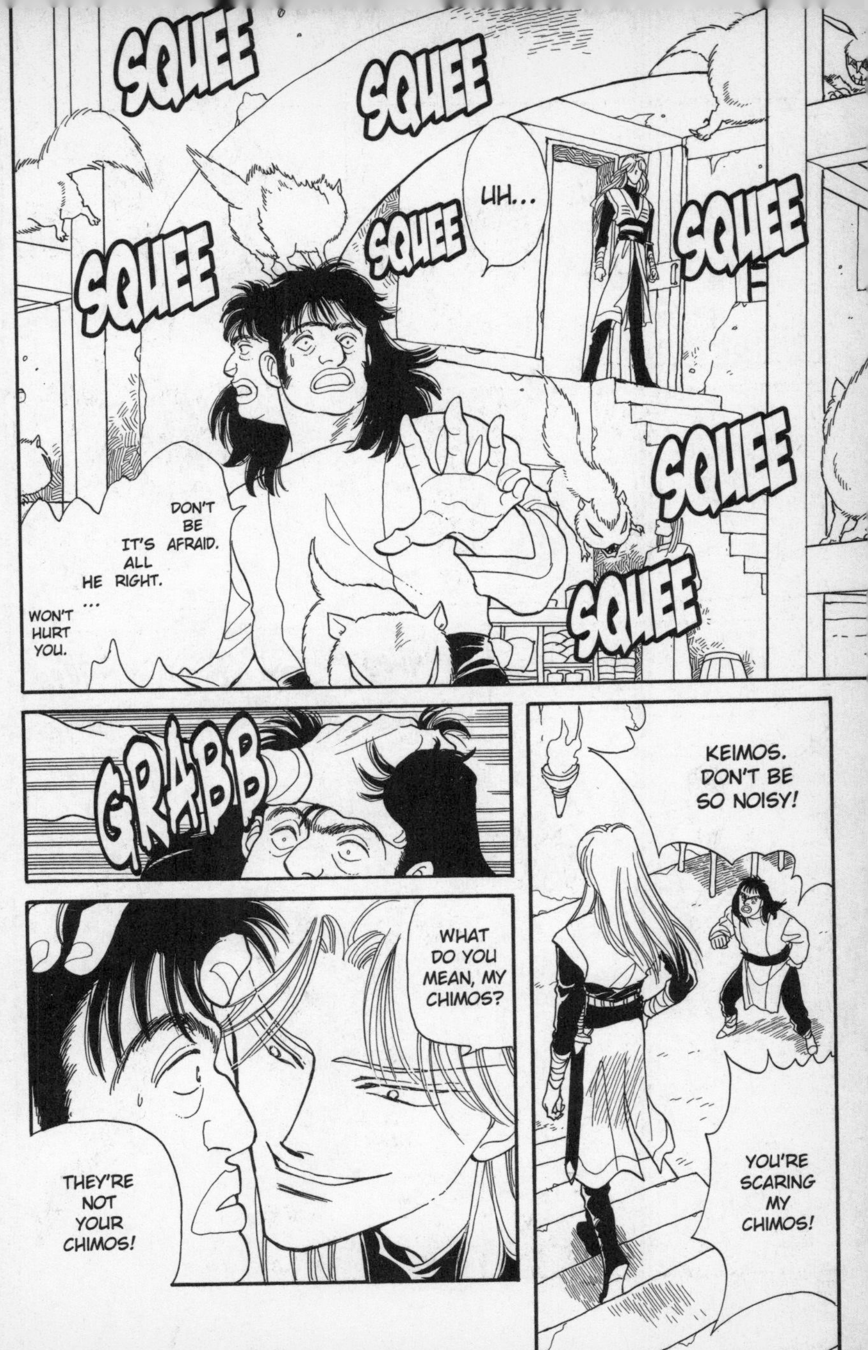
SQUEE
UH...
SQUEE
SQUEE
SQUEE
SQUEE
SQUEE
SQUEE
SQUEE
DON'T BE AFRAID. IT'S ALL RIGHT. HE ... WON'T HURT YOU.
KEIMOS. DON'T BE SO NOISY!
YOU'RE SCARING MY CHIMOS!
GRABB
WHAT DO YOU MEAN, MY CHIMOS?
THEY'RE NOT YOUR CHIMOS!

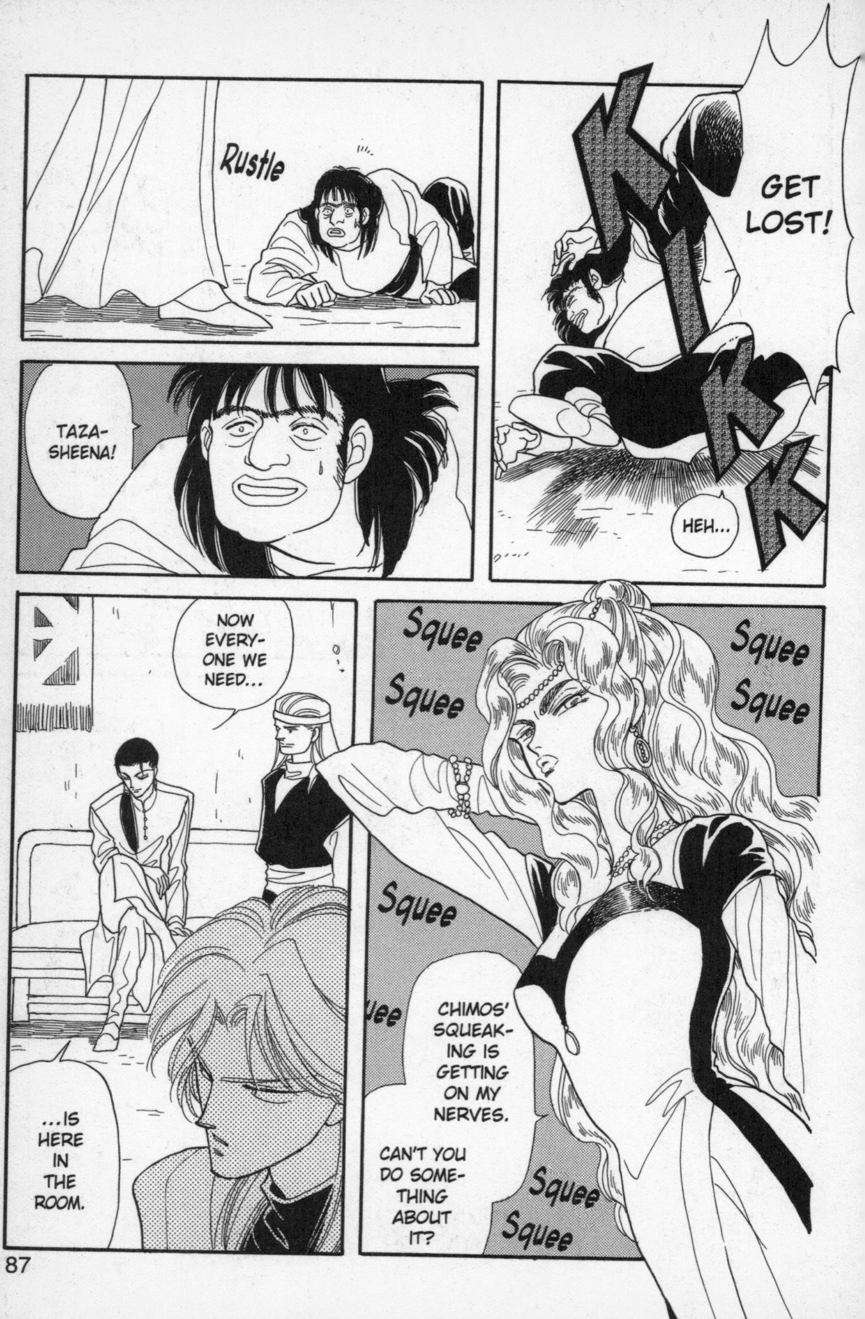
GET LOST!
KKKK
HEH...
Rustle
TAZA-SHEENA!
Squee Squee Squee Squee Squee Squee Squee Squee
CHIMOS' SQUEAKING IS GETTING ON MY NERVES.
CAN'T YOU DO SOMETHING ABOUT IT?
NOW EVERYONE WE NEED...
...IS HERE IN THE ROOM.

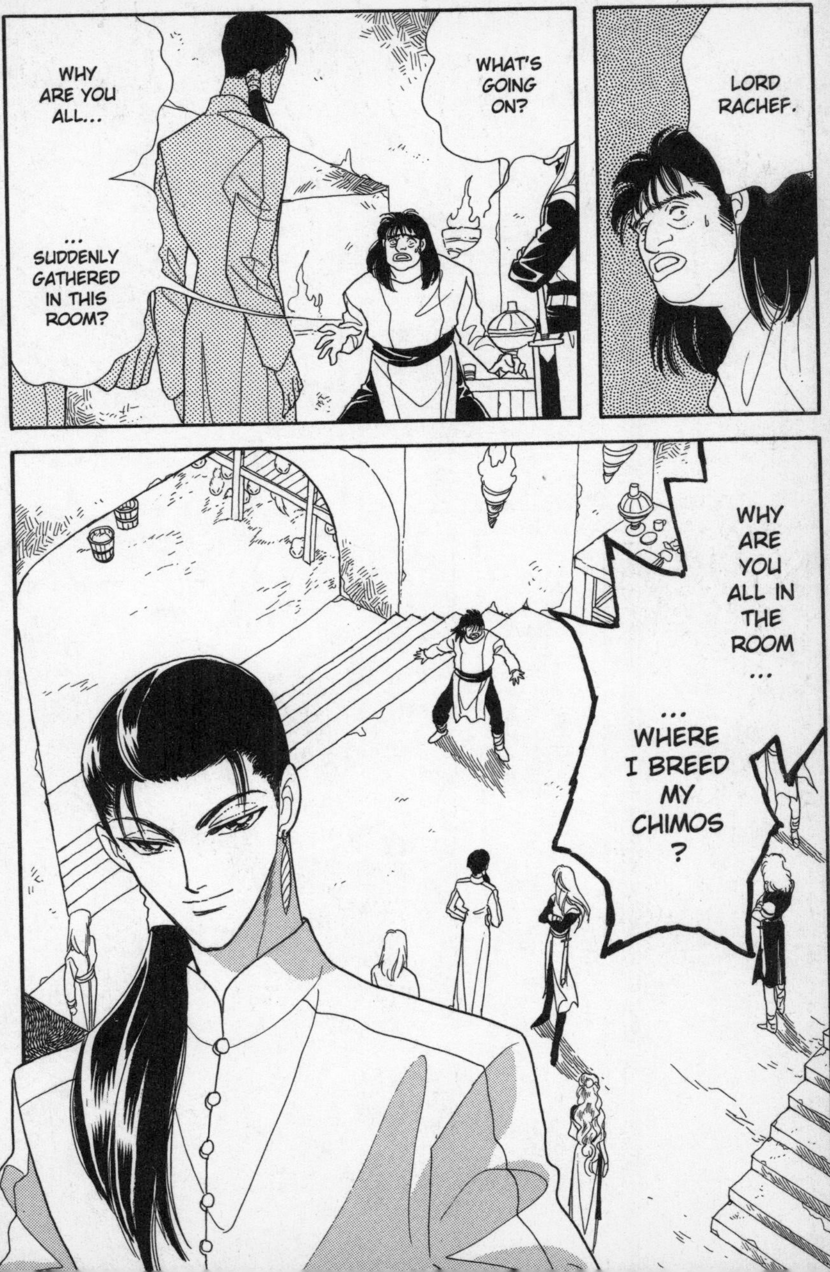
LORD RACHEF.
WHAT'S GOING ON?
WHY ARE YOU ALL...
...SUDDENLY GATHERED IN THIS ROOM?
WHY ARE YOU ALL IN THE ROOM...
...WHERE I BREED MY CHIMOS?

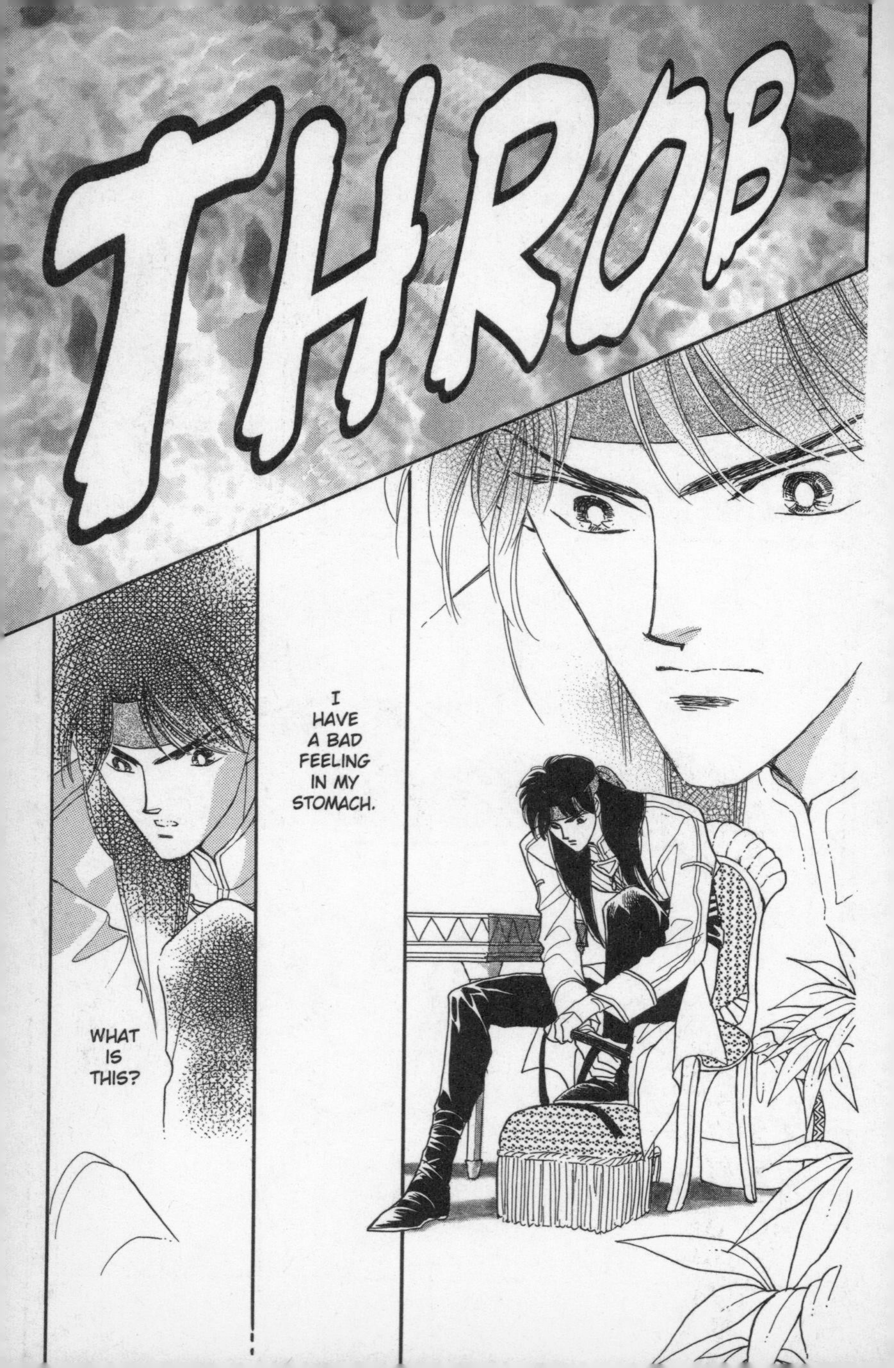
THROB
I HAVE A BAD FEELING IN MY STOMACH.
WHAT IS THIS?

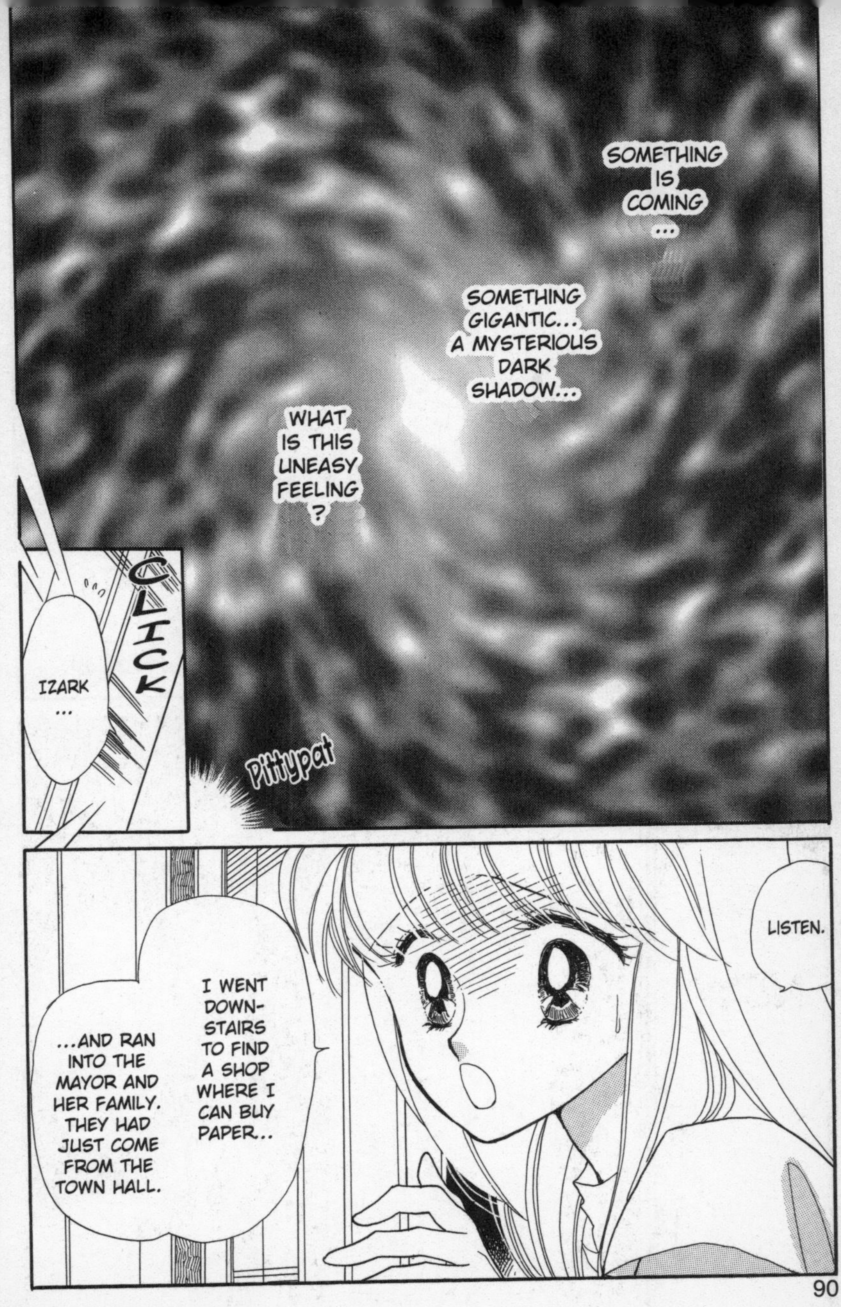
SOMETHING IS COMING ...
SOMETHING GIGANTIC... A MYSTERIOUS DARK SHADOW...
WHAT IS THIS UNEASY FEELING ?
Pittypat
CLICK
IZARK ...
LISTEN.
I WENT DOWN-STAIRS TO FIND A SHOP WHERE I CAN BUY PAPER...
...AND RAN INTO THE MAYOR AND HER FAMILY. THEY HAD JUST COME FROM THE TOWN HALL.

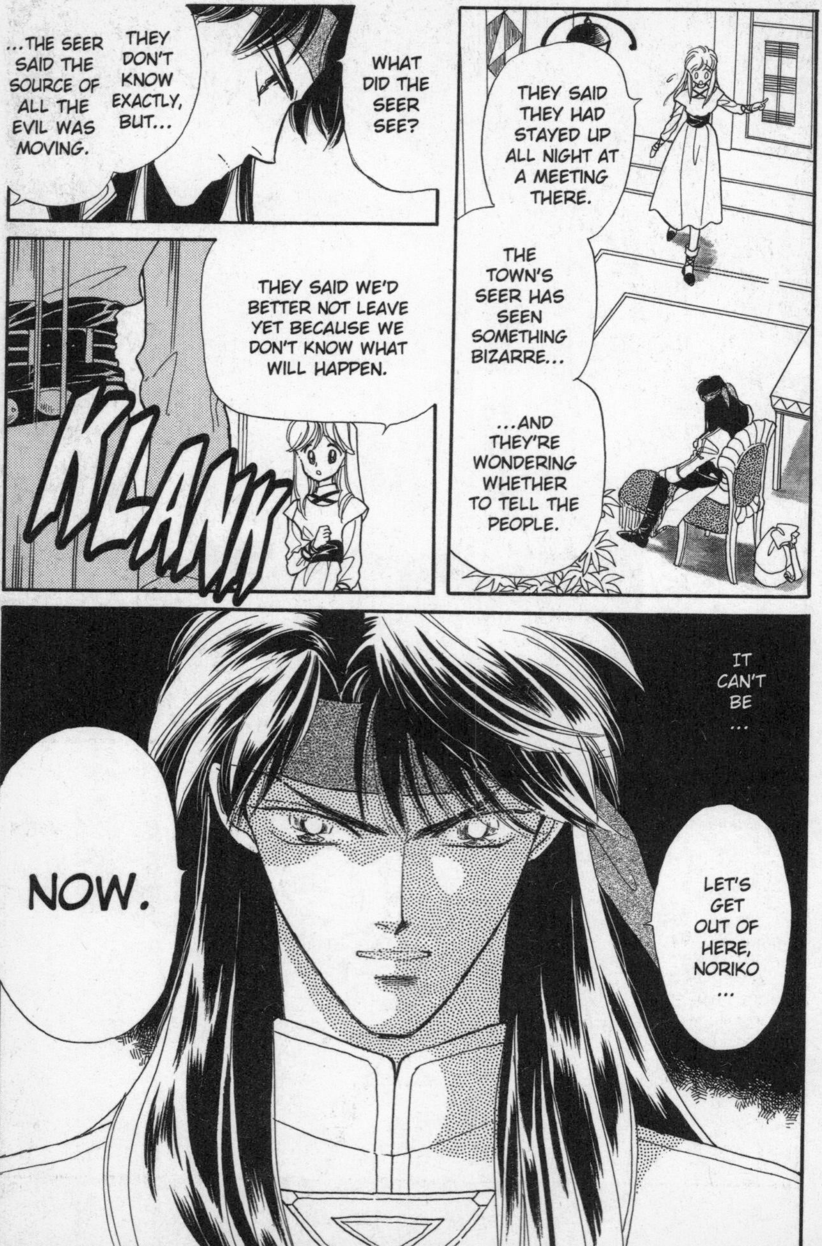
THEY SAID THEY HAD STAYED UP ALL NIGHT AT A MEETING THERE.
THE TOWN'S SEER HAS SEEN SOMETHING BIZARRE...
...AND THEY'RE WONDERING WHETHER TO TELL THE PEOPLE.
WHAT DID THE SEER SEE?
THEY DON'T KNOW EXACTLY, BUT...
...THE SEER SAID THE SOURCE OF ALL THE EVIL WAS MOVING.
THEY SAID WE'D BETTER NOT LEAVE YET BECAUSE WE DON'T KNOW WHAT WILL HAPPEN.
KLANK
IT CAN'T BE...
LET'S GET OUT OF HERE, NORIKO...
NOW.

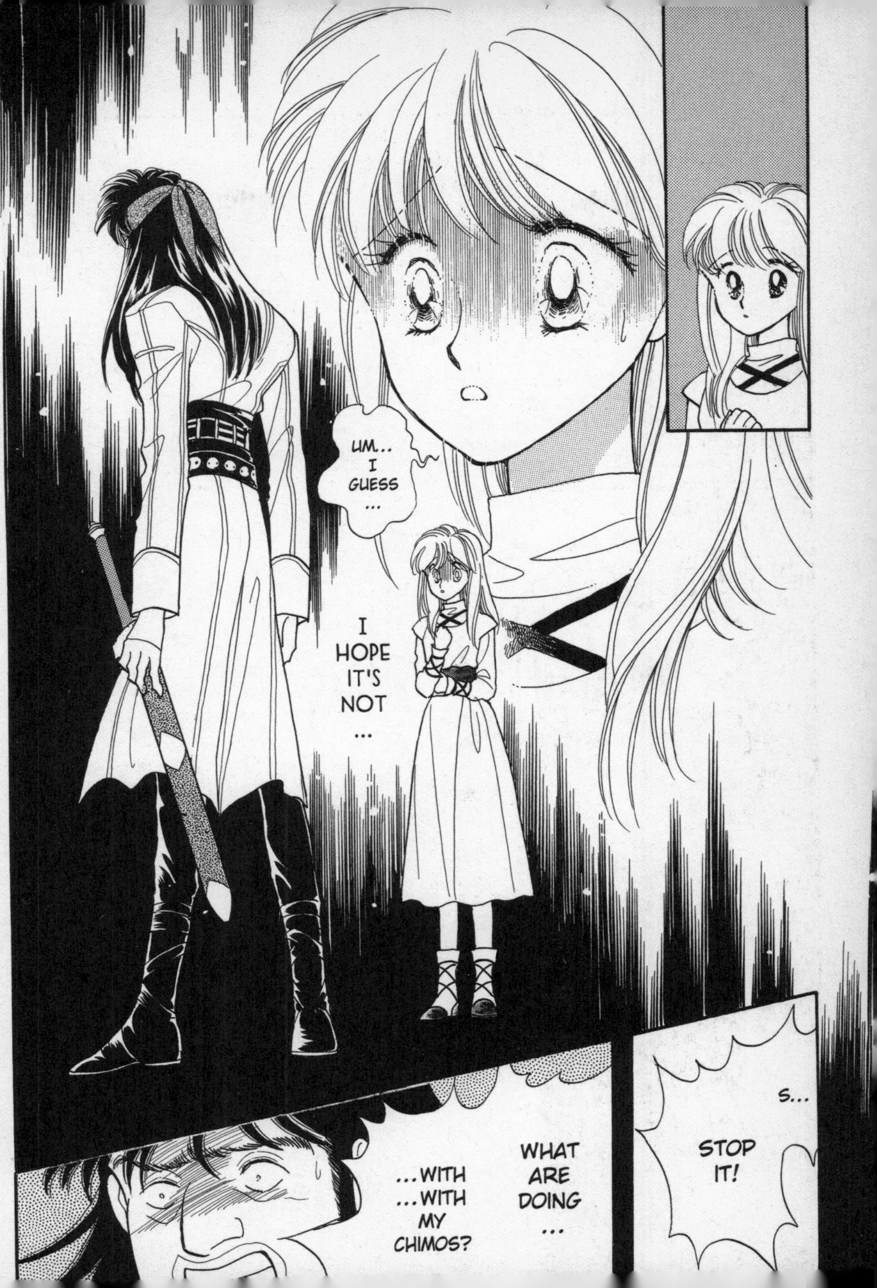
UM... I GUESS ...
I HOPE IT'S NOT ...
S...
STOP IT!
WHAT ARE DOING ...
...WITH ...WITH MY CHIMOS?

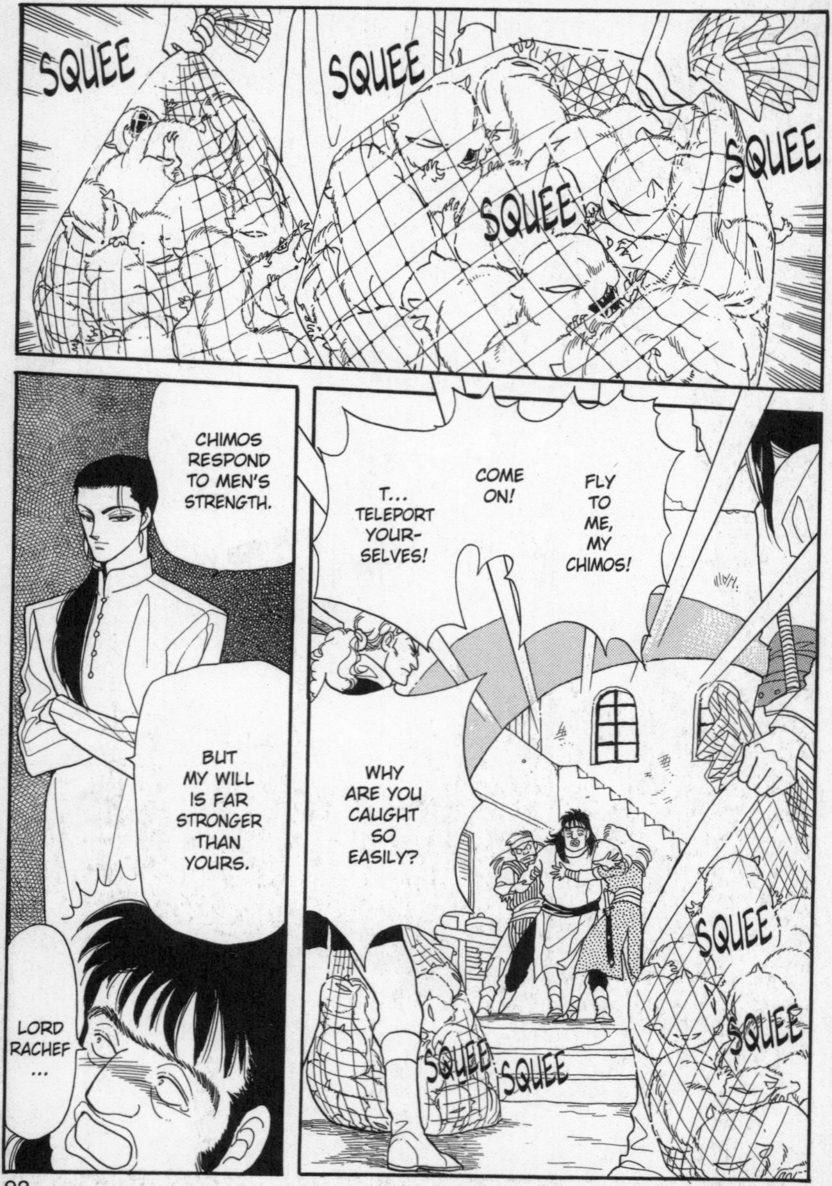
SQUEE
SQUEE
SQUEE
SQUEE
FLY TO ME, MY CHIMOS!
COME ON!
T... TELEPORT YOUR-SELVES!
WHY ARE YOU CAUGHT SO EASILY?
SQUEE
SQUEE
SQUEE
SQUEE
CHIMOS RESPOND TO MEN'S STRENGTH.
BUT MY WILL IS FAR STRONGER THAN YOURS.
LORD RACHEF ...

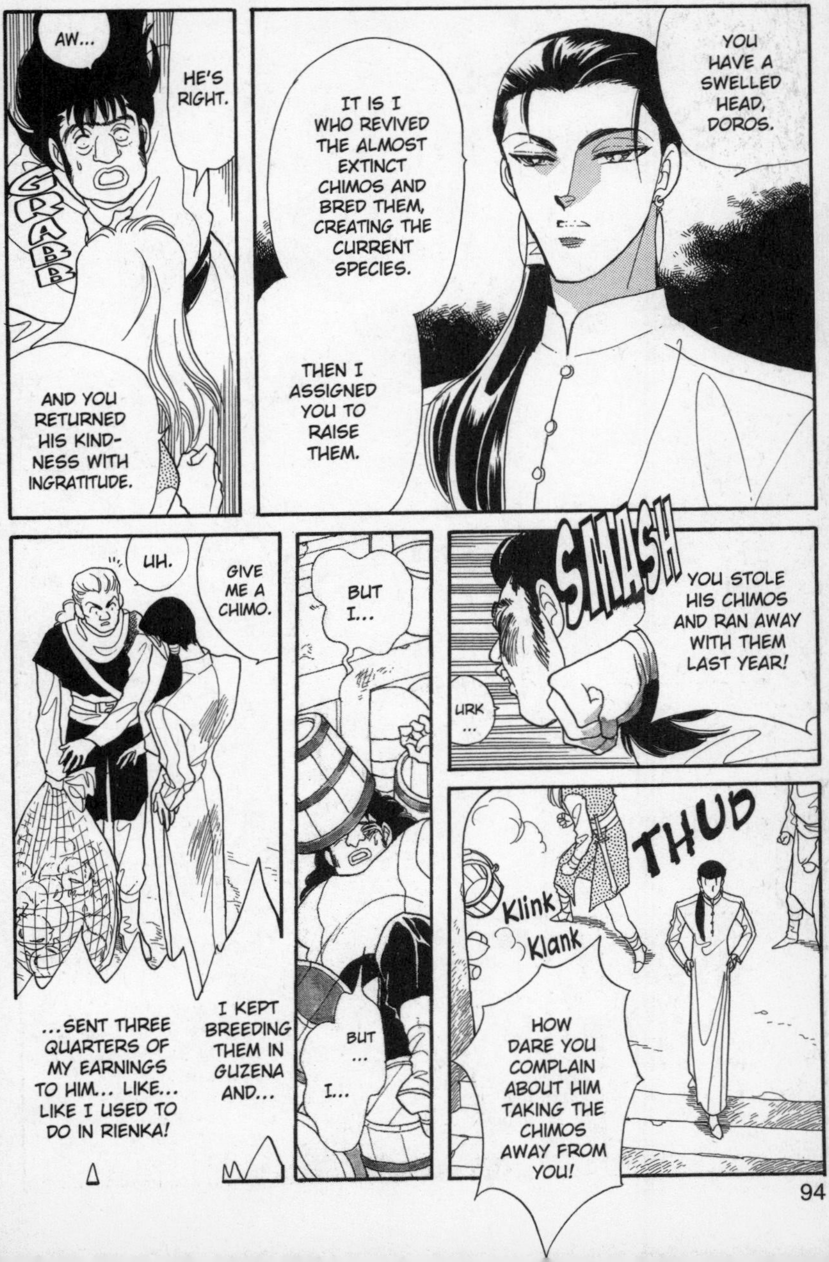
YOU HAVE A SWELLED HEAD, DOROS.
IT IS I WHO REVIVED THE ALMOST EXTINCT CHIMOS AND BRED THEM, CREATING THE CURRENT SPECIES.
THEN I ASSIGNED YOU TO RAISE THEM.
AW...
HE'S RIGHT.
GRABBB
AND YOU RETURNED HIS KINDNESS WITH INGRATITUDE.
SMASH
YOU STOLE HIS CHIMOS AND RAN AWAY WITH THEM LAST YEAR!
URK ...
THUD
Klink
Klank
HOW DARE YOU COMPLAIN ABOUT HIM TAKING THE CHIMOS AWAY FROM YOU!
BUT I...
BUT ... I...
I KEPT BREEDING THEM IN GUZENA AND...
GIVE ME A CHIMO.
UH.
...SENT THREE QUARTERS OF MY EARNINGS TO HIM... LIKE... LIKE I USED TO DO IN RIENKA!

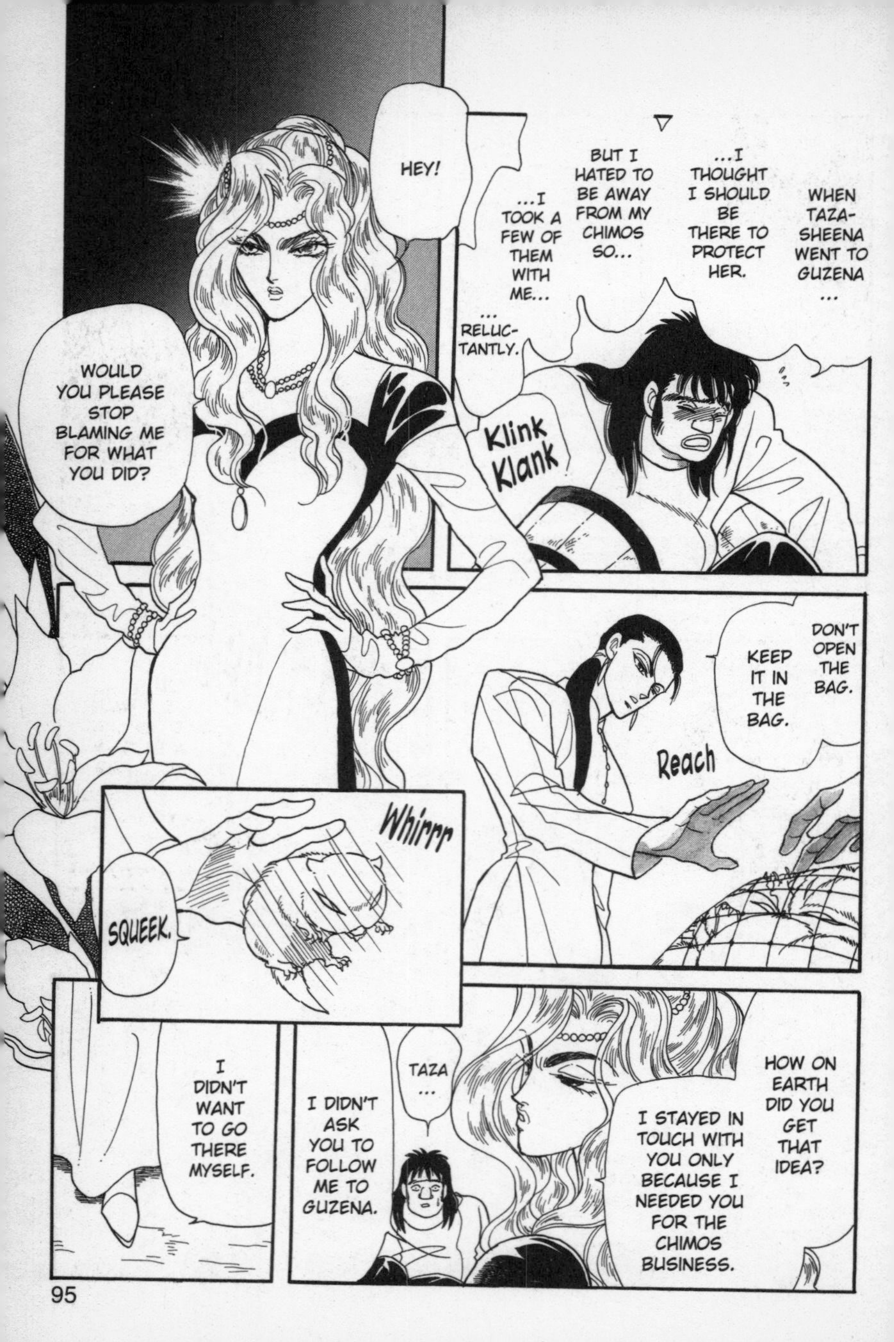
WHEN TAZA-SHEENA WENT TO GUZENA ...
...I THOUGHT I SHOULD BE THERE TO PROTECT HER.
BUT I HATED TO BE AWAY FROM MY CHIMOS SO...
...I TOOK A FEW OF THEM WITH ME...
...RELUCTANTLY.
Klink Klank
DON'T OPEN THE BAG.
KEEP IT IN THE BAG.
Reach
HEY!
WOULD YOU PLEASE STOP BLAMING ME FOR WHAT YOU DID?
Whirrr
SQUEEK.
HOW ON EARTH DID YOU GET THAT IDEA?
I STAYED IN TOUCH WITH YOU ONLY BECAUSE I NEEDED YOU FOR THE CHIMOS BUSINESS.
TAZA ...
I DIDN'T ASK YOU TO FOLLOW ME TO GUZENA.
I DIDN'T WANT TO GO THERE MYSELF.

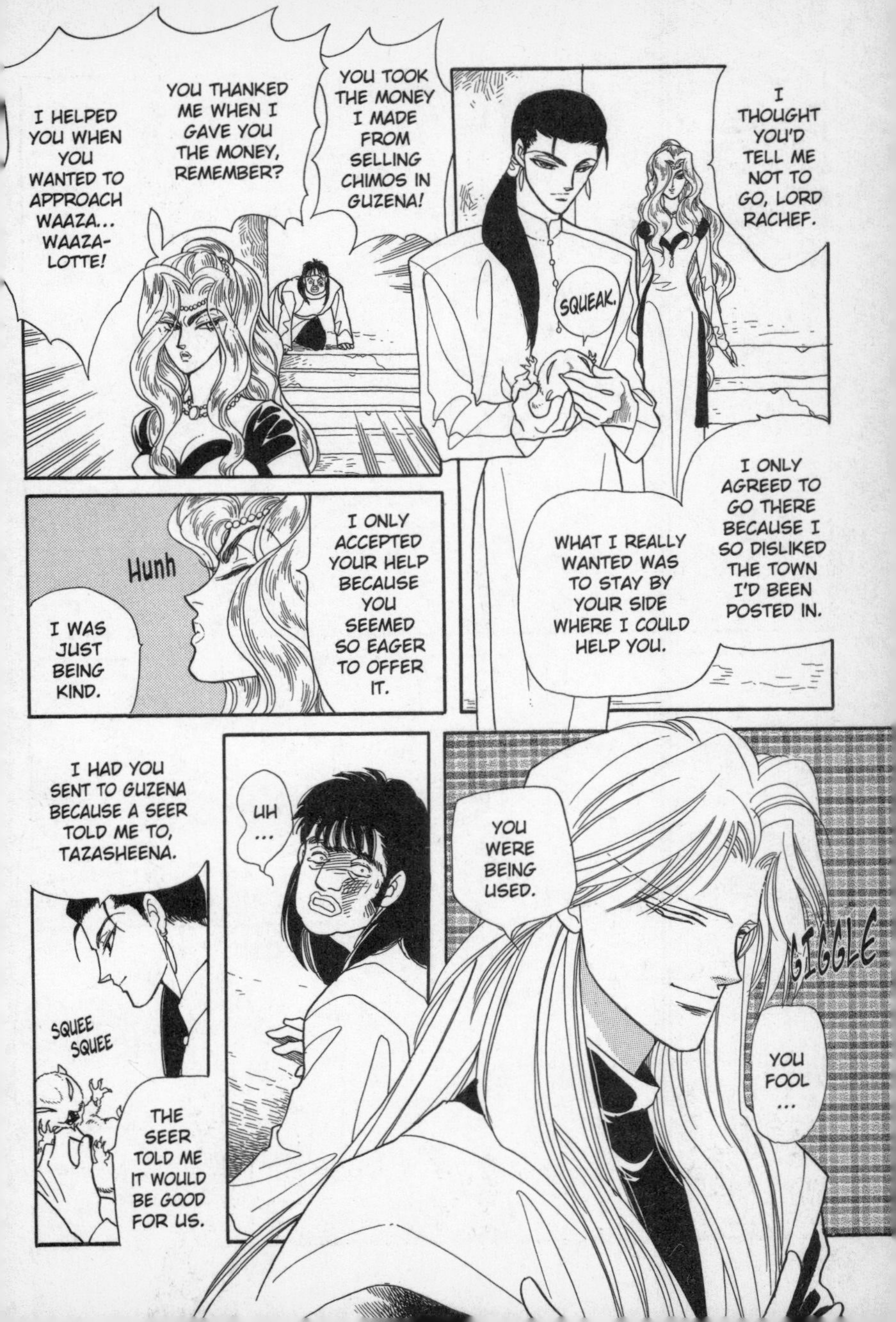
I THOUGHT YOU'D TELL ME NOT TO GO, LORD RACHEF.
SQUEAK.
I ONLY AGREED TO GO THERE BECAUSE I SO DISLIKED THE TOWN I'D BEEN POSTED IN.
WHAT I REALLY WANTED WAS TO STAY BY YOUR SIDE WHERE I COULD HELP YOU.
YOU TOOK THE MONEY I MADE FROM SELLING CHIMOS IN GUZENA!
YOU THANKED ME WHEN I GAVE YOU THE MONEY, REMEMBER?
I HELPED YOU WHEN YOU WANTED TO APPROACH WAAZA... WAAZA-LOTTE!
I ONLY ACCEPTED YOUR HELP BECAUSE YOU SEEMED SO EAGER TO OFFER IT.
Hunh
I WAS JUST BEING KIND.
YOU WERE BEING USED.
GIGGLE
YOU FOOL ...
UH ...
I HAD YOU SENT TO GUZENA BECAUSE A SEER TOLD ME TO, TAZASHEENA.
SQUEE SQUEE
THE SEER TOLD ME IT WOULD BE GOOD FOR US.

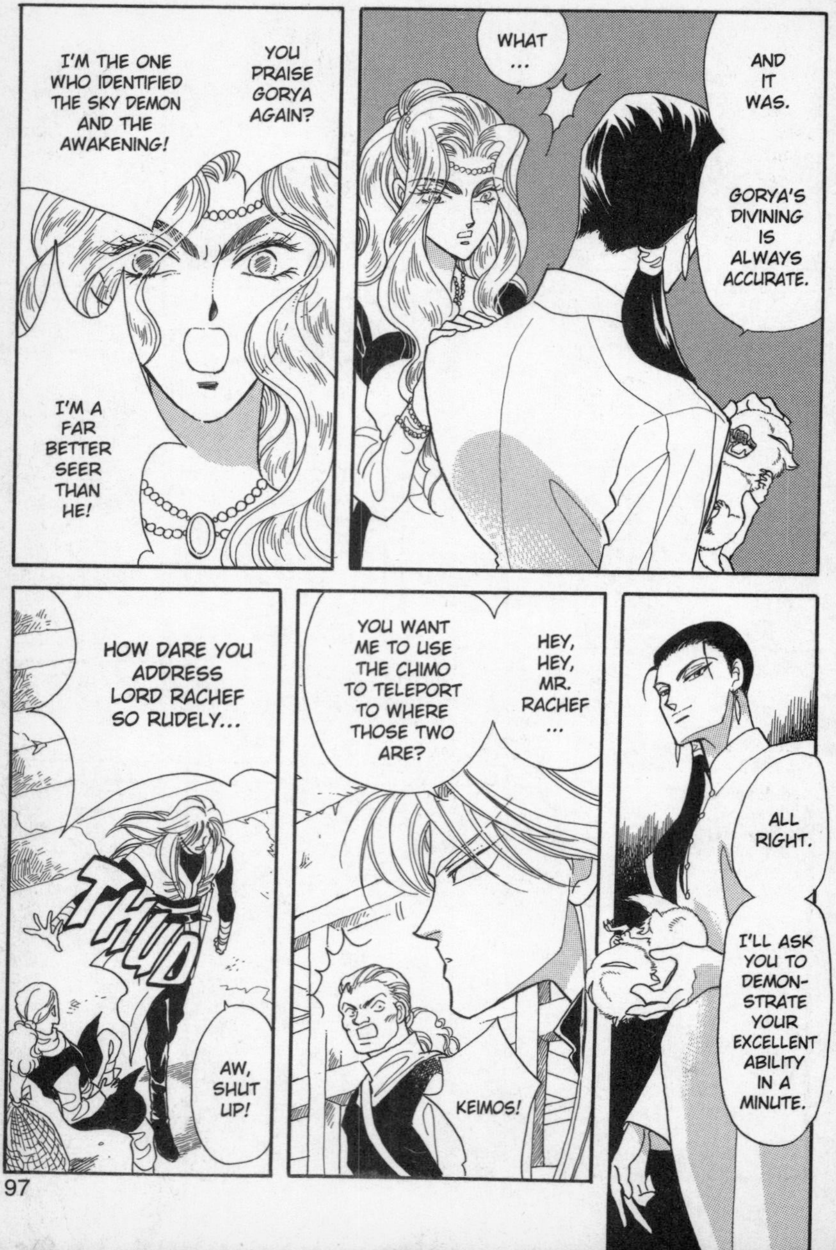
AND IT WAS.
GORYA'S DIVINING IS ALWAYS ACCURATE.
WHAT ...
YOU PRAISE GORYA AGAIN?
I'M THE ONE WHO IDENTIFIED THE SKY DEMON AND THE AWAKENING!
I'M A FAR BETTER SEER THAN HE!
ALL RIGHT.
I'LL ASK YOU TO DEMON-STRATE YOUR EXCELLENT ABILITY IN A MINUTE.
HEY, HEY, MR. RACHEF ...
YOU WANT ME TO USE THE CHIMO TO TELEPORT TO WHERE THOSE TWO ARE?
KEIMOS!
HOW DARE YOU ADDRESS LORD RACHEF SO RUDELY...
THUD
AW, SHUT UP!

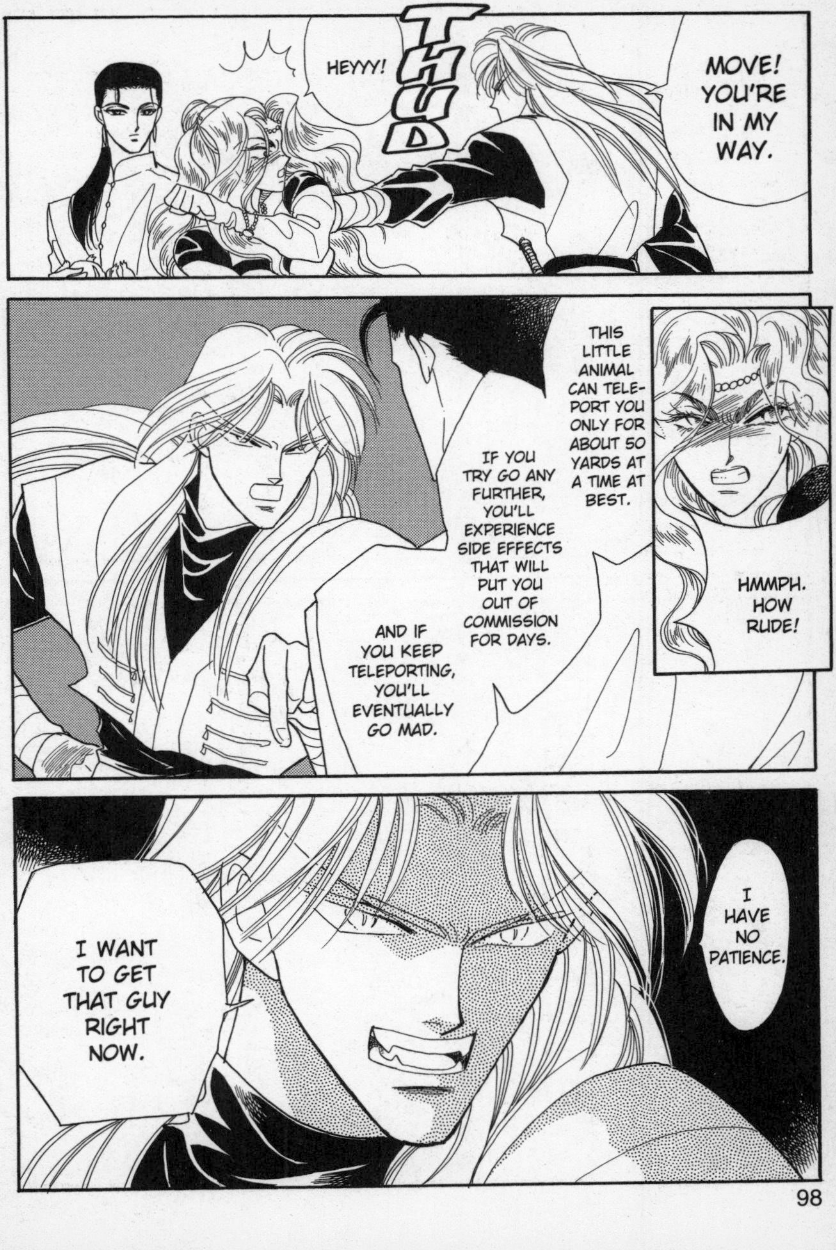
MOVE! YOU'RE IN MY WAY.
THUD
HEYYY!
HMMPH. HOW RUDE!
THIS LITTLE ANIMAL CAN TELE-PORT YOU ONLY FOR ABOUT 50 YARDS AT A TIME AT BEST.
IF YOU TRY GO ANY FURTHER, YOU'LL EXPERIENCE SIDE EFFECTS THAT WILL PUT YOU OUT OF COMMISSION FOR DAYS.
AND IF YOU KEEP TELEPORTING, YOU'LL EVENTUALLY GO MAD.
I HAVE NO PATIENCE.
I WANT TO GET THAT GUY RIGHT NOW.

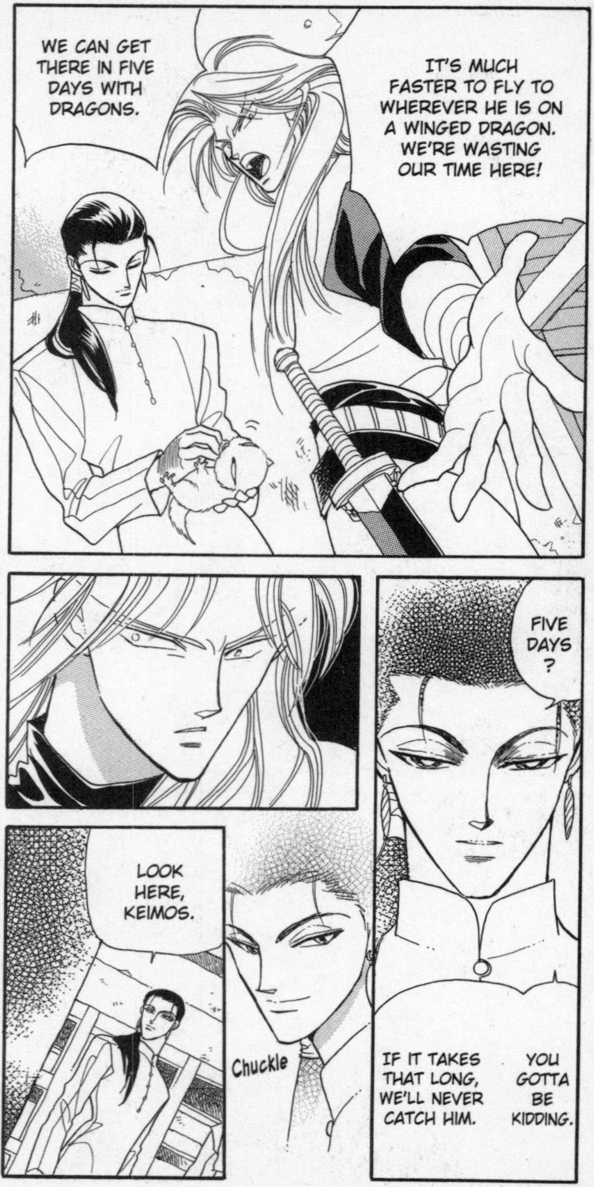
IT'S MUCH FASTER TO FLY TO WHEREVER HE IS ON A WINGED DRAGON. WE'RE WASTING OUR TIME HERE!
WE CAN GET THERE IN FIVE DAYS WITH DRAGONS.
FIVE DAYS ?
YOU GOTTA BE KIDDING.
IF IT TAKES THAT LONG, WE'LL NEVER CATCH HIM.
LOOK HERE, KEIMOS.
Chuckle

A Cat Story (3)

Every time I ran into the calico cat, I'd stare at it or talk to it. One day, I got on my bicycle without noticing that the cat was there. I was just leaving my house when I saw the her sitting right in front of me with her paws neatly together.

When I said, "Wow, you startled me. I didn't know you were there," she seemed satisfied and walked away.

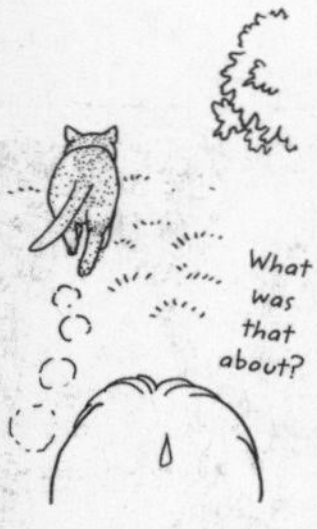
What was that about?

After that, the cat went back to her old ways and either ignored me or ran away whenever she saw me.

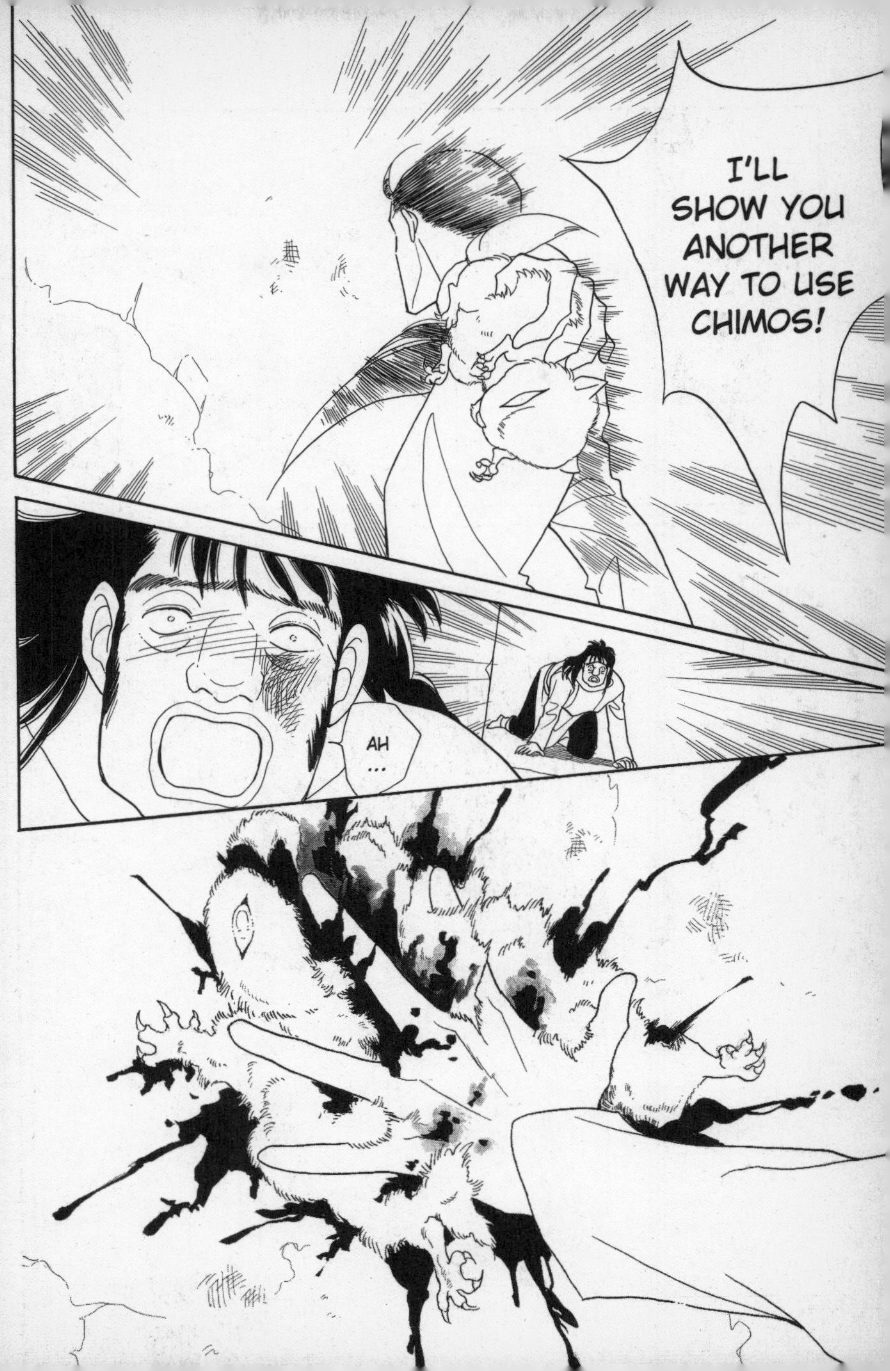
I'LL SHOW YOU ANOTHER WAY TO USE CHIMOS!
AH ...

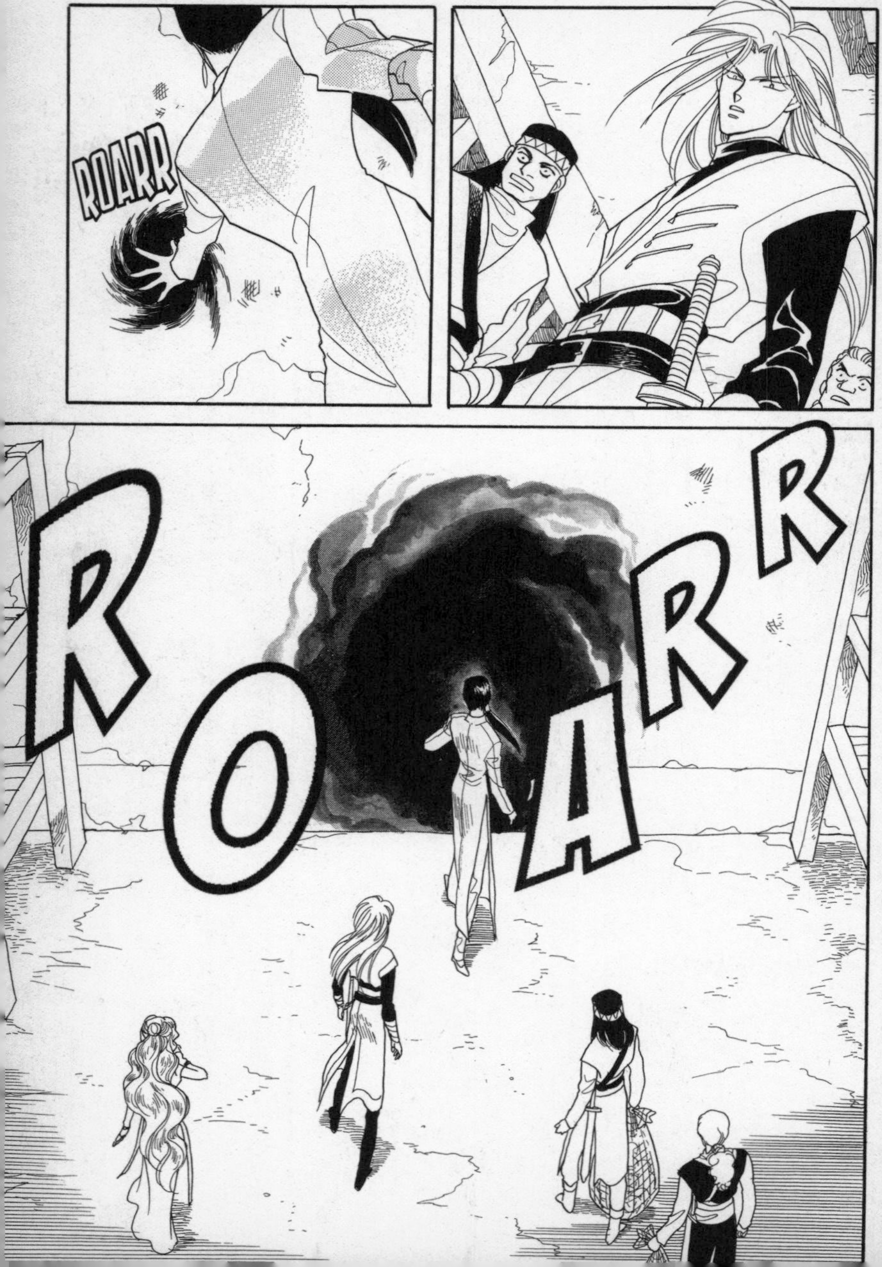
ROARR
ROARR

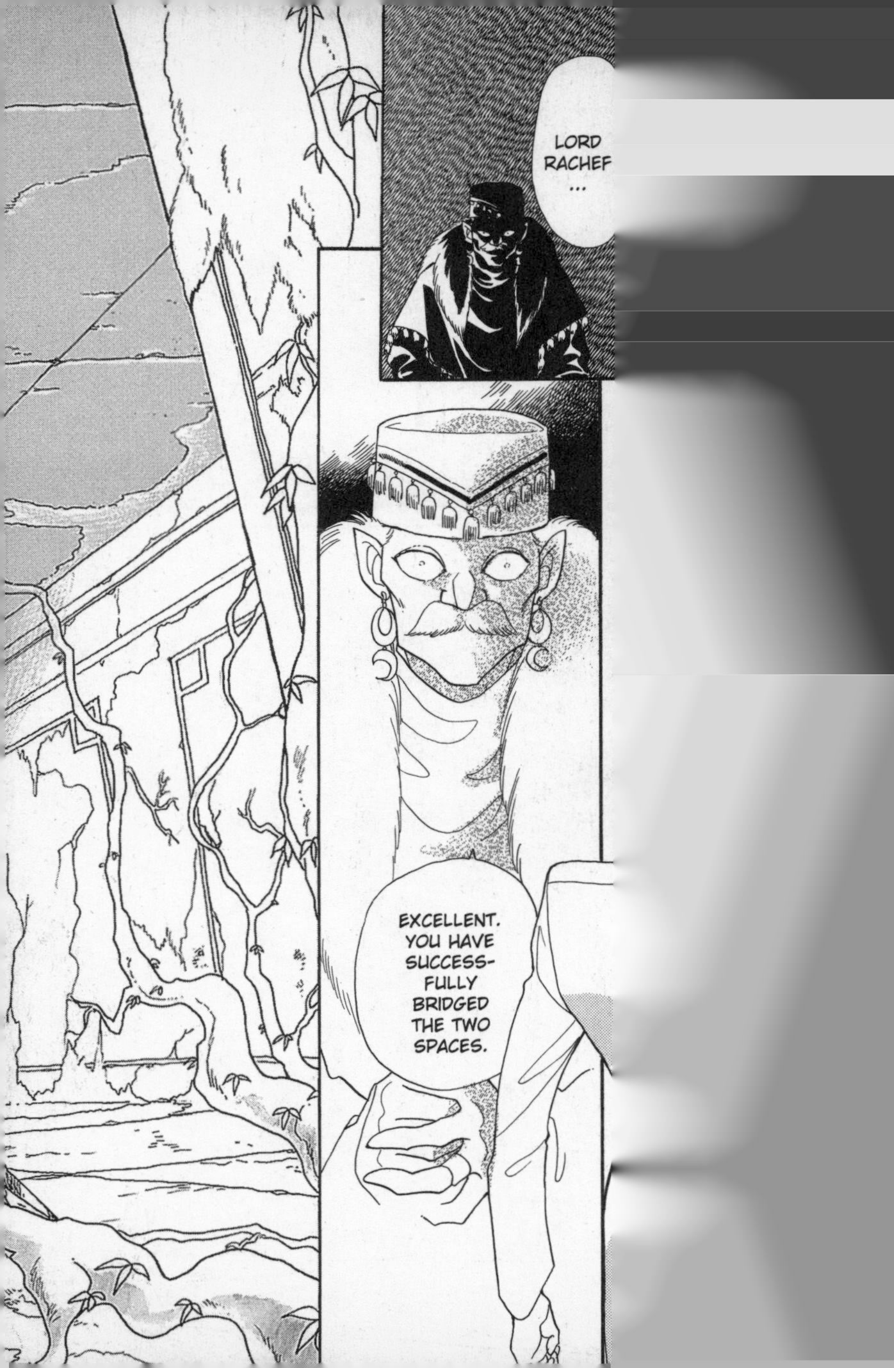
LORD RACHEF ...
EXCELLENT. YOU HAVE SUCCESS-FULLY BRIDGED THE TWO SPACES.

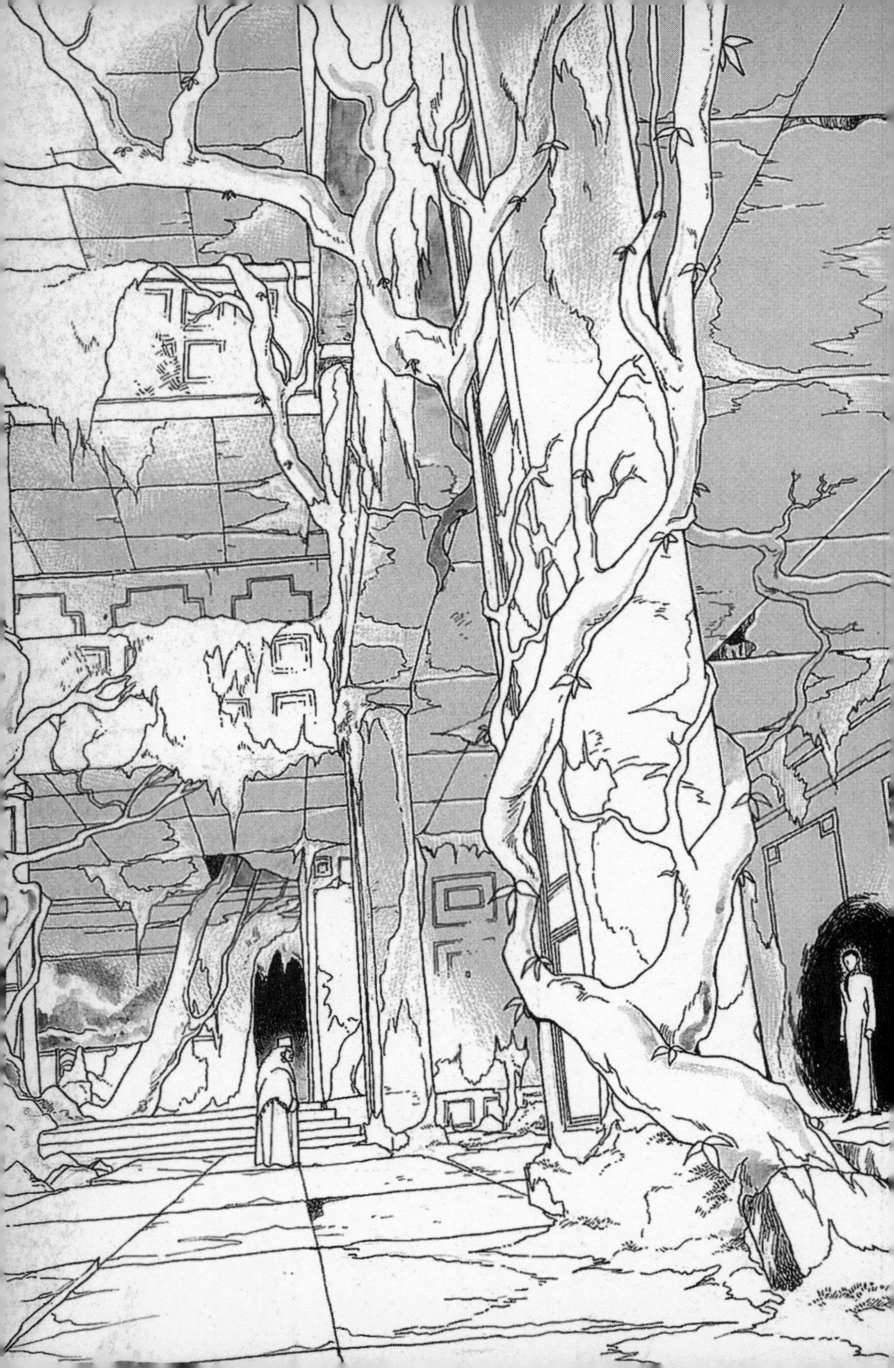

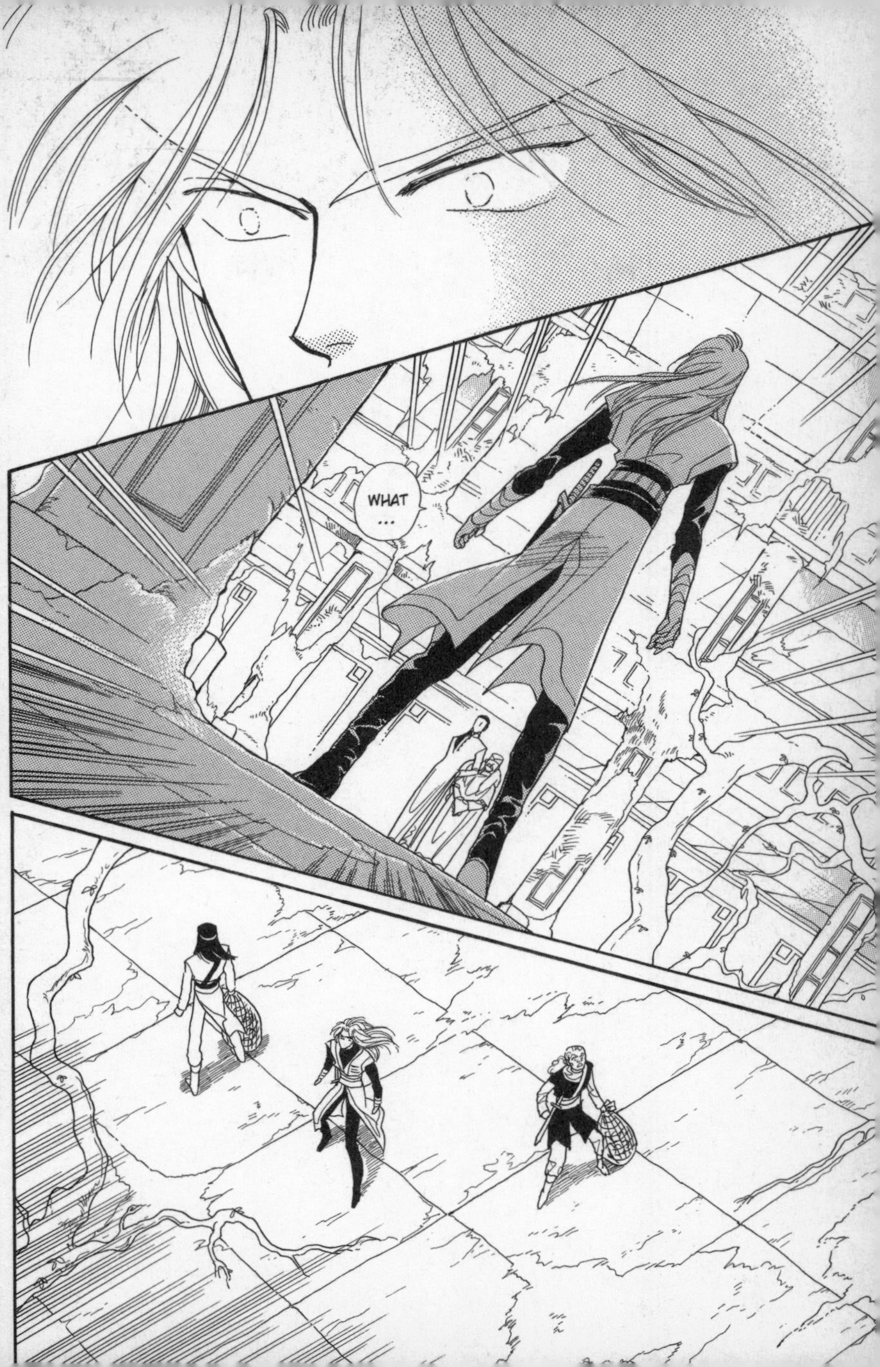
WHAT ...

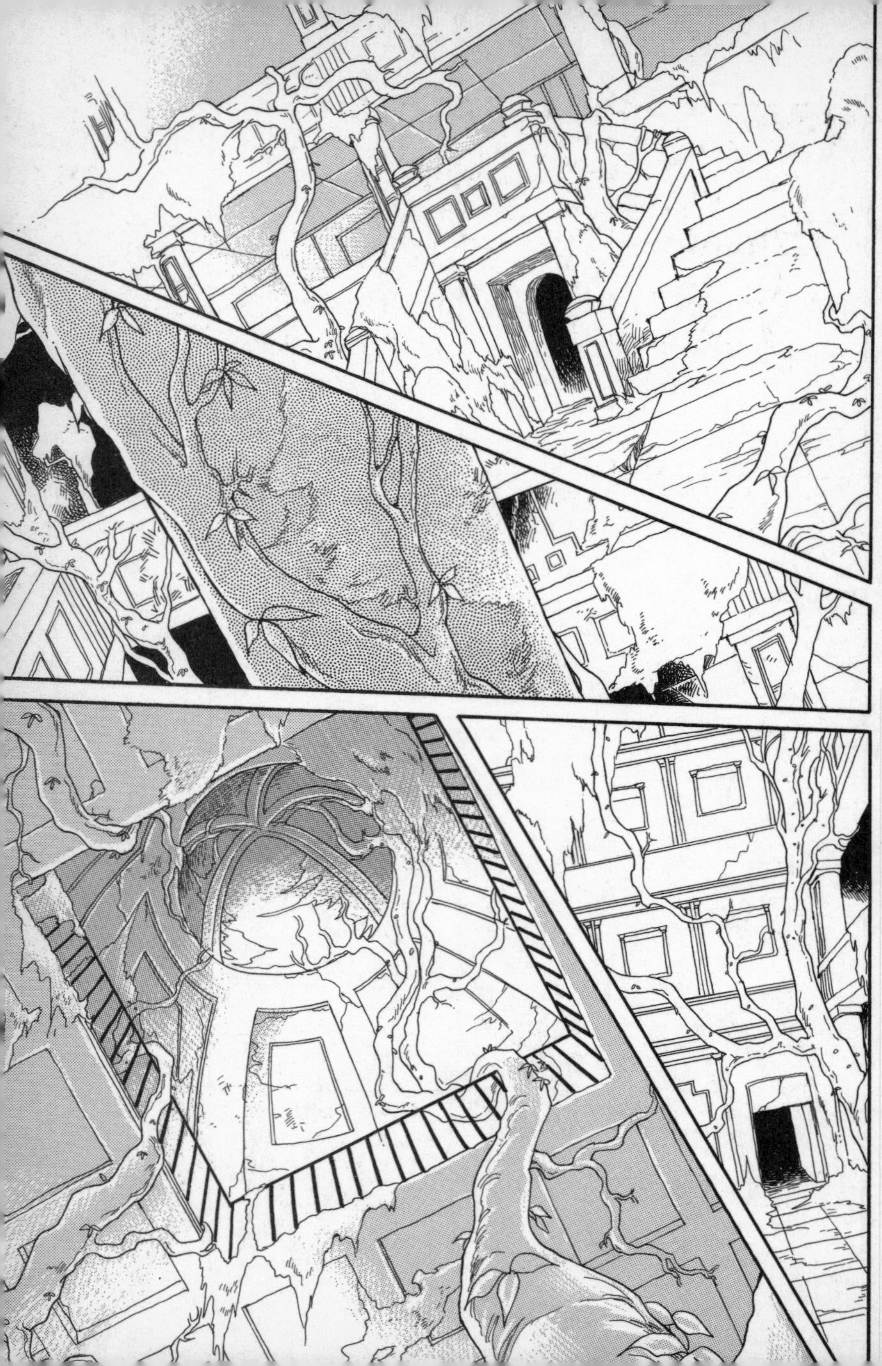

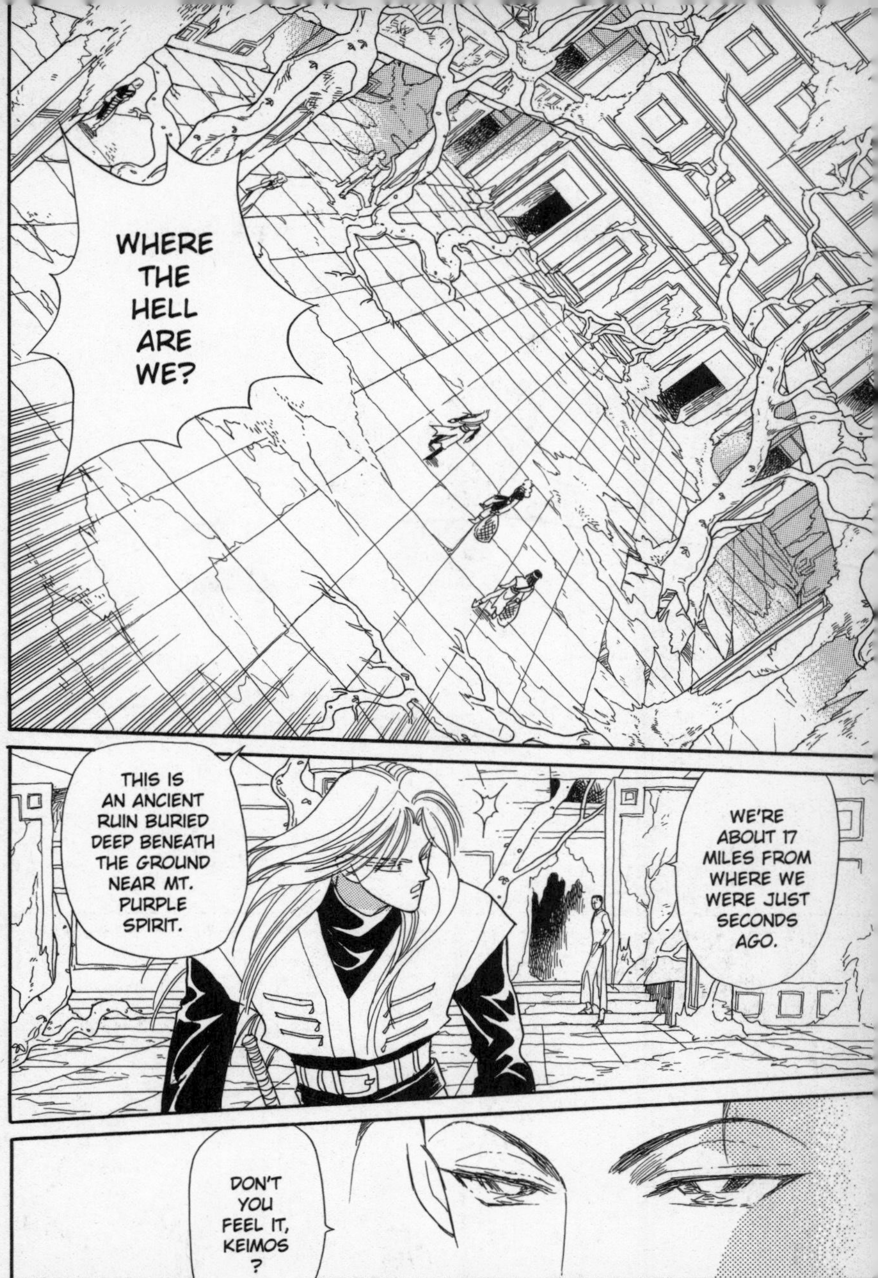
WHERE THE HELL ARE WE?
WE'RE ABOUT 17 MILES FROM WHERE WE WERE JUST SECONDS AGO.
THIS IS AN ANCIENT RUIN BURIED DEEP BENEATH THE GROUND NEAR MT. PURPLE SPIRIT.
DON'T YOU FEEL IT, KEIMOS?

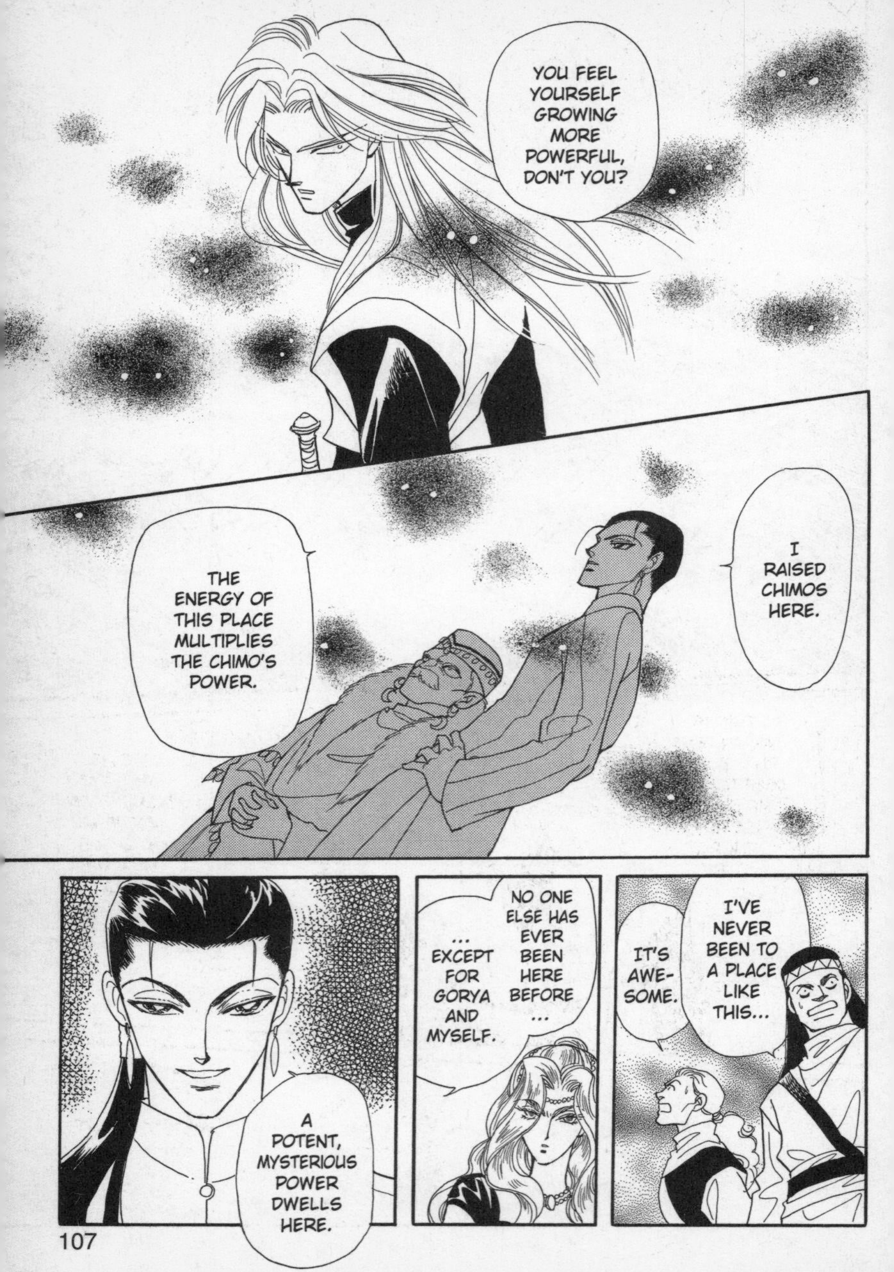
YOU FEEL YOURSELF GROWING MORE POWERFUL, DON'T YOU?
I RAISED CHIMOS HERE.
THE ENERGY OF THIS PLACE MULTIPLIES THE CHIMO'S POWER.
I'VE NEVER BEEN TO A PLACE LIKE THIS...
IT'S AWE-SOME.
NO ONE ELSE HAS EVER BEEN HERE BEFORE ...
... EXCEPT FOR GORYA AND MYSELF.
A POTENT, MYSTERIOUS POWER DWELLS HERE.

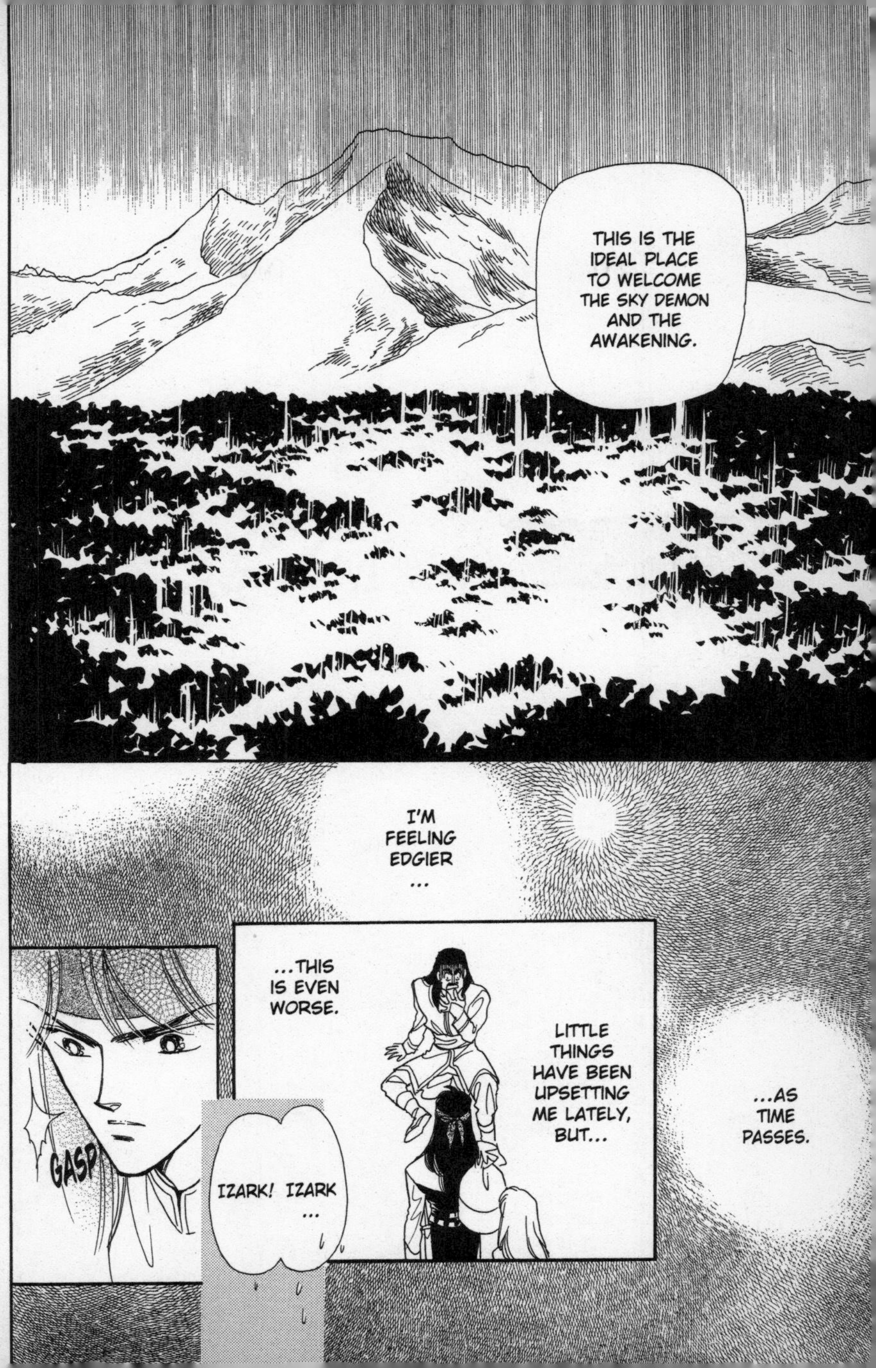
THIS IS THE IDEAL PLACE TO WELCOME THE SKY DEMON AND THE AWAKENING.
I'M FEELING EDGIER ...
...AS TIME PASSES.
LITTLE THINGS HAVE BEEN UPSETTING ME LATELY, BUT...
...THIS IS EVEN WORSE.
IZARK! IZARK ...
GASP

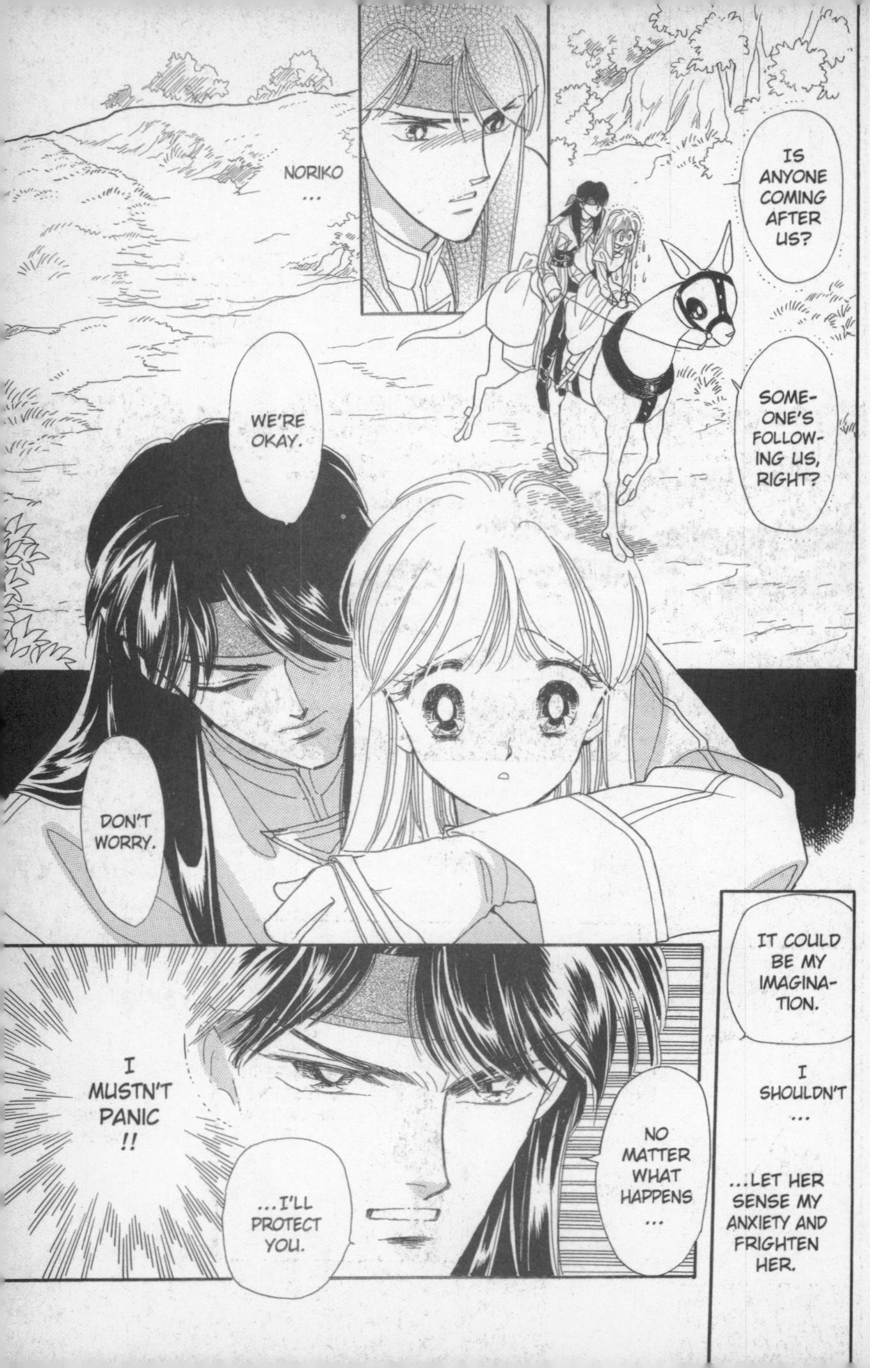
IS ANYONE COMING AFTER US?
SOME-ONE'S FOLLOW-ING US, RIGHT?
NORIKO ...
WE'RE OKAY.
DON'T WORRY.
IT COULD BE MY IMAGINA-TION.
I SHOULDN'T ...
...LET HER SENSE MY ANXIETY AND FRIGHTEN HER.
NO MATTER WHAT HAPPENS ...
...I'LL PROTECT YOU.
I MUSTN'T PANIC !!

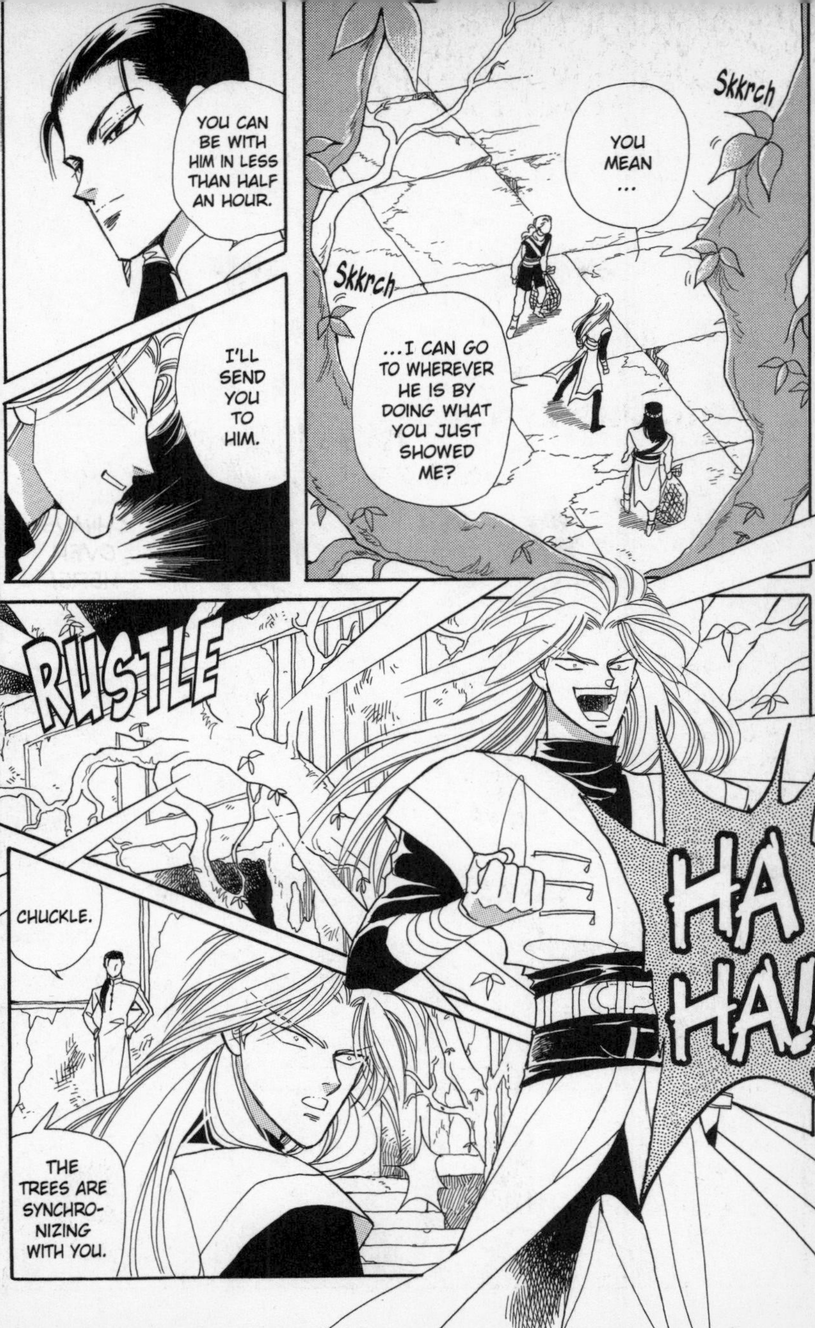
Skkrch
YOU MEAN ...
Skkrch
...I CAN GO TO WHEREVER HE IS BY DOING WHAT YOU JUST SHOWED ME?
YOU CAN BE WITH HIM IN LESS THAN HALF AN HOUR.
I'LL SEND YOU TO HIM.
HA HA!
RUSTLE
CHUCKLE.
THE TREES ARE SYNCHRO-NIZING WITH YOU.

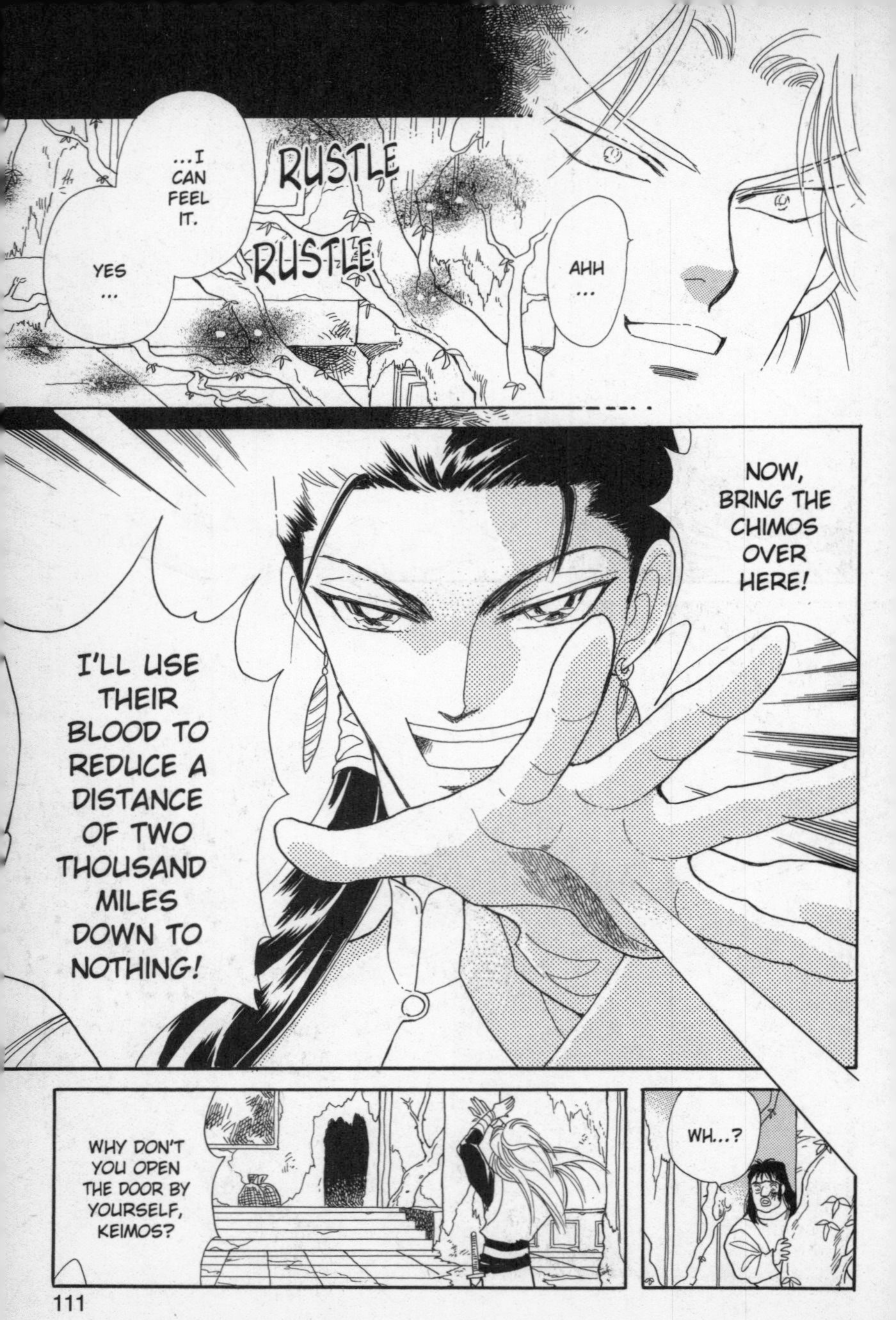
AHH ...
RUSTLE
RUSTLE
...I CAN FEEL IT.
YES ...
NOW, BRING THE CHIMOS OVER HERE!
I'LL USE THEIR BLOOD TO REDUCE A DISTANCE OF TWO THOUSAND MILES DOWN TO NOTHING!
WH...?
WHY DON'T YOU OPEN THE DOOR BY YOURSELF, KEIMOS?

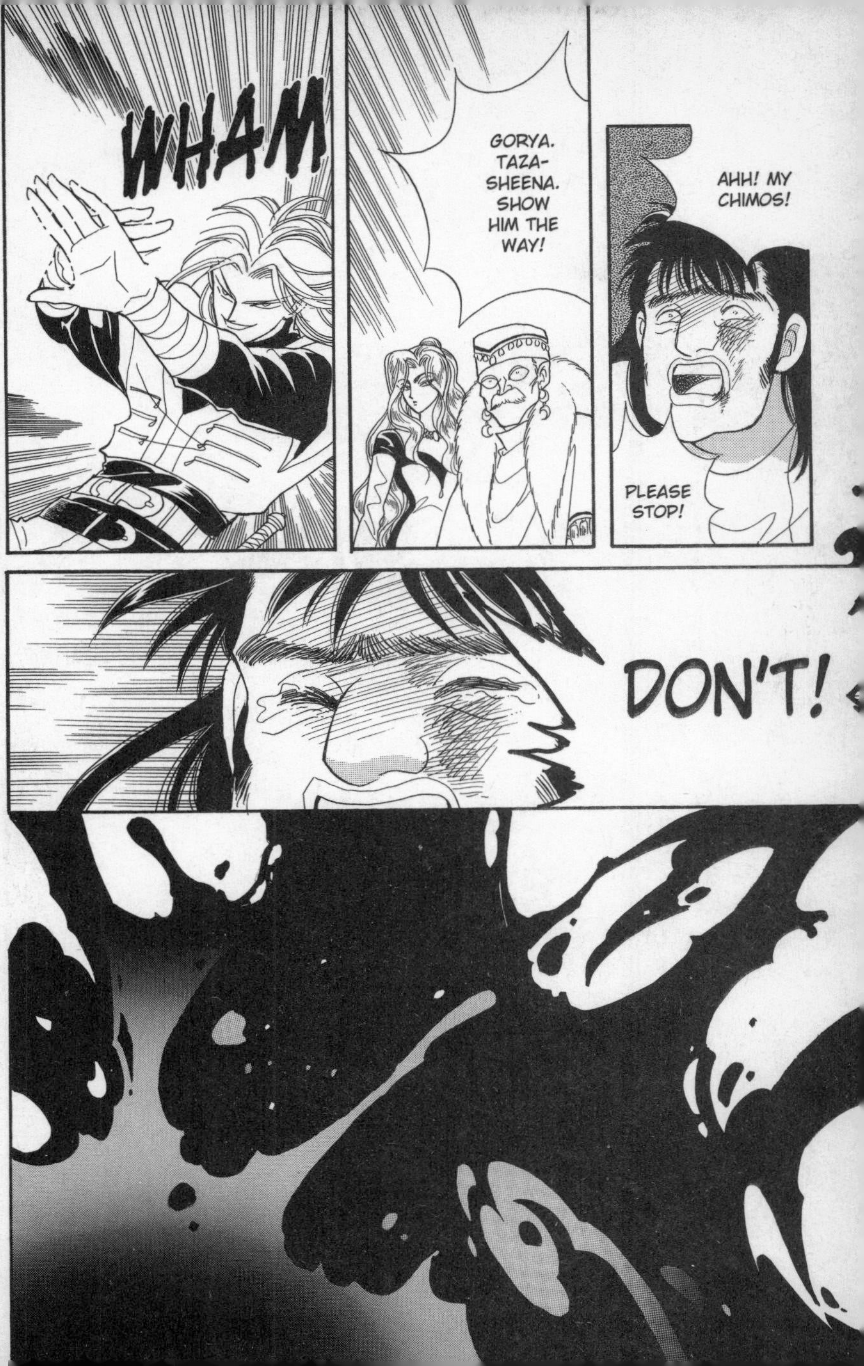
AHH! MY CHIMOS!
PLEASE STOP!
GORYA. TAZA-SHEENA. SHOW HIM THE WAY!
WHAM
DON'T!

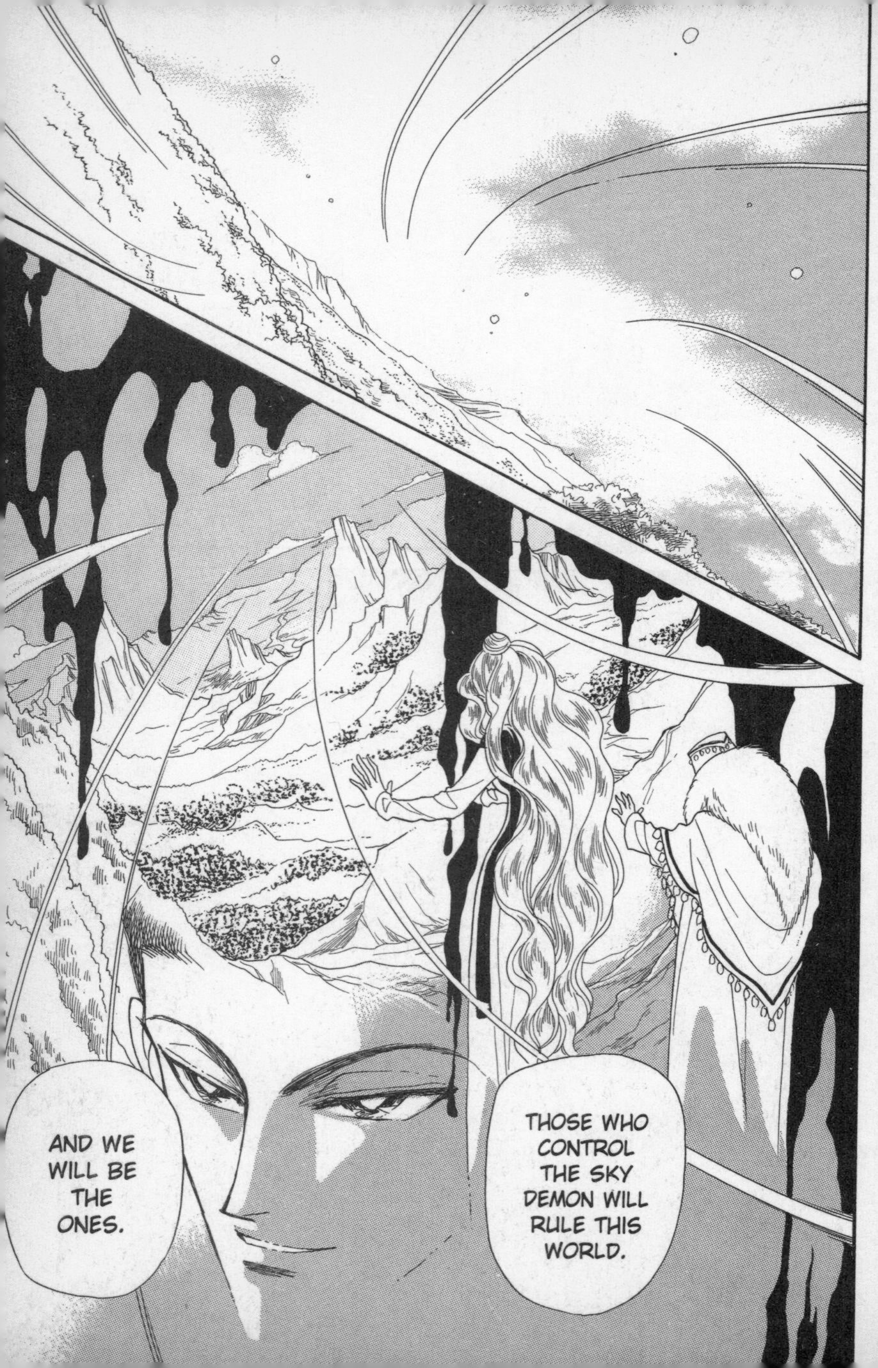
THOSE WHO CONTROL THE SKY DEMON WILL RULE THIS WORLD.
AND WE WILL BE THE ONES.

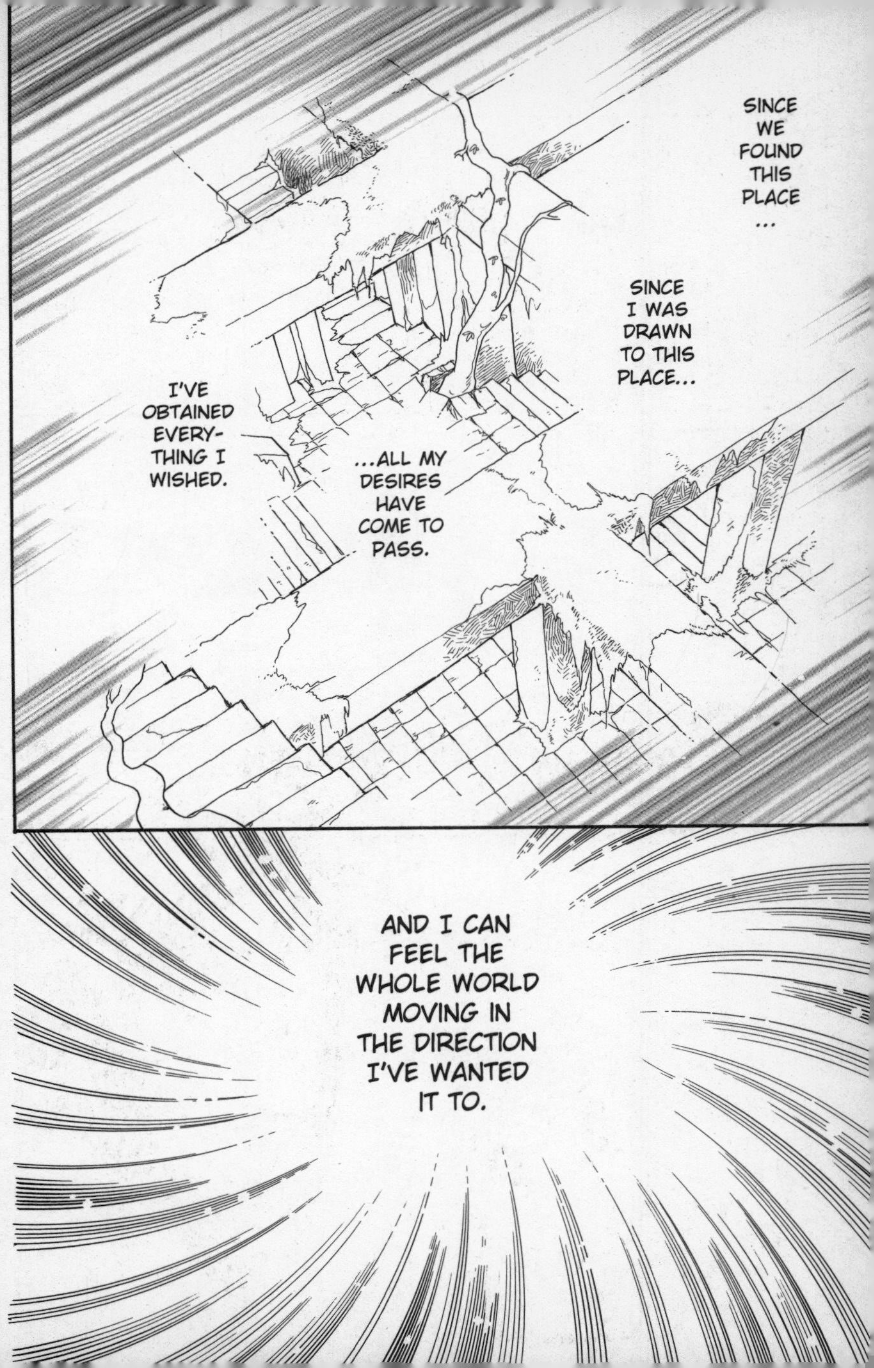
SINCE WE FOUND THIS PLACE...
SINCE I WAS DRAWN TO THIS PLACE...
...ALL MY DESIRES HAVE COME TO PASS.
I'VE OBTAINED EVERY-THING I WISHED.
AND I CAN FEEL THE WHOLE WORLD MOVING IN THE DIRECTION I'VE WANTED IT TO.

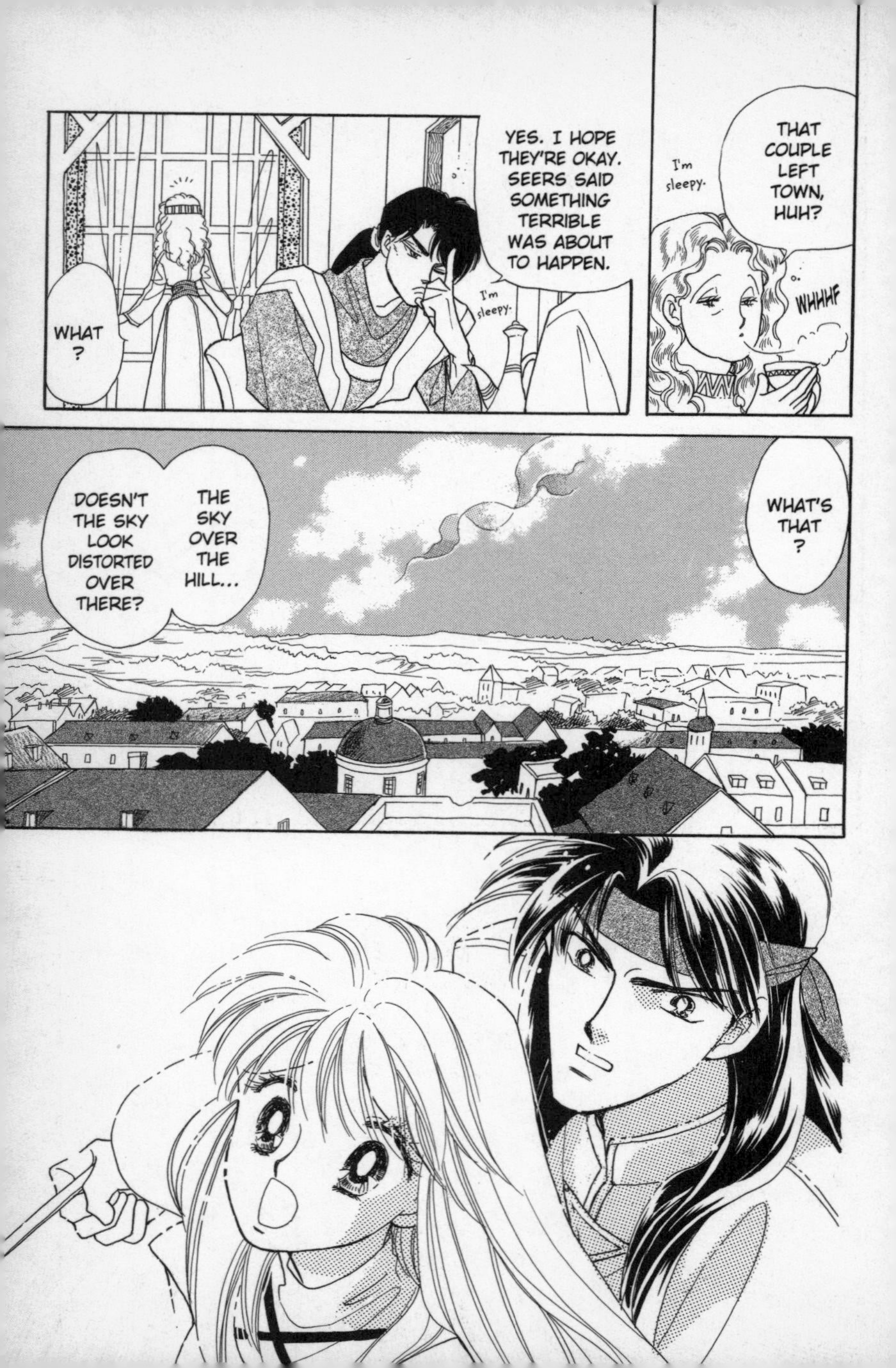
THAT COUPLE LEFT TOWN, HUH?
I'm sleepy.
WHHHF
YES. I HOPE THEY'RE OKAY. SEERS SAID SOMETHING TERRIBLE WAS ABOUT TO HAPPEN.
I'm sleepy.
WHAT?
WHAT'S THAT?
THE SKY OVER THE HILL...
DOESN'T THE SKY LOOK DISTORTED OVER THERE?

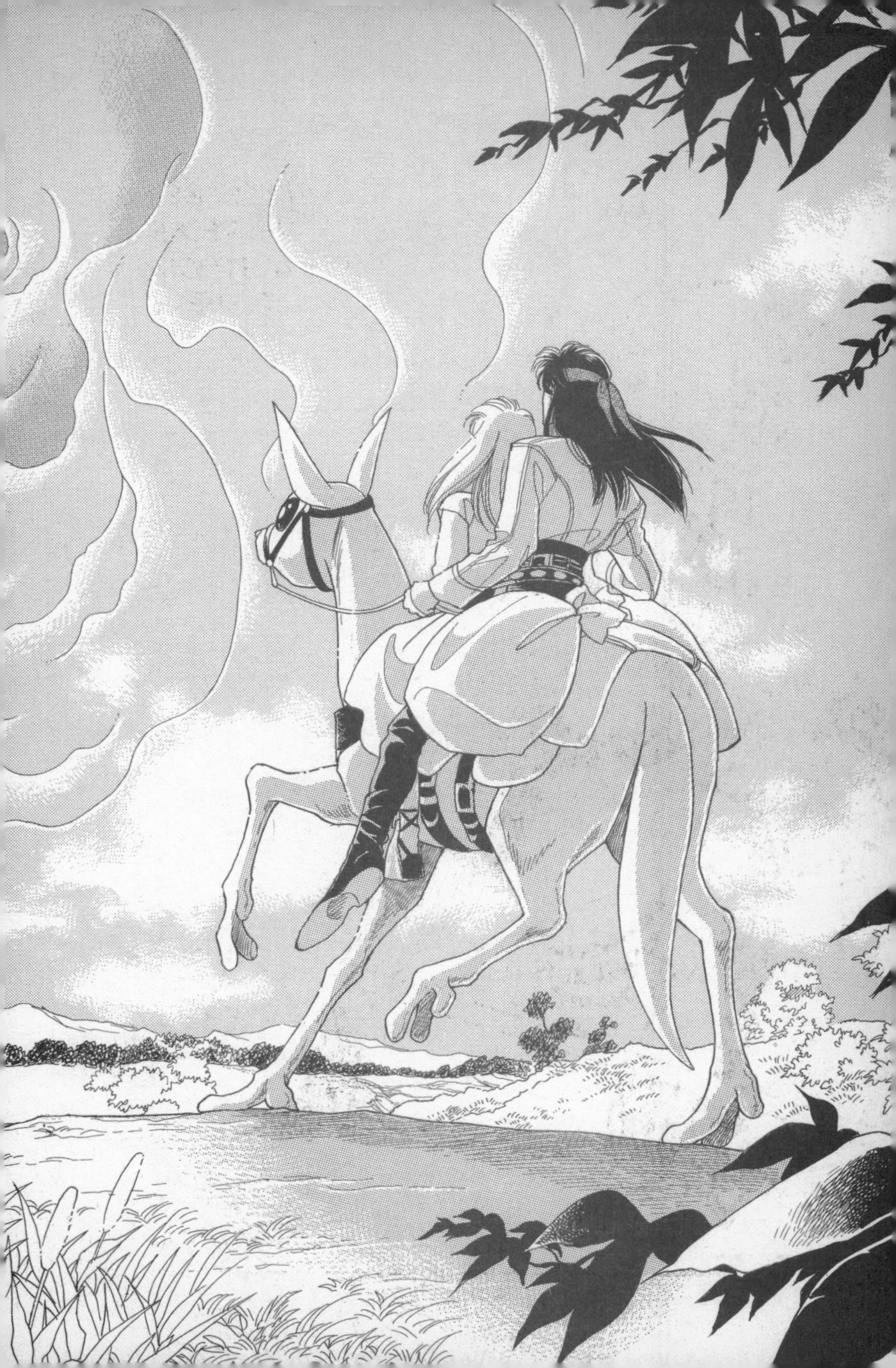

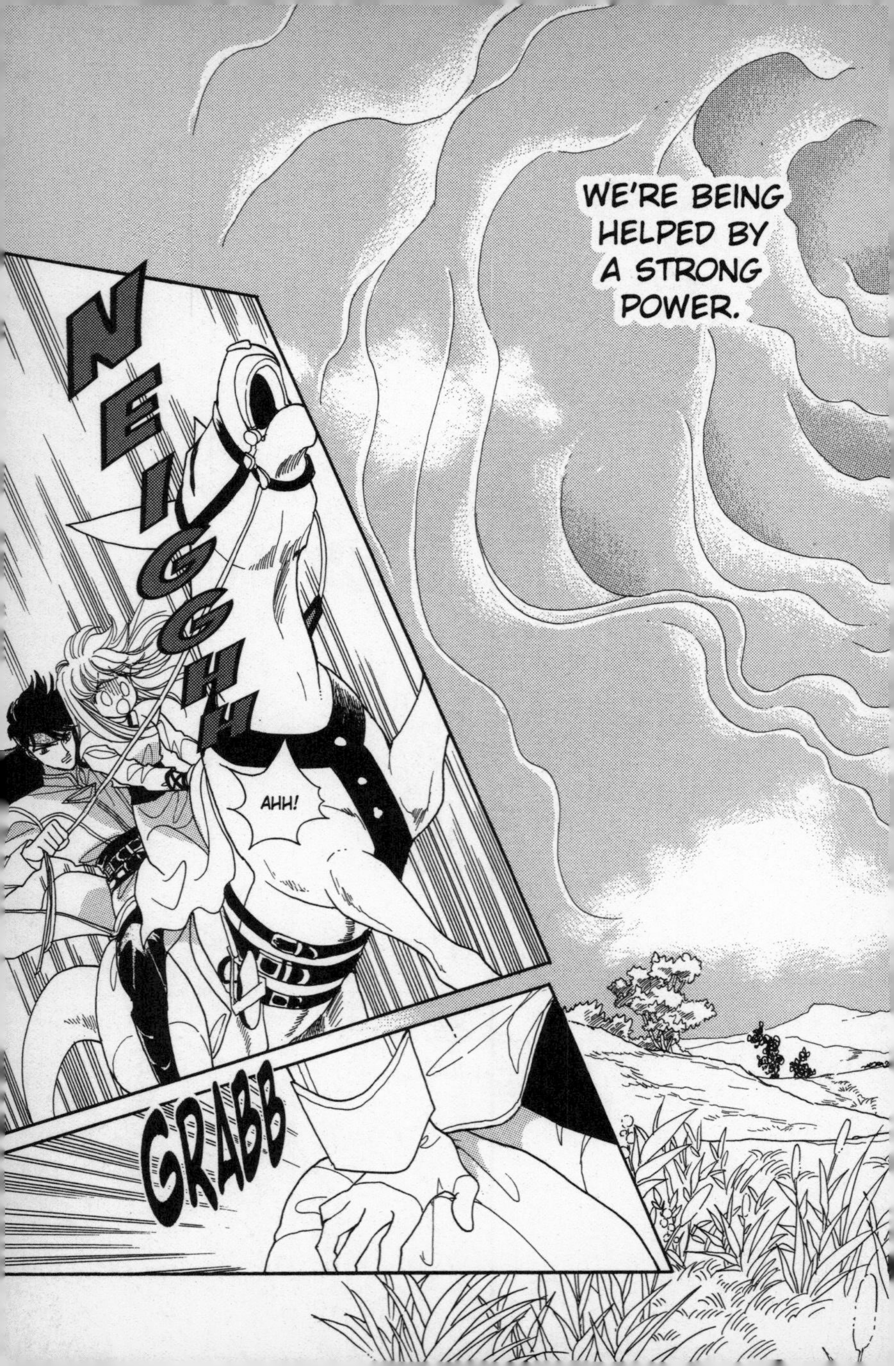
WE'RE BEING HELPED BY A STRONG POWER.
NEIGHHH
AHH!
GRABB

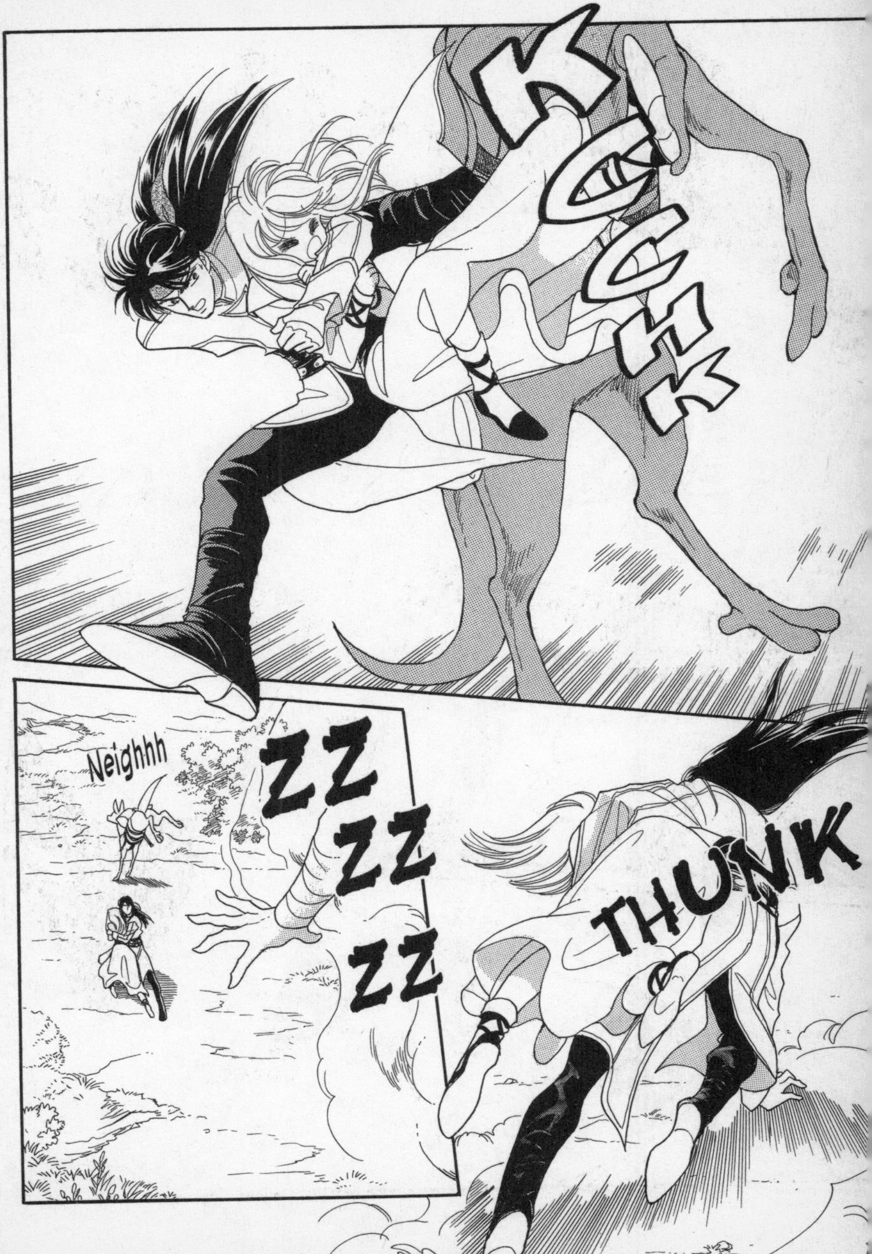
THUNK
ZZ
ZZ
ZZ
Neighhh

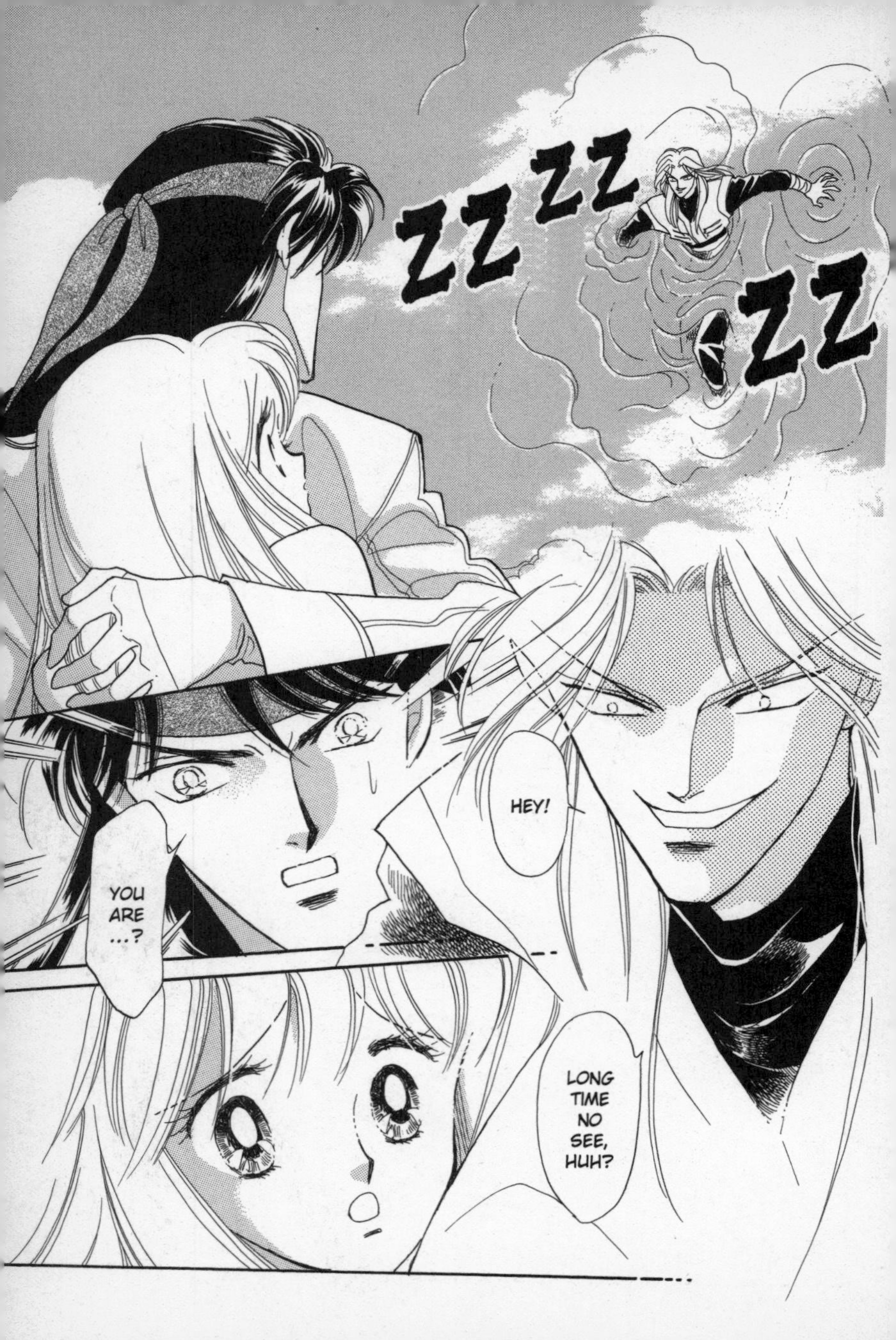
ZZ ZZZ ZZ
HEY!
YOU ARE ...?
LONG TIME NO SEE, HUH?

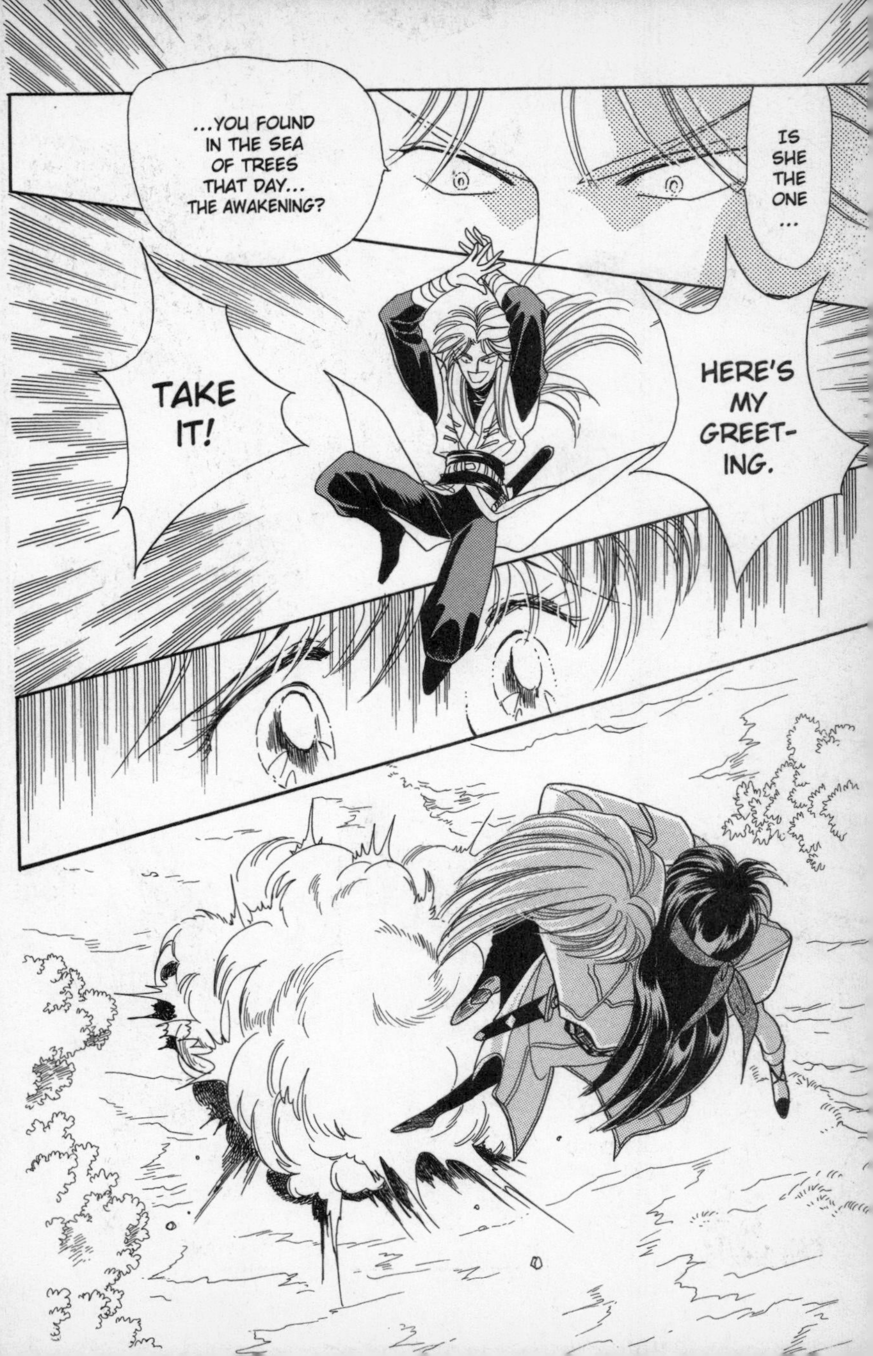
IS SHE THE ONE...
...YOU FOUND IN THE SEA OF TREES THAT DAY... THE AWAKENING?
HERE'S MY GREET-ING.
TAKE IT!

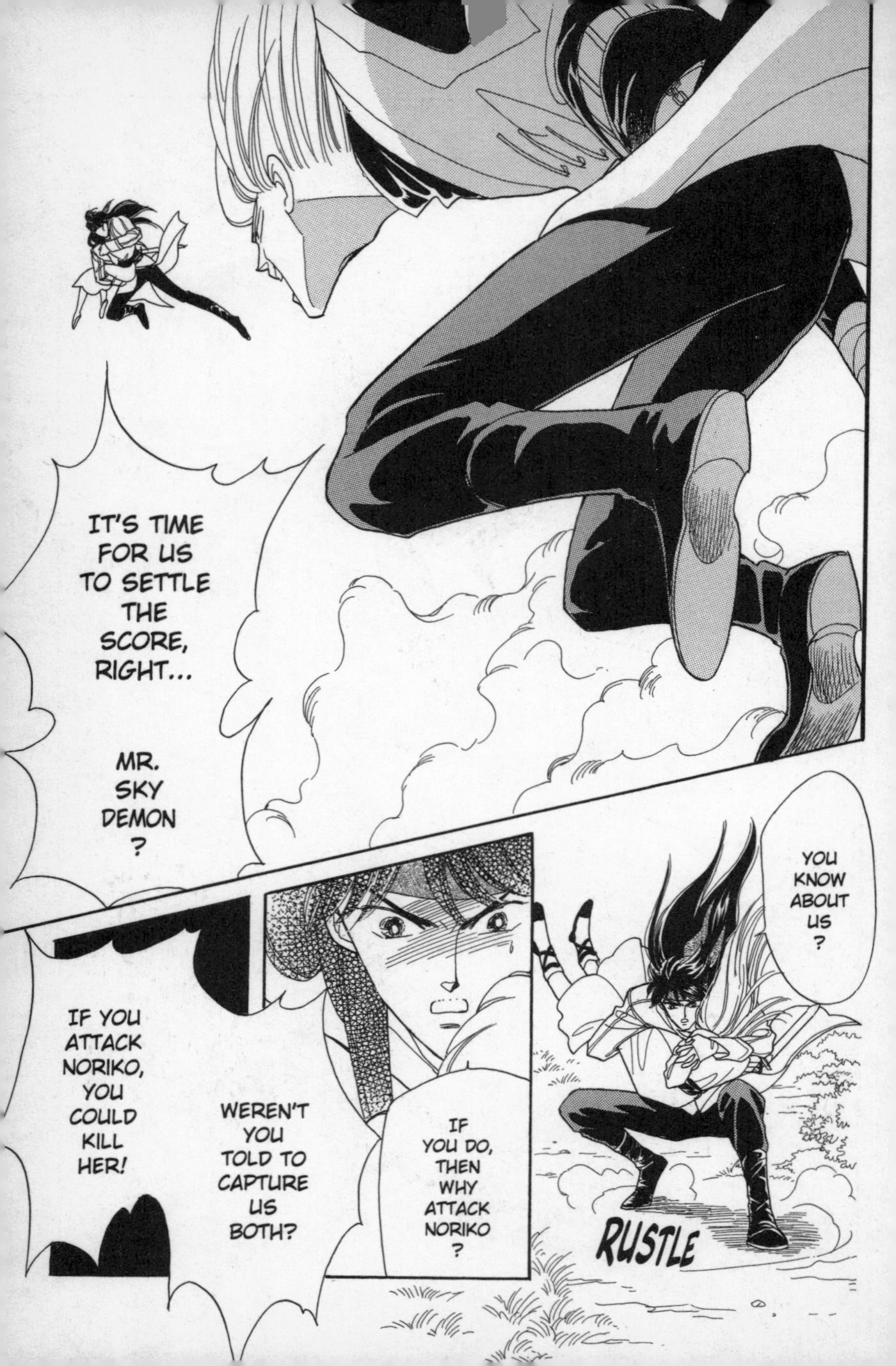
IT'S TIME FOR US TO SETTLE THE SCORE, RIGHT... MR. SKY DEMON?
YOU KNOW ABOUT US?
RUSTLE
IF YOU DO, THEN WHY ATTACK NORIKO?
WEREN'T YOU TOLD TO CAPTURE US BOTH?
IF YOU ATTACK NORIKO, YOU COULD KILL HER!

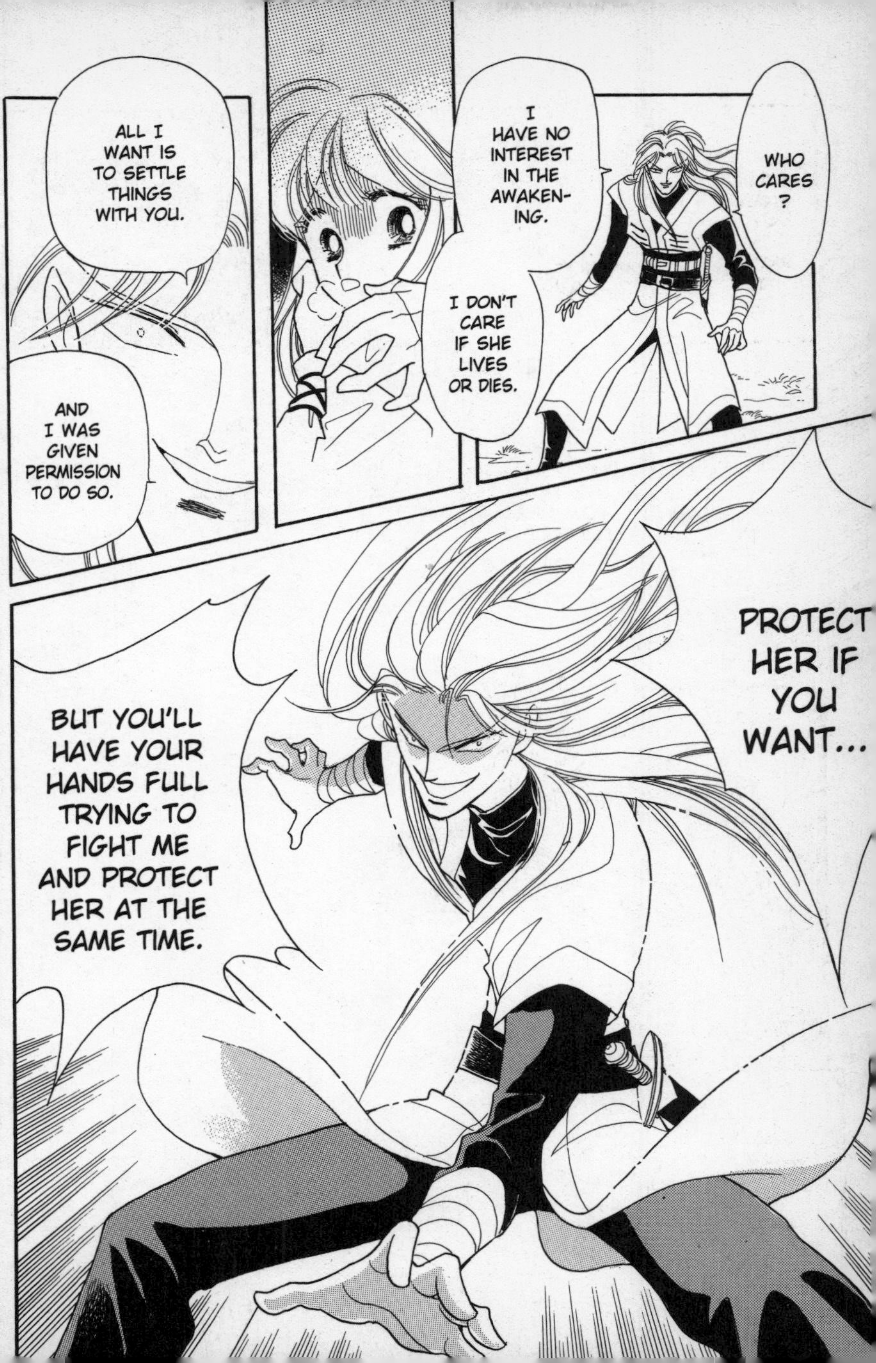
WHO CARES?
I HAVE NO INTEREST IN THE AWAKENING.
I DON'T CARE IF SHE LIVES OR DIES.
ALL I WANT IS TO SETTLE THINGS WITH YOU.
AND I WAS GIVEN PERMISSION TO DO SO.
PROTECT HER IF YOU WANT...
BUT YOU'LL HAVE YOUR HANDS FULL TRYING TO FIGHT ME AND PROTECT HER AT THE SAME TIME.

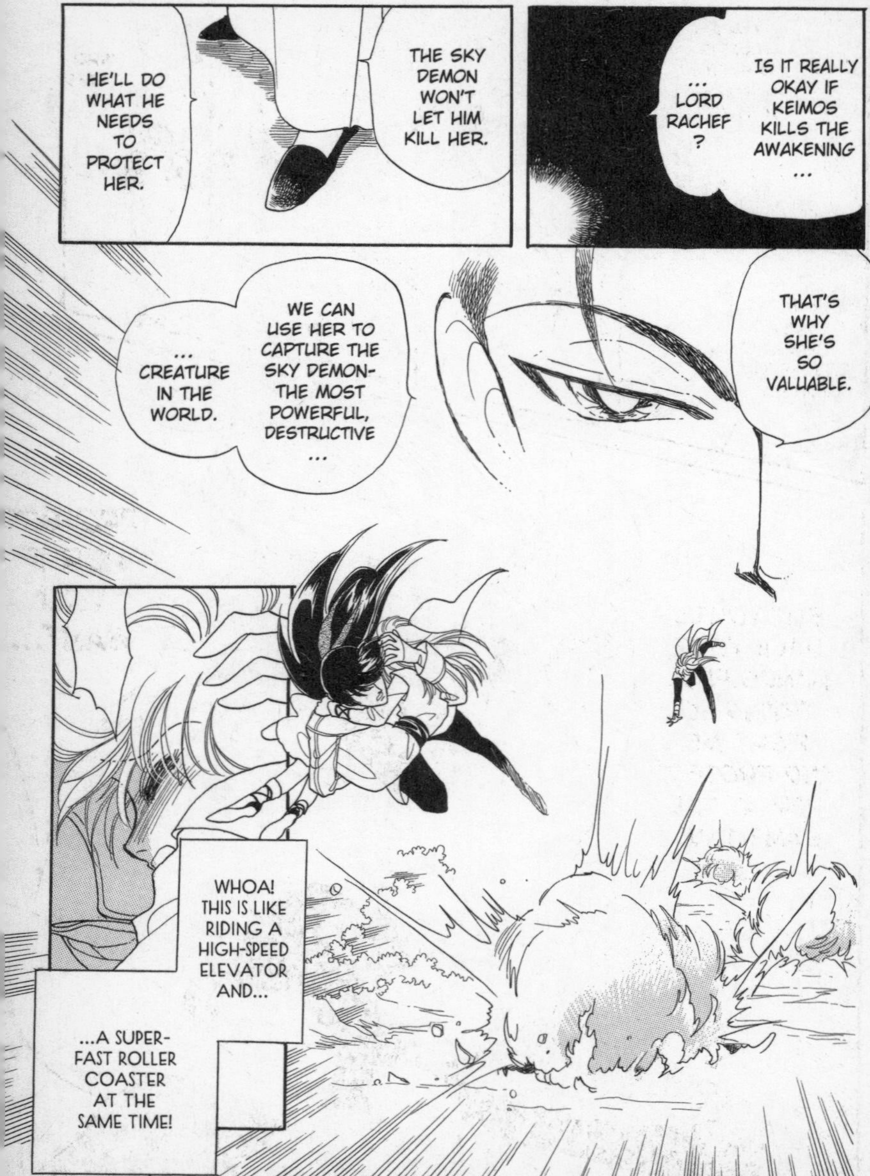
IS IT REALLY OKAY IF KEIMOS KILLS THE AWAKENING ...
... LORD RACHEF ?
THE SKY DEMON WON'T LET HIM KILL HER.
HE'LL DO WHAT HE NEEDS TO PROTECT HER.
THAT'S WHY SHE'S SO VALUABLE.
WE CAN USE HER TO CAPTURE THE SKY DEMON- THE MOST POWERFUL, DESTRUCTIVE ...
... CREATURE IN THE WORLD.
WHOA! THIS IS LIKE RIDING A HIGH-SPEED ELEVATOR AND...
...A SUPER-FAST ROLLER COASTER AT THE SAME TIME!

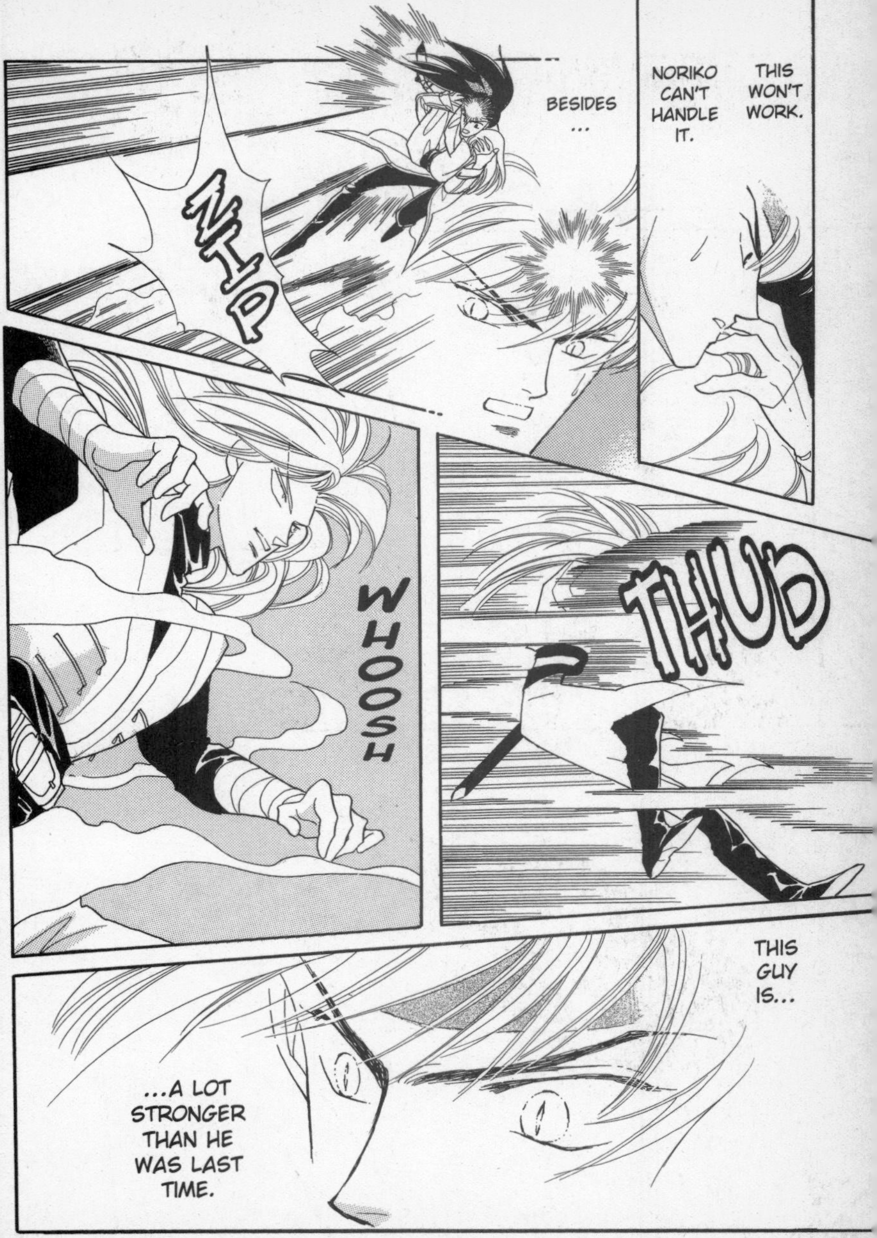
THIS WON'T WORK.
NORIKO CAN'T HANDLE IT.
BESIDES ...
ZIP
THUD
WHOOSH
THIS GUY IS...
...A LOT STRONGER THAN HE WAS LAST TIME.

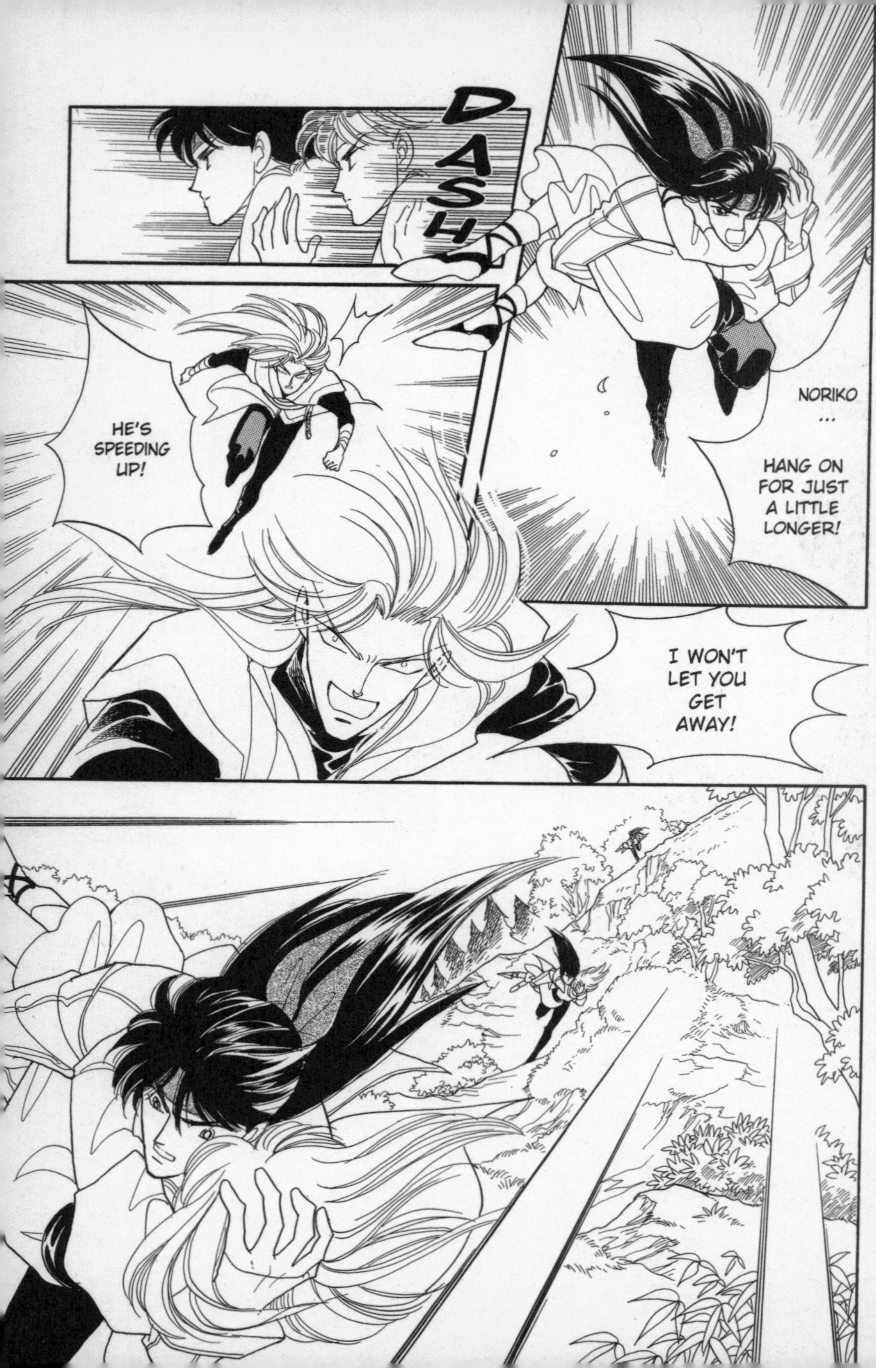
DASH
NORIKO ...
HANG ON FOR JUST A LITTLE LONGER!
I WON'T LET YOU GET AWAY!
HE'S SPEEDING UP!

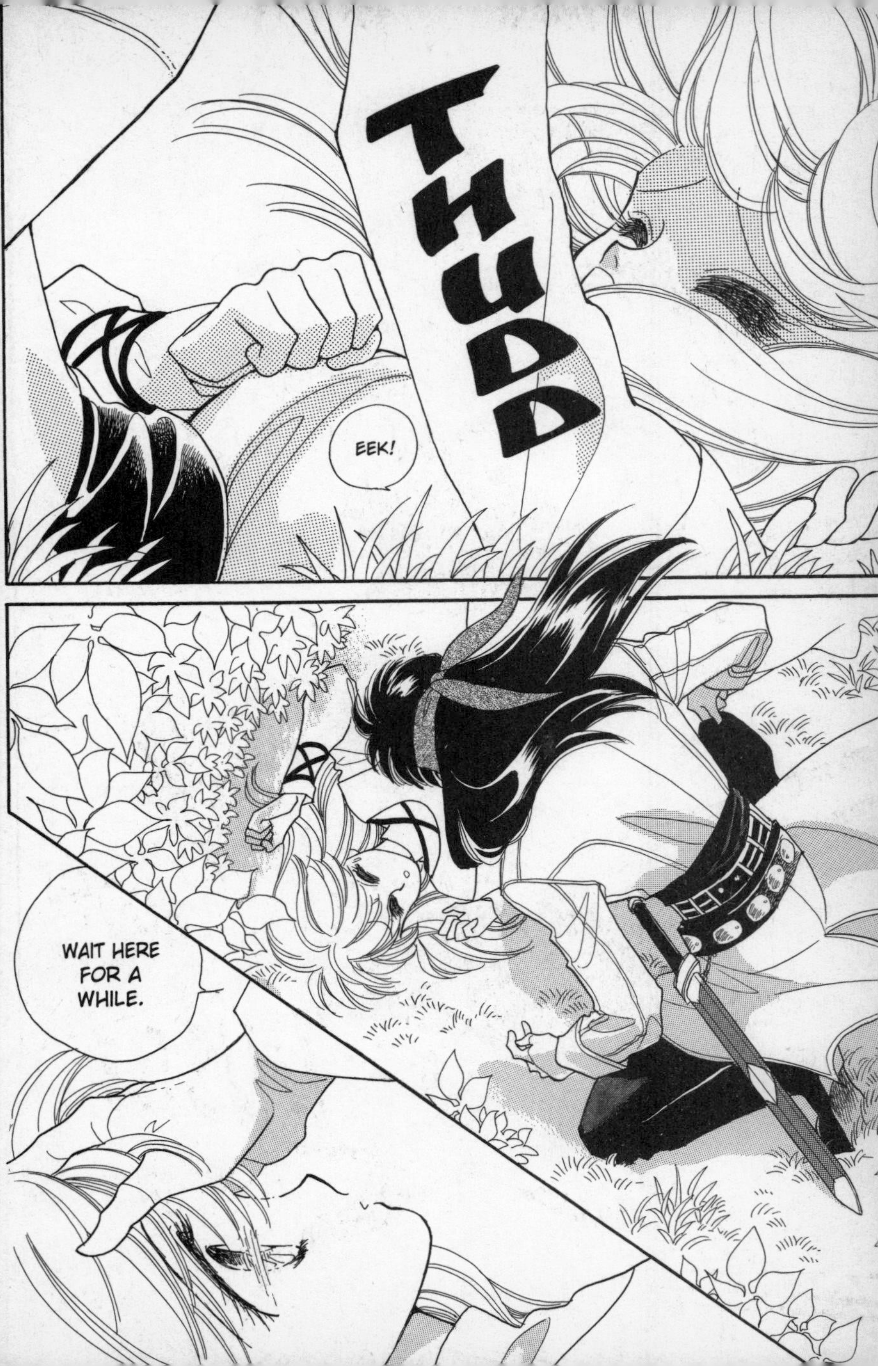
THUDD
EEK!
WAIT HERE FOR A WHILE.

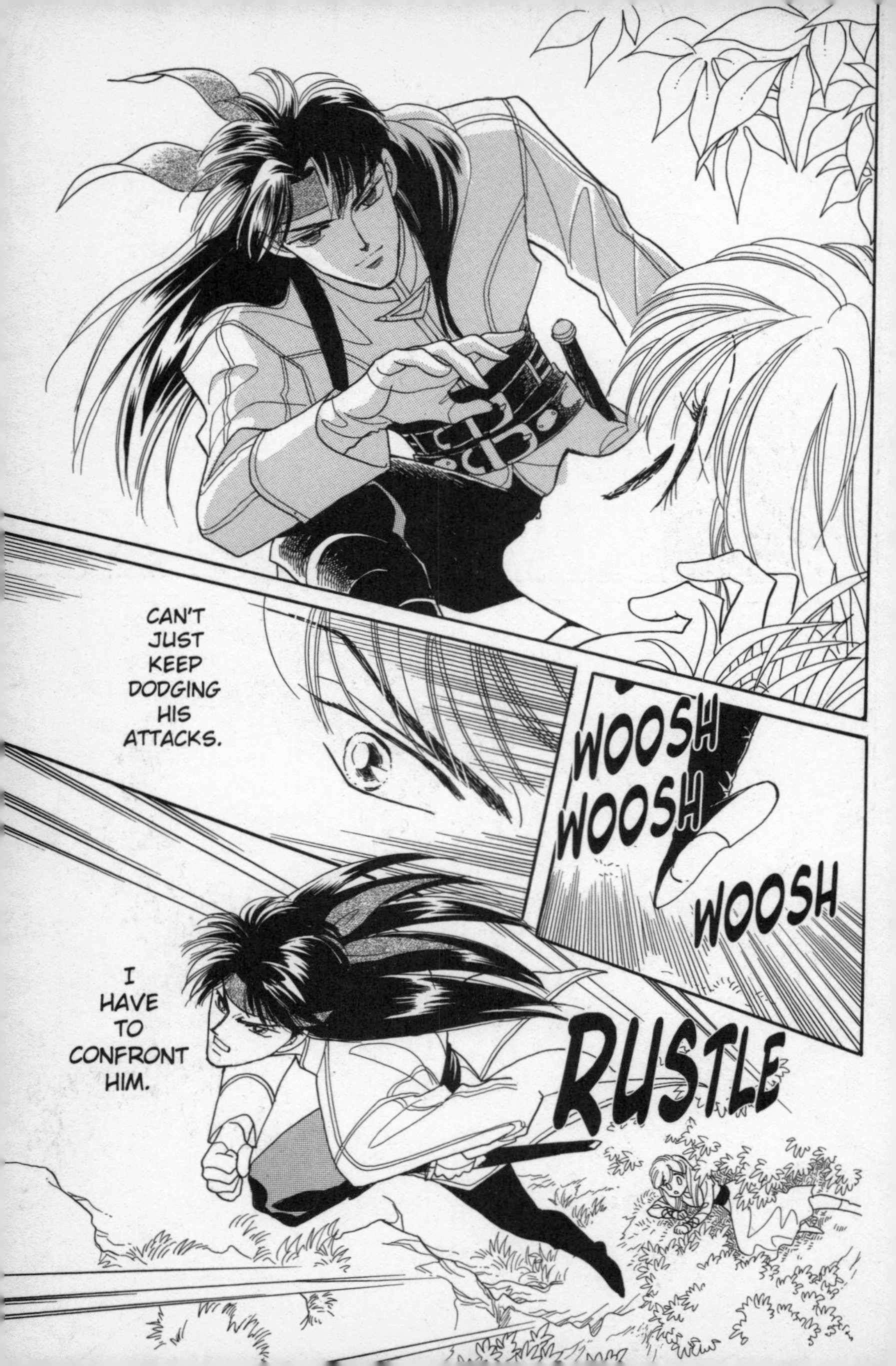
WOOSH
WOOSH
WOOSH
CAN'T JUST KEEP DODGING HIS ATTACKS.
RUSTLE
I HAVE TO CONFRONT HIM.

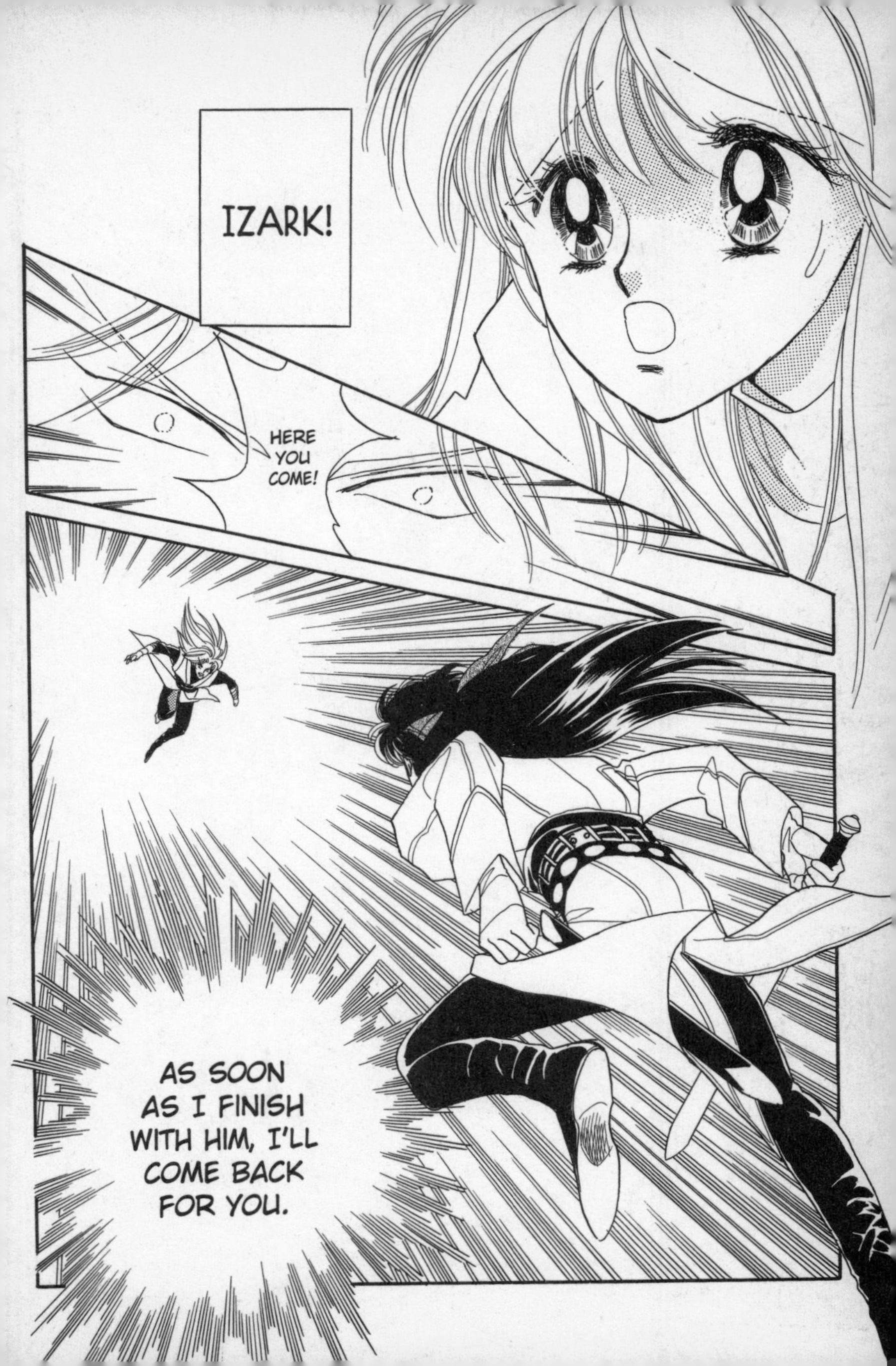
IZARK!
HERE YOU COME!
AS SOON AS I FINISH WITH HIM, I'LL COME BACK FOR YOU.

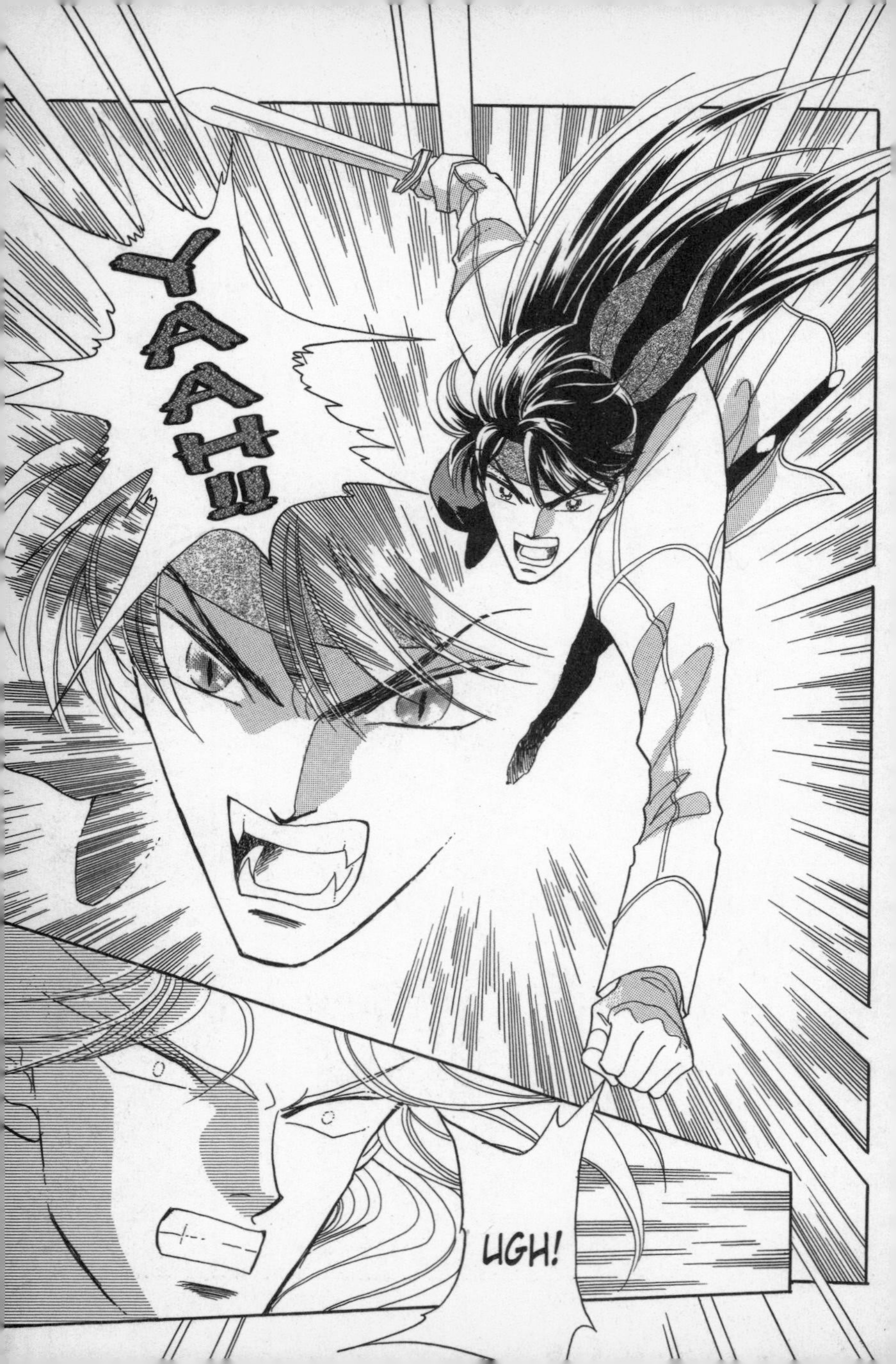
YAAH!!
UGH!

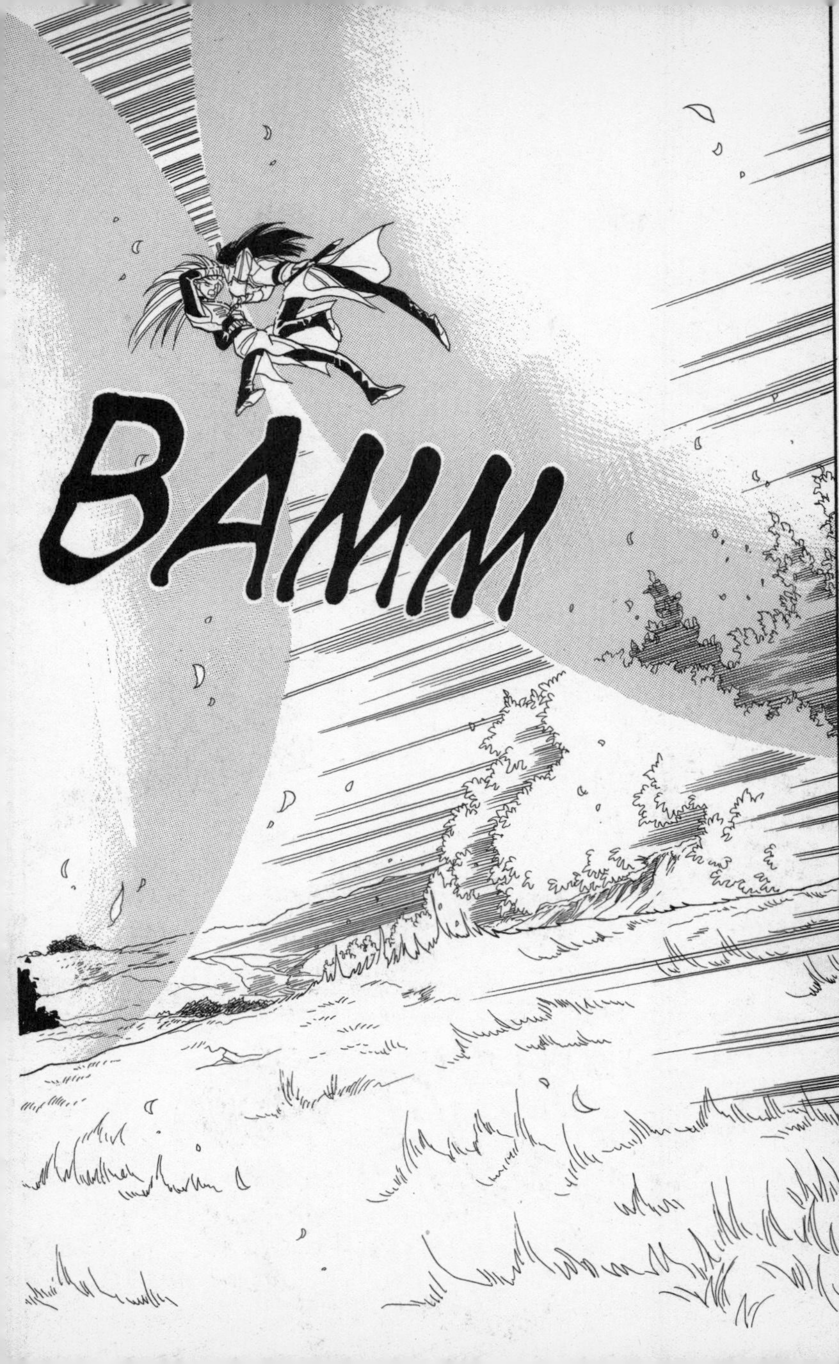
BAMM

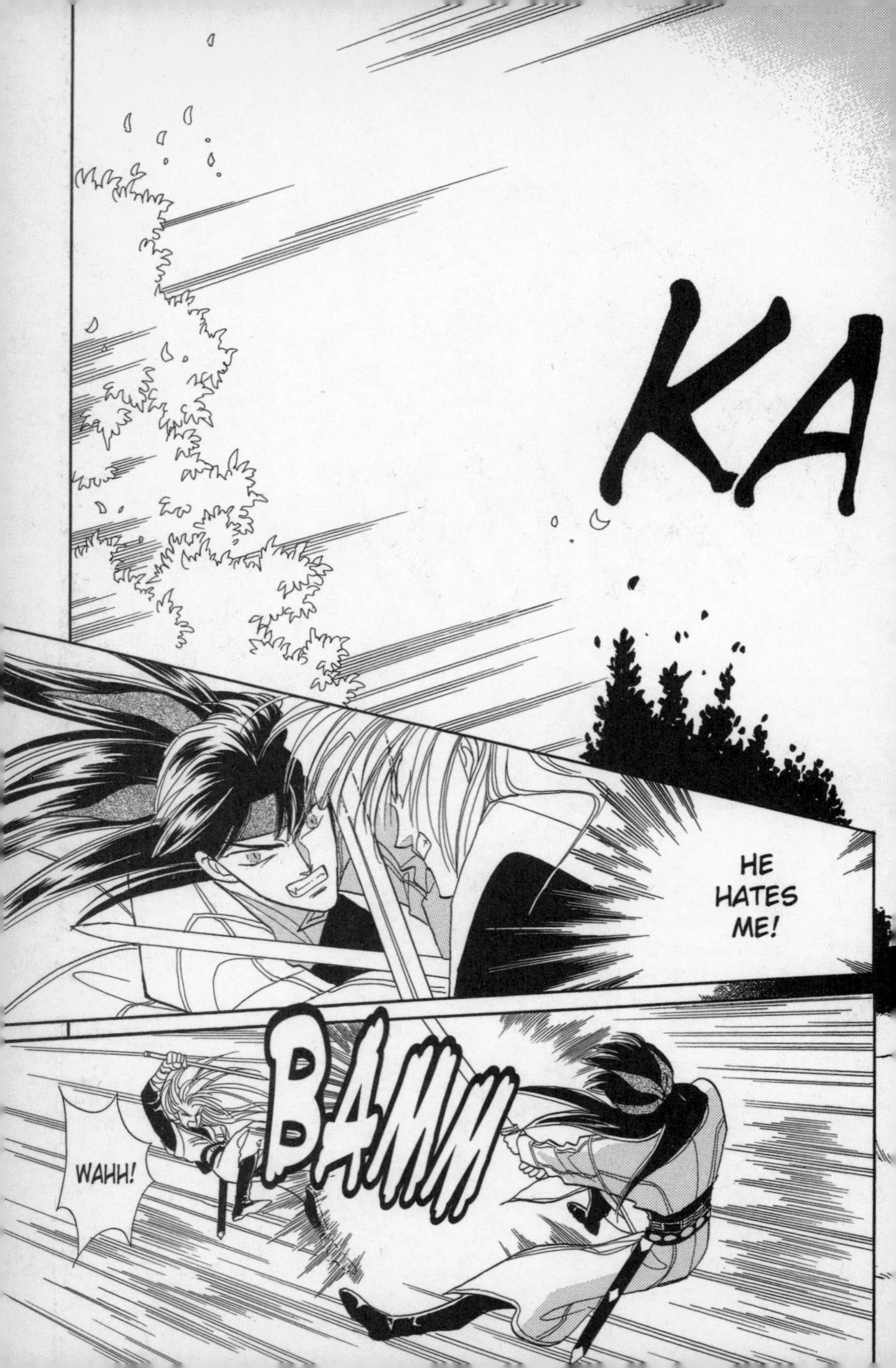
KA
HE HATES ME!
BAMM
WAHH!

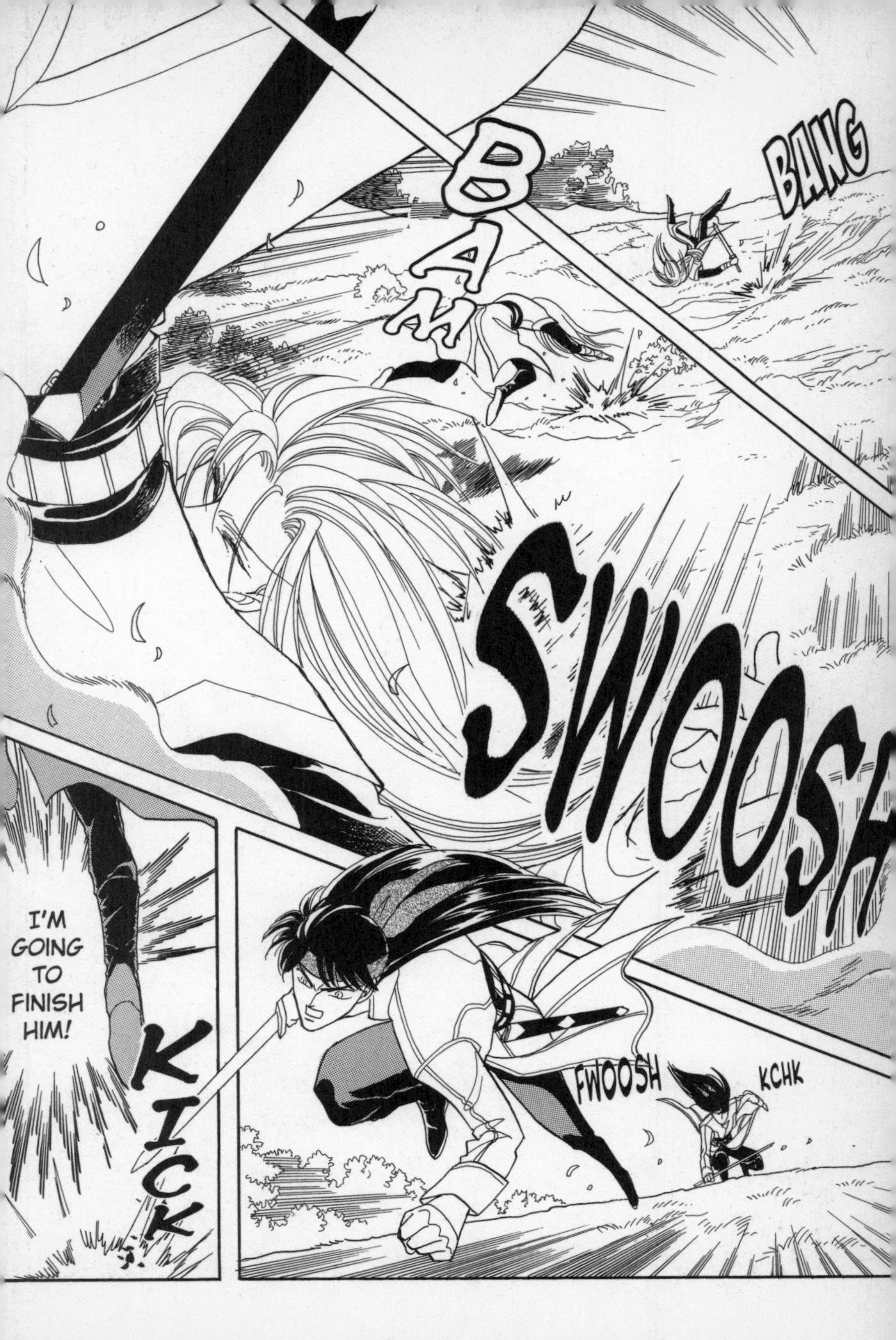
BANG
BAM
SWOOSH
KCHK
FWOOSH
KICK
I'M GOING TO FINISH HIM!

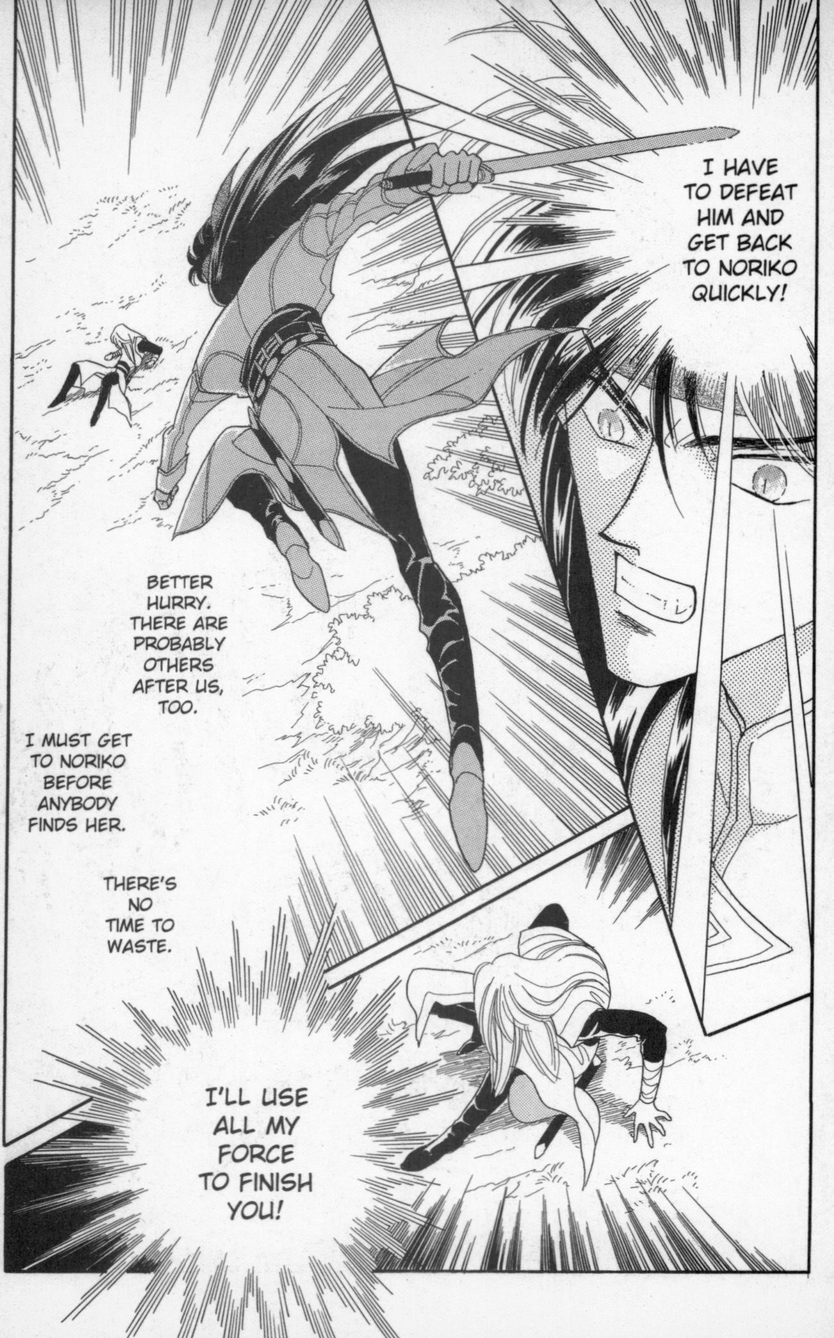
I HAVE TO DEFEAT HIM AND GET BACK TO NORIKO QUICKLY!
BETTER HURRY. THERE ARE PROBABLY OTHERS AFTER US, TOO.
I MUST GET TO NORIKO BEFORE ANYBODY FINDS HER.
THERE'S NO TIME TO WASTE.
I'LL USE ALL MY FORCE TO FINISH YOU!

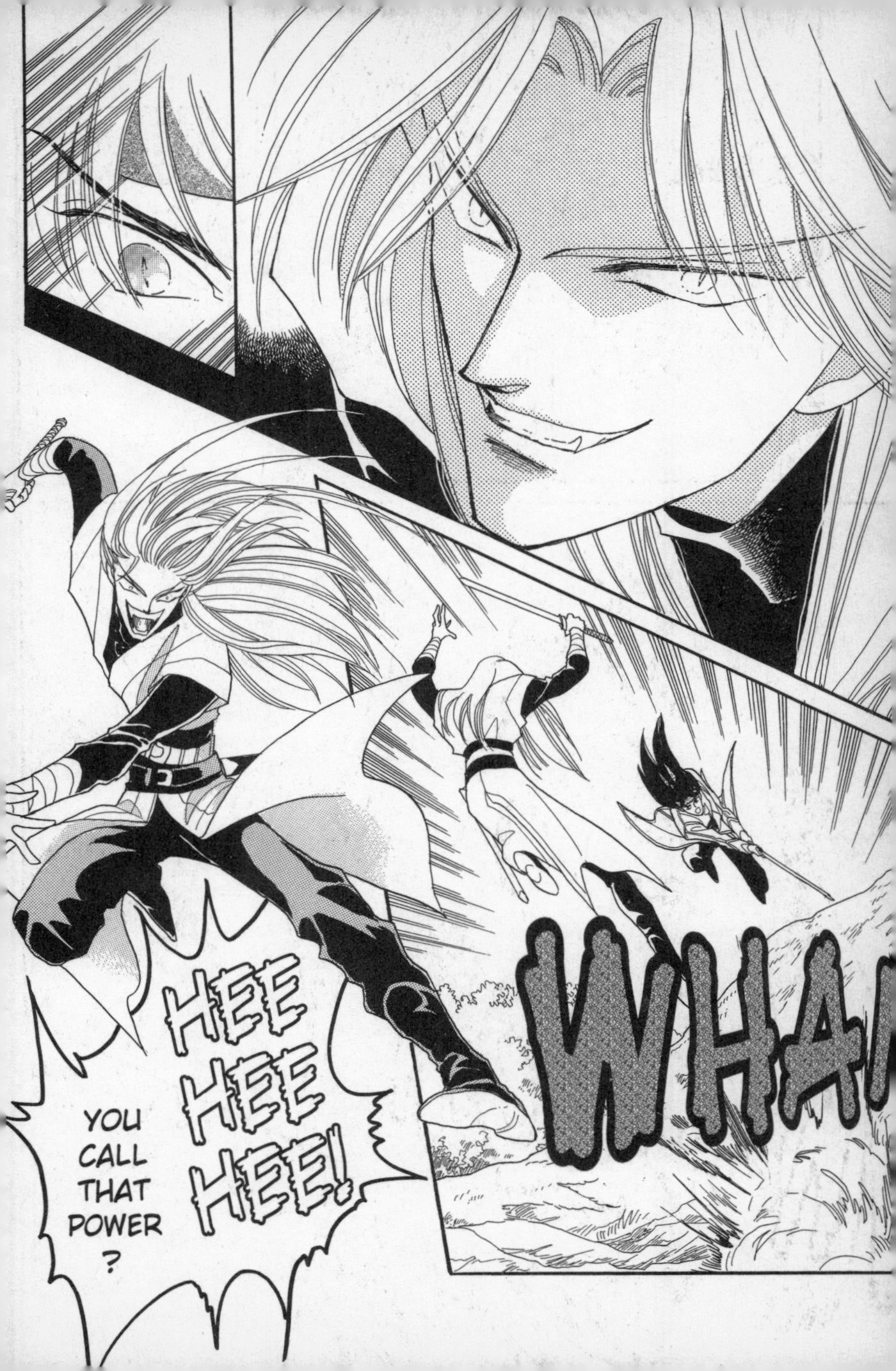
WHA
HEE HEE HEE!
YOU CALL THAT POWER?

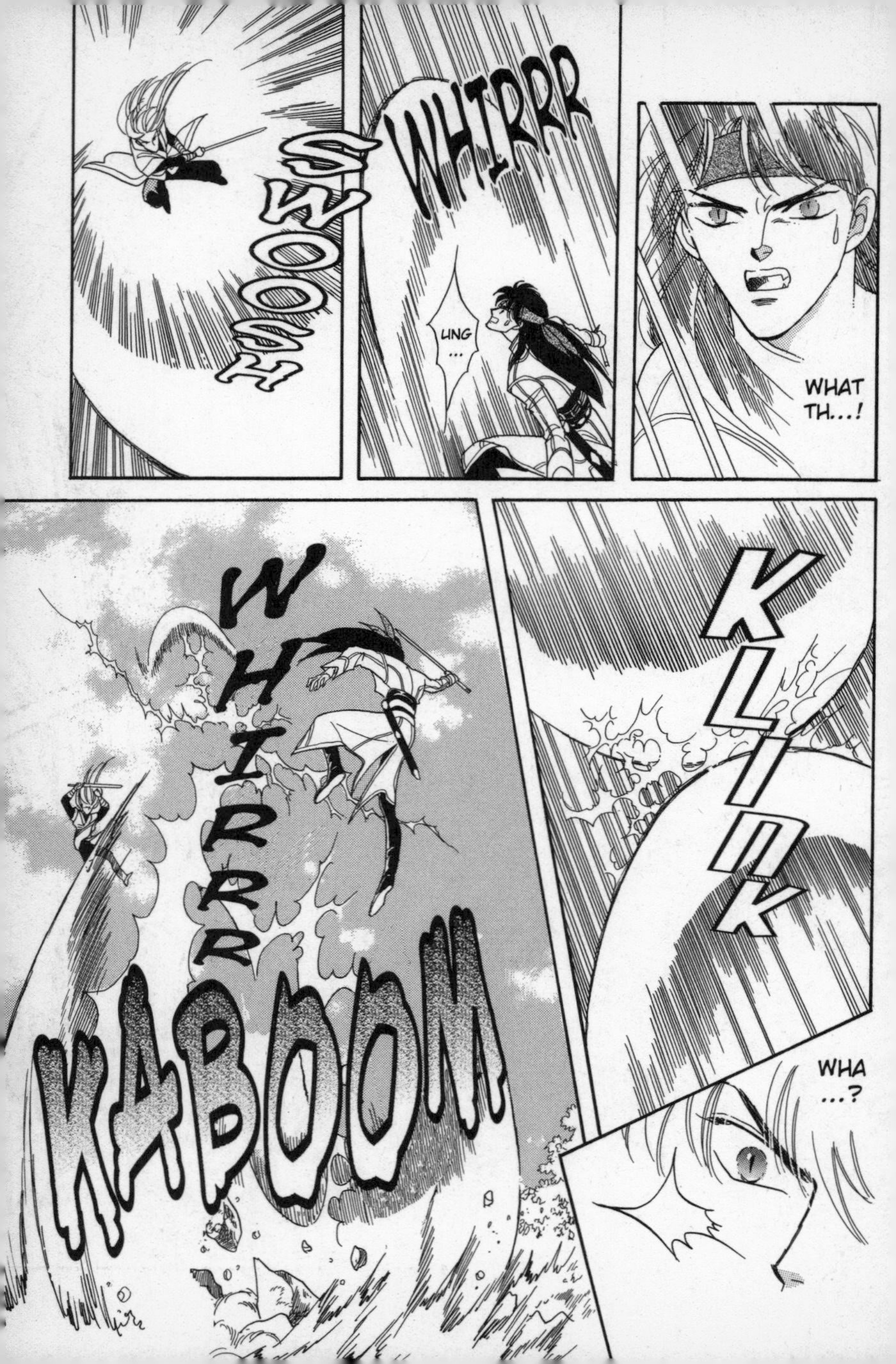
WHAT TH...!
WHIRRR
UNG ...
SWOOSH
KLINK
WHA ...?
WHIRRR
KABOOM

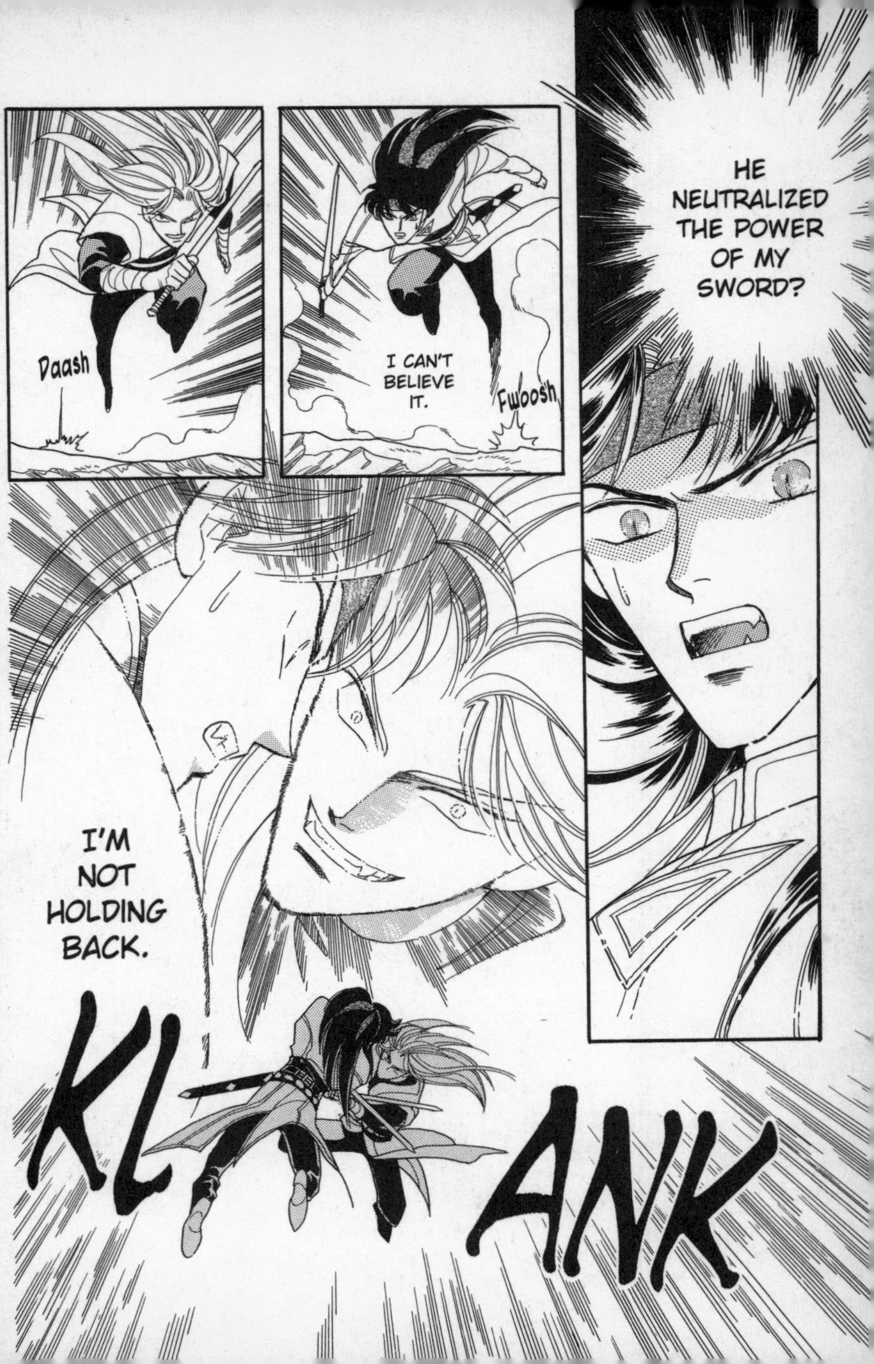
HE NEUTRALIZED THE POWER OF MY SWORD?
I CAN'T BELIEVE IT.
Fwoosh
Daash
I'M NOT HOLDING BACK.
KL ANK

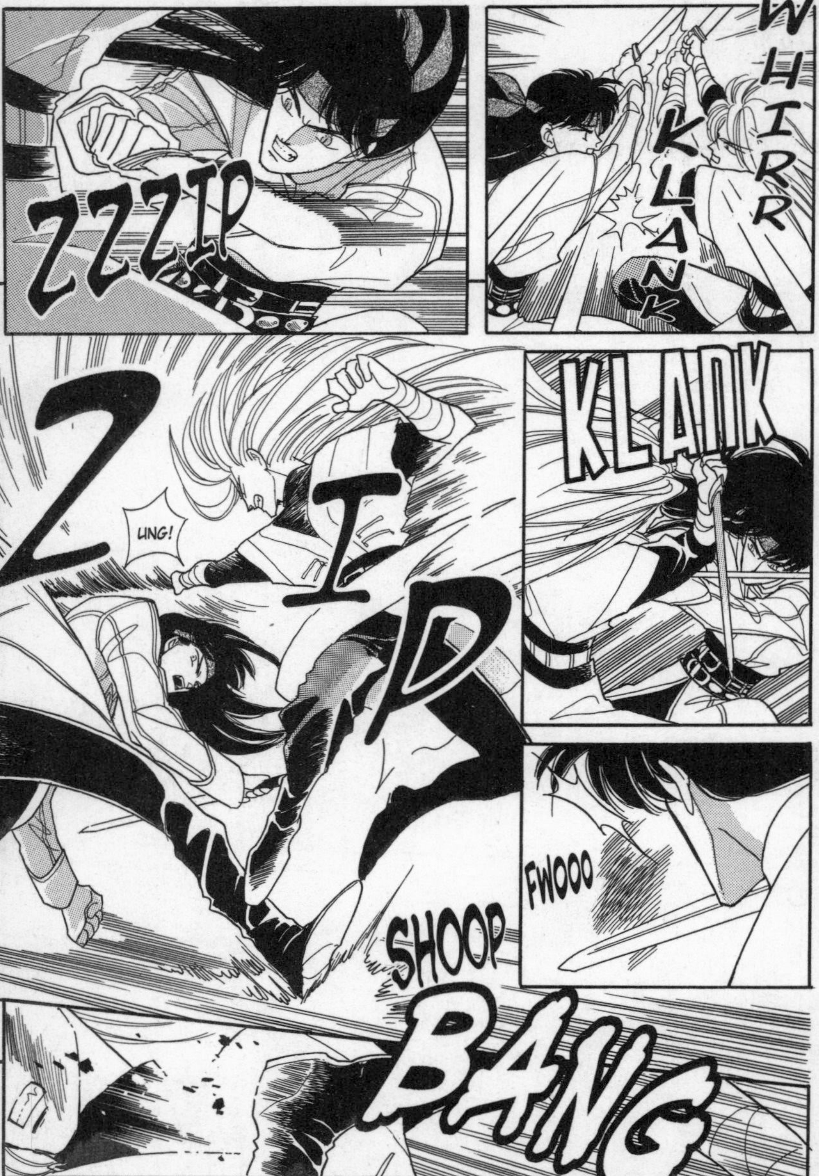
WHIRR
KLANK
ZZZIP
KLANK
FWOOO
ZIP
UNG!
SHOOP
BANG

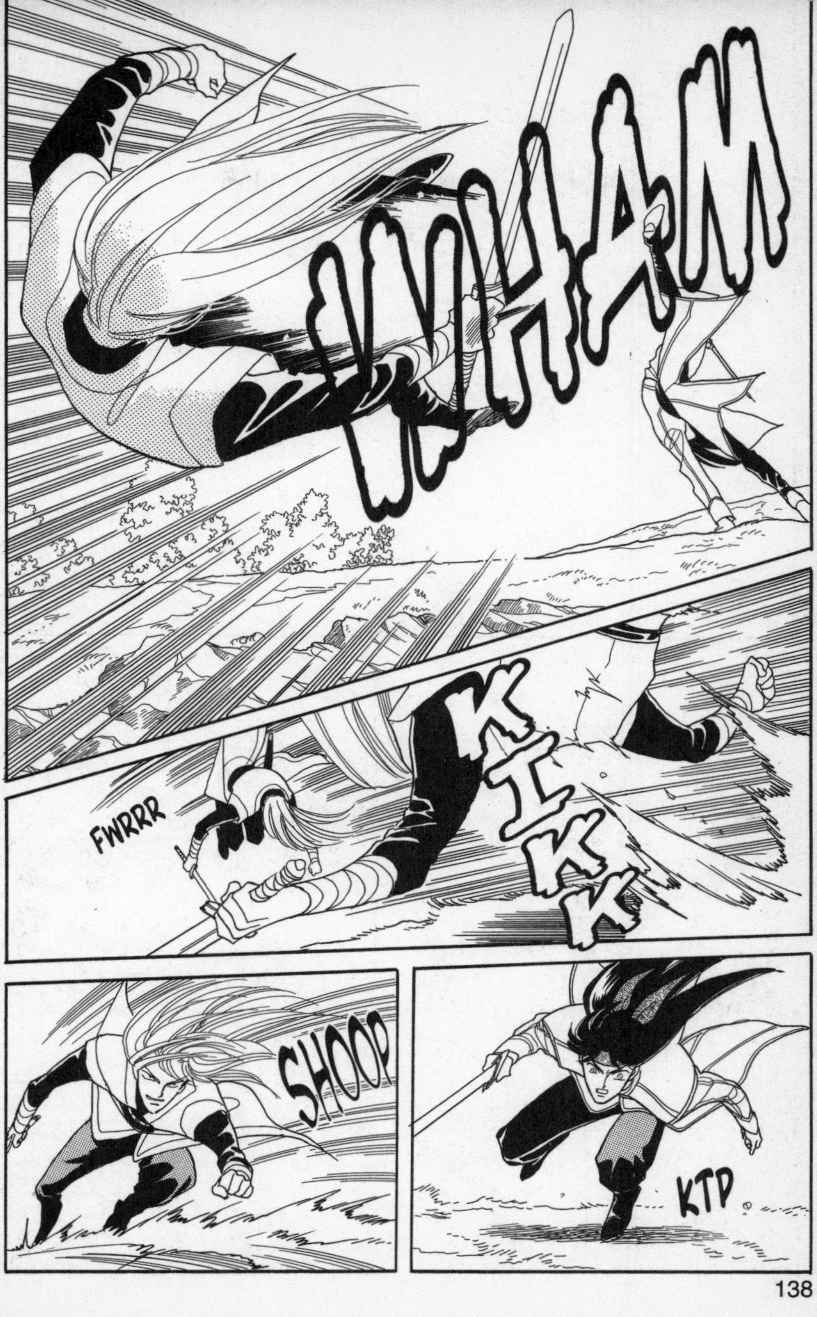
WHAM
KIKK
FWRRR
KTP
SHOOP

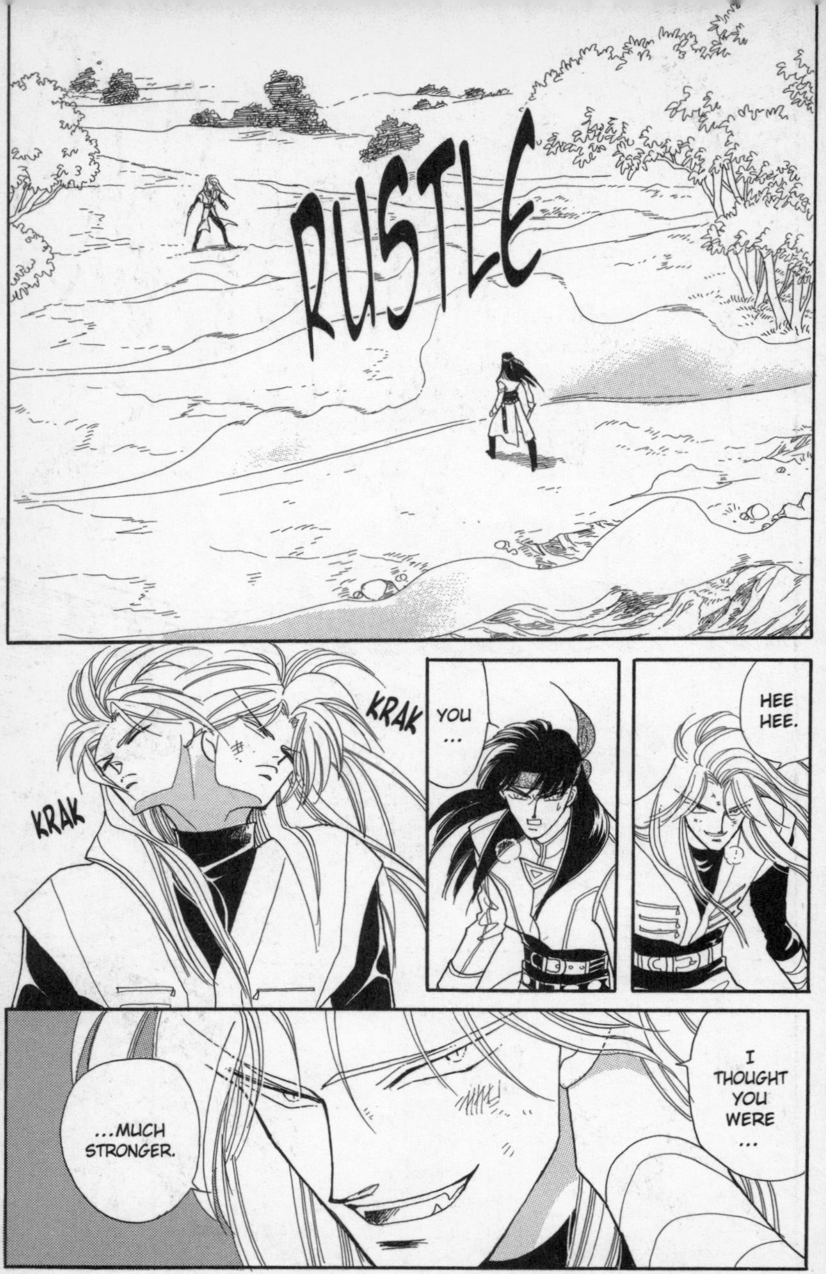
RUSTLE
HEE HEE.
YOU ...
KRAK
KRAK
I THOUGHT YOU WERE ...
...MUCH STRONGER.

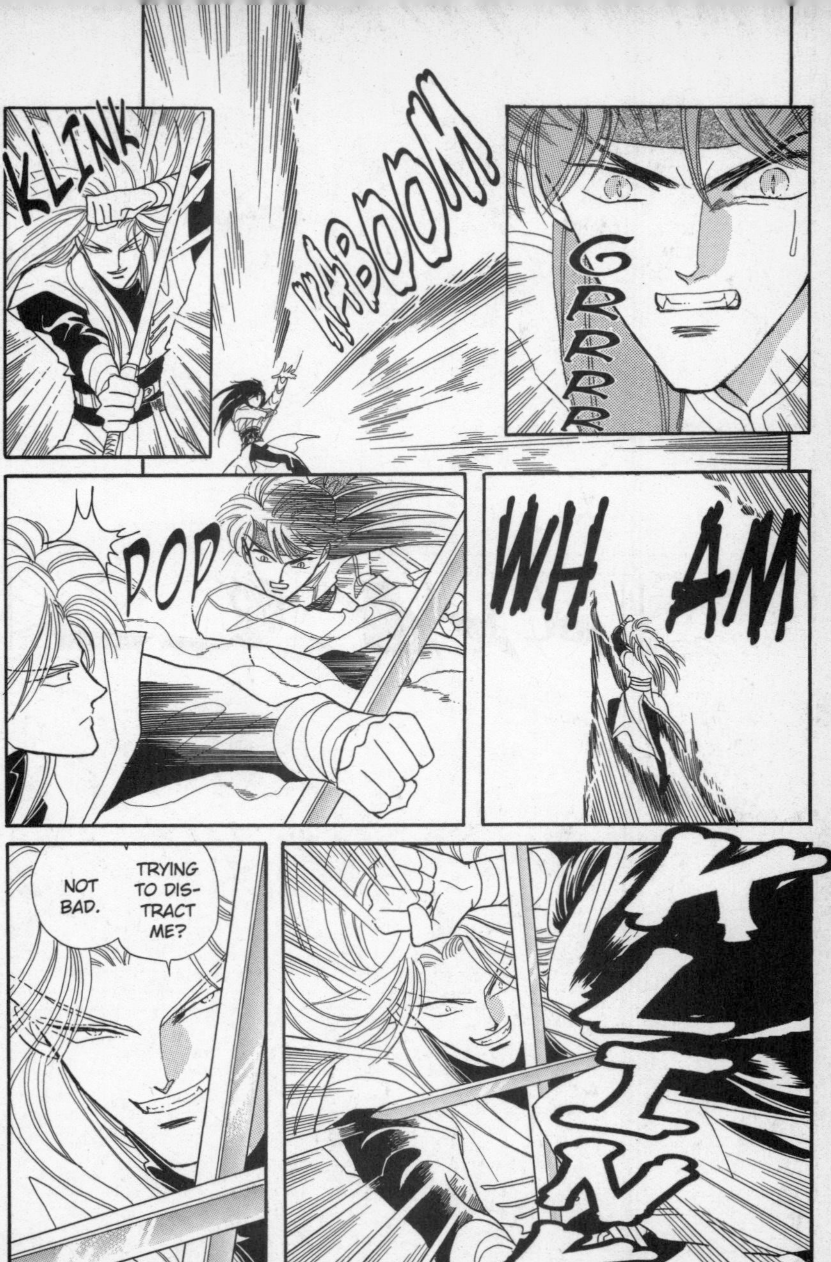
GRRRR
KABOOOM
KLINK
WH AM
POP
TRYING TO DIS-TRACT ME?
NOT BAD.

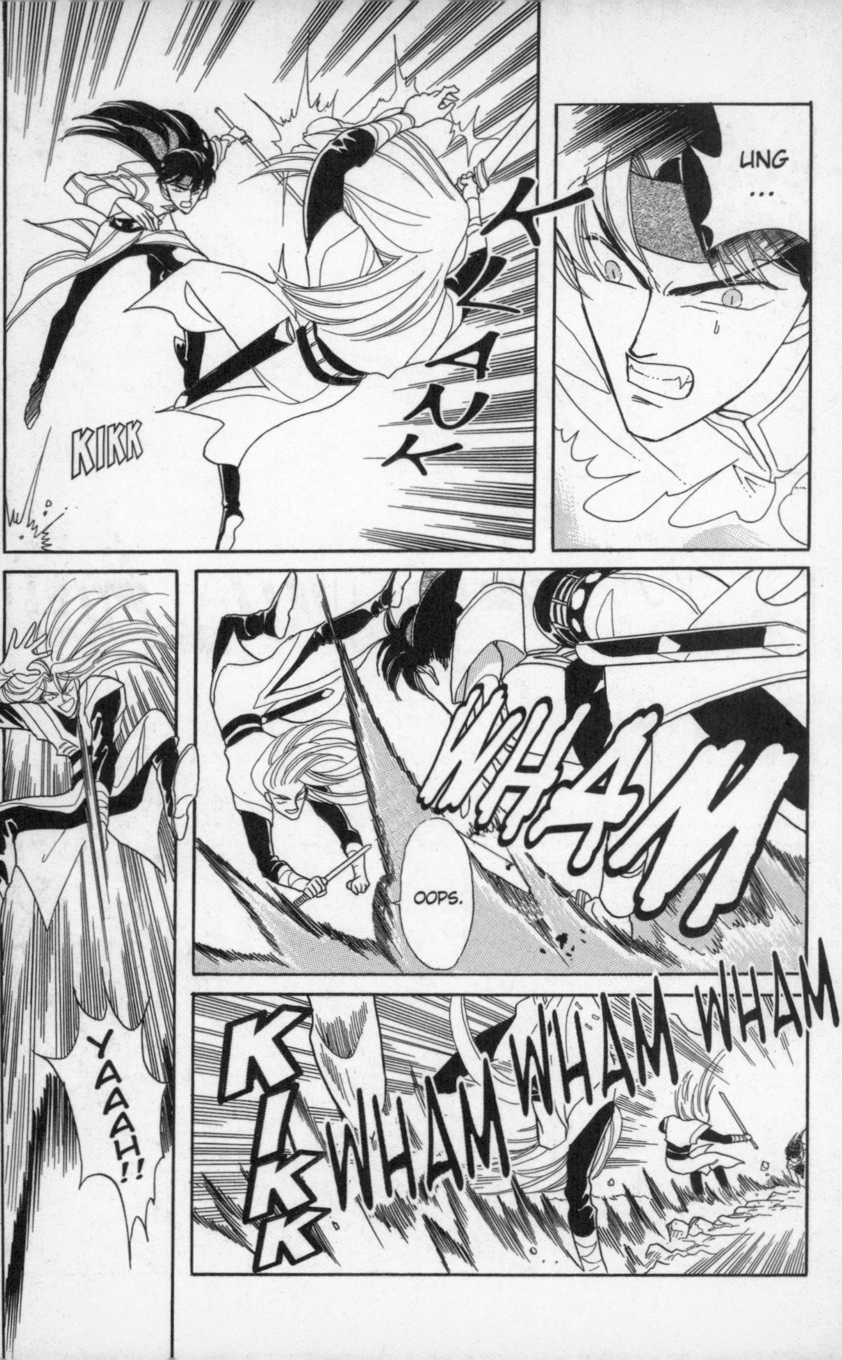
UNG
...
KLAUK
KIKK
WHAM
OOPS.
KIKK
WHAM WHAM WHAM WHAM
YAAAH!!

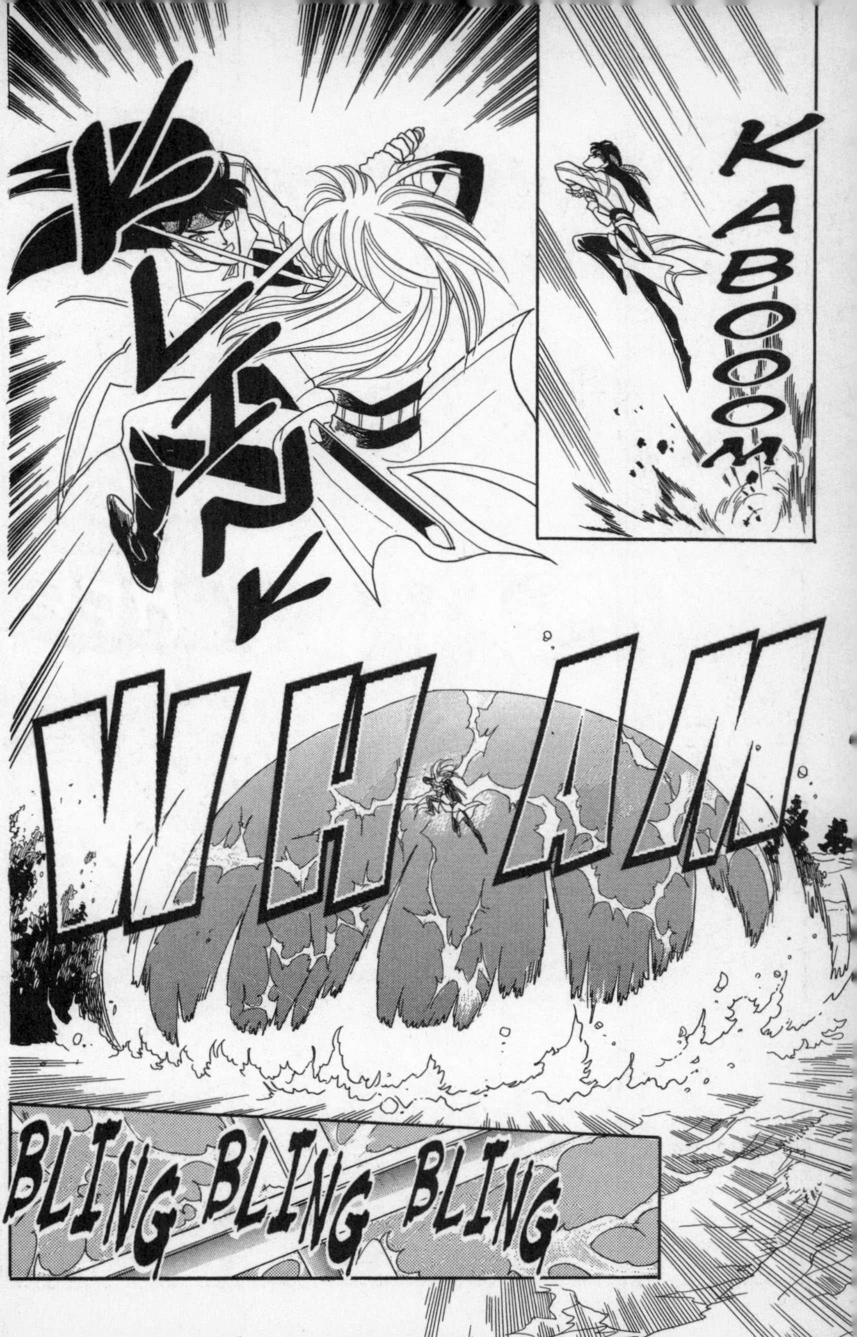
KABOOOOM
WHAM
BLING BLING BLING

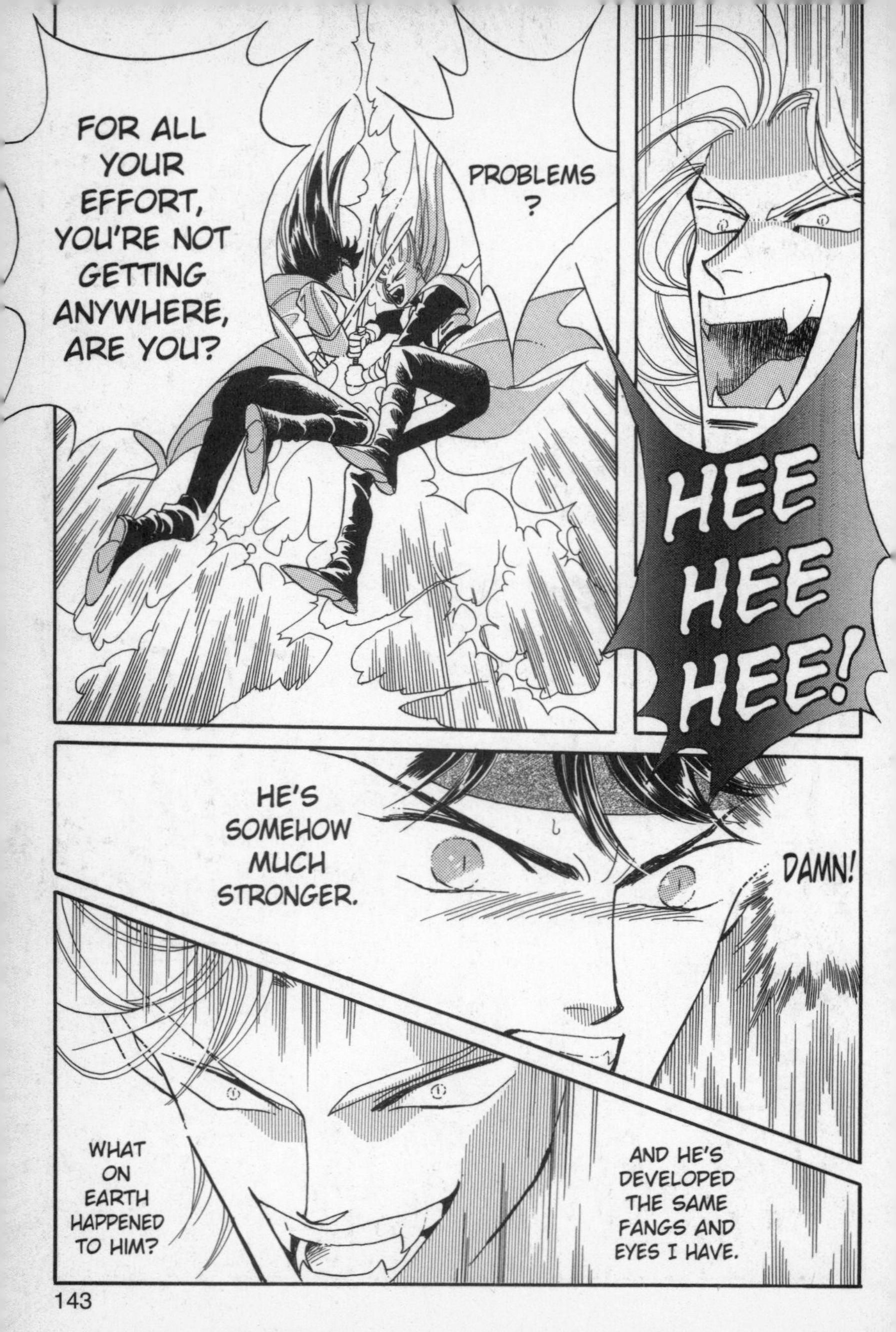
HEE HEE HEE!
FOR ALL YOUR EFFORT, YOU'RE NOT GETTING ANYWHERE, ARE YOU?
PROBLEMS ?
DAMN!
HE'S SOMEHOW MUCH STRONGER.
AND HE'S DEVELOPED THE SAME FANGS AND EYES I HAVE.
WHAT ON EARTH HAPPENED TO HIM?

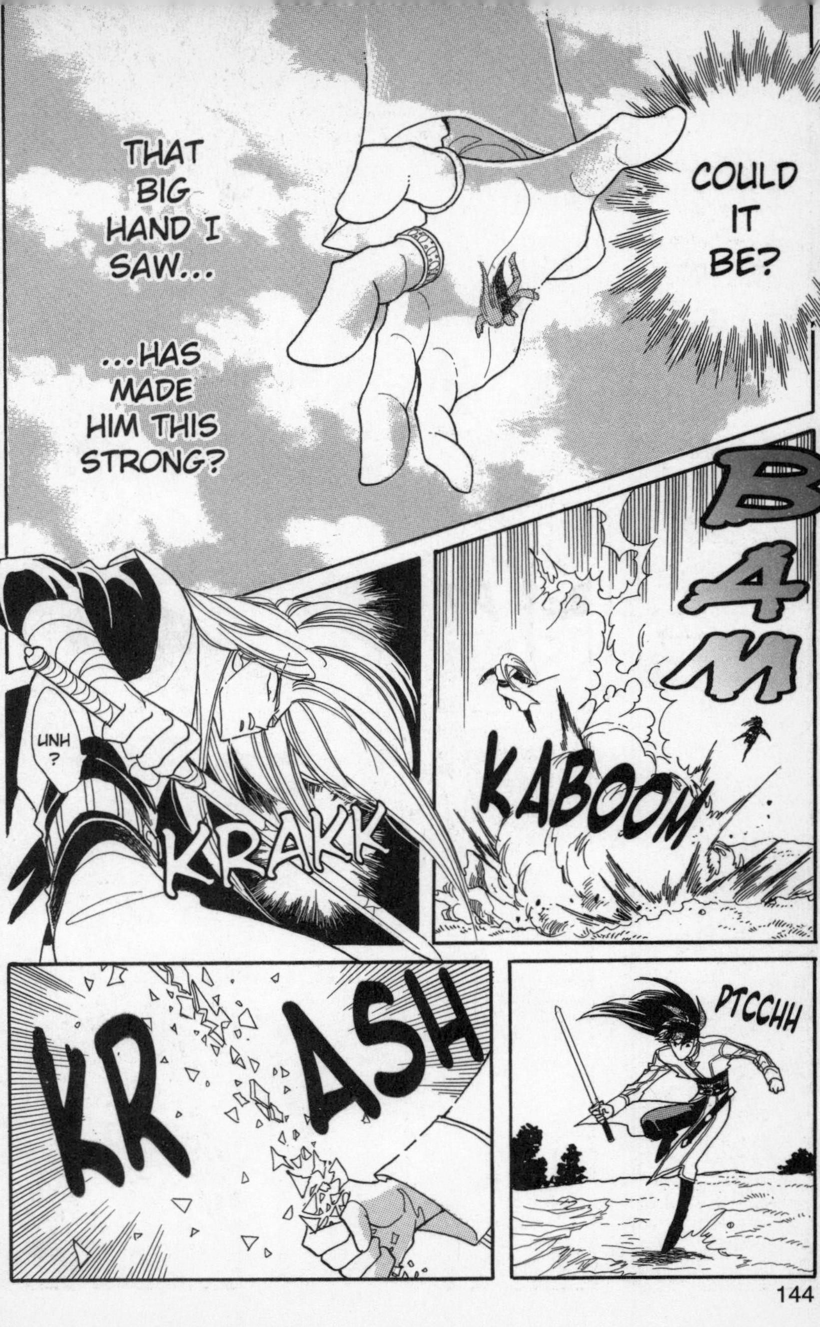
COULD IT BE?
THAT BIG HAND I SAW...
...HAS MADE HIM THIS STRONG?
BAM
KABOOM
UNH?
KRAKK
DTCCHH
KRASH

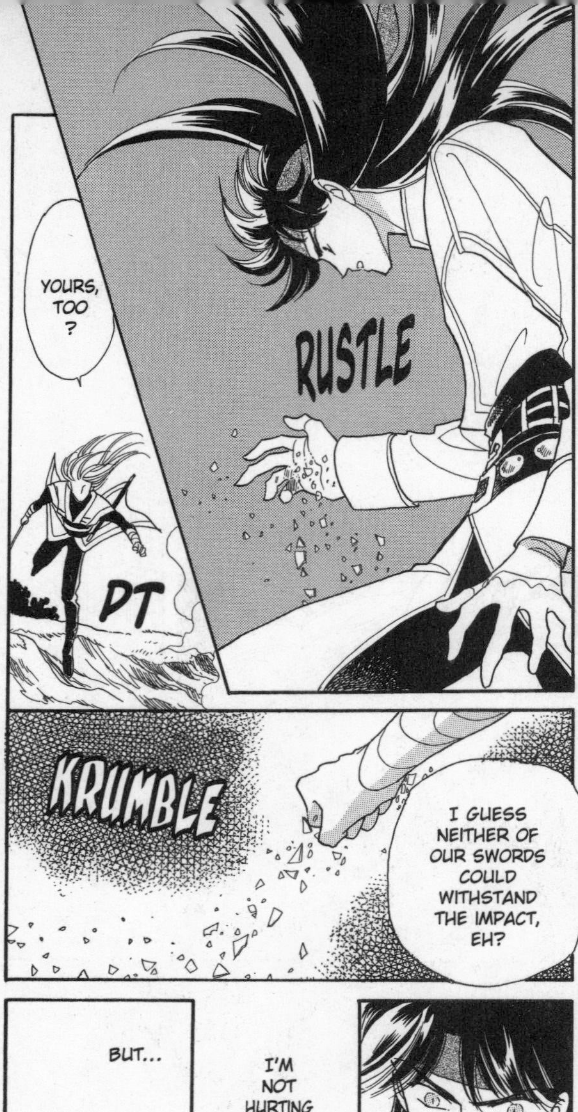
RUSTLE
YOURS, TOO ?
DT
I GUESS NEITHER OF OUR SWORDS COULD WITHSTAND THE IMPACT, EH?
KRUMBLE
I'M NOT HURTING HIM ...
BUT...
...I CAN'T DRAW OUT ANY MORE FORCE...

Cat Story (4)

This is about a brown cat that hasn't come to my yard lately.

One day my mother went out to our backyard and screamed when she saw that this brown cat had just pooped. The cat used to leave its poop in our yard uncovered, but that day, it covered its poop very carefully while watching out for my mother.

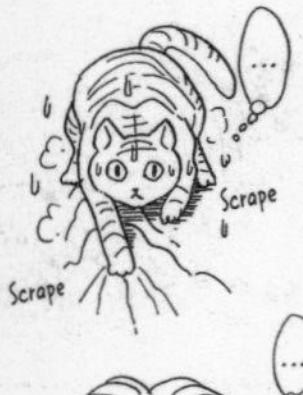
...
Scrape
Scrape
...

It didn't change the fact that the cat had pooped in our yard, but it must have felt it was being more polite by covering it with sand.

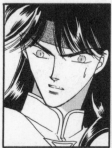

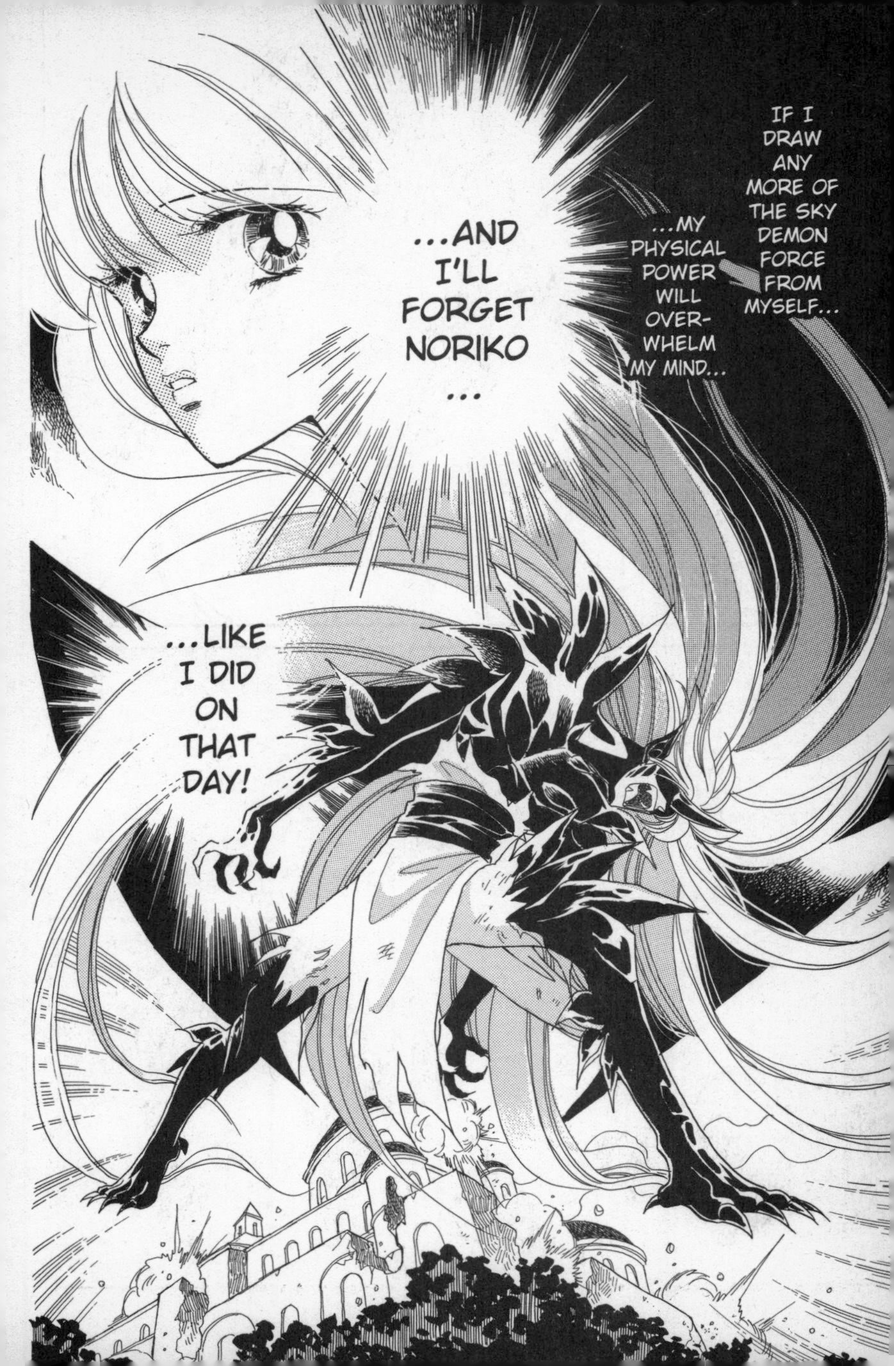
IF I DRAW ANY MORE OF THE SKY DEMON FORCE FROM MYSELF...
...MY PHYSICAL POWER WILL OVER-WHELM MY MIND...
...AND I'LL FORGET NORIKO ...
...LIKE I DID ON THAT DAY!

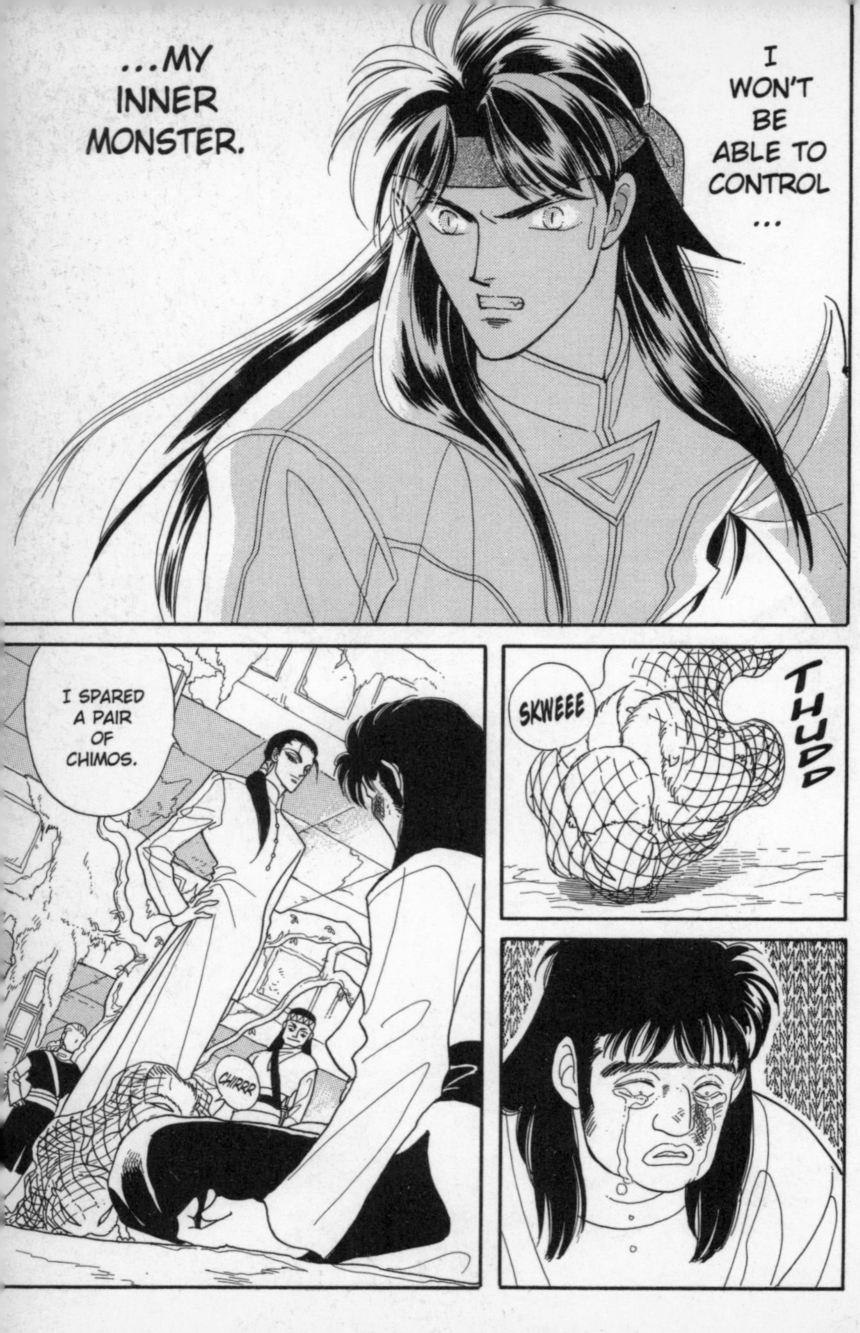
I WON'T BE ABLE TO CONTROL ...
...MY INNER MONSTER.
SKWEEE
THUDD
I SPARED A PAIR OF CHIMOS.
CHIRRR

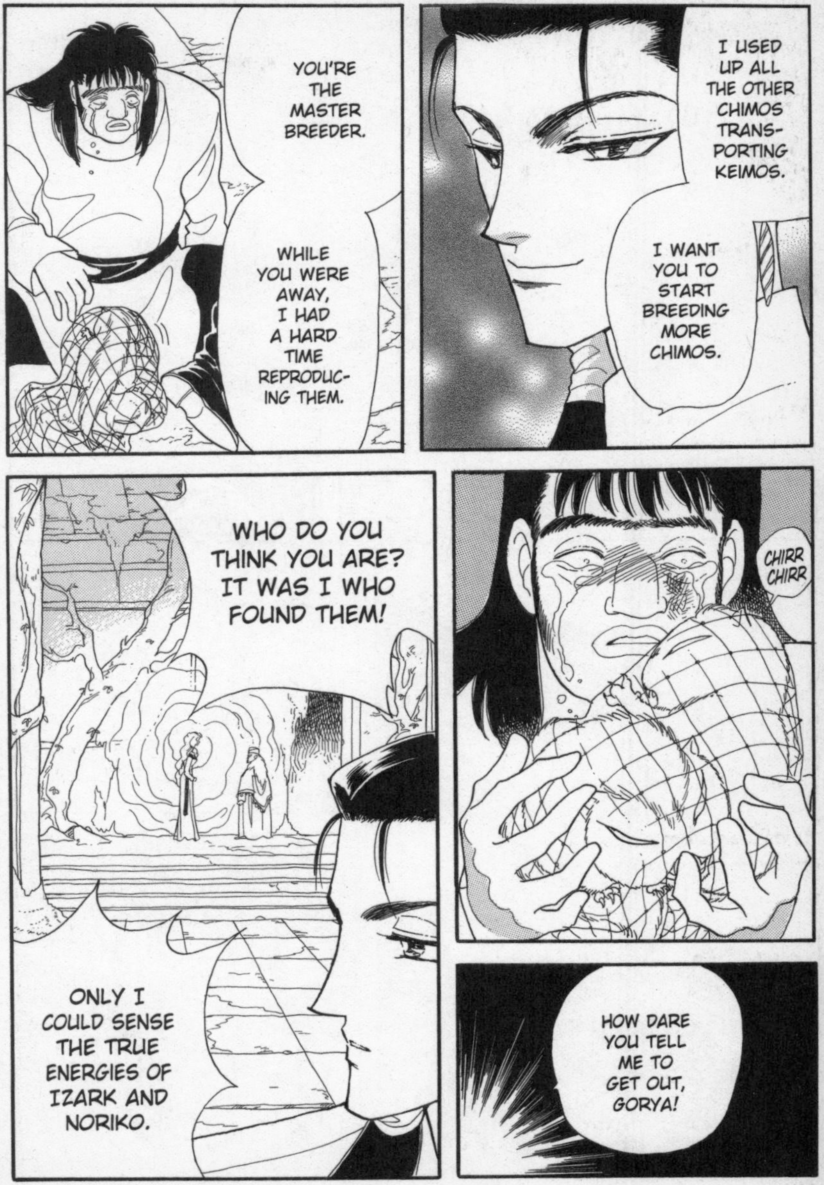
I USED UP ALL THE OTHER CHIMOS TRANS-PORTING KEIMOS.
I WANT YOU TO START BREEDING MORE CHIMOS.
YOU'RE THE MASTER BREEDER.
WHILE YOU WERE AWAY, I HAD A HARD TIME REPRODUC-ING THEM.
CHIRR CHIRR
HOW DARE YOU TELL ME TO GET OUT, GORYA!
WHO DO YOU THINK YOU ARE? IT WAS I WHO FOUND THEM!
ONLY I COULD SENSE THE TRUE ENERGIES OF IZARK AND NORIKO.

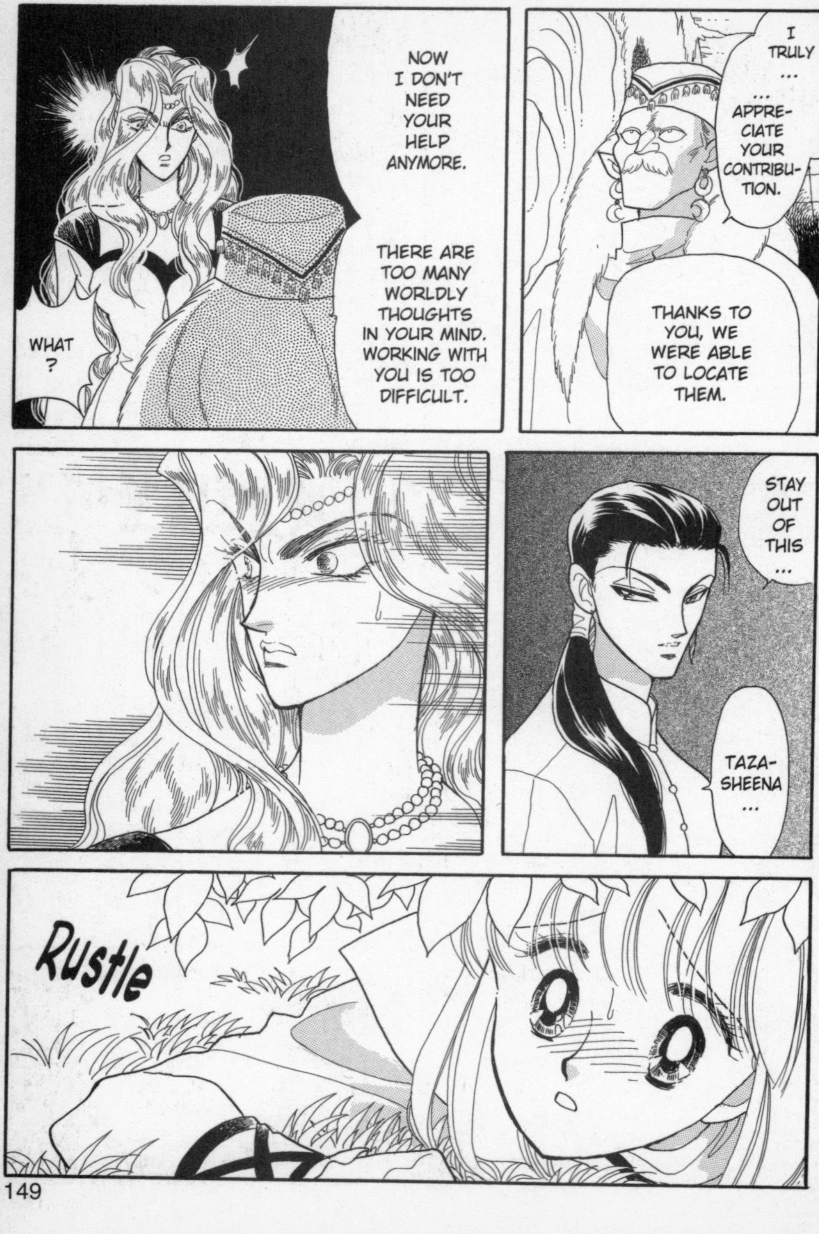
I TRULY ... ... APPRECIATE YOUR CONTRIBUTION.
THANKS TO YOU, WE WERE ABLE TO LOCATE THEM.
NOW I DON'T NEED YOUR HELP ANYMORE.
THERE ARE TOO MANY WORLDLY THOUGHTS IN YOUR MIND. WORKING WITH YOU IS TOO DIFFICULT.
WHAT ?
STAY OUT OF THIS ...
TAZA-SHEENA ...
Rustle

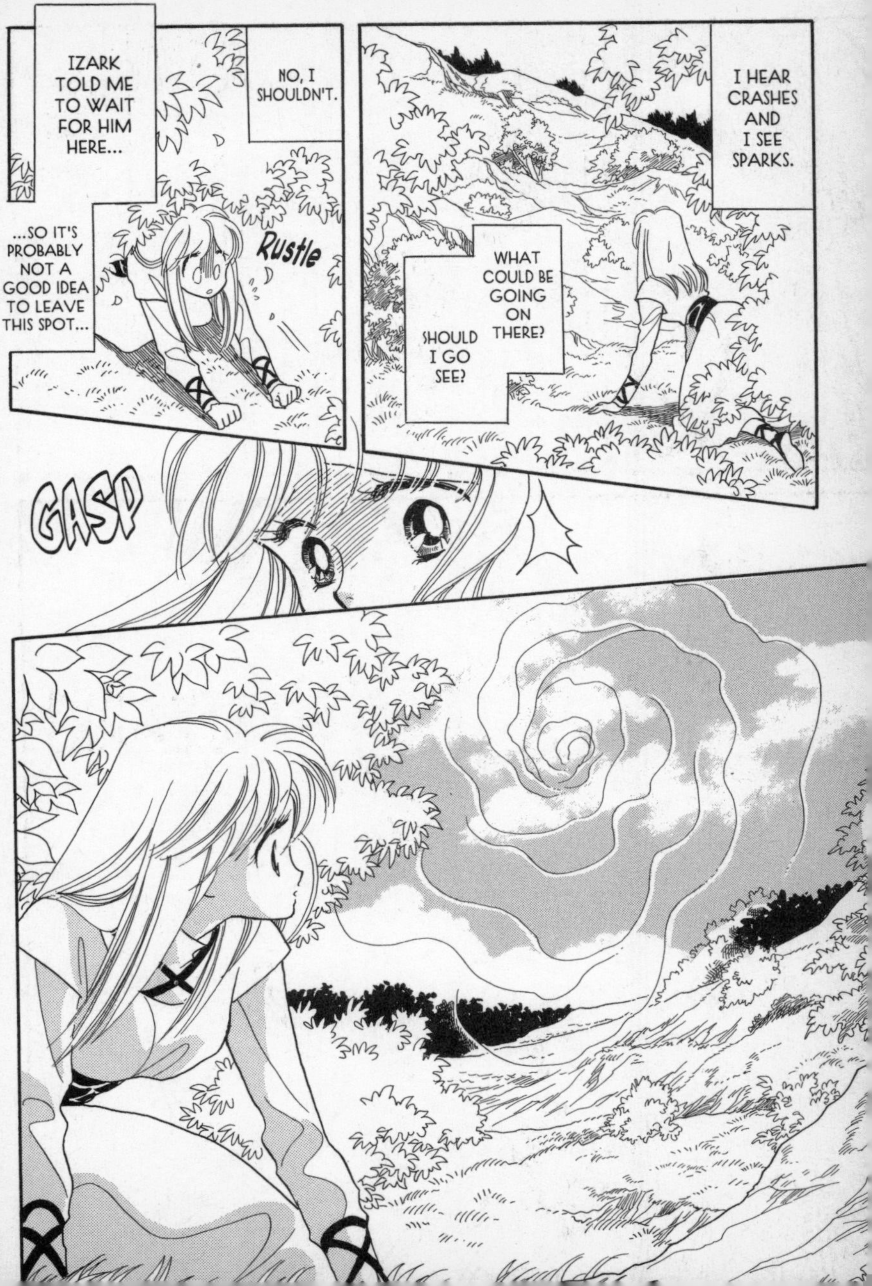
I HEAR CRASHES AND I SEE SPARKS.
WHAT COULD BE GOING ON THERE?
SHOULD I GO SEE?
NO, I SHOULDN'T.
IZARK TOLD ME TO WAIT FOR HIM HERE...
...SO IT'S PROBABLY NOT A GOOD IDEA TO LEAVE THIS SPOT...
Rustle
GASP

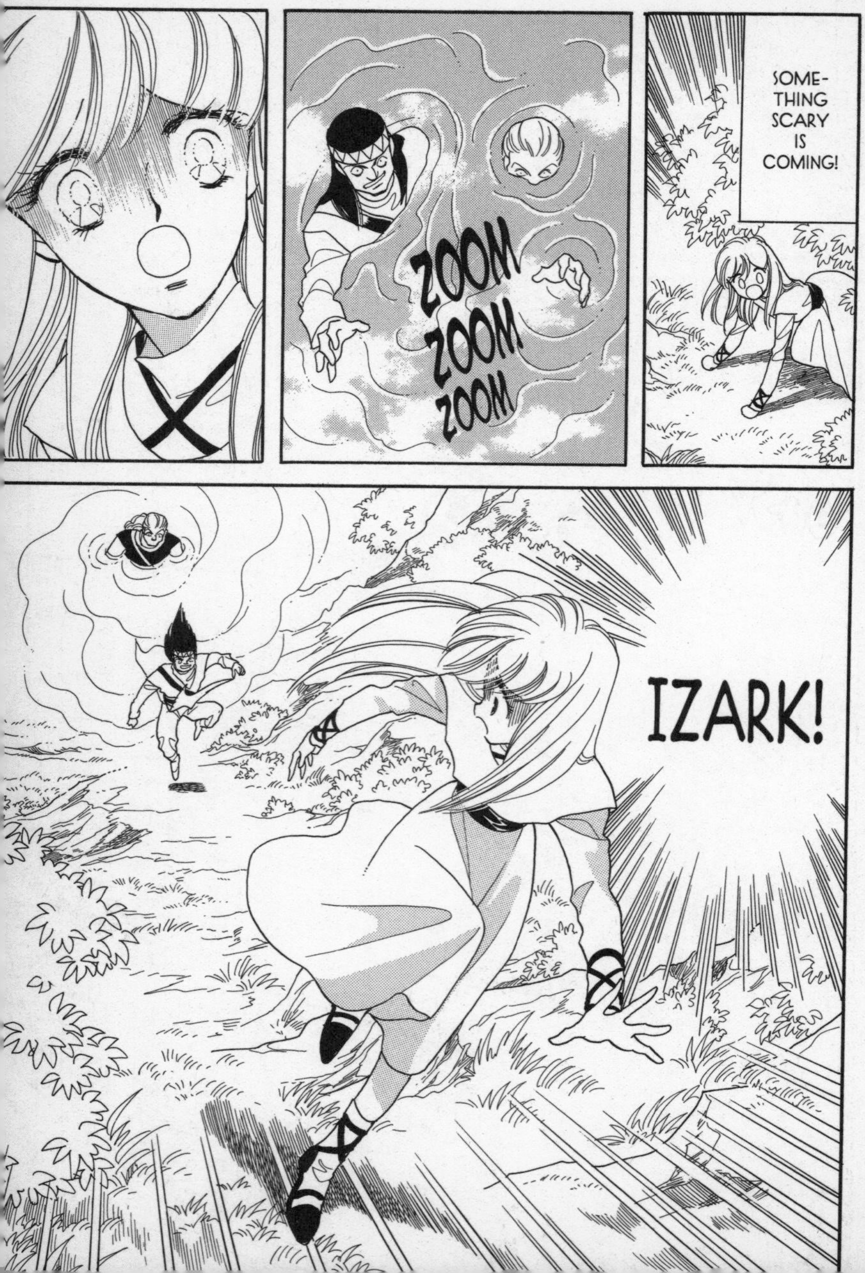
SOME-
THING
SCARY
IS
COMING!
ZOOM
ZOOM
ZOOM
IZARK!

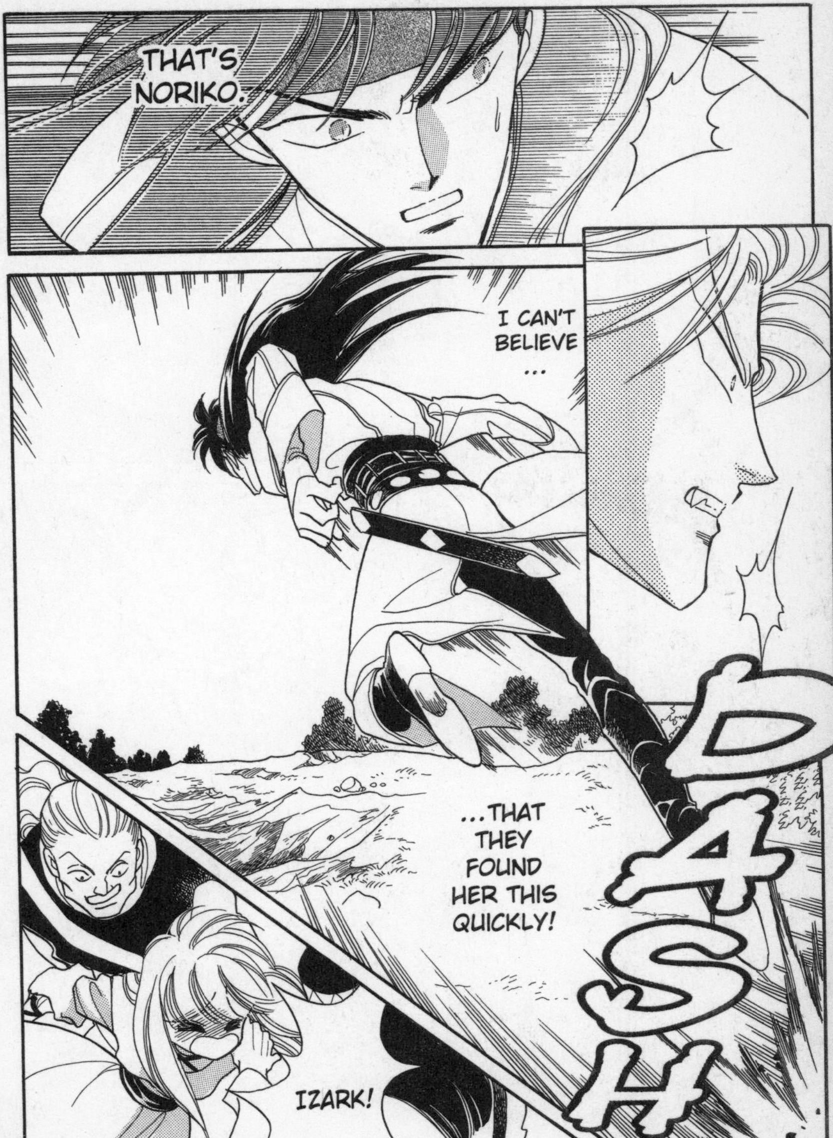
THAT'S NORIKO.
I CAN'T BELIEVE ...
...THAT THEY FOUND HER THIS QUICKLY!
DASH
IZARK!

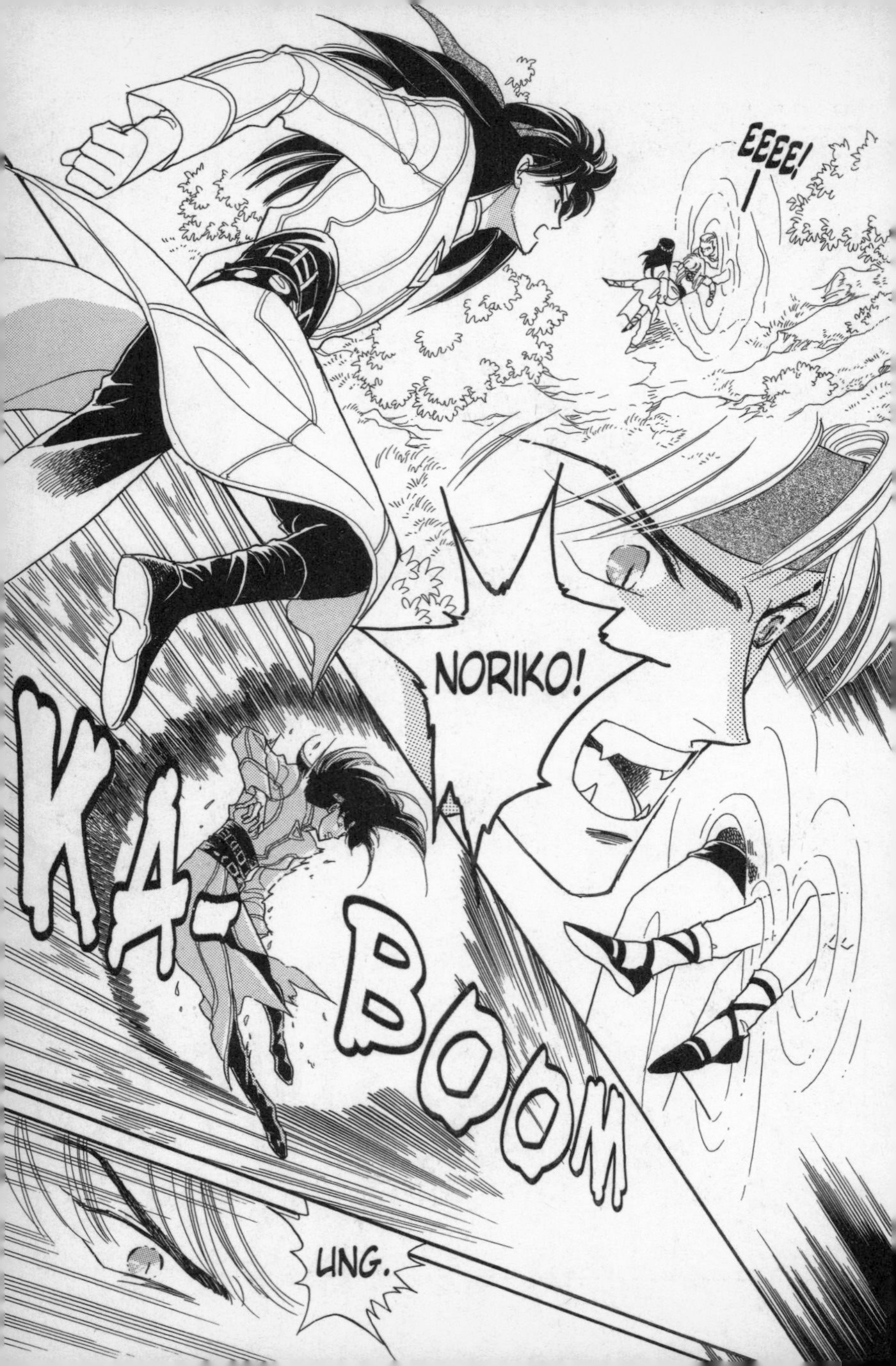
EEEE!
NORIKO!
KA-BOOM
UNG.

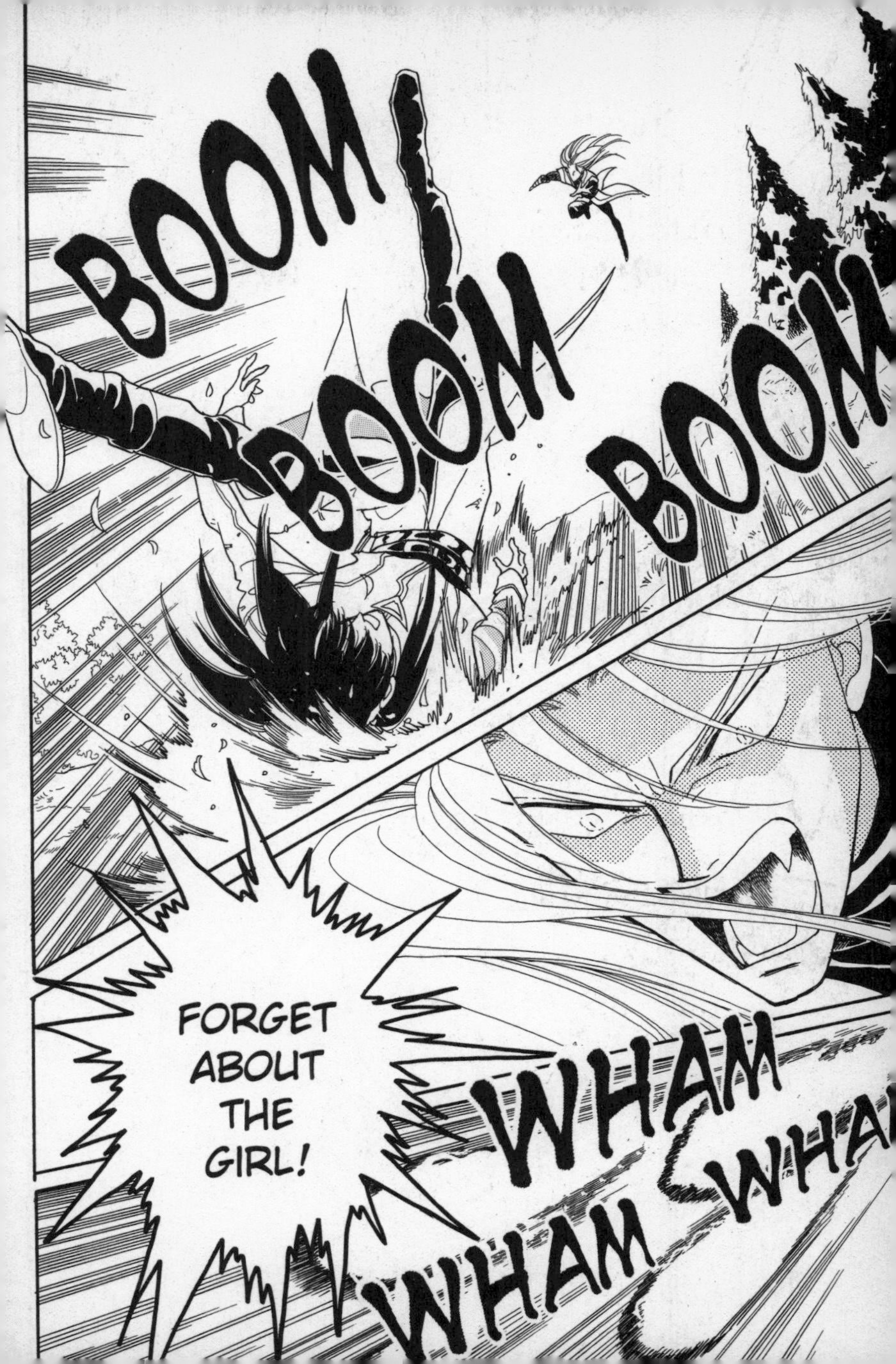
BOOM
BOOM
BOOM
FORGET ABOUT THE GIRL!
WHAM
WHAM

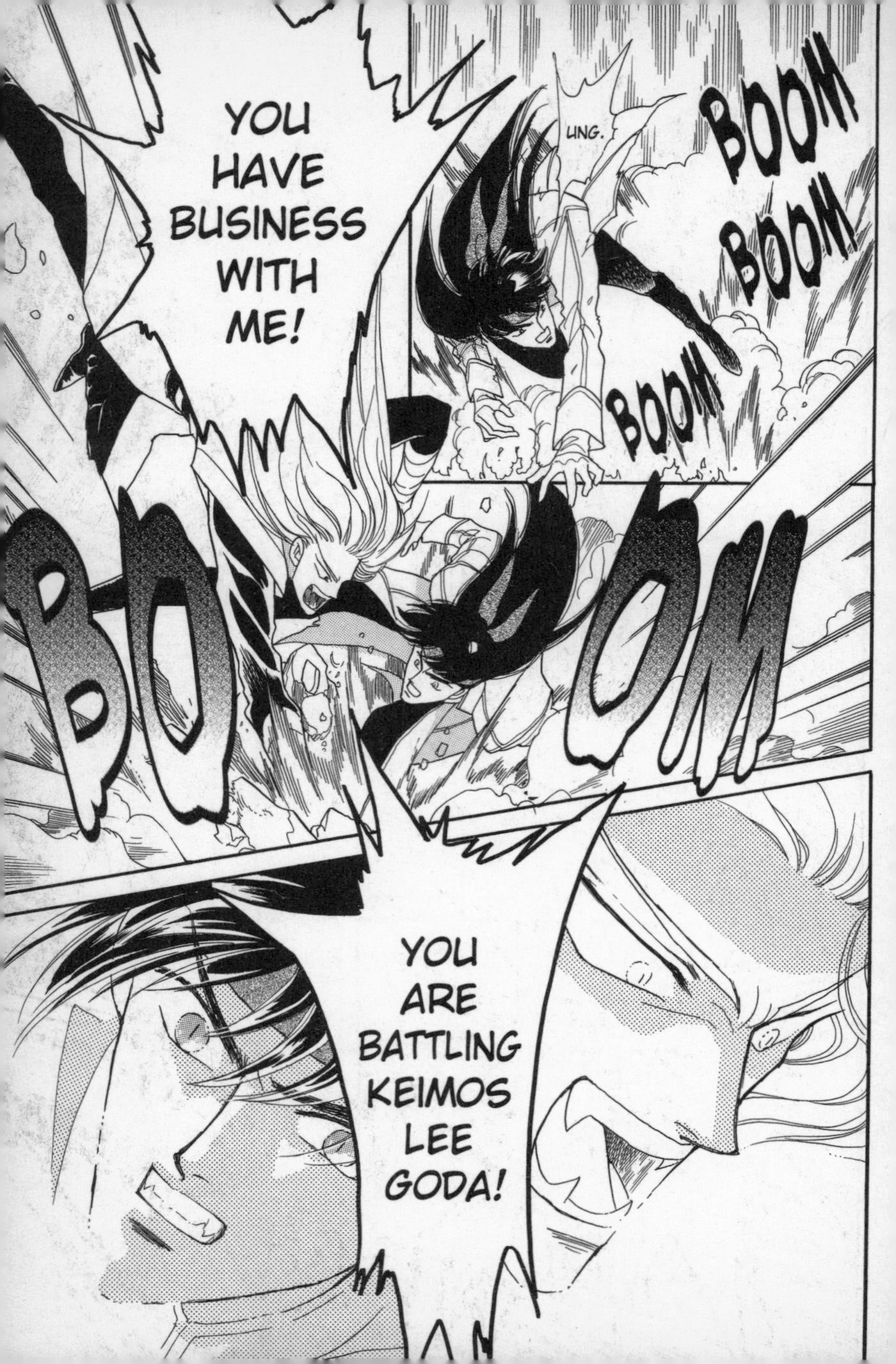
UNG.
BOOM
BOOM
BOOM
YOU HAVE BUSINESS WITH ME!
BOOM
YOU ARE BATTLING KEIMOS LEE GODA!

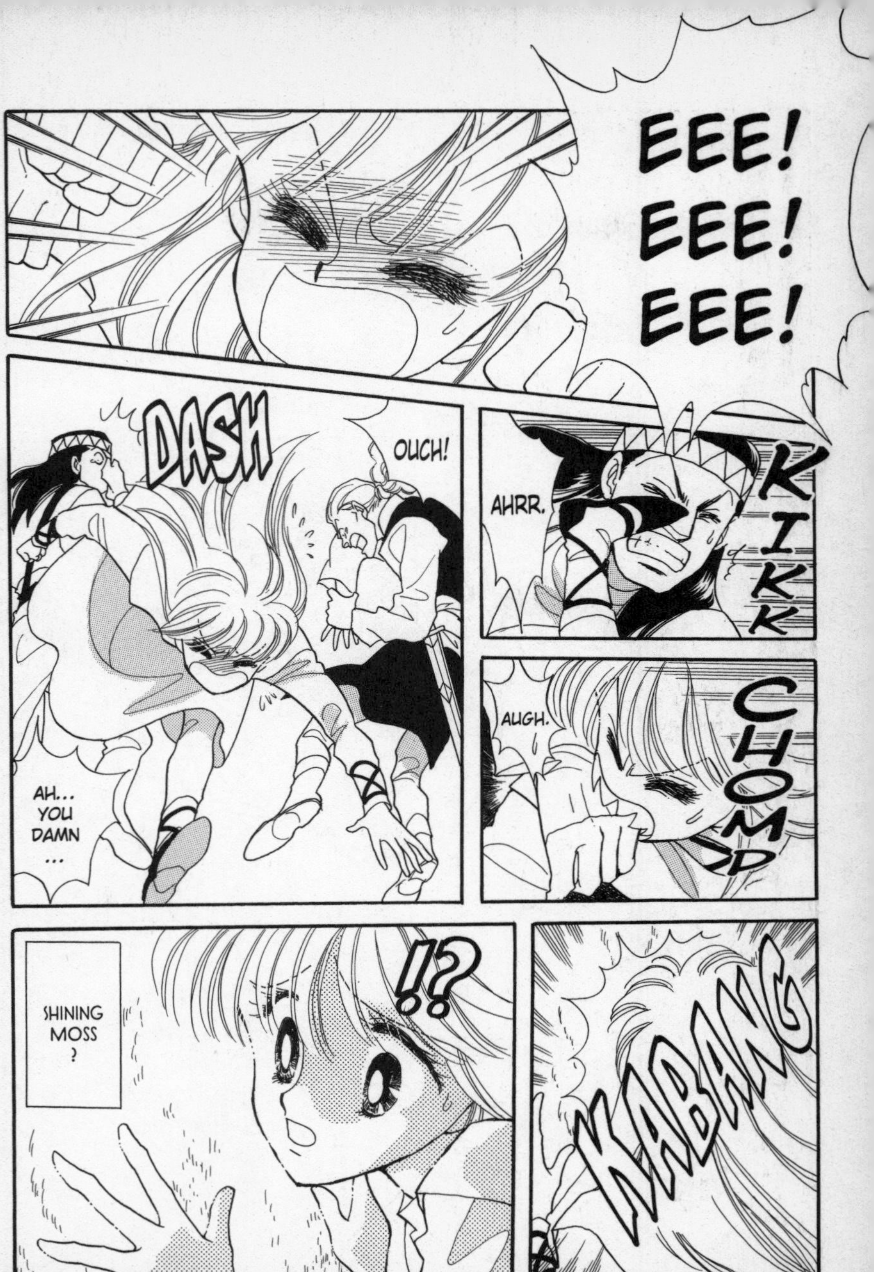
EEE!
EEE!
EEE!
AHRR.
KIKK
AUGH.
CHOMP
OUCH!
DASH
AH... YOU DAMN ...
KABANG
!?
SHINING MOSS ?

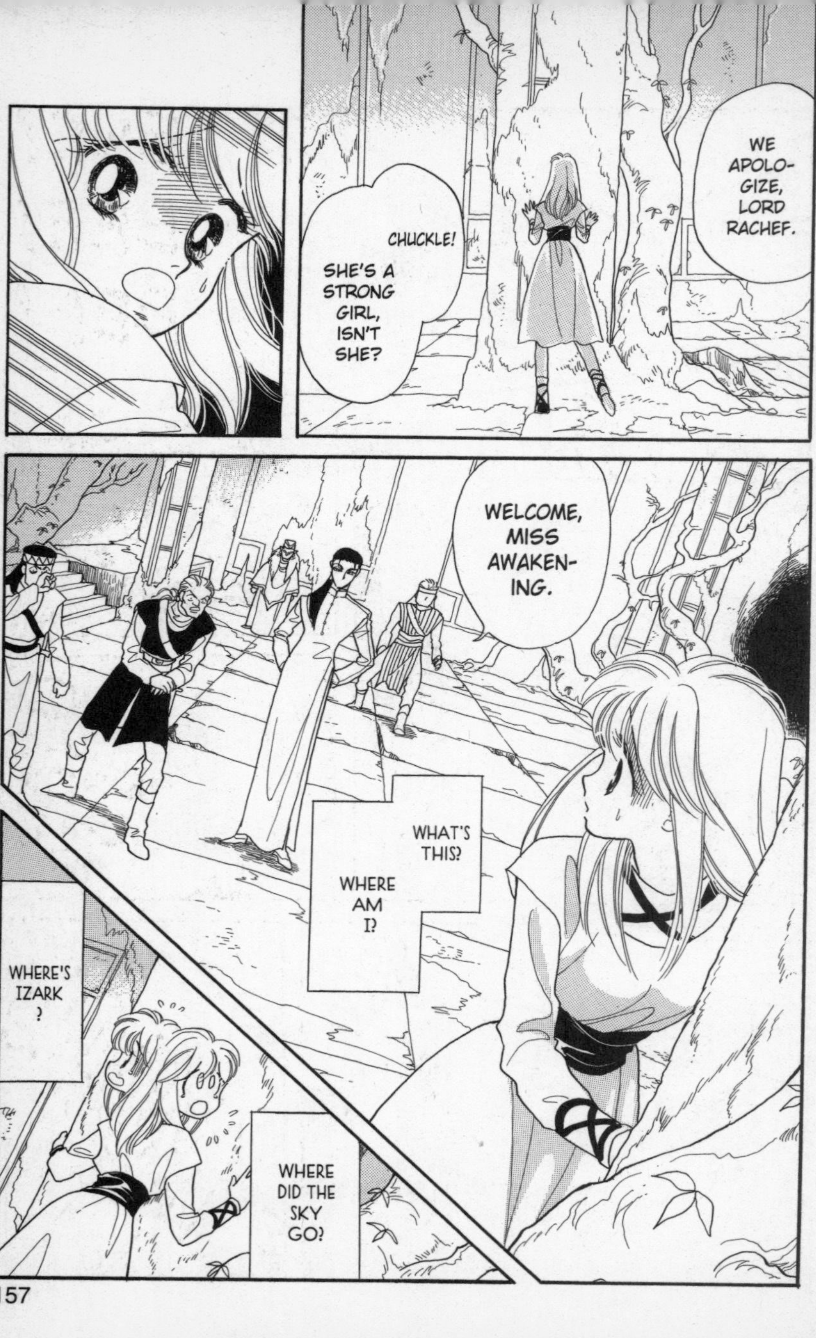
WE APOLOGIZE, LORD RACHEF.
CHUCKLE! SHE'S A STRONG GIRL, ISN'T SHE?
WELCOME, MISS AWAKENING.
WHAT'S THIS? WHERE AM I?
WHERE'S IZARK ?
WHERE DID THE SKY GO?

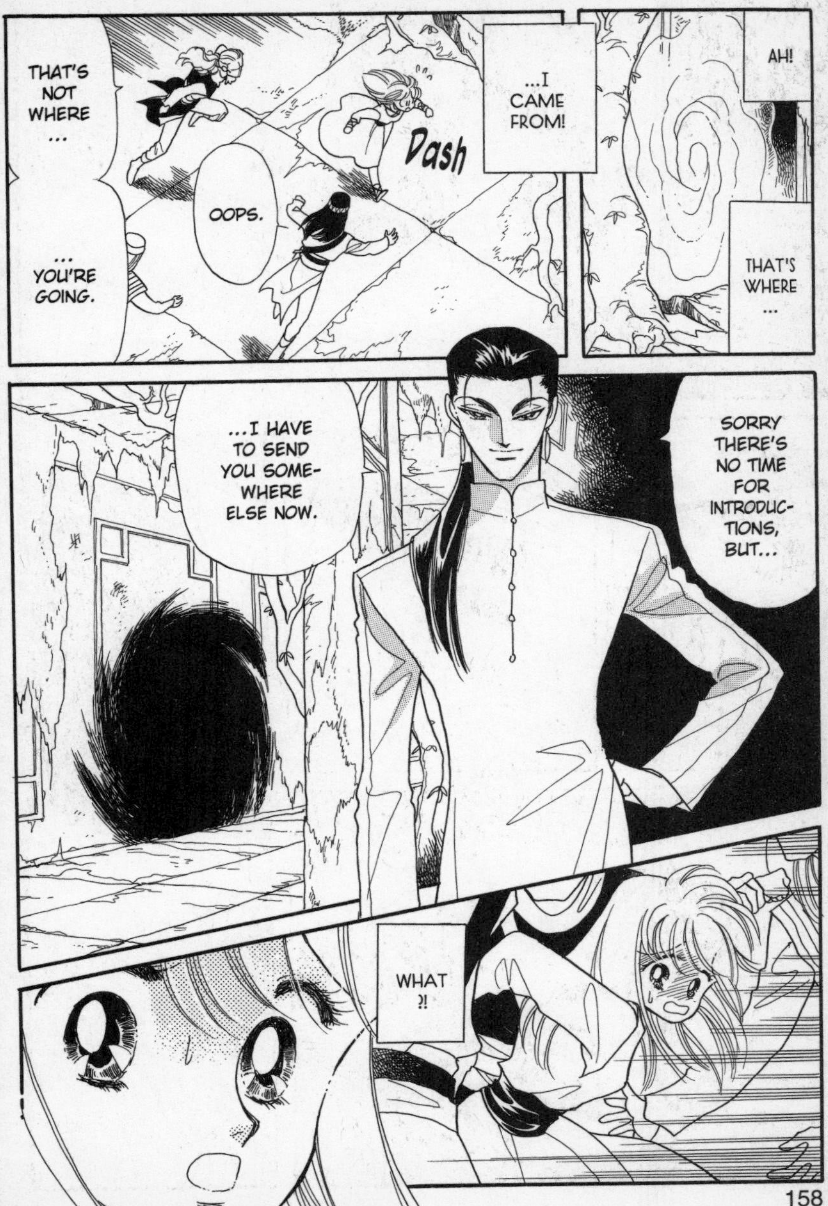
AH!
THAT'S WHERE ...
...I CAME FROM!
Dash
OOPS.
THAT'S NOT WHERE ...
... YOU'RE GOING.
SORRY THERE'S NO TIME FOR INTRODUCTIONS, BUT...
...I HAVE TO SEND YOU SOMEWHERE ELSE NOW.
WHAT ?!

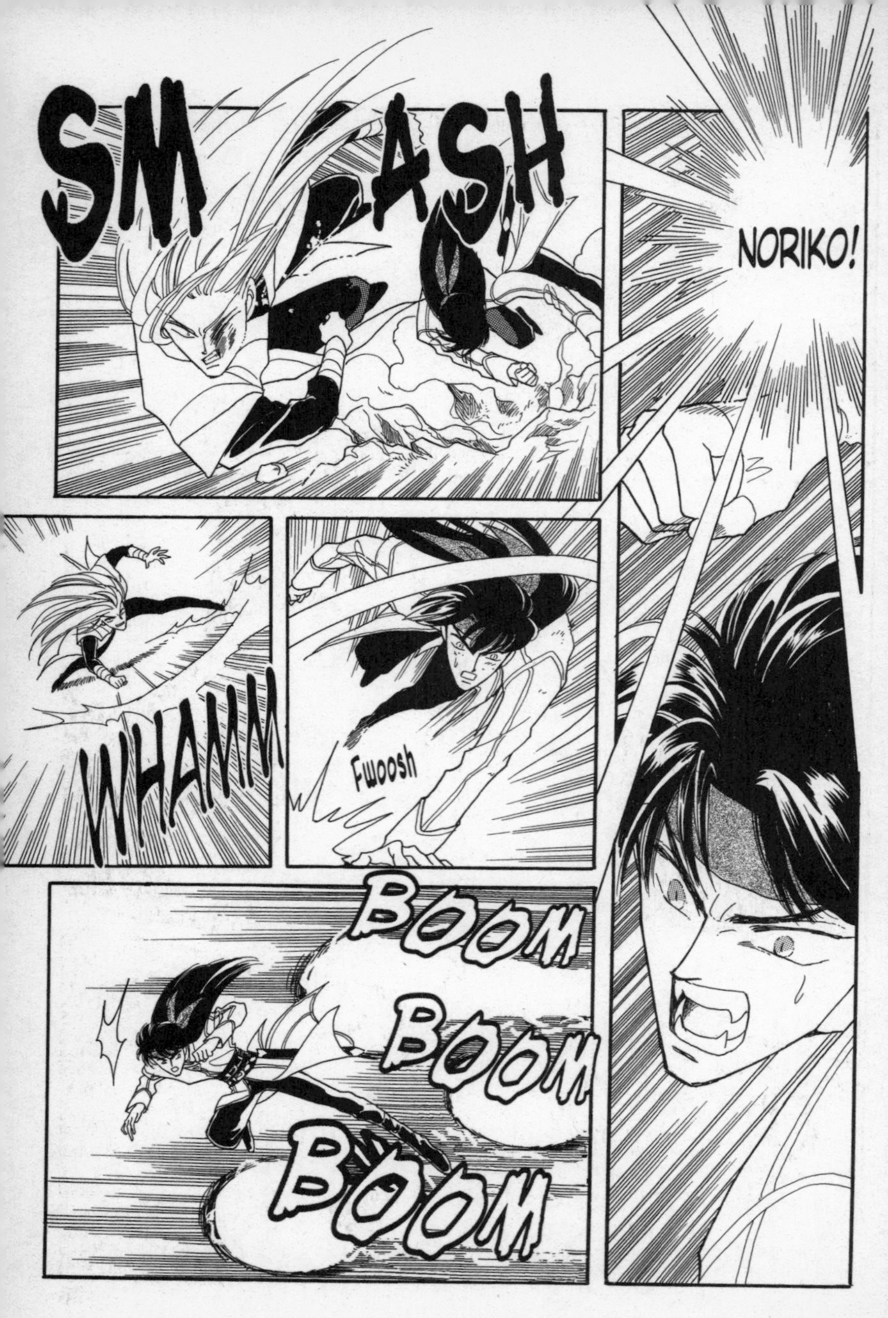
NORIKO!
SMASH
Fwoosh
WHAMM
BOOM
BOOM
BOOM

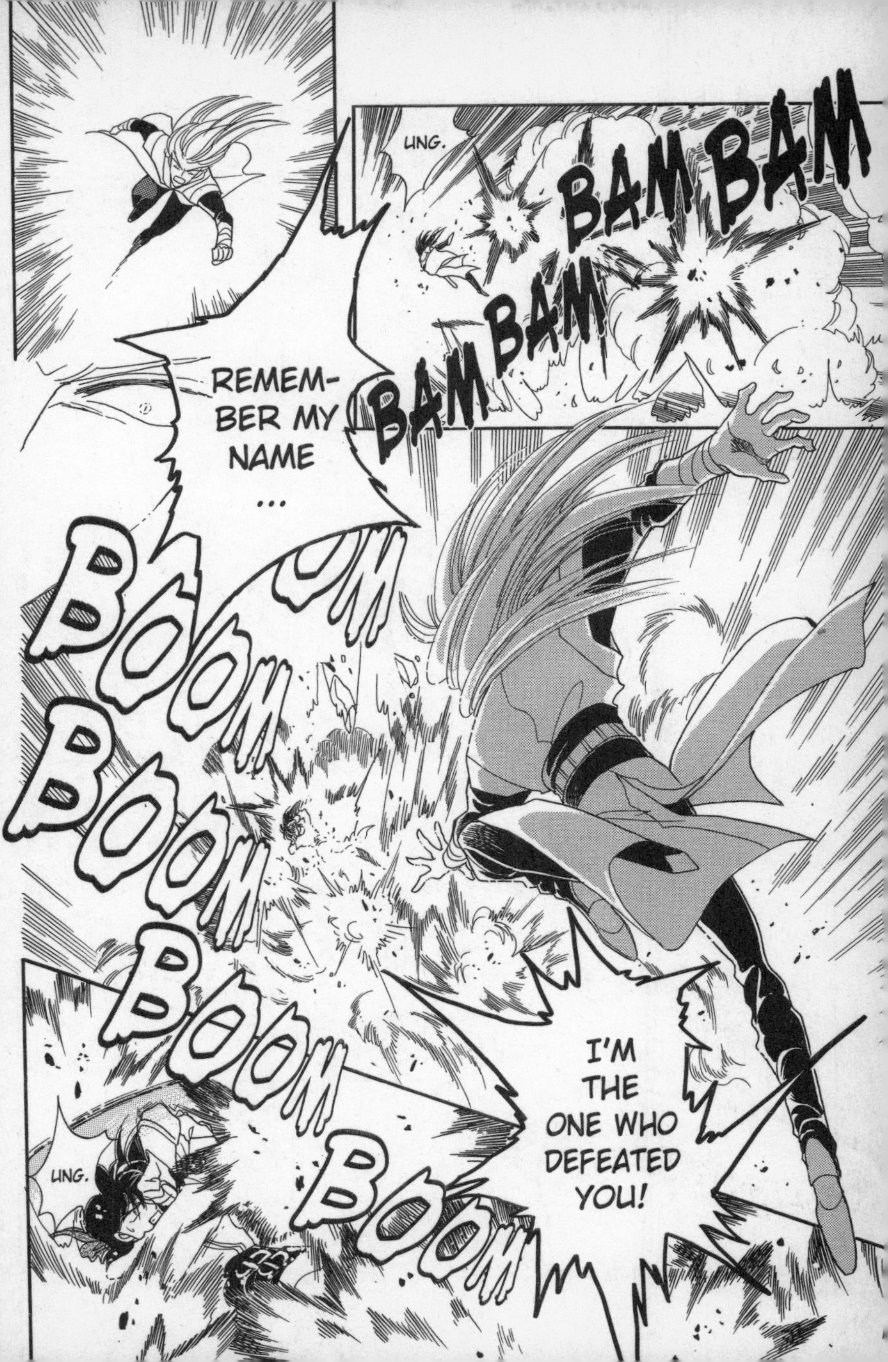
UNG.
BAM BAM BAM BAM
REMEMBER MY NAME ...
I'M THE ONE WHO DEFEATED YOU!
BOOM BOOM BOOM BOOM
UNG.

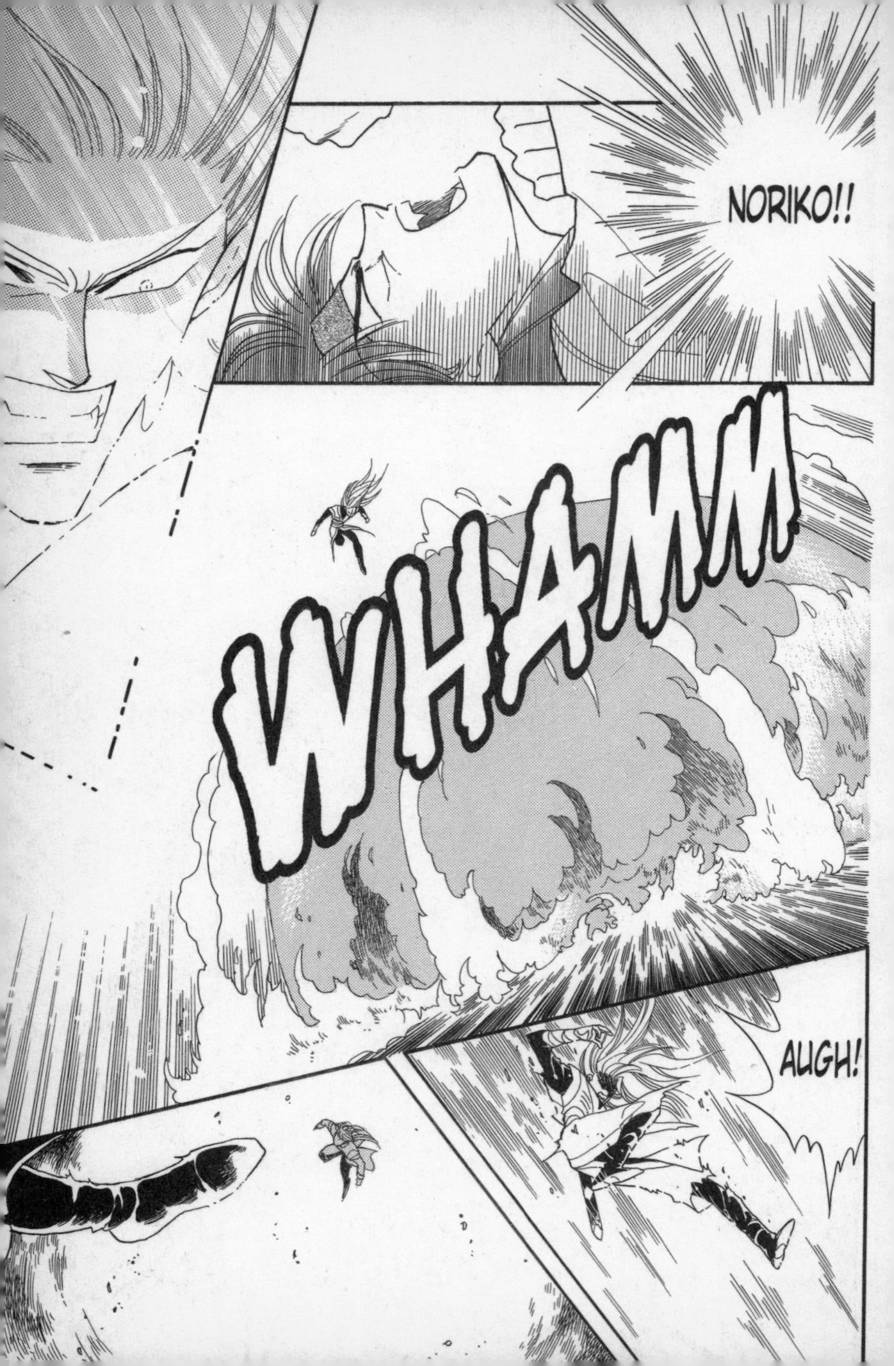
NORIKO!!
WHAMM
AUGH!

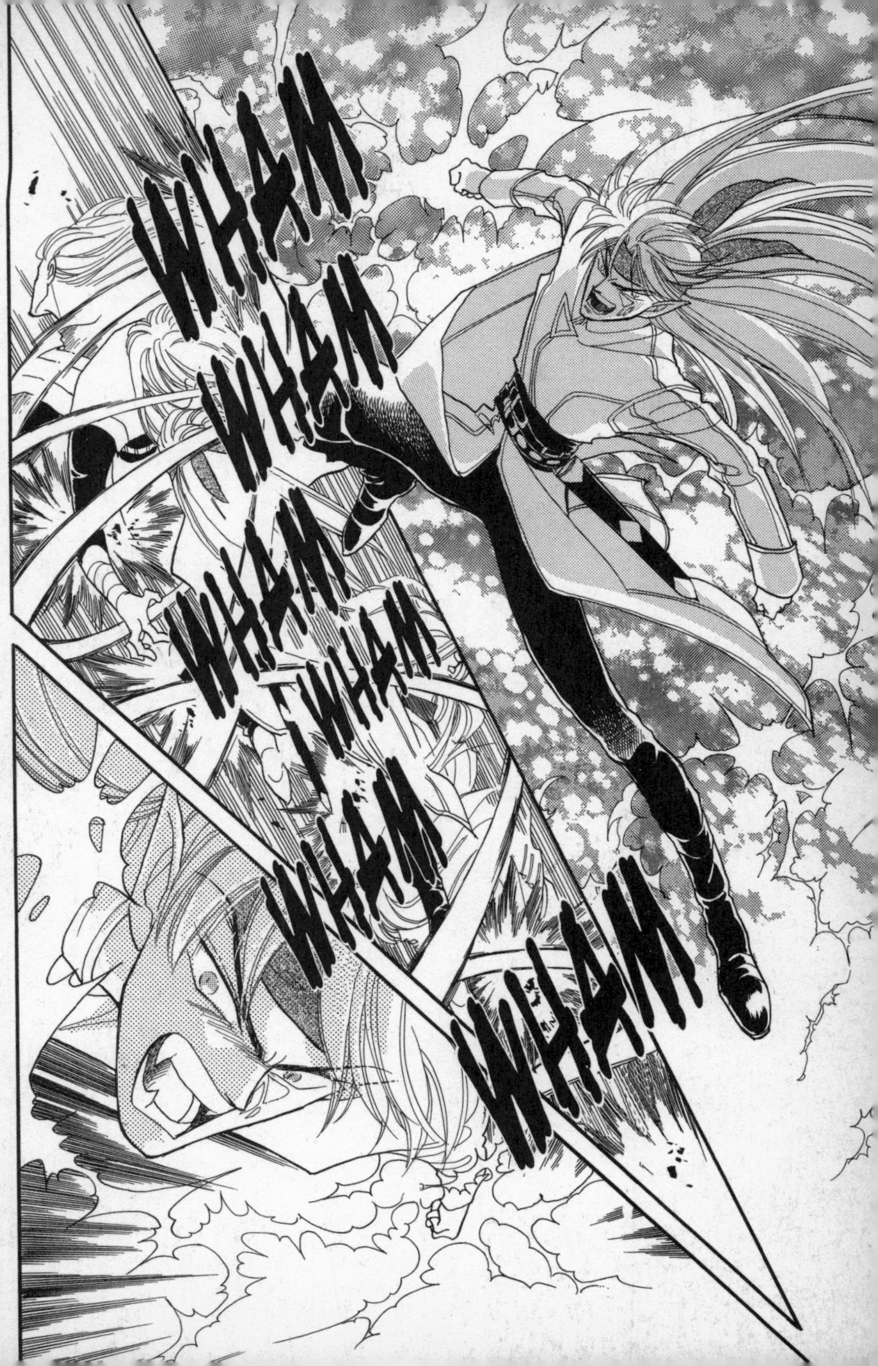
WHAM
WHAM
WHAM
WHAM
WHAM
WHAM

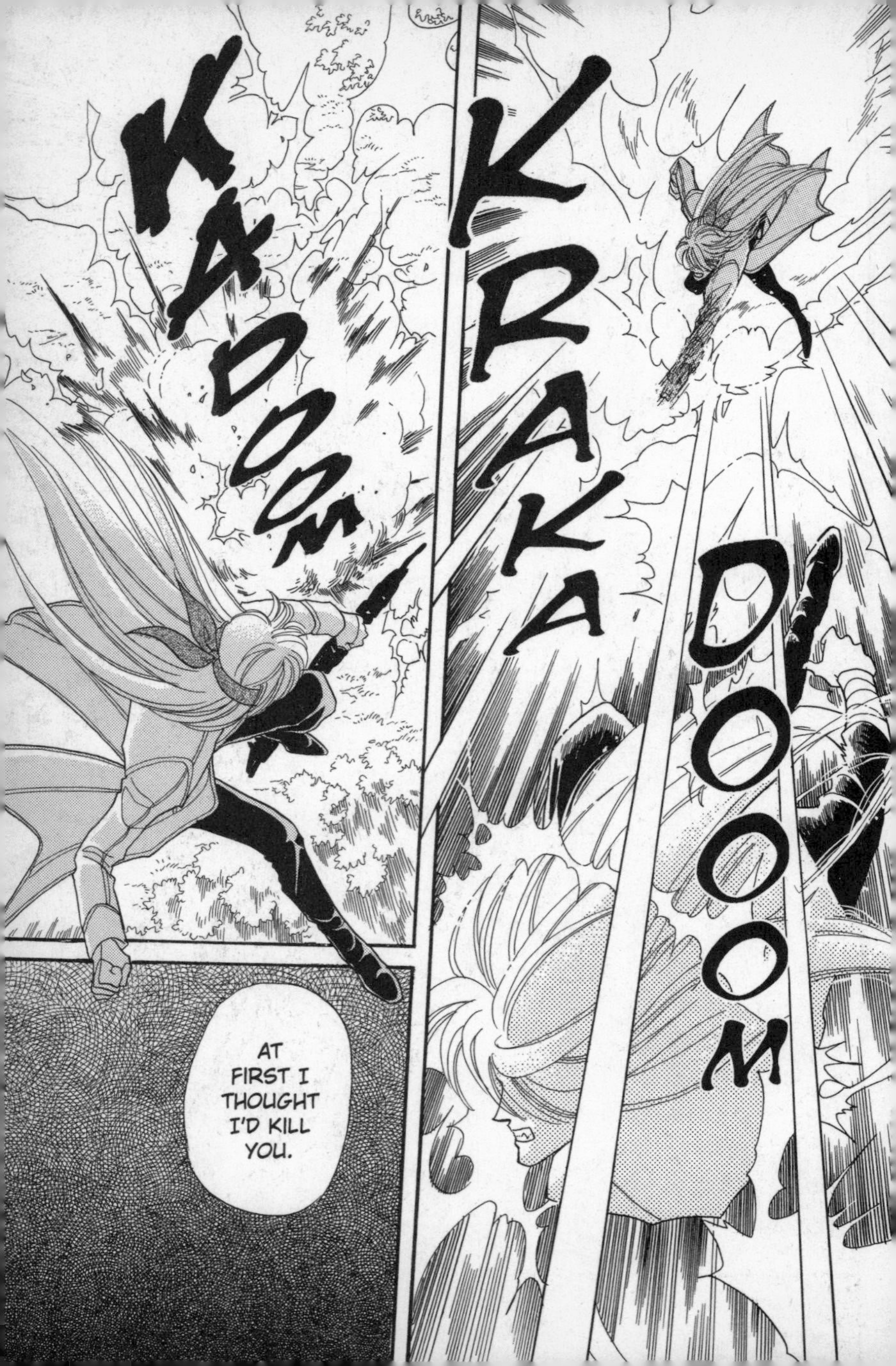
KRAKA
DOOOM
KADOOM!
AT FIRST I THOUGHT I'D KILL YOU.

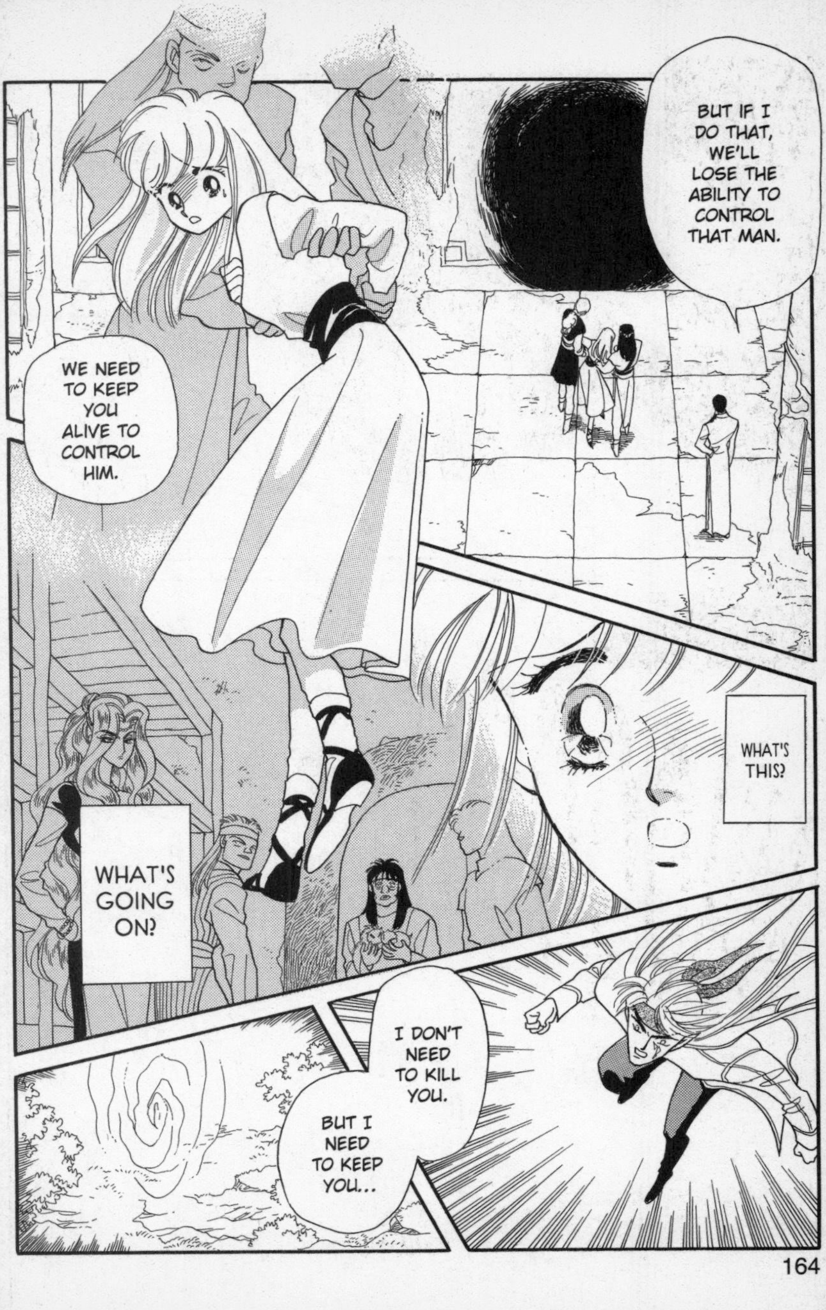
BUT IF I DO THAT, WE'LL LOSE THE ABILITY TO CONTROL THAT MAN.
WHAT'S THIS?
WE NEED TO KEEP YOU ALIVE TO CONTROL HIM.
WHAT'S GOING ON?
I DON'T NEED TO KILL YOU.
BUT I NEED TO KEEP YOU...

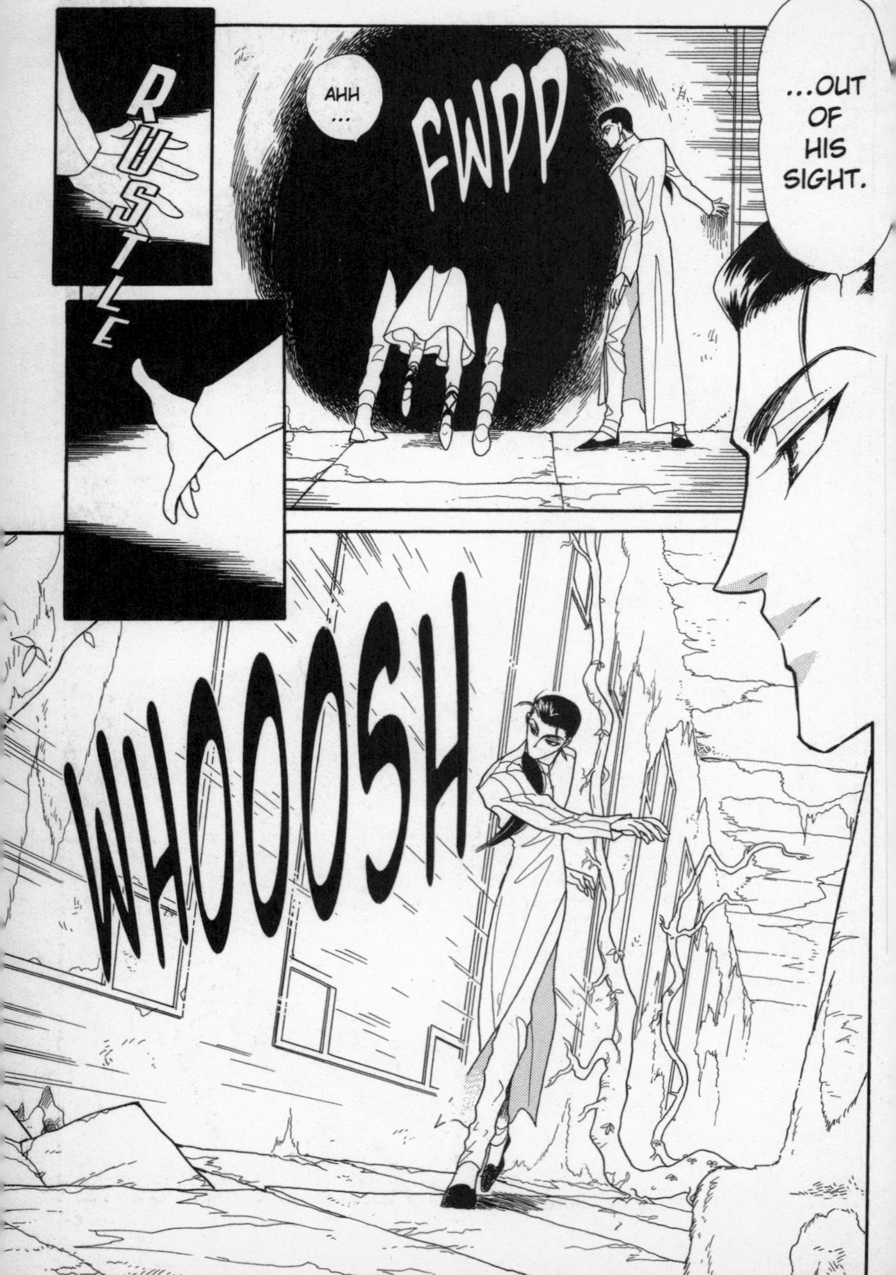
...OUT OF HIS SIGHT.
AHH ...
FWPP
RUSTLE
WHOOOSH

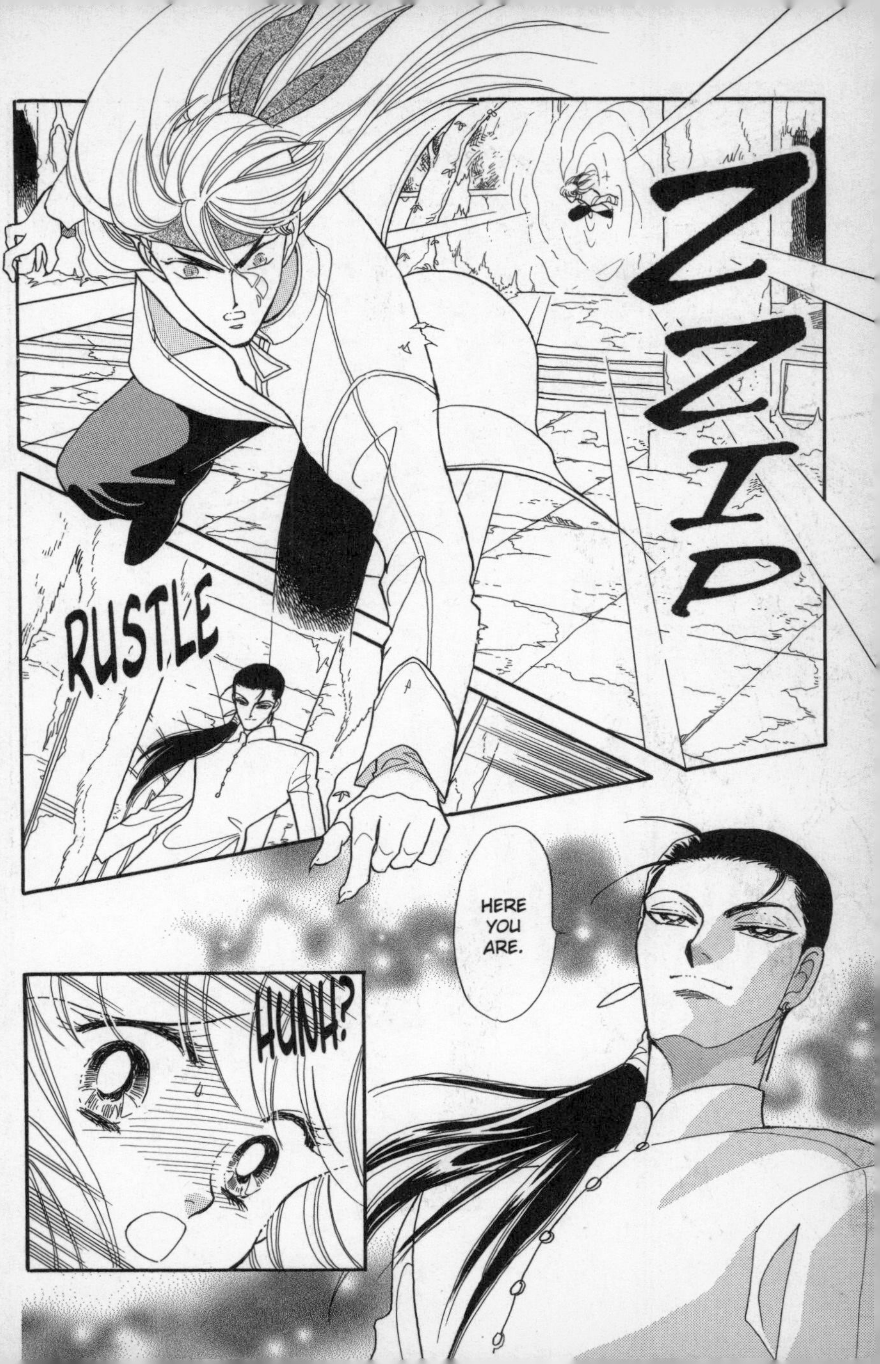
ZZIP
RUSTLE
HERE YOU ARE.
HUNH?

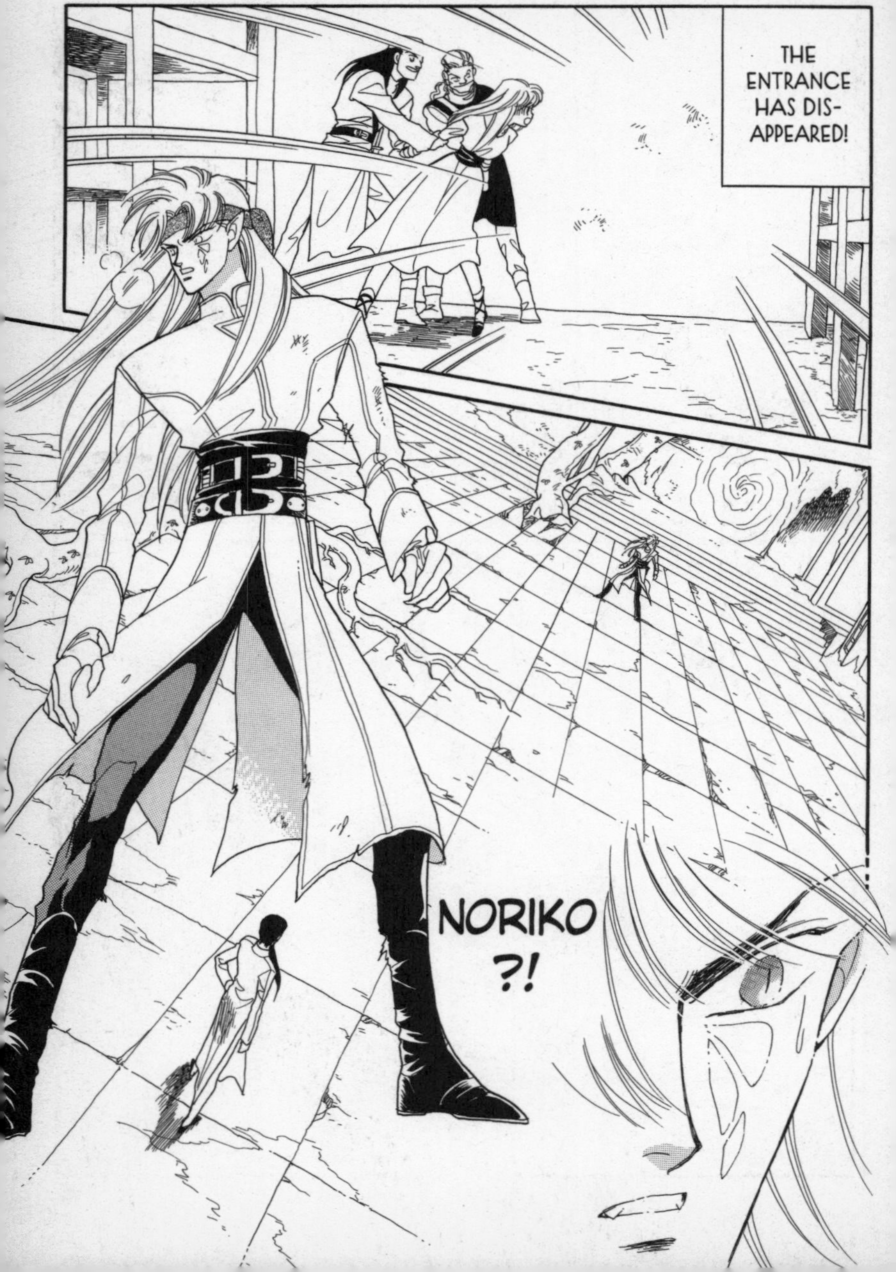
THE ENTRANCE HAS DIS-APPEARED!
NORIKO ?!

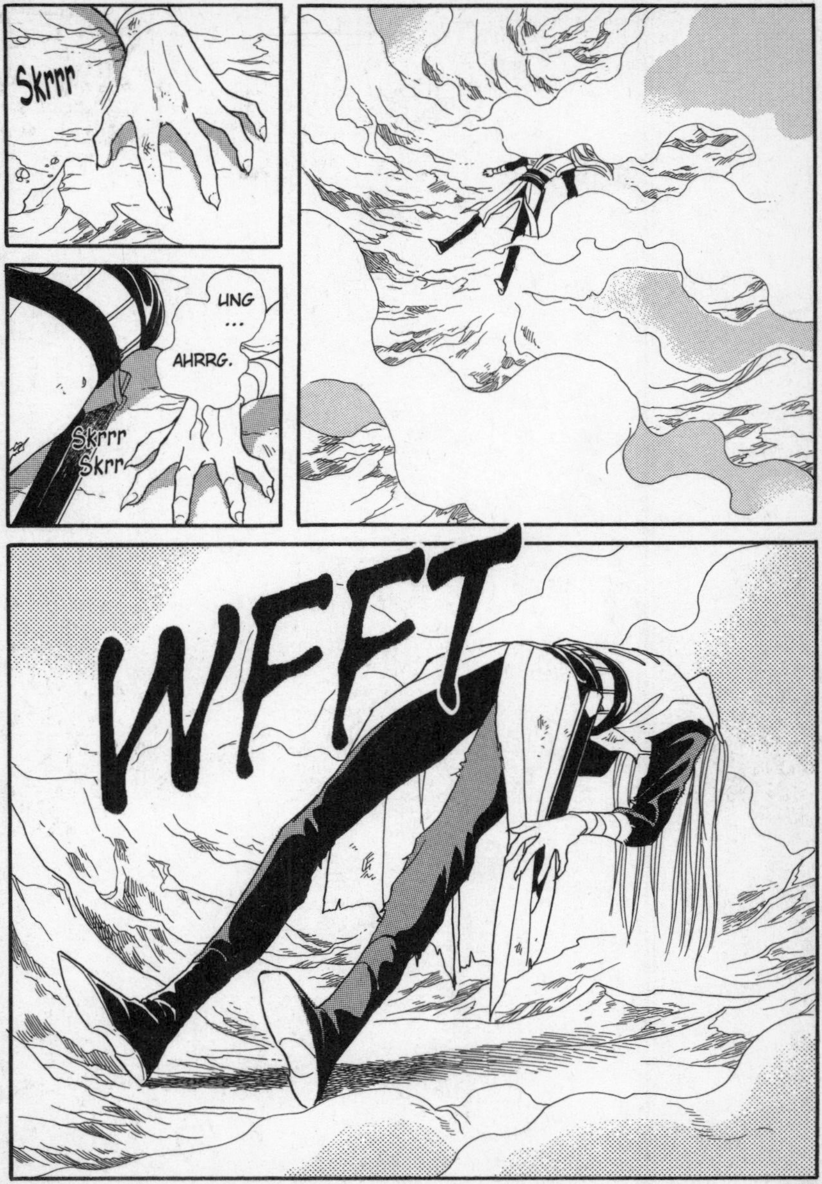
Skrrr
UNG ... AHRRG.
Skrrr
Skrr
WFFT

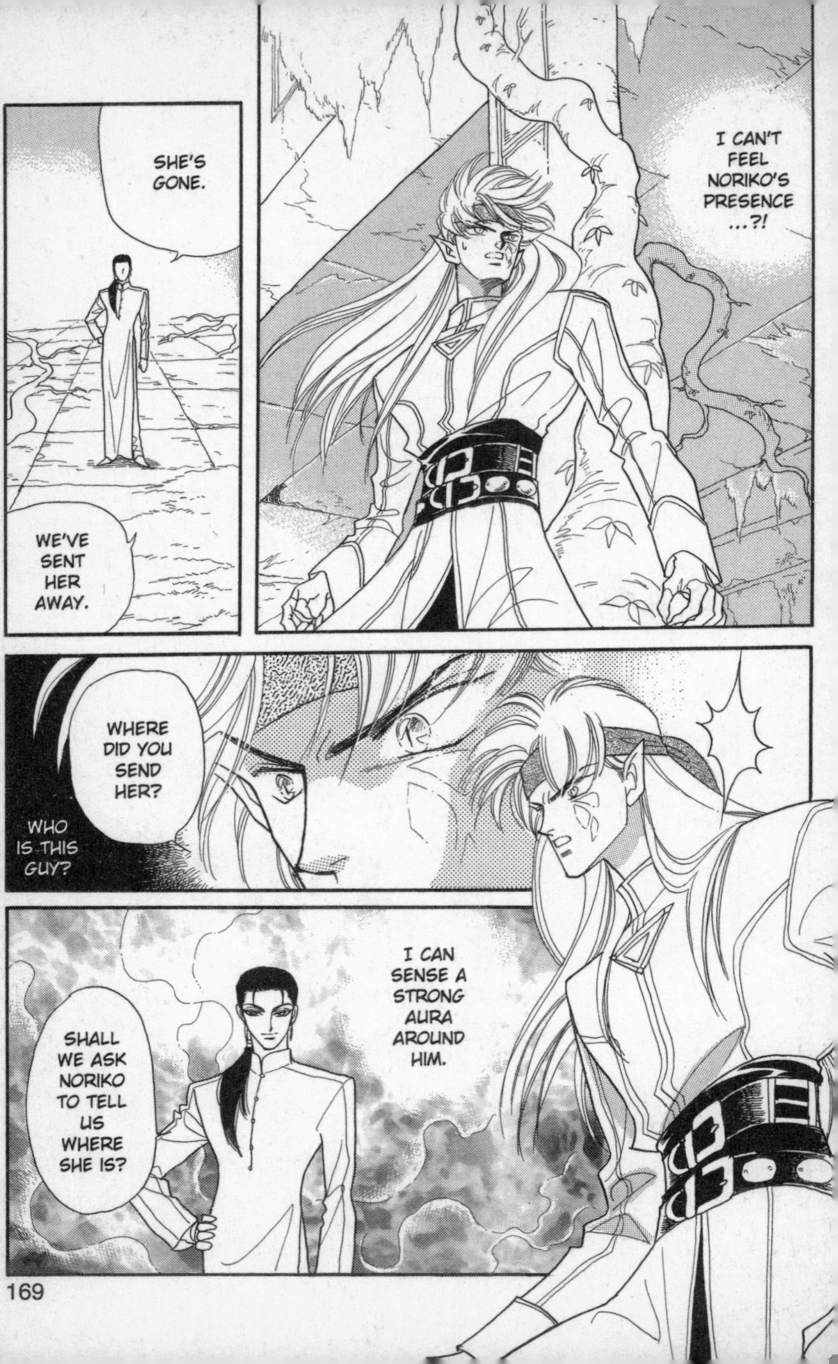
I CAN'T FEEL NORIKO'S PRESENCE ...?!
SHE'S GONE.
WE'VE SENT HER AWAY.
WHERE DID YOU SEND HER?
WHO IS THIS GUY?
I CAN SENSE A STRONG AURA AROUND HIM.
SHALL WE ASK NORIKO TO TELL US WHERE SHE IS?

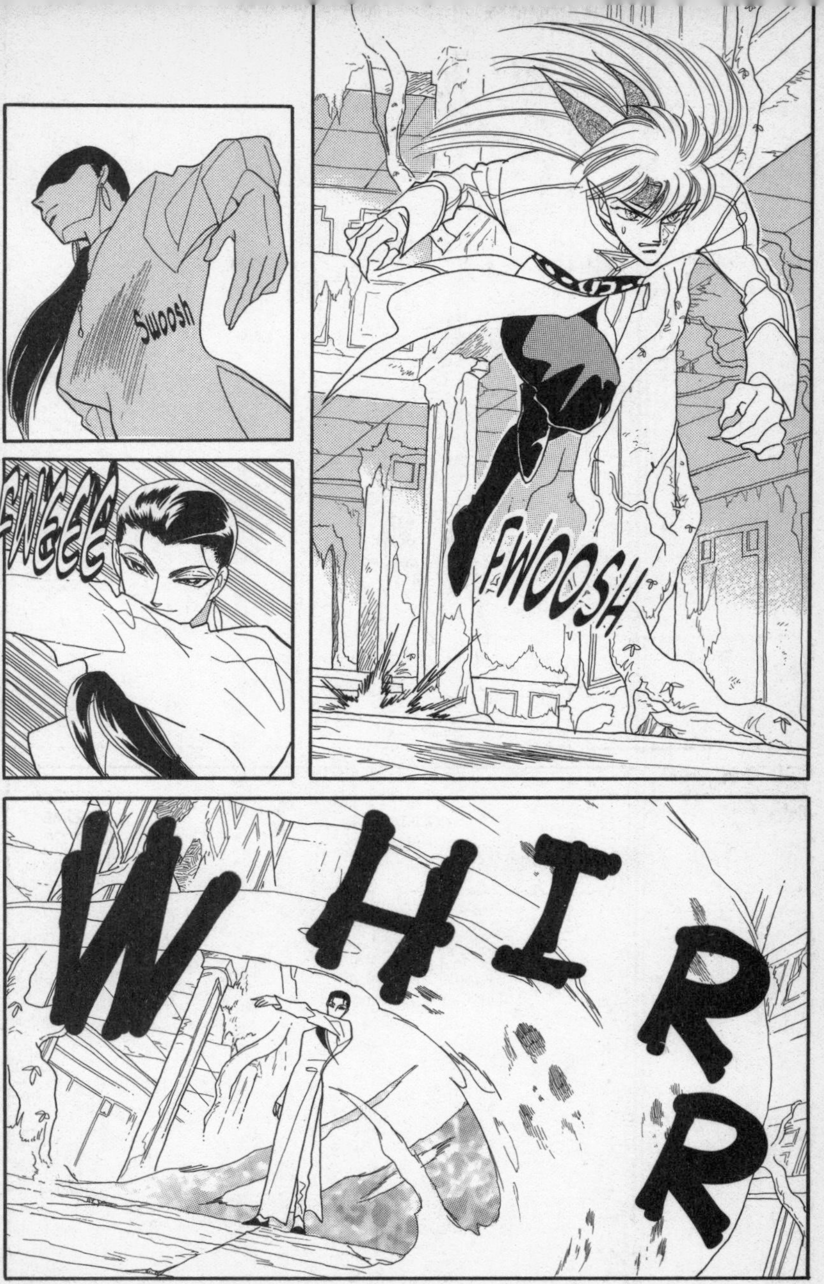
FWOOSH
Swoosh
FWEEE
WHIRR

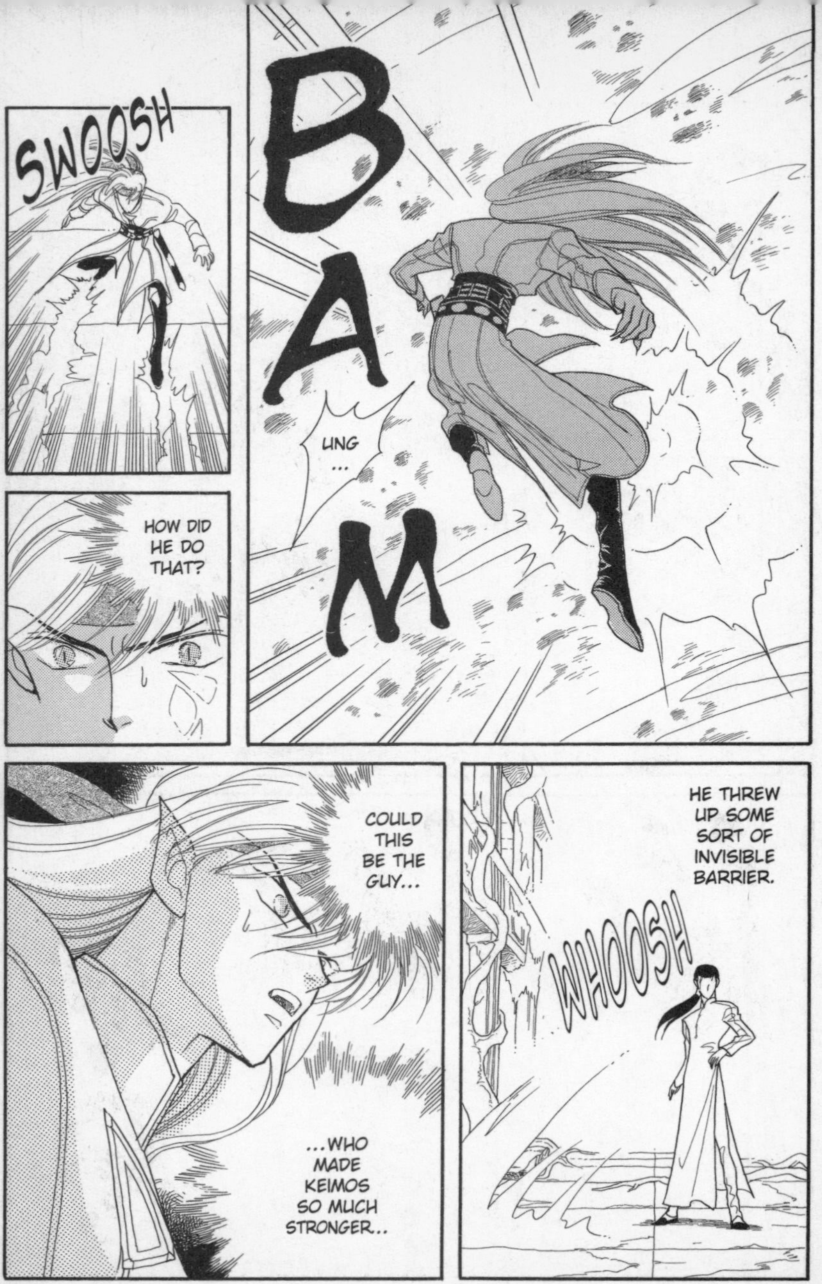

BAM
UNG...
SWOOSH
HOW DID HE DO THAT?
HE THREW UP SOME SORT OF INVISIBLE BARRIER.
WHOOSH
COULD THIS BE THE GUY...
...WHO MADE KEIMOS SO MUCH STRONGER...

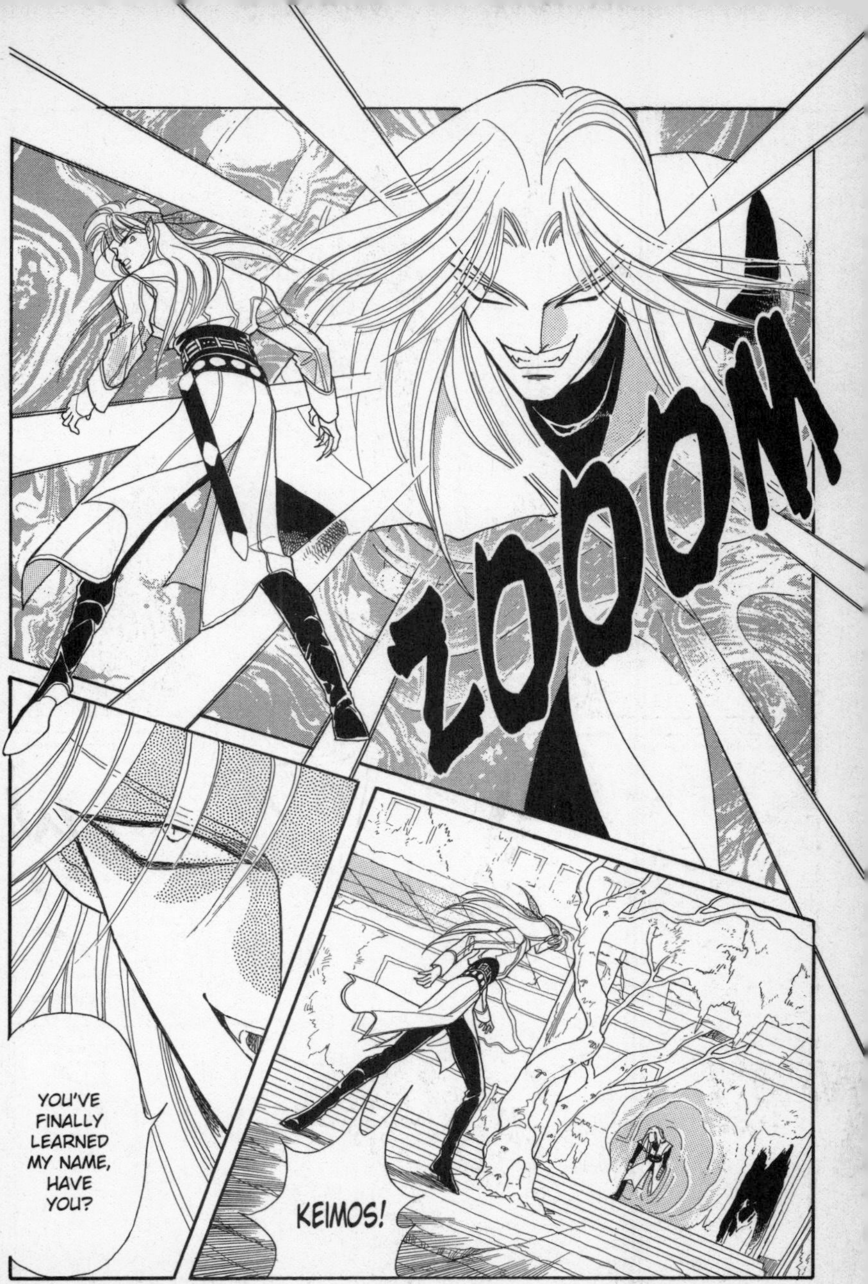
ZOOOOM
KEIMOS!
YOU'VE FINALLY LEARNED MY NAME, HAVE YOU?

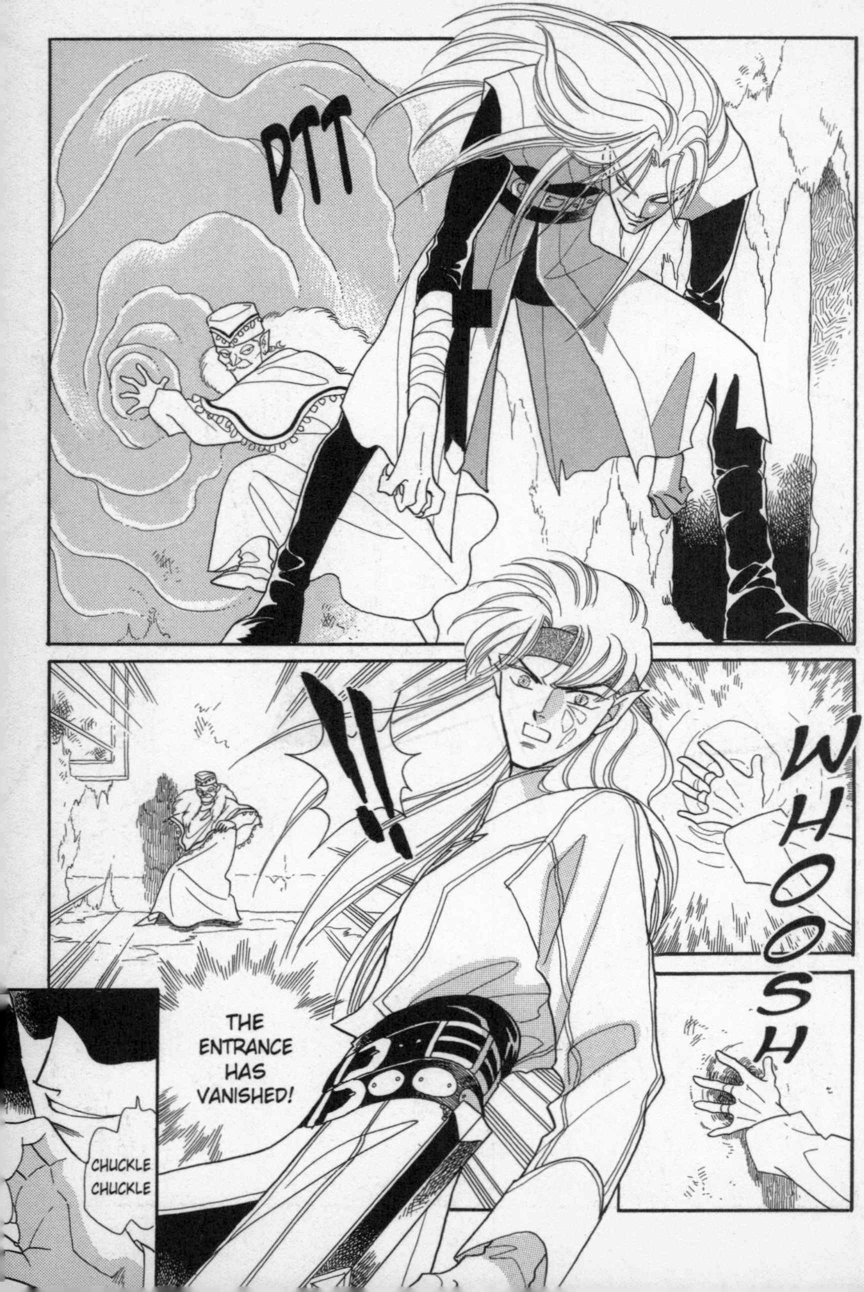
DTT
WHOOSH
!!
THE ENTRANCE HAS VANISHED!
CHUCKLE CHUCKLE

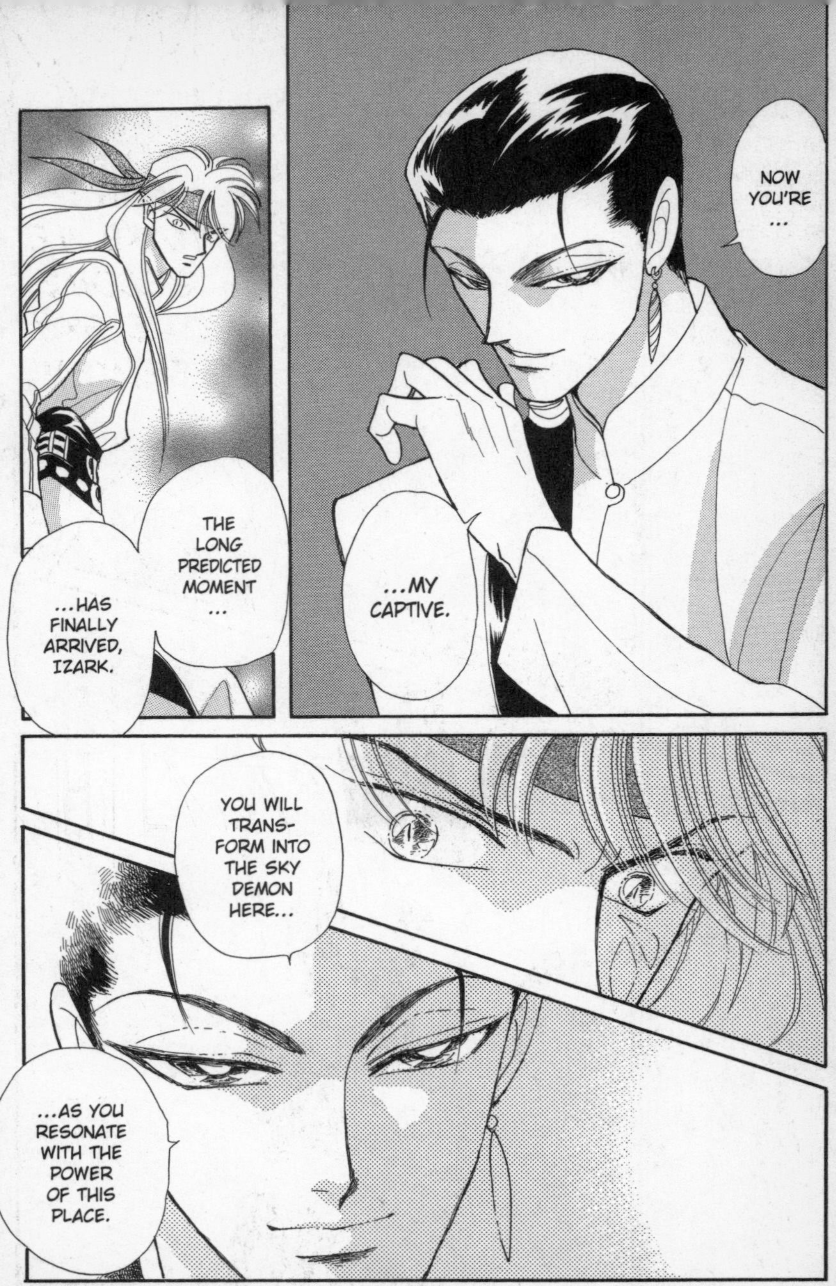
NOW YOU'RE ...
...MY CAPTIVE.
THE LONG PREDICTED MOMENT ...
...HAS FINALLY ARRIVED, IZARK.
YOU WILL TRANS-FORM INTO THE SKY DEMON HERE...
...AS YOU RESONATE WITH THE POWER OF THIS PLACE.

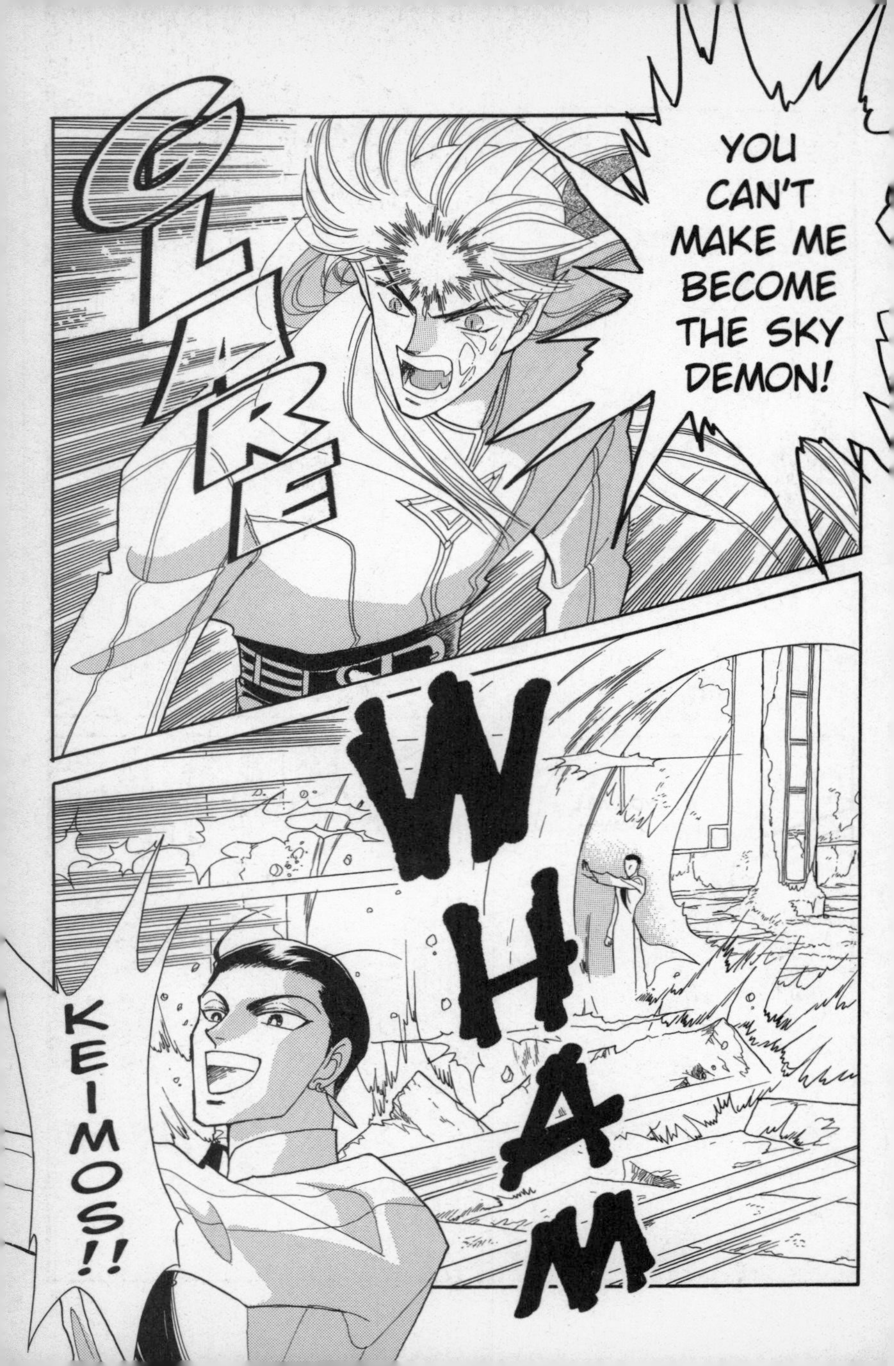
YOU CAN'T MAKE ME BECOME THE SKY DEMON!
CLARE
WHAM
KEIMOS!!

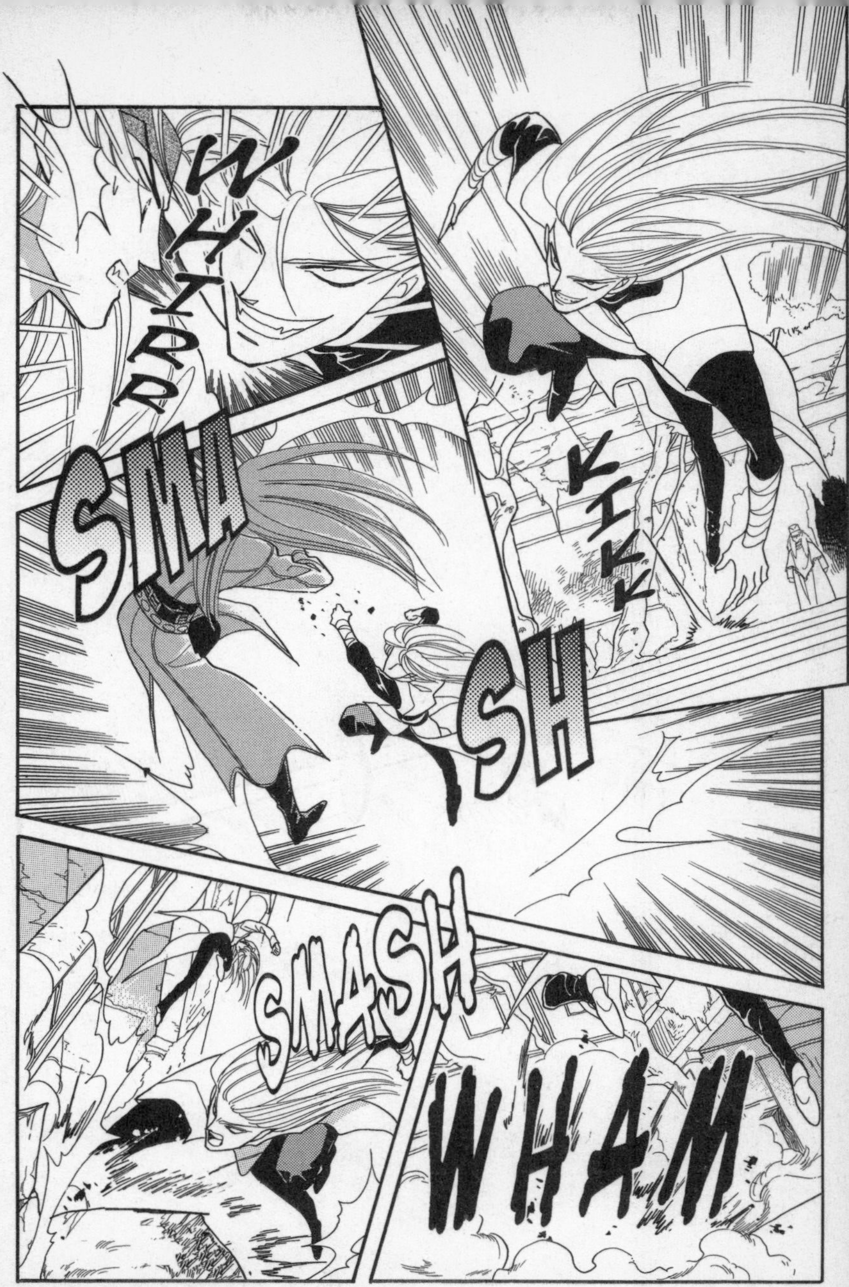
KIKK
WHIRR
SMA
SH
WHAM
SMASH

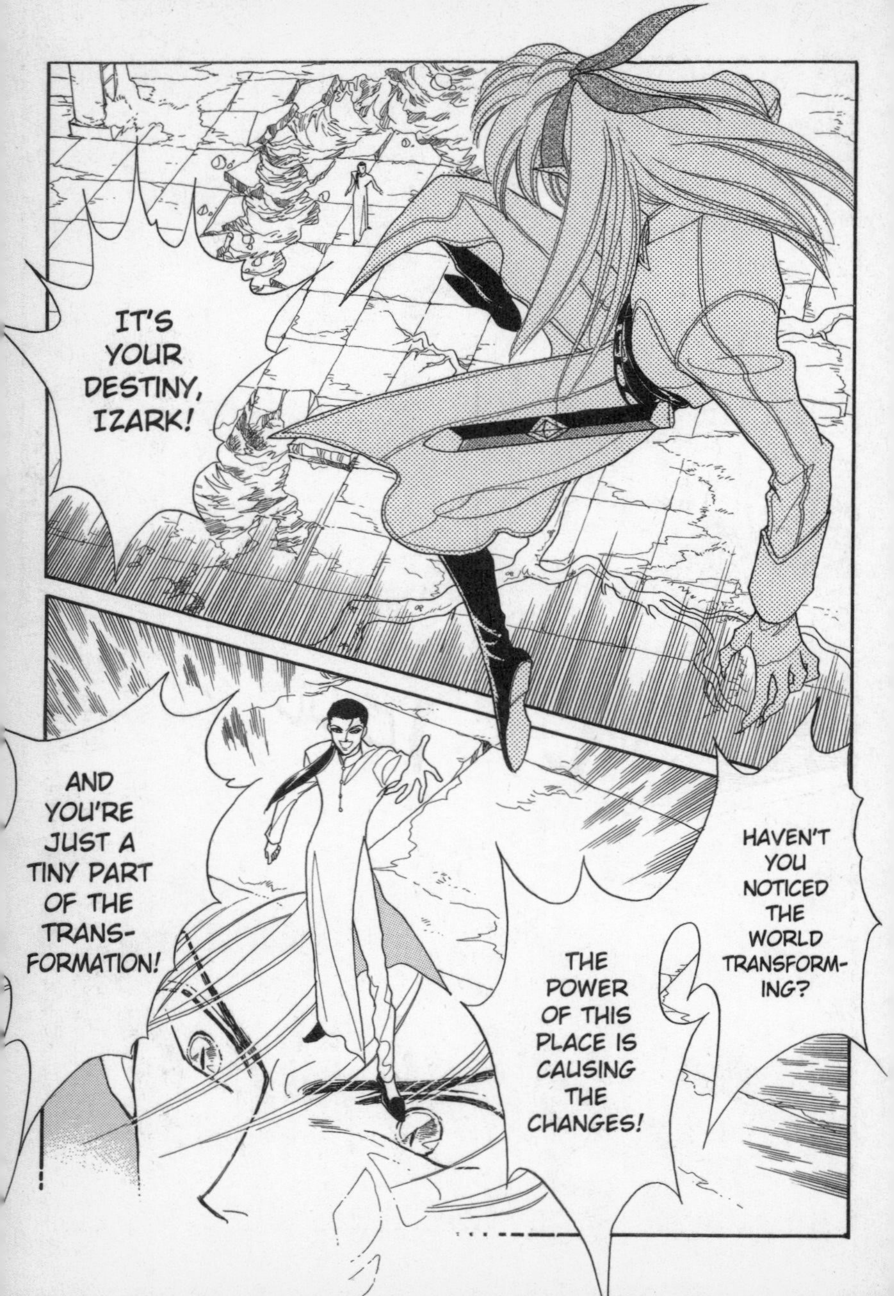
IT'S YOUR DESTINY, IZARK!
HAVEN'T YOU NOTICED THE WORLD TRANSFORMING?
THE POWER OF THIS PLACE IS CAUSING THE CHANGES!
AND YOU'RE JUST A TINY PART OF THE TRANSFORMATION!

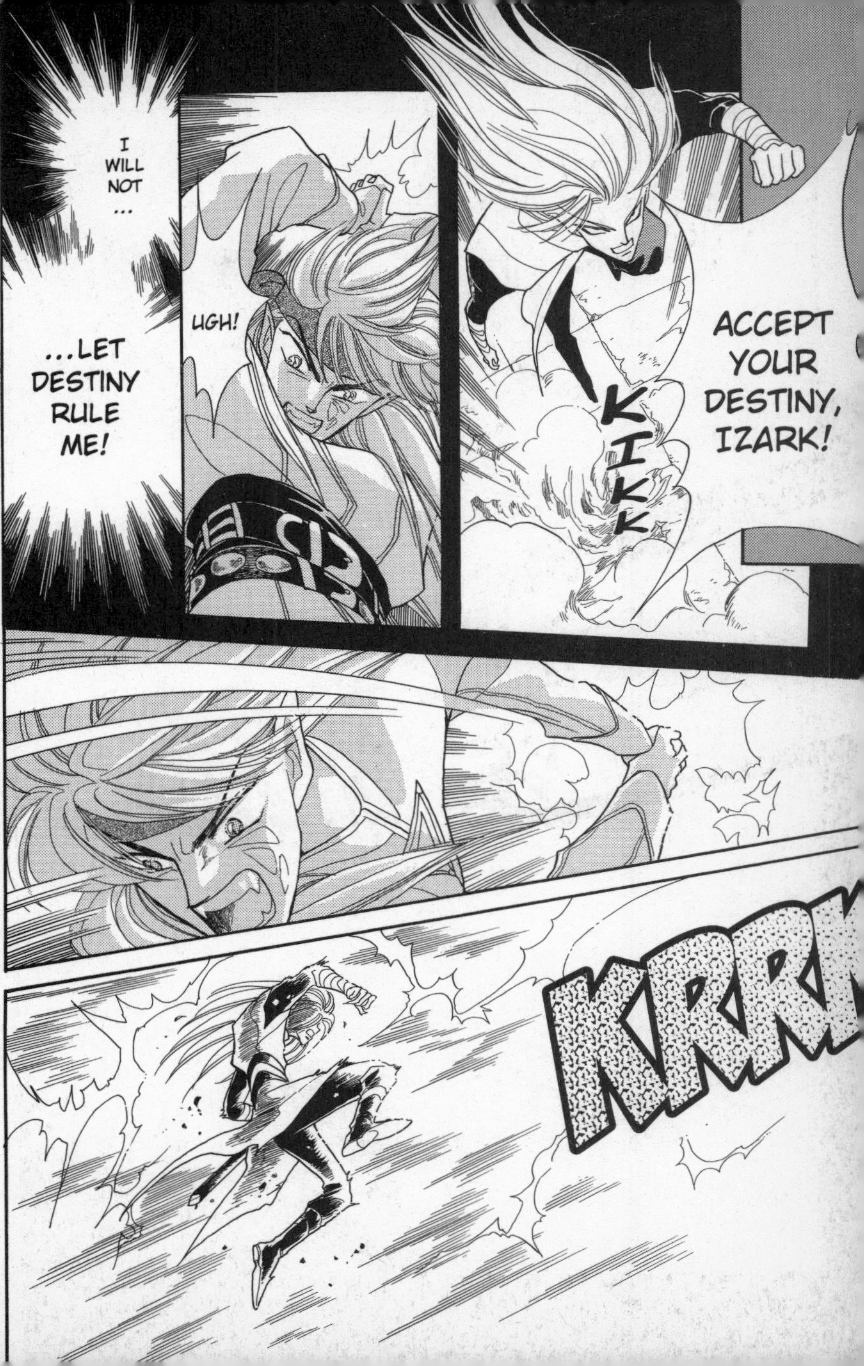
ACCEPT YOUR DESTINY, IZARK!
KIKK
UGH!
I WILL NOT ...
...LET DESTINY RULE ME!
KRRK

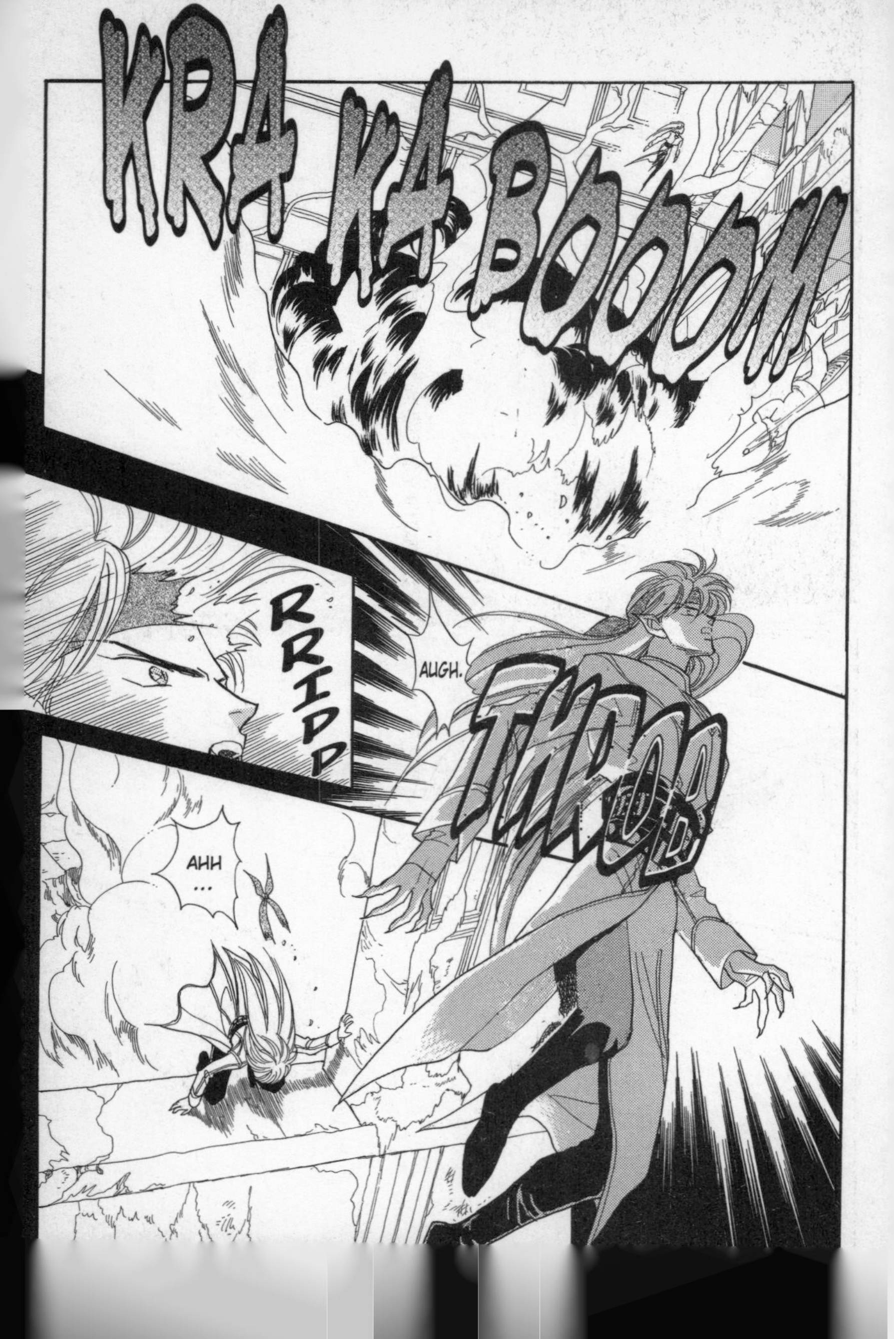
KRA KA BOOOM
AUGH.
THOOB
RRIPP
AHH ...

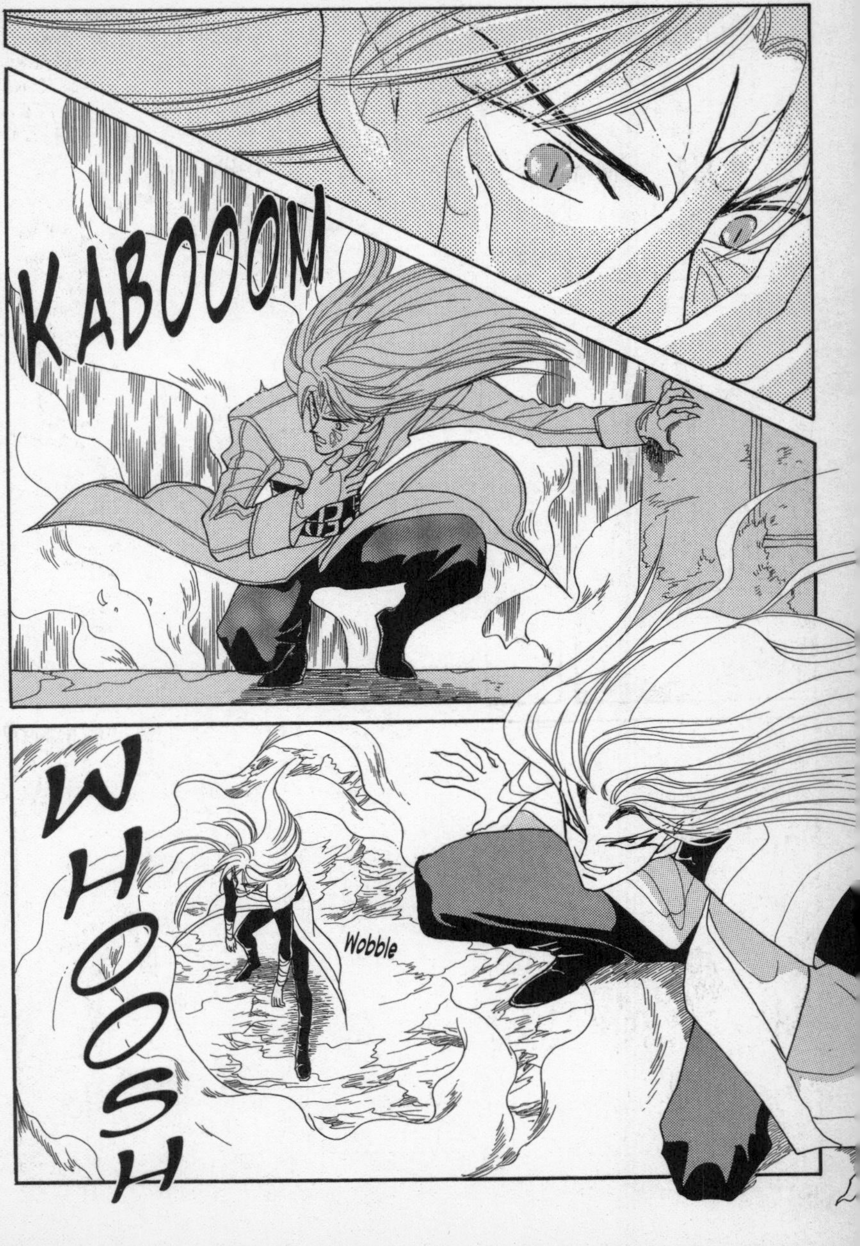
KABOOOM
Wobble
WHOOOSH

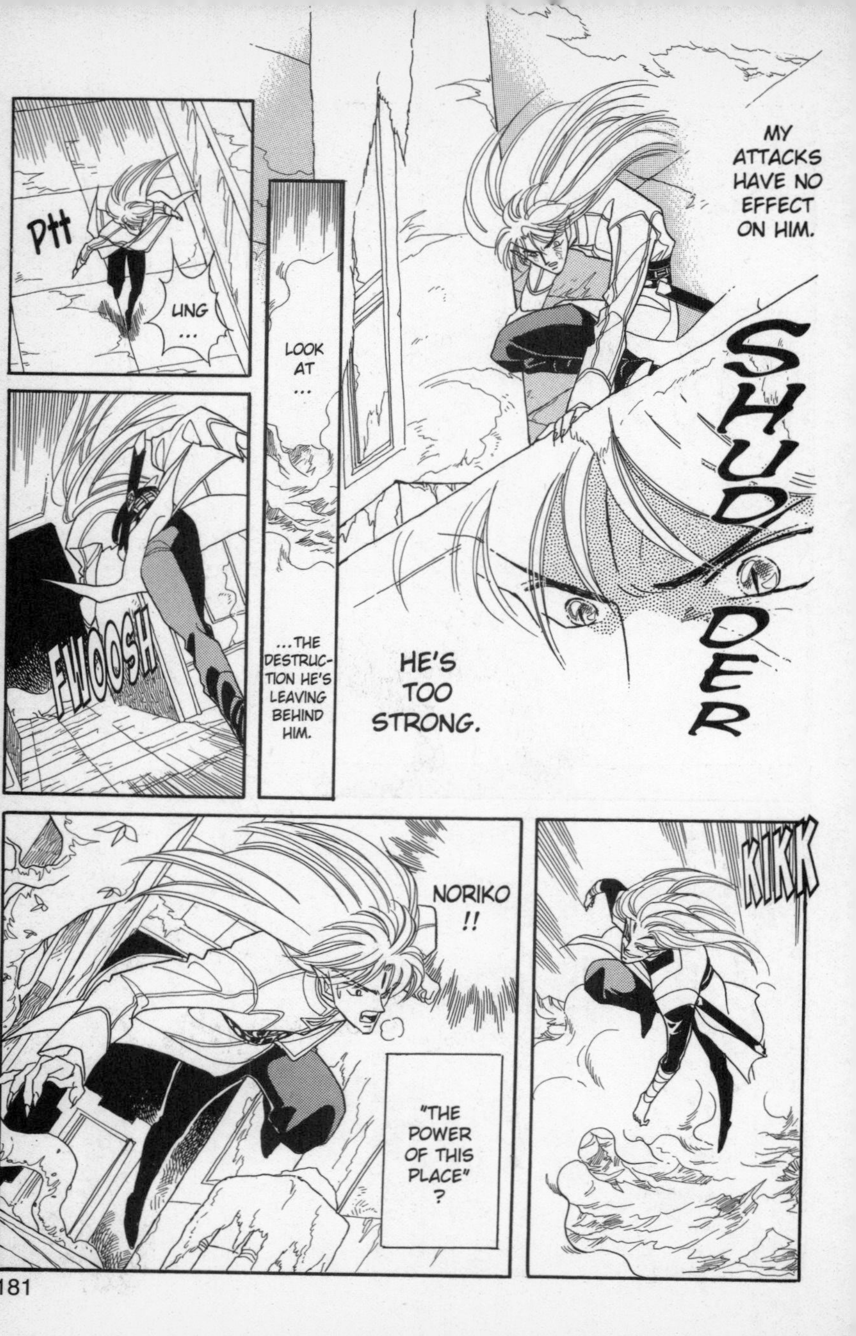
MY ATTACKS HAVE NO EFFECT ON HIM.
SHUDDER
HE'S TOO STRONG.
LOOK AT ...
...THE DESTRUCTION HE'S LEAVING BEHIND HIM.
Ptt
UNG ...
FWOOSH
KIKK
NORIKO !!
"THE POWER OF THIS PLACE" ?

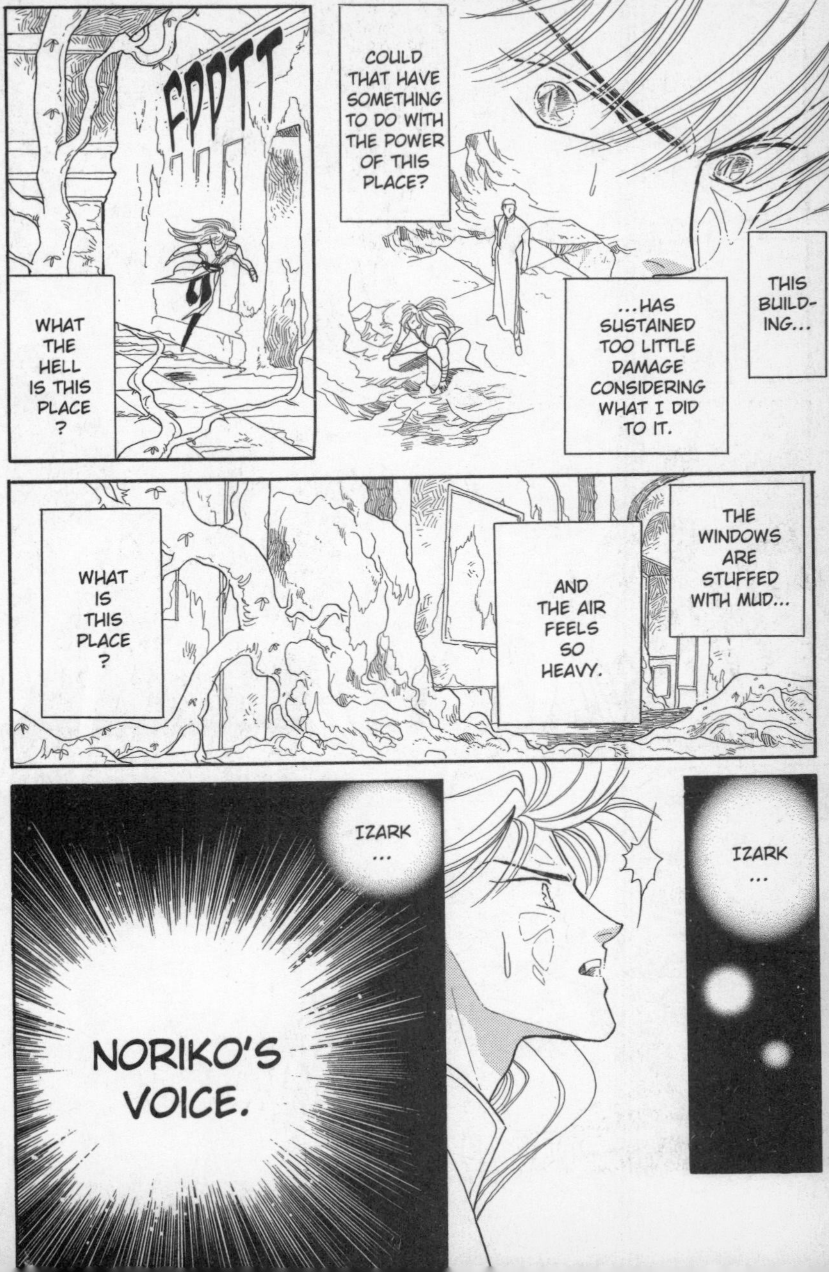
THIS BUILDING...
...HAS SUSTAINED TOO LITTLE DAMAGE CONSIDERING WHAT I DID TO IT.
COULD THAT HAVE SOMETHING TO DO WITH THE POWER OF THIS PLACE?
FPPTT
WHAT THE HELL IS THIS PLACE?
THE WINDOWS ARE STUFFED WITH MUD...
AND THE AIR FEELS SO HEAVY.
WHAT IS THIS PLACE?
IZARK...
IZARK...
NORIKO'S VOICE.

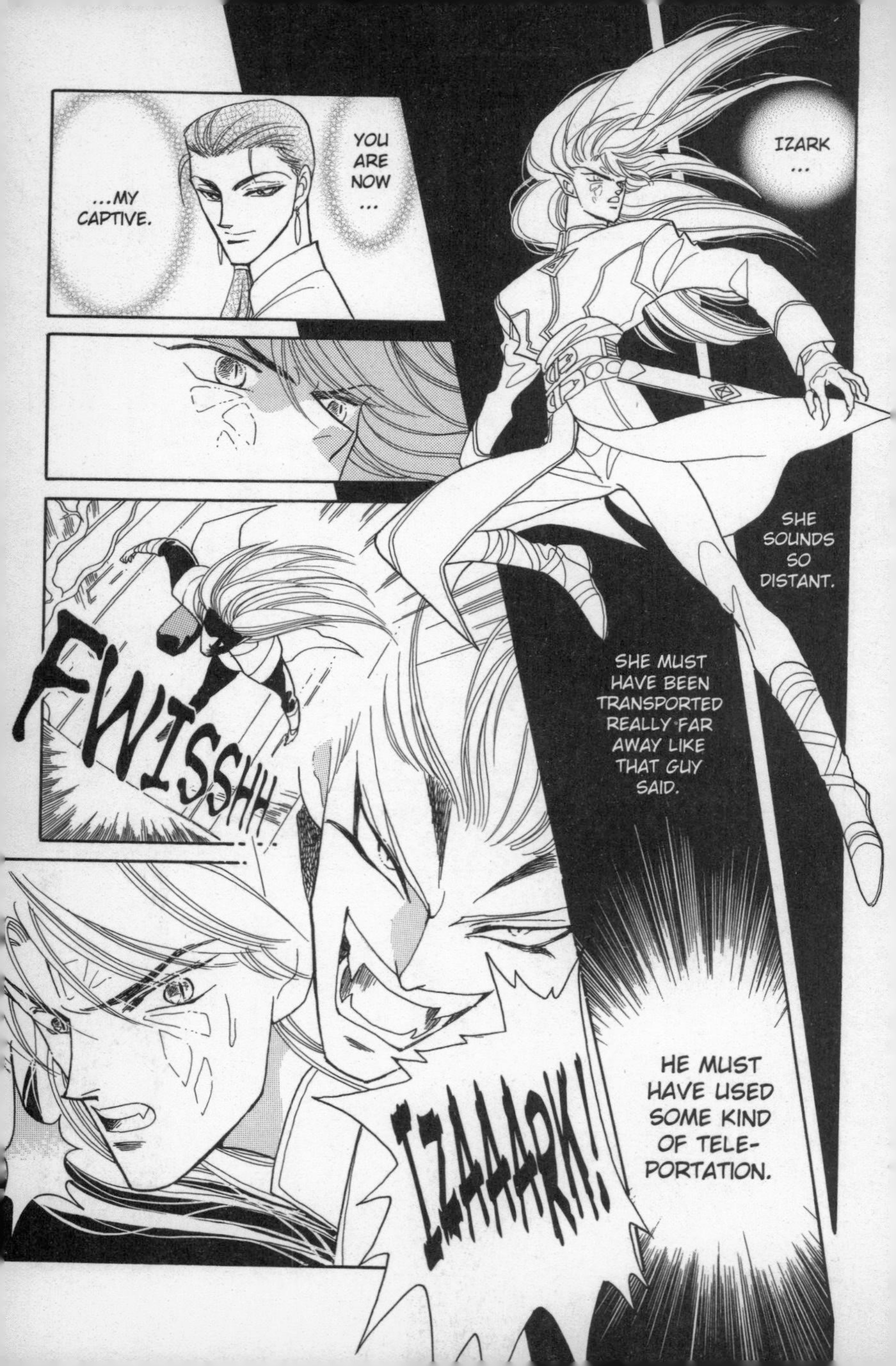
IZARK ...
SHE SOUNDS SO DISTANT.
SHE MUST HAVE BEEN TRANSPORTED REALLY FAR AWAY LIKE THAT GUY SAID.
YOU ARE NOW ...
...MY CAPTIVE.
FWISSHH
HE MUST HAVE USED SOME KIND OF TELE-PORTATION.
IZAAARK!

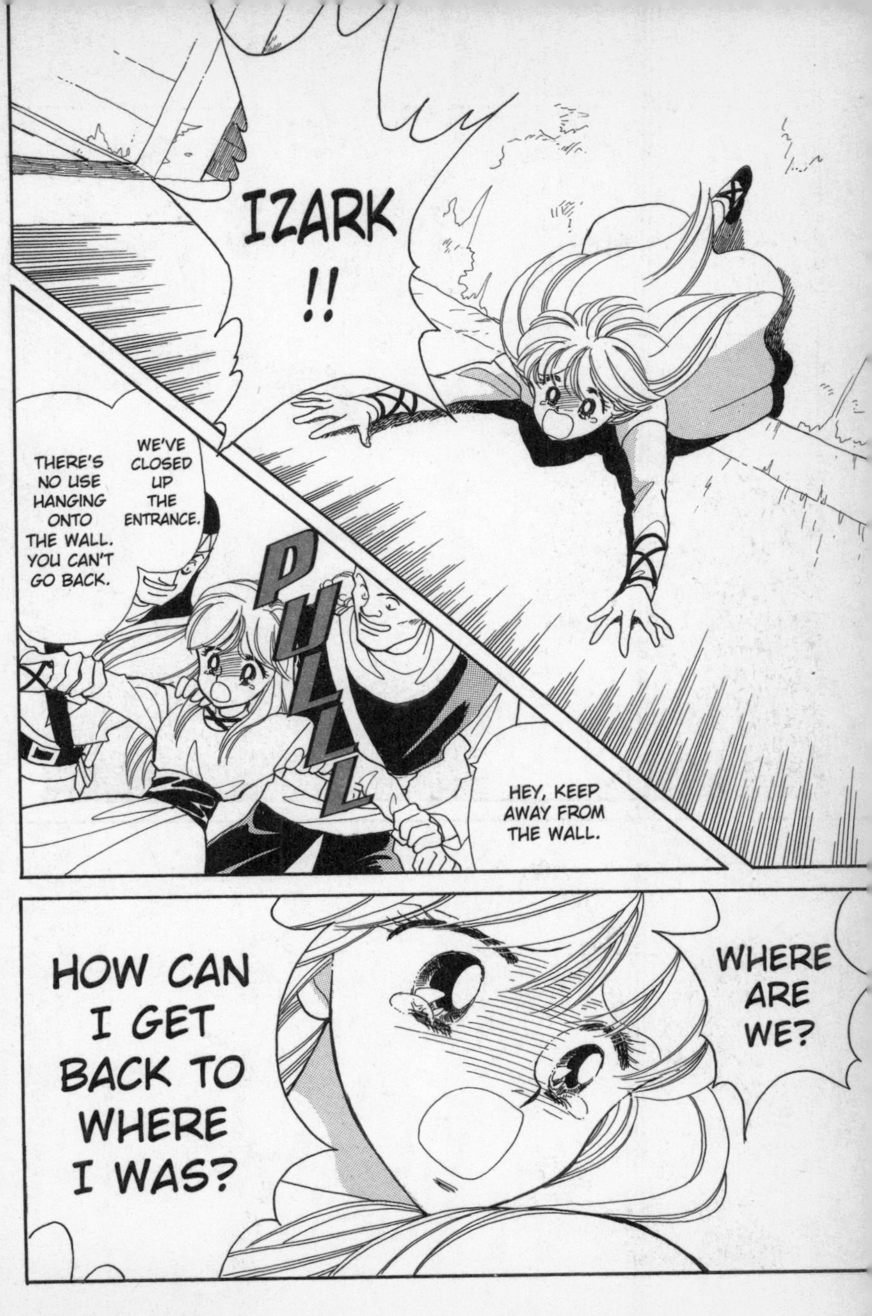
IZARK !!
WE'VE CLOSED UP THE ENTRANCE.
THERE'S NO USE HANGING ONTO THE WALL. YOU CAN'T GO BACK.
PULL
HEY, KEEP AWAY FROM THE WALL.
WHERE ARE WE?
HOW CAN I GET BACK TO WHERE I WAS?

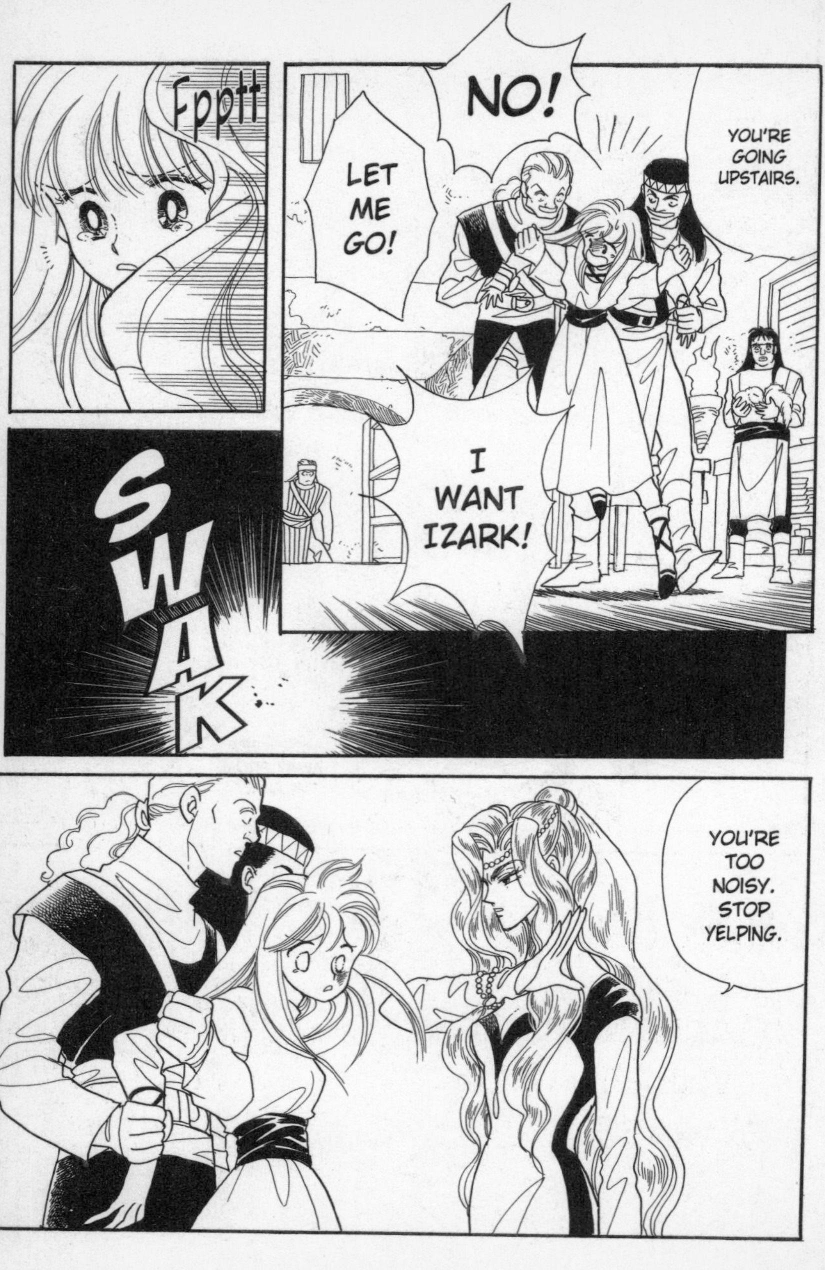
YOU'RE GOING UPSTAIRS.
NO!
LET ME GO!
I WANT IZARK!
Fpptt
SWAK
YOU'RE TOO NOISY. STOP YELPING.

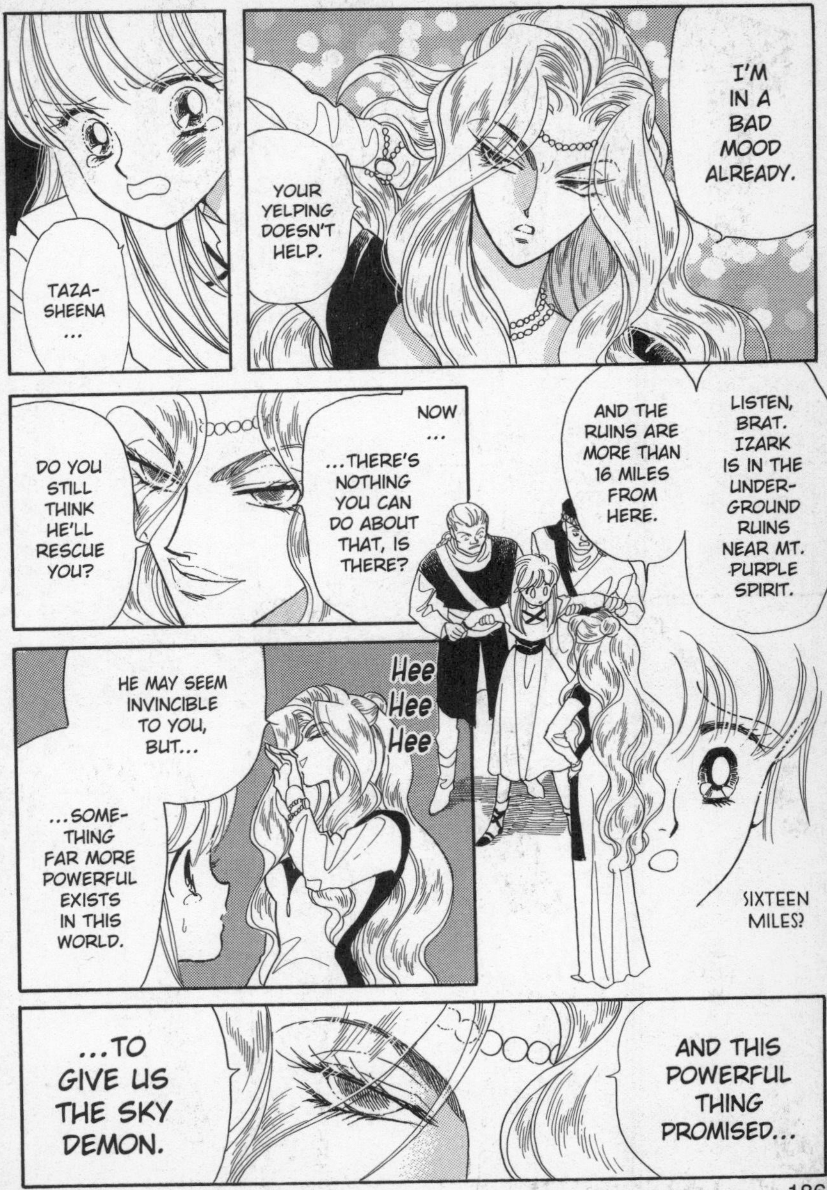
I'M IN A BAD MOOD ALREADY.
YOUR YELPING DOESN'T HELP.
TAZA-SHEENA ...
LISTEN, BRAT. IZARK IS IN THE UNDERGROUND RUINS NEAR MT. PURPLE SPIRIT.
AND THE RUINS ARE MORE THAN 16 MILES FROM HERE.
SIXTEEN MILES?
NOW ...
...THERE'S NOTHING YOU CAN DO ABOUT THAT, IS THERE?
DO YOU STILL THINK HE'LL RESCUE YOU?
Hee Hee Hee
HE MAY SEEM INVINCIBLE TO YOU, BUT...
...SOMETHING FAR MORE POWERFUL EXISTS IN THIS WORLD.
AND THIS POWERFUL THING PROMISED...
...TO GIVE US THE SKY DEMON.

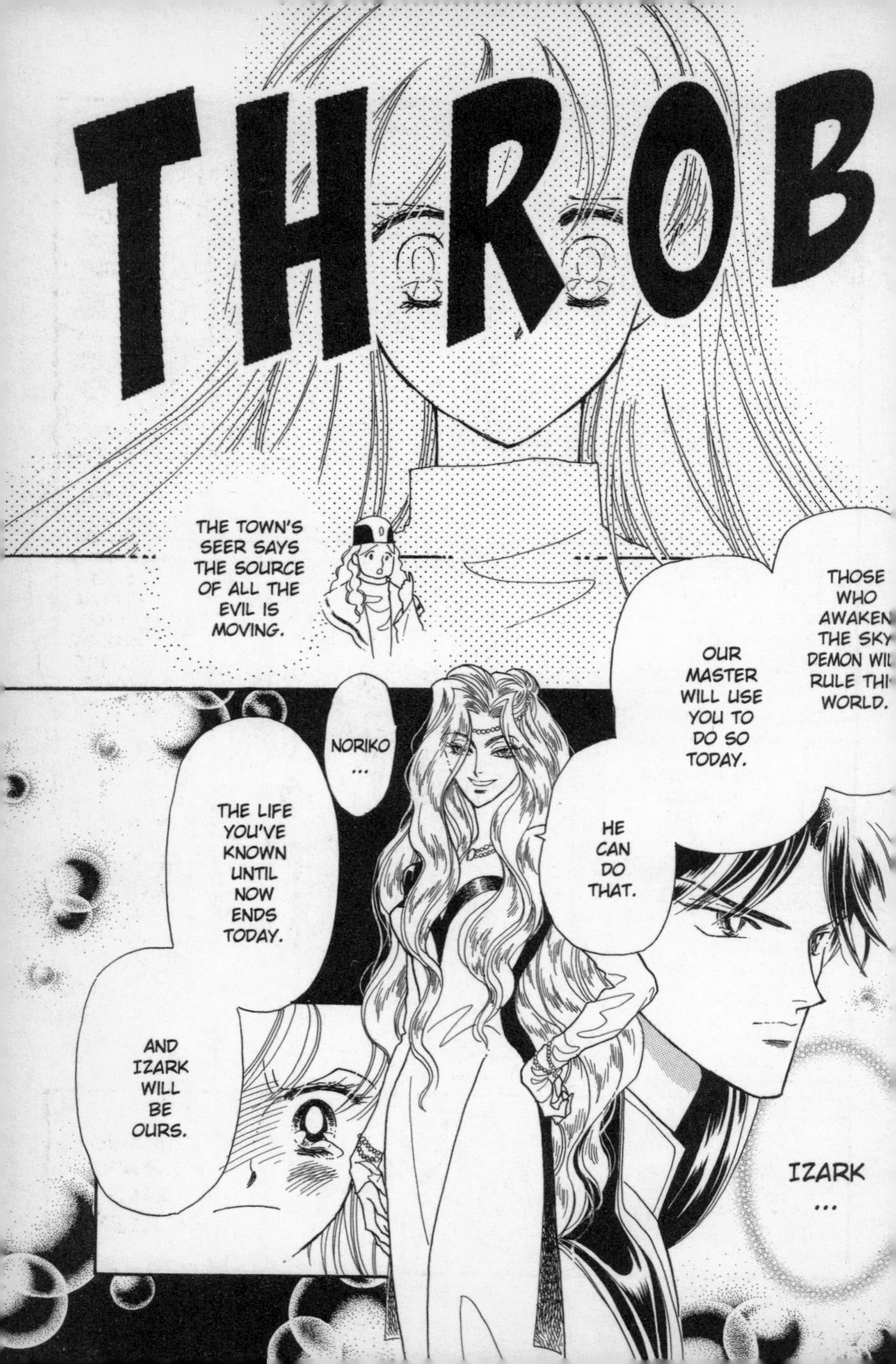
THROB
THE TOWN'S SEER SAYS THE SOURCE OF ALL THE EVIL IS MOVING.
THOSE WHO AWAKEN THE SKY DEMON WIL RULE THI WORLD.
OUR MASTER WILL USE YOU TO DO SO TODAY.
HE CAN DO THAT.
NORIKO ...
THE LIFE YOU'VE KNOWN UNTIL NOW ENDS TODAY.
AND IZARK WILL BE OURS.
IZARK ...

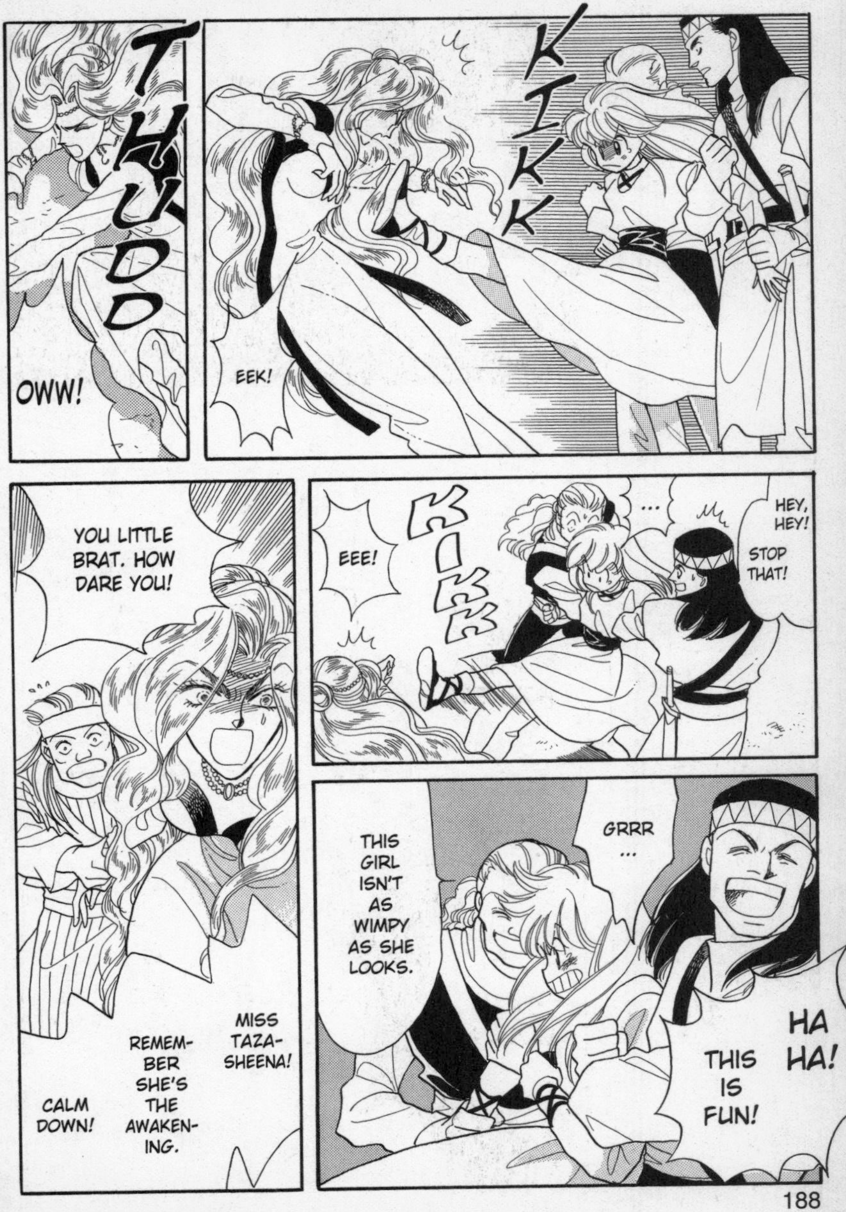
KIKK
EEK!
THUDD
OWW!
HEY, HEY!
STOP THAT!
...
KIKK
EEE!
HA HA!
THIS IS FUN!
GRRR ...
THIS GIRL ISN'T AS WIMPY AS SHE LOOKS.
YOU LITTLE BRAT. HOW DARE YOU!
MISS TAZA-SHEENA!
REMEM-BER SHE'S THE AWAKEN-ING.
CALM DOWN!

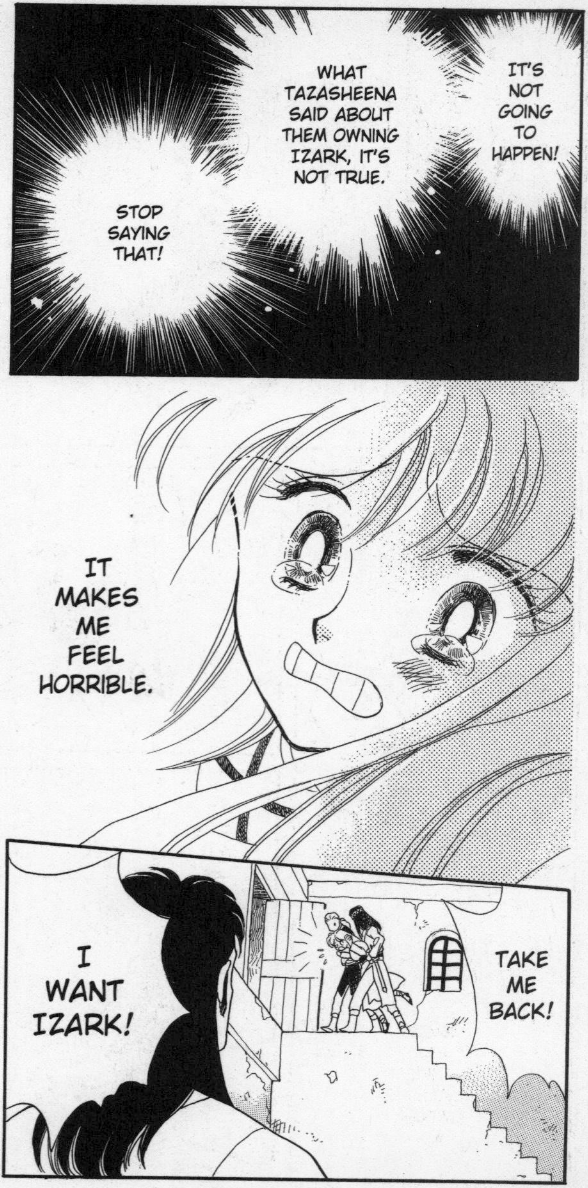
IT'S NOT GOING TO HAPPEN!
WHAT TAZASHEENA SAID ABOUT THEM OWNING IZARK, IT'S NOT TRUE.
STOP SAYING THAT!
IT MAKES ME FEEL HORRIBLE.
TAKE ME BACK!
I WANT IZARK!

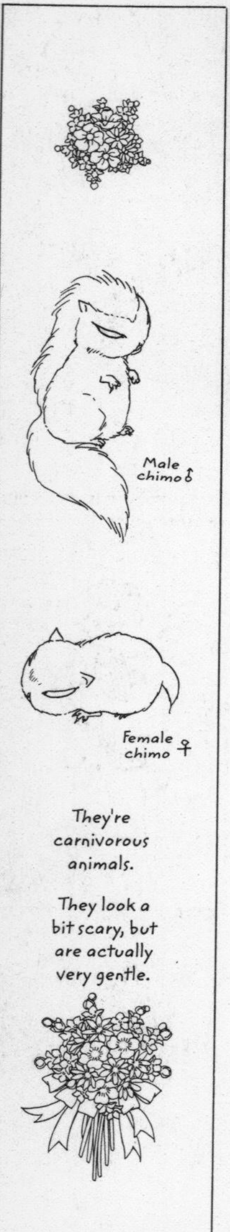
Male chimo ♂
Female chimo ♀
They're carnivorous animals.
They look a bit scary, but are actually very gentle.

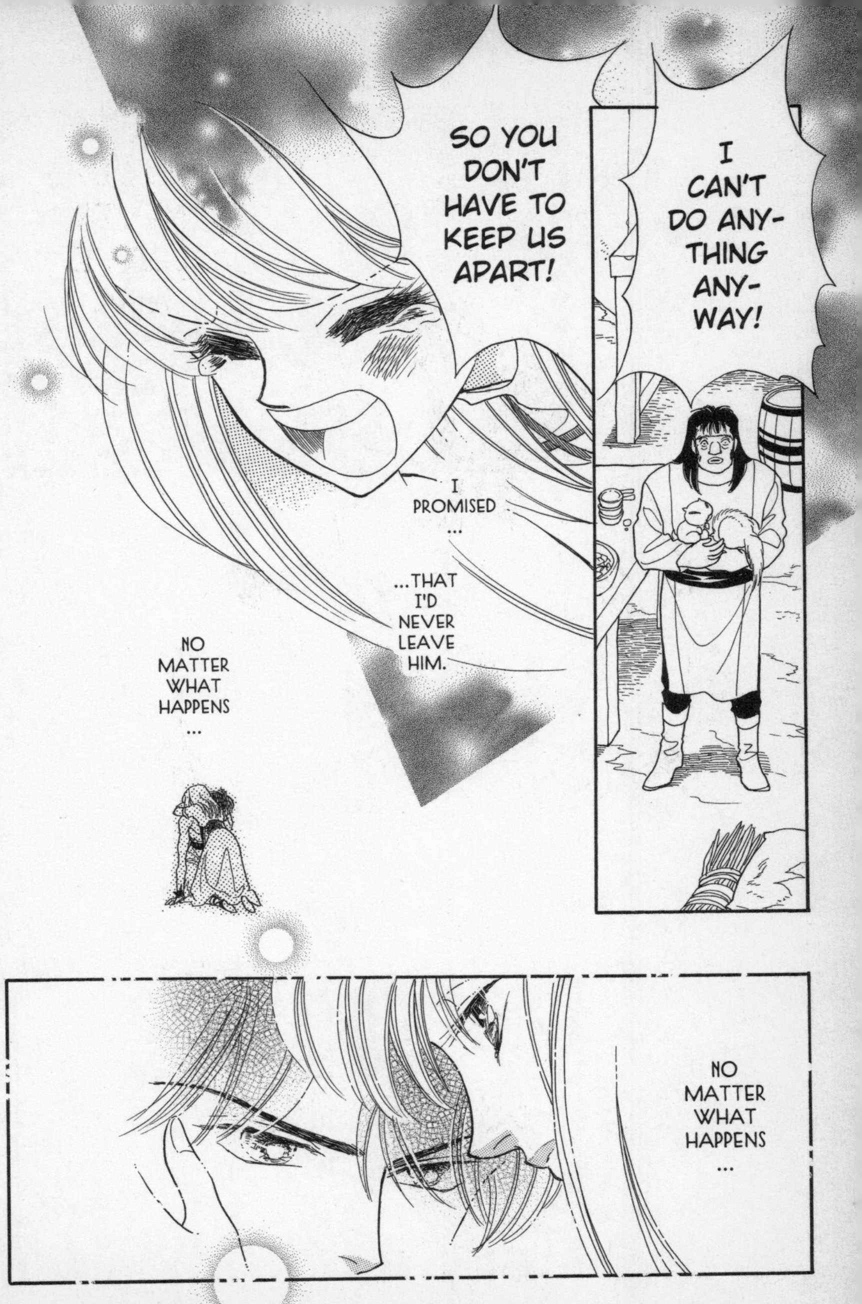
I CAN'T DO ANY-THING ANY-WAY!
SO YOU DON'T HAVE TO KEEP US APART!
I PROMISED ...
...THAT I'D NEVER LEAVE HIM.
NO MATTER WHAT HAPPENS ...
NO MATTER WHAT HAPPENS ...

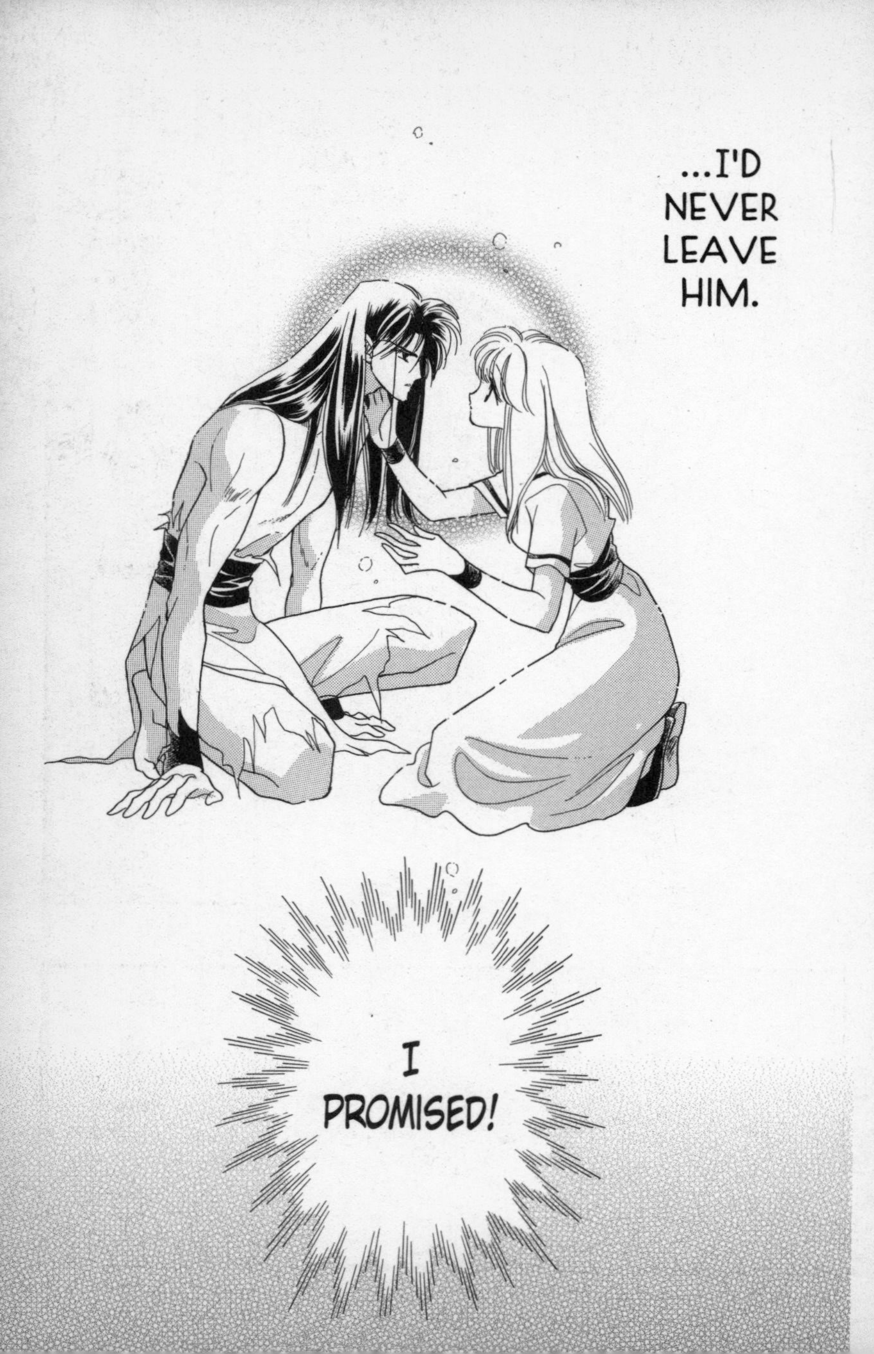
...I'D NEVER LEAVE HIM.
I PROMISED!

# COVER ILLUSTRATION COLLECTION

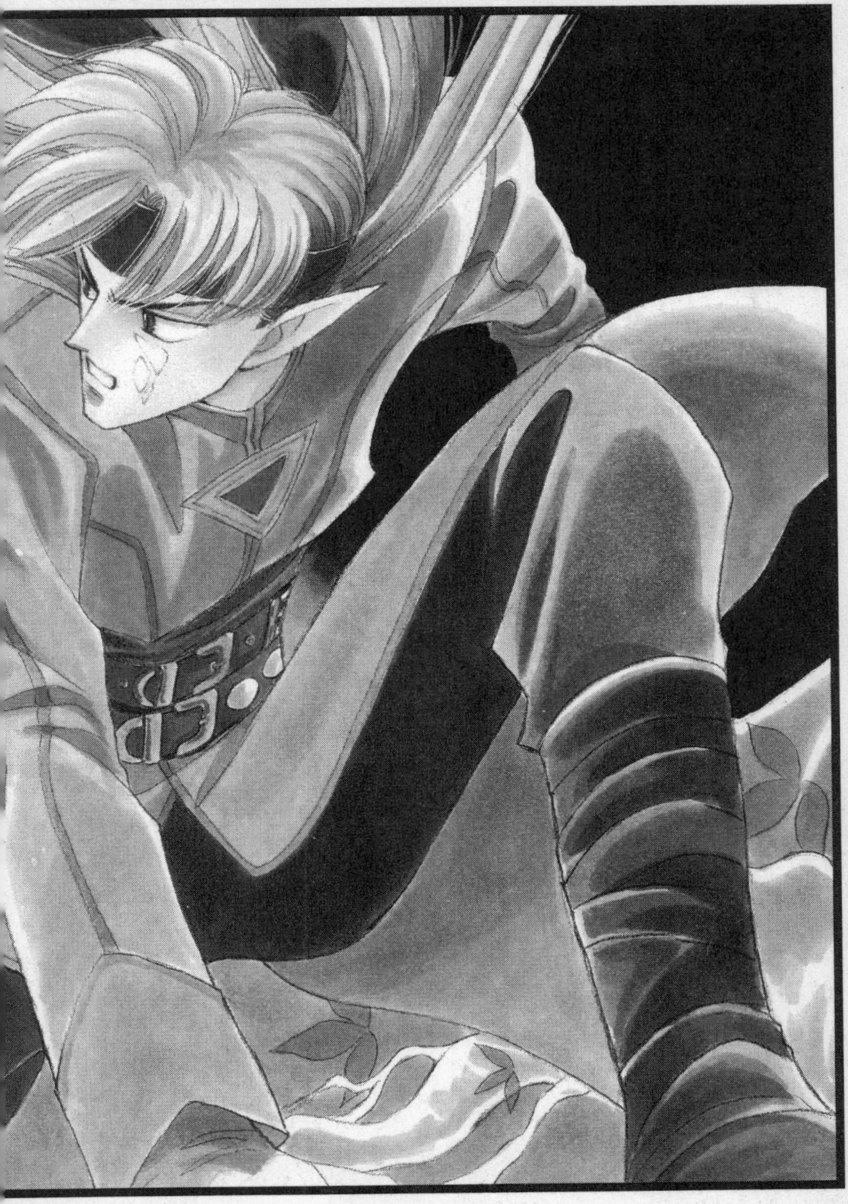

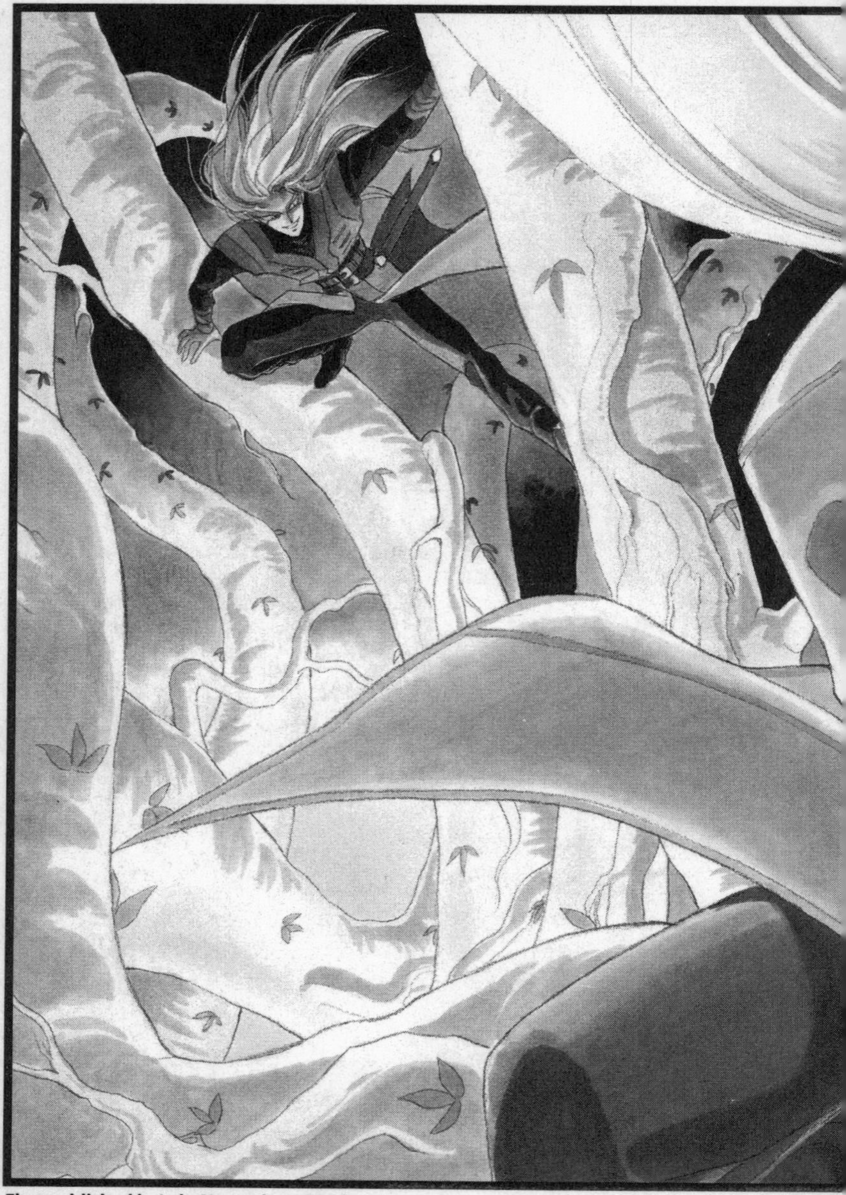

First published in *Lala*, November 1997 issue

First published in *Lala*, July 1997 issue

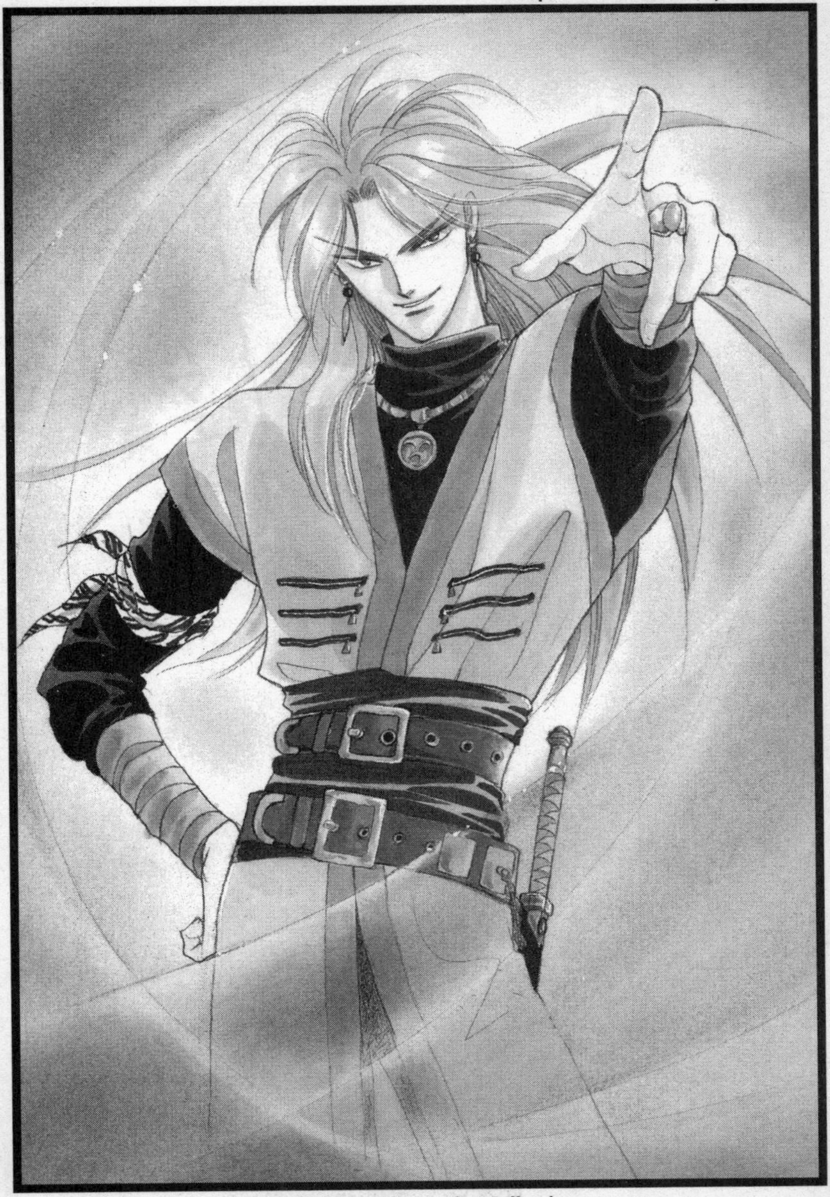

End of Cover Illustration Collection

**From Far Awa**
**Vol.**
Shôjo Editio

Story and Art b
Kyoko Hikaw

English Adaptation/Trina Robbin
Translation/Yuko Sawad
Touch-Up Art & Lettering/Walden Wor
Cover & Graphic Design/Andrea Ric
Editors/Eric Searleman & Joel End

Editor in Chief, Books/Alvin L
Editor in Chief, Magazines/Marc Weidenbau
VP of Publishing Licensing/Rika Inouy
VP of Sales/Gonzalo Ferrey
Sr. VP of Marketing/Liza Coppol
Publisher/Hyoe Narit

Printed in Canad

Published by VIZ Media, LL
P.O. Box 7701
San Francisco, CA 9410

10 9 8 7 6 5 4 3
First printing, December 200
Second printing, June 200

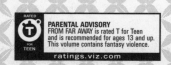

www.viz.com

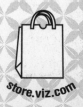

store.viz.com

# EDITOR RECOMMENDATIONS

Did you enjoy this volume of ***FROM FAR AWAY***? If so, here are three more titles the editor thinks you'd like.

RED RIVER
1 story and art by Chie Shinohara

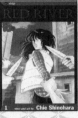

***RED RIVER***
by Chie Shinohara
All Yuri wants to do is go to high school and fall in love. Her life changes dramatically when she suddenly gets whisked away to a magical Middle-Eastern village. Added bonus: lots of sex and romance!

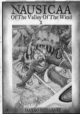

NAUSICAÄ
Of The Valley Of The Wind
1
HAYAO MIYAZAKI



***NAUSICAÄ OF THE VALLEY OF THE WIND***
by Hayao Miyazaki
A young girl accepts her destiny to save the world from an ecological disaster. Written and drawn by the Academy Award-winning film director. Highly recommended!

INUYASHA
vol. 21



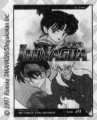

***INUYASHA***
by Rumiko Takahashi
World's collide when a plucky teenager finds herself trapped in an ancient Japanese fairy tale. Historical fantasy from the beloved creator of ***Ranma 1/2***.

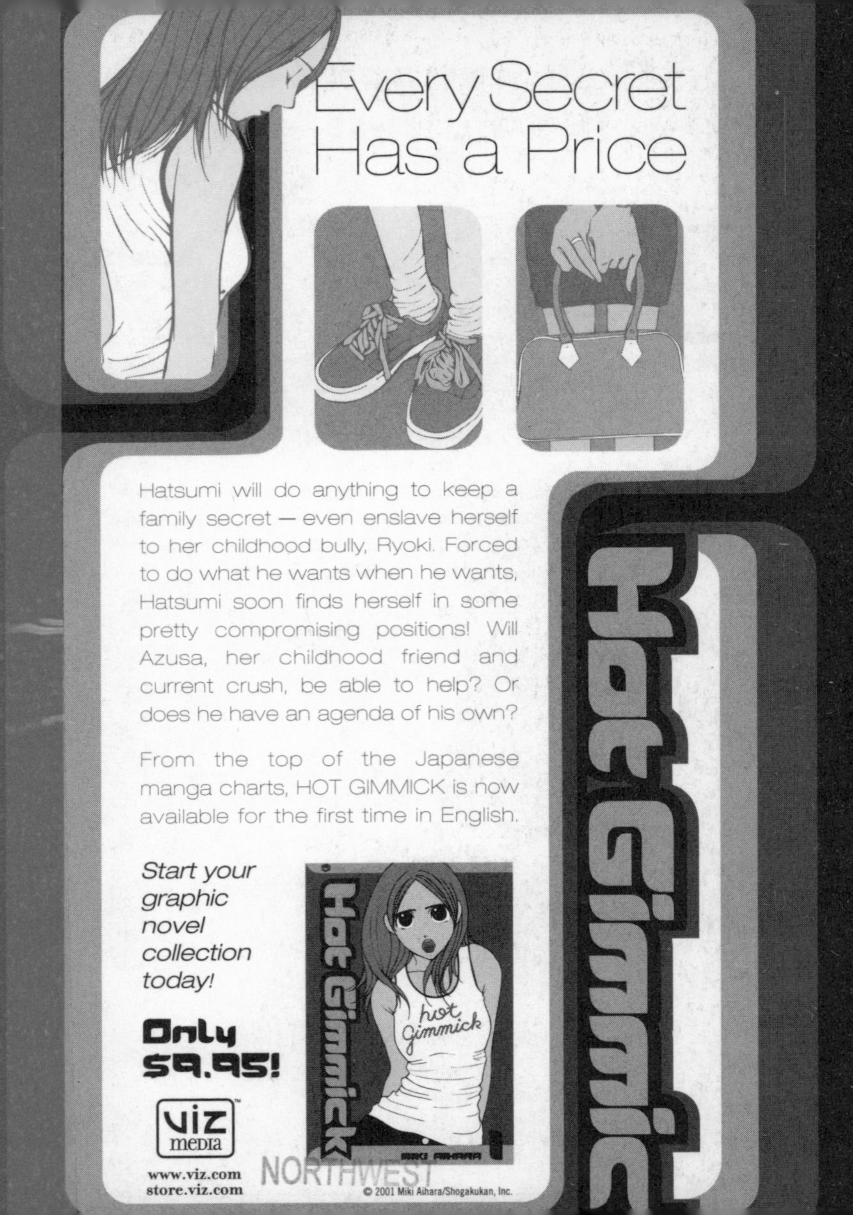
Every Secret Has a Price
Hatsumi will do anything to keep a family secret — even enslave herself to her childhood bully, Ryoki. Forced to do what he wants when he wants, Hatsumi soon finds herself in some pretty compromising positions! Will Azusa, her childhood friend and current crush, be able to help? Or does he have an agenda of his own?
From the top of the Japanese manga charts, HOT GIMMICK is now available for the first time in English.
Start your graphic novel collection today!
Only $9.95!
Hot Gimmick
Hot Gimmick
hot Gimmick
MIKI AIHARA
1
viz media
www.viz.com
store.viz.com
NORTHWEST
© 2001 Miki Aihara/Shogakukan, Inc.

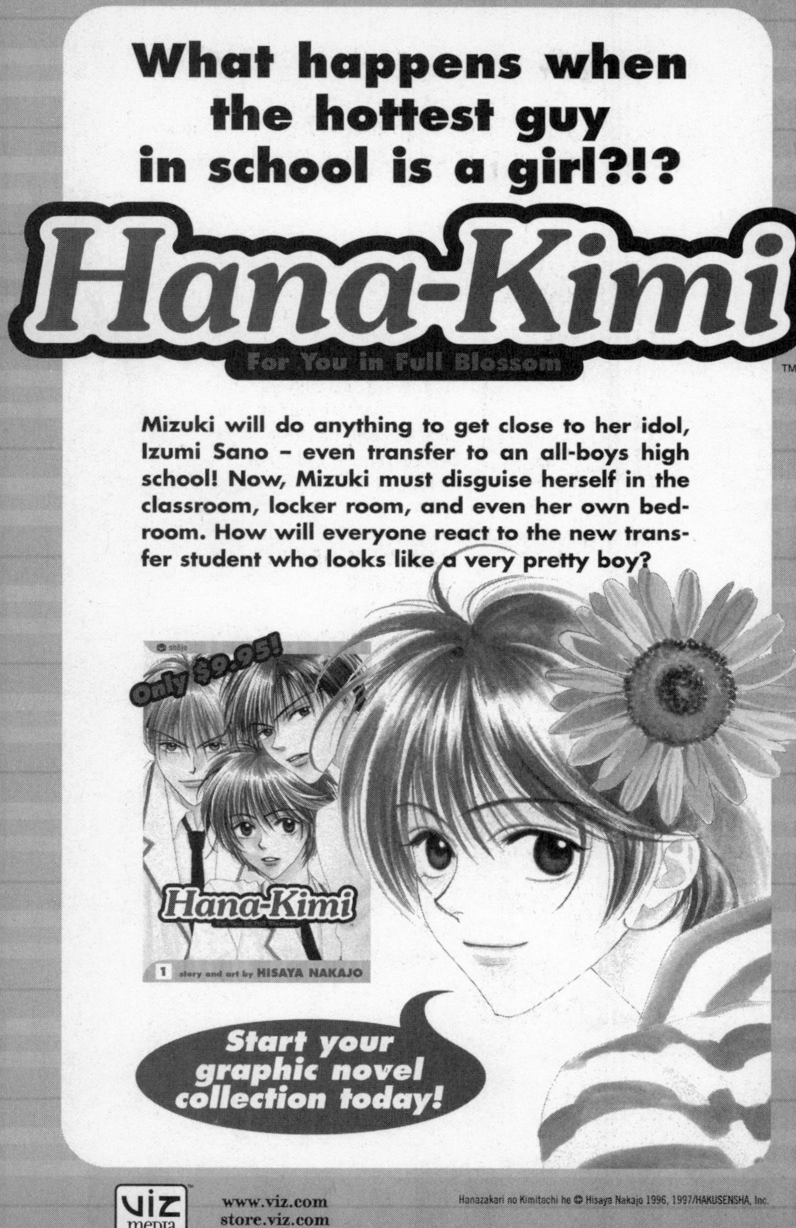

What happens when the hottest guy in school is a girl?!?
Hana-Kimi
For You in Full Blossom
™
Mizuki will do anything to get close to her idol, Izumi Sano – even transfer to an all-boys high school! Now, Mizuki must disguise herself in the classroom, locker room, and even her own bedroom. How will everyone react to the new transfer student who looks like a very pretty boy?
Only $9.95!
Hana-Kimi
1 story and art by HISAYA NAKAJO
Start your graphic novel collection today!
viz media
www.viz.com
store.viz.com
Hanazakari no Kimitachi he © Hisaya Nakajo 1996, 1997/HAKUSENSHA, Inc.

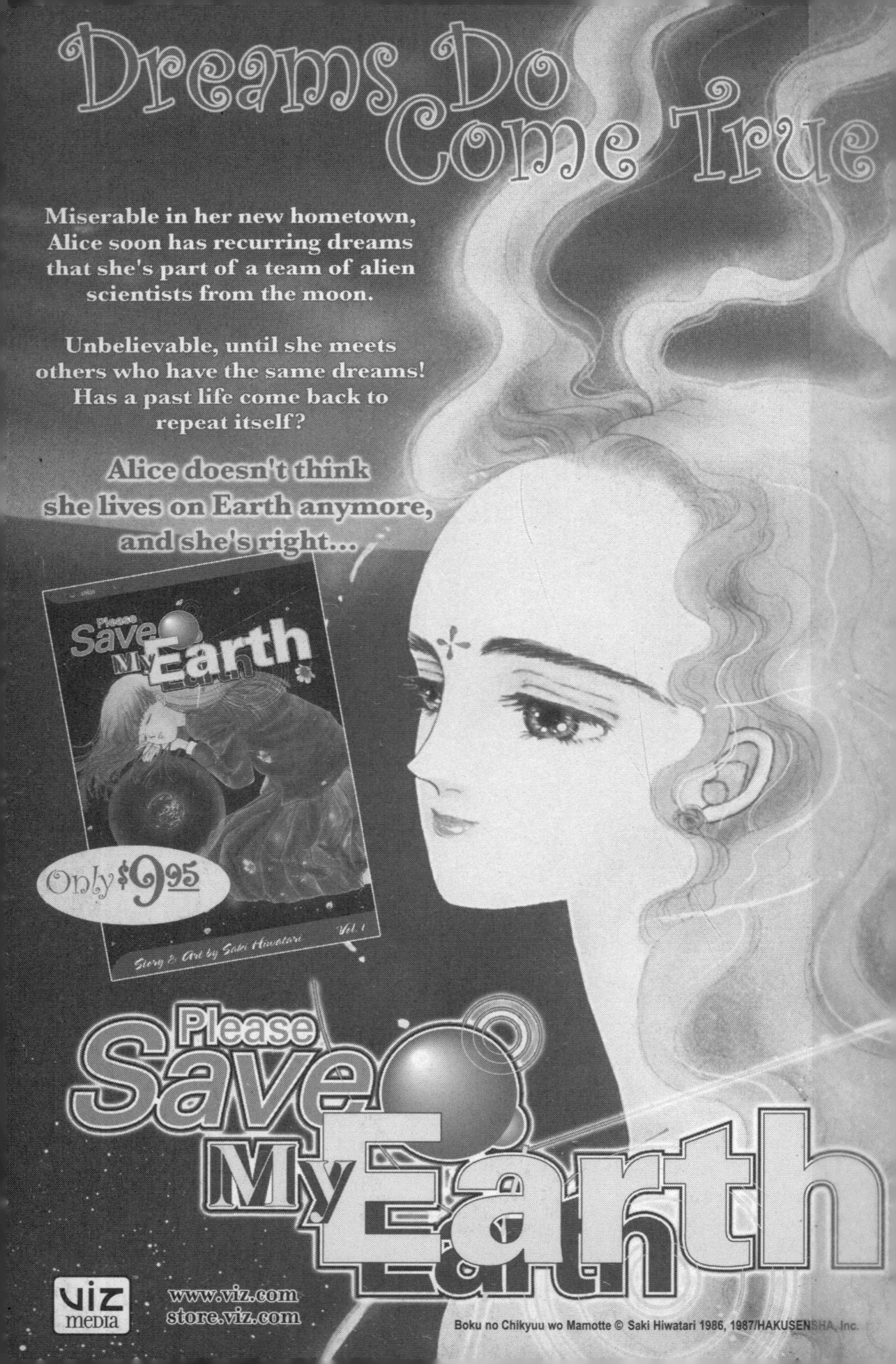

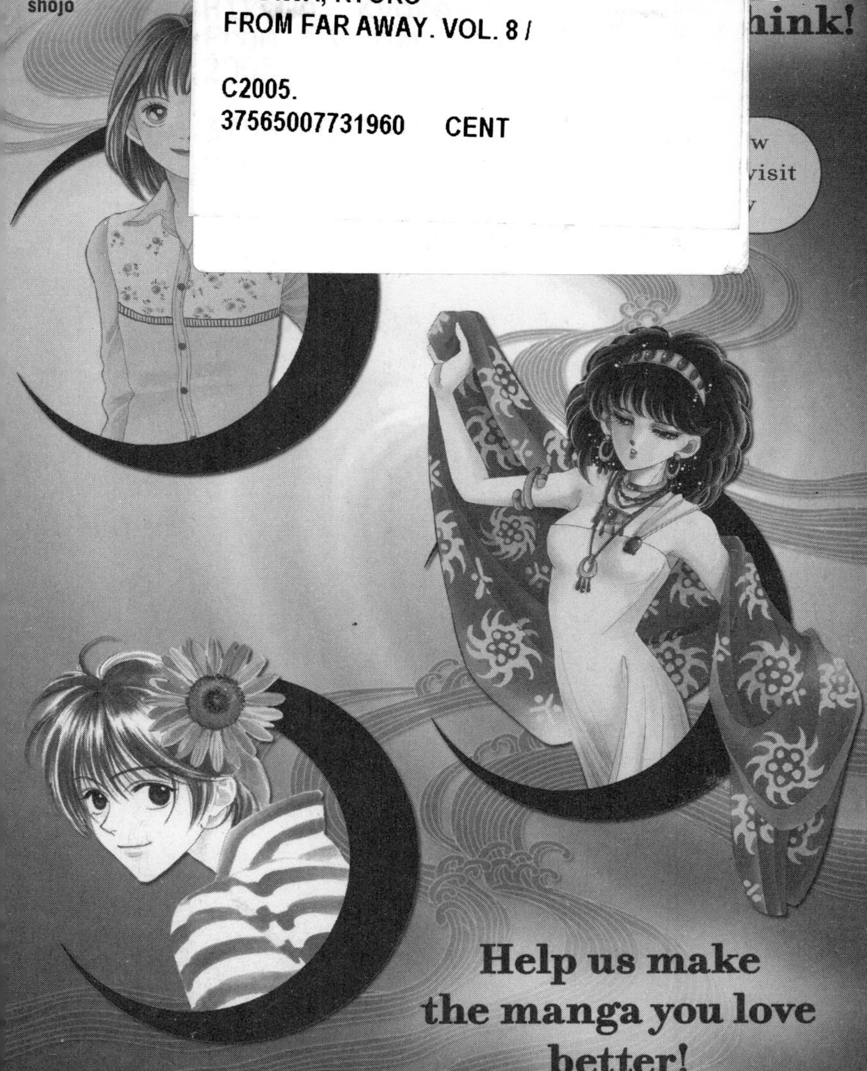
w
visit
v

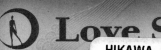